THE
LATINO
ENCYCLOPEDIA

THE
LATINO
ENCYCLOPEDIA

Volume 3

Florida – Lopez, Nancy

Editors

RICHARD CHABRÁN AND RAFAEL CHABRÁN

Marshall Cavendish
New York • London • Toronto

Published By
Marshall Cavendish Corporation
99 White Plains Road
Tarrytown, New York 10591-9001
United States of America

∞ The paper in these volumes conforms to the American National Standard for Permanence of Paper for Printed Library Materials, Z39.48-1984.

Library of Congress Cataloging-in-Publication Data

The Latino encyclopedia / editors, Richard Chabrán, and Rafael Chabrán,
    p. cm.
  Includes bibliographical references and index.
   1. Hispanic Americans—Encyclopedias. I. Chabrán, Richard II. Chabrán, Rafael
E184.S75L357 1995
973′ .0468′003—dc20   95-13144
ISBN 0-7614-0125-3 (set).   CIP
ISBN 0-7614-0128-8 (vol. 3).

First Printing

Contents

CONTENTS

THE
LATINO
ENCYCLOPEDIA

Florida: The fourth most populous state in the United States (1990 census), Florida is home to the nation's largest community of Cuban Americans.

History. On April 15, 1513, Spanish explorer Juan PONCE DE LEÓN landed in the region of the St. John's River. He named the area "Florida" in honor of *Pascuas floridas*, the Easter season. Over then next three decades, the Florida coast was extensively explored by such Spaniards as Alonzo ÁLVAREZ DE PIÑEDA, Pánfilo de NARVÁEZ, and Hernando DE SOTO. The Spanish mission and settlement of St. Augustine were established in 1565, and by the end of the century, missions dotted the coastline.

Florida has always been torn between influences from north and south. Originally believed by the Spaniards to be a single land mass with Cuba, the colony was governed by Spain from Havana and was traded back and forth with England during the American revolutionary period (1763-1783). In 1821, both East and West Florida were ceded by Spain to the United States, and in 1845 Florida was admitted to the Union as the twenty-seventh state.

Early Hispanic Settlement. Early Hispanic settlement was centered in Key West and Tampa, where Cuban cigar manufacturers opened factories and attracted Cuban workers in the 1860's (*see* CIGAR MANUFACTURING). By the 1890's, one-third of Tampa's population was composed of Cuban cigar workers. Prior to and during the Spanish-American War, Cuban revolutionary José MARTÍ made frequent visits to Tampa, Key West, Jacksonville, and St. Augustine to gather support and raise funds for the national liberation movement.

Well into the twentieth century, Hispanic populations in Florida were concentrated in Tampa and Key West. Hispanic theater activity in TAMPA and neighboring YBOR CITY, nexus of the Cuban community, was vibrant. In 1936 and 1937, Tampa was the site of the Federal Theatre Project's only Hispanic theater company, established under the Works Progress Administration (WPA). The area also contained a strong network of Hispanic societies that provided various benefits and social activities.

Cuban Exodus. In the 1930's, Miami began to emerge as a center of Cuban American culture as exiles, many of them educated professionals, began to flee the political turmoil of President Gerardo Machado's government. The wealthier arrivals had business contacts in Miami and soon became established in the city's business community. On the city's northwest side, the suburb of Hialeah also absorbed many immigrants.

In 1950, there were about six thousand CUBAN AMERICANS in Miami. Only 27 percent of the Cuban

Hernando de Soto landing at Tampa Bay, Florida, in 1539. (Library of Congress)

Americans in the United States lived in Florida; 45 percent lived in New York and New Jersey, still the primary Cuban destination. Between 1953 and 1959, another spurt of immigrants arrived, fleeing the rule of Fulgencio Batista.

The largest exodus, however, began in 1960, after Fidel CASTRO successfully overthrew Batista's regime. Many immigrants settled in New York and New Jersey, but by far the largest number went to MIAMI and the surrounding communities of Dade County. Between 1959 and 1980, an estimated 794,000 Cubans immigrated to the United States. By 1970, about 46 percent of Cuban Americans in the United States were in Florida; by 1980, the figure had risen to 59 percent.

The immigrants who fled Castro differed from their predecessors in that they anticipated returning to their homeland, after Castro's expected overthrow, in a few years at the most (*see* CUBAN IMMIGRATION). They chose Florida over New York for its mild climate, inexpensive housing, and already established Cuban community.

In the early 1960's, downtown Miami was in disrepair. The poor but ambitious arrivals grabbed the affordable commercial and residential real estate and turned Southwest Eighth Street into a Cuban district. The area soon became known as CALLE OCHO and LITTLE HAVANA. Immigrants of the educated middle classes had to work their way up in their chosen fields; many a political militant was transformed over the years into an ethnic entrepreneur.

In 1961, President John F. Kennedy established the CUBAN REFUGEE PROGRAM (CRP) to ease the burden on South Florida by relocating selected refugees, usually those with better skills or English proficiency, to other states. Of nearly half a million arrivals registered with the CRP in its first two decades, 61 percent were relocated outside Florida.

By 1981, the Miami area led the state with 585,000 Cuban Americans, followed by Orlando and Ft. Lauderdale with fifteen thousand each, Tampa with eight thousand, and Key West with two thousand. About 87 percent of the state's Cuban American residents lived

Little Havana has served as an initial settlement point for Cuban Americans. (Martin Hutner)

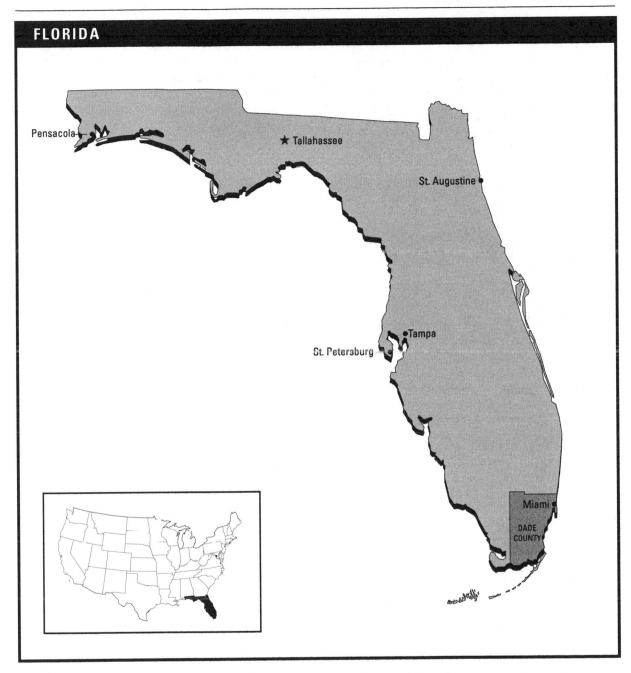

FLORIDA

Pensacola

★ Tallahassee

St. Augustine

Tampa

St. Petersburg

Miami

DADE COUNTY

in Dade County. With a total 1980 population of 1,625,000, the metropolitan area was approximately 35 percent Hispanic. The only city in the world with a larger Cuban population than Miami was Havana itself.

The relief Florida received from the CRP in the 1960's was temporary. In the 1970's and 1980's, many of those who had been relocated returned to Miami. A 1978 survey in the *Miami Herald* found that 40 percent of the city's Cuban Americans fit this profile. The returnees did not settle into Little Havana but concentrated in western suburbs such as Sweetwater and West Miami and in Hialeah to the north. No longer an isolated ghetto, Little Havana was a port of entry for the community to spread into other parts of the city.

The Cuban exodus and the resulting growth of Little Havana made Miami an attractive destination for other Latin American immigrants. In addition to 585,000 Cuban Americans, Miami was home to some 100,000 other Latinos in 1981.

Latino Population of Florida, 1990

Total number of Latinos = 1,574,143; 12% of population

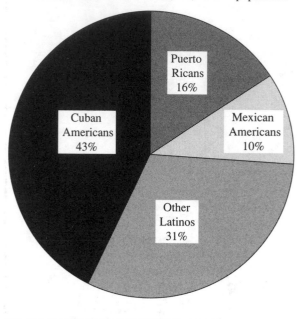

Source: Data are from Marlita A. Reddy, ed., *Statistical Record of Hispanic Americans* (Detroit: Gale Research, 1993), Table 106.

Miami's liberal political base was dramatically altered by the influx of Cuban Americans with their virulent anticommunist sentiment. The city became a center of anti-Castro organizing, and in 1961 a U.S.-supported grassroots attempt to topple Castro was aborted during the BAY OF PIGS INVASION. Anti-Castro feelings have remained high: In 1978, President Jimmy Carter's efforts to initiate a dialogue between the Cuban Americans and the Castro government were strongly rebuffed. Meanwhile, Cuban Americans moved into Florida politics. In 1978, the election of Jorge E. VALDÉS made Sweetwater the first city in the country with a Cuban American mayor. Hialeah soon followed with Mayor Raúl Martinez.

The 1980's. In the spring of 1980, a large-scale attempt by Cubans to escape their homeland led to the MARIEL BOAT LIFT. The effort, aided by the United States with Castro's embarrassed approval, brought 125,000 Cubans to Florida by summer's end. Many of the arrivals were poor, and nearly half had criminal records. The Jimmy Carter Administration welcomed them, offering permanent resident status and other services and benefits.

Simultaneously, the arrival of Haitian refugees in small, crowded boats exacerbated tensions while blurring linguistic and racial lines. Fears fanned by the Mariel boat lift and the Haitian influx led Dade County voters to repeal a standing resolution making Spanish the county's official second language. In 1988, an English-only amendment was added to the state constitution (*see* ENGLISH-ONLY CONTROVERSY).

Nevertheless, in 1984, three Cuban Americans were elected to the state legislature in Tallahassee. Robert MARTÍNEZ, the mayor of Tampa, was elected governor in 1986. In 1986, Xavier SUÁREZ became mayor of Miami.

In the late 1980's and the early 1990's, Florida again played the role of base camp for Latin American revolutionaries, as the U.S.-supported contras attempting to topple the Sandinista government in Nicaragua were headquartered in the city. The failure of that undeclared war resulted in a flood of Nicaraguan refugees who reached Florida via Guatemala, Mexico, and Texas. For a period, U.S. bus companies scheduled extra buses from the Mexican border directly to Miami. As many as three hundred Nicaraguans arrived daily. Unlike the Mariel immigrants, the Nicaraguans were not welcomed; they were treated as illegal aliens. The Nicaraguan immigrants established their own enclave in Sweetwater.

The 1990's. More than a million Hispanics were living in Florida by 1993. In 1990, the Miami-Ft. Lauderdale metropolitan area had a population of nearly 3.2 million, and MIAMI was the eleventh-largest city in the United States. About one-third of the area's population was Hispanic; Anglos made up 29 percent of the population. Miami itself had a population that was almost half Hispanic.

Dade County became effectively bilingual and bicultural. An annual spring festival in Little Havana is Carnaval Miami, similar to the world-famous Carnaval in Rio de Janeiro, Brazil. SANTERÍA, a form of Afro-Cuban religious worship and ritual, is also very popular, with many *botánicas* selling religious relics and ritual items.

Two daily newspapers serve the Latino communities: *El Nuevo Herald*, a Spanish edition of the *Miami Herald* that has been editorially independent since 1988; and *El Diario Las Americas*. On television, there are several Spanish channels, and the SPANISH INTERNATIONAL NETWORK has anchored its nightly national news program out of Miami. The situation comedy *Que Pasa* was developed by Miami Cubans and became a staple on public television for several years. In the 1980's, Miami boasted seven Hispanic radio stations.

Politics. The focus on Castro and the homeland makes Miami's Latinos strongly anti-communist and

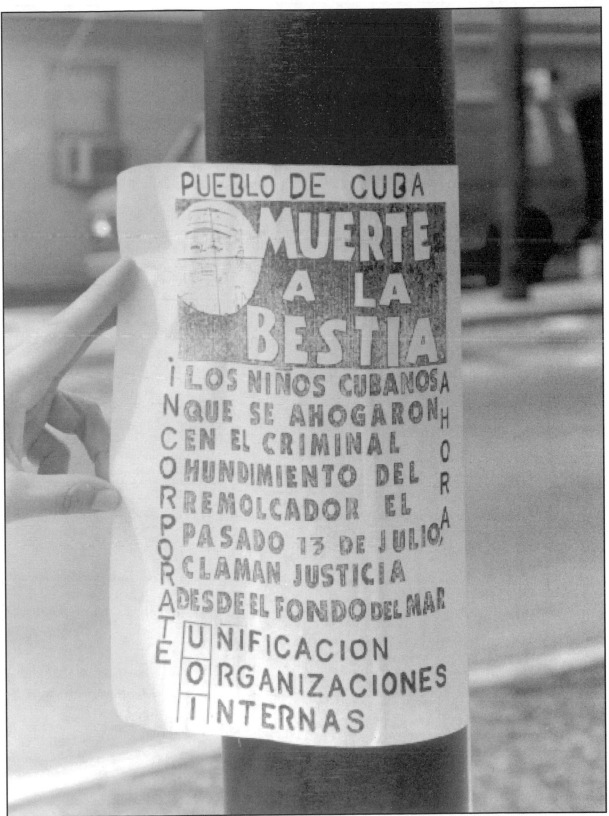

Miami's Latinos have taken up a variety of political causes. (Martin Hutner)

strongly Republican. In 1990, Latinos held demonstrations during the visit of Nelson Mandela, the leader of South Africa's liberation movement, protesting Mandela's support of the Cuban regime. Latino political organizations include the CUBAN AMERICAN NATIONAL FOUNDATION, established in 1980 by Jorge MAS CANOSA, and the foundation's political action arm, the Free Cuba Committee; the SPANISH AMERICAN LEAGUE AGAINST DISCRIMINATION (SALAD); the Cuban National Liberation Front; and the Veterans Association of Brigade 2506, made up of men who survived the invasion of the Bay of Pigs.

The conservatism of Florida's Cuban Americans is matched by that of the area's Nicaraguan community, not because of a shared Hispanic heritage but because both have fled extreme left-wing ideologies. Given the city's historical position in Latin American politics, it is appropriate that Miami's Woodlawn Cemetery holds former Cuban presidents Carlos Prío Socarrás and Gerardo Machado and former Nicaraguan president Anastasio Somoza.

In Miami, the distinct Latino groups tend to be segregated. In addition to the large Cuban majority, there are well-established communities of people from Mexico, Puerto Rico, the Dominican Republic, Colombia, Venezuela, Nicaragua, Panama, and Argentina. Latinos in Miami tend to be better educated and more affluent and cosmopolitan than those in most other American cities.

Business. Latinos have helped to expand Miami's business connections with the world. Between 1975 and 1985, Florida experienced a tripling of its international trade, half of which is conducted with Latin America. Miami's economic boom of the 1980's was

Latinos have thrived in both mainstream business enterprises and more traditional ones, including those targeted to Latino markets. (Martin Hutner)

aided by trade dollars from Venezuela, Colombia, Chile, and Argentina. As a result, Miami is one of the only U.S. cities with a foreign policy of its own.

Dade County has nine Hispanic chambers of commerce. There are many Latino-owned firms, most of which operate on a small scale. In 1980, the Miami metropolitan area was second only to the Los Angeles metropolitan area in the number of Hispanic-owned businesses (*see* BUSINESS AND CORPORATE ENTER PRISE). More than one-third of Miami's banks were Latino-owned. There is also extensive business in illicit drugs, with Cubans and Colombians among the leading traffickers.

Ethnic tensions in Miami sometimes run high among Hispanics, African Americans, and Anglos. Although anti-Latino sentiment is strong among Anglos, the Latino population is also often perceived as having elbowed African Americans out of minority privileges. Florida's African Americans tend to have much lower standards of living—in terms of education, services, employment, and income—than Anglos, with Hispanics falling in the middle. The communities are geographically and socioeconomically separate. Occasional outbreaks of violence in the African American community are sometimes related to Hispanics.

—*Barry Mann*

SUGGESTED READINGS:

• Boswell, Thomas D., and James R. Curtis. *The Cuban-American Experience: Culture, Images, and Perspectives*. Totowa, N.J.: Rowman & Allanheld, 1983. In this statistical and sociological examination of Cubans in the United States, Boswell and Curtis give equal coverage to the Miami and metropolitan New York/New Jersey communities. Scholarly, with occasional bursts of colorful and anecdotal writing.

• Portes, Alejandro, and Alex Stepick. *City on the Edge: The Transformation of Miami*. Berkeley: University of California Press, 1993. A comprehensive and lucid discussion of the effect Hispanics have had on Miami, including the Mariel boat lift and interethnic relations. The authors effectively interweave statistics, interviews, and original survey material and attempt to develop a prognosis for the city's future.

• Rieff, David. *Going to Miami: Exiles, Tourists, and Refugees in the New America*. Boston: Little, Brown, 1987. A compelling portrait of Miami's many communities and faces: part travelogue, part hard-hitting journalism, part fanciful impressions. Rieff draws on historical knowledge, candid interviews, and a keen sense of observation to explore the Cuban mind-set, ethnic problems, and other timely issues.

• Shofner, Jerrell. *Florida Portrait: A Pictorial History of Florida*. Sarasota, Fla.: Pineapple Press, 1990. A simple, straightforward, and engaging exploration of Florida's past and present through words and a wealth of historical photos, with occasional references to the role of Hispanics.

• Weyr, Thomas. *Hispanic U.S.A.: Breaking the Melting Pot*. New York: Harper & Row, 1988. Weyr focuses on people and places across the Hispanic American spectrum in this strident and heavily anecdotal volume. Many interviews and extended quotes, and a strong emphasis on Hispanics in politics and business. Frequent references to Florida and a small section devoted to Miami.

Florit, Eugenio (b. Oct. 15, 1903, Madrid, Spain): Poet, playwright, and critic. Florit, a black Cuban poet, was born into a literary family that moved to Cuba in 1918. As an adolescent in the LaSalle School, Florit read voraciously and wrote poetry. By 1927, he had been graduated from law school.

Florit's *Treinta y dos poemas brevas* (1927; thirty-two short poems) and a Cuban journal, *Revista de avance* (1928-1930), were published privately. After his graduation from law school, he helped to organize the second International Conference on Emigration and Immigration and worked in the Cuban Department of State. *Reino (Kingdom)* was published in 1938. A trip to New York to be honored by the Hispanic Institute led to his appointment as an auxiliary consul to promote Hispanic culture.

An invitation to teach at Columbia University launched a career in teaching. Florit retired from Columbia in 1969 but retained an emeritus professorship; he also taught at Barnard College and at Middlebury College in Vermont. During the 1940's and 1950's, he was the central figure in Hispanic writing in New York.

Folk arts and crafts: In the context of ethnic cultures, folk art refers to community-based visual artistic traditions or crafts that are learned informally and passed on to succeeding generations. Folk art serves both a practical and an aesthetic function as an intimate symbol of a culture or subculture. Examples of Latino folk art include the carved santos of Hispanos in New Mexico, the handmade Carnaval (Mardi Gras) masks and costumes of Puerto Ricans in New York, the conga drum making of Cuban Americans in Miami, and the wrought ironwork of Mexican Americans in Los Angeles and Denver.

Equipment used by vaqueros *and* charros *is often handmade.* (Ruben G. Mendoza)

Unlike fine art, which is generally taught and learned in schools, folk art is cultivated through apprenticeships involving face-to-face interaction and practical experience. Creators of fine art often strive for uniqueness and personal expression through their art, but practitioners of folk art often work within a structure that does not validate or applaud unnecessary experimental deviations. Nevertheless, ethnic folk art does evolve, absorbing the influences of other cultures, including aspects of popular and elite arts.

In order to survive, folk art must remain important in the daily life of an ethnic group, meeting both utilitarian needs and aesthetic demands. Some of the strongest traditions in Latino folk art fulfill religious needs in highly individualistic, ethnically accented ways that mainstream popular culture cannot provide. For example, many homes in the Mexican American barrio in San Antonio, Texas, have outdoor Catholic shrines called *capillas* that incorporate various media in a folk assemblage. Many contemporary Latino and non-Latino artists have been inspired by the forms, motifs, and styles of Latino folk art.

Leather Work. Some folk art arises out of the needs of traditional occupations, such as the Mexican or Mexican American VAQUERO (cowboy). Since the Spanish colonial era, the equipment of the *vaquero* has been a fundamental part of his work. This equipment, including saddles, saddle blankets and bags, spurs, boots, and whips, was and is often handmade by blacksmiths and leatherworkers to fit the specific needs of the individual, his horse, and his duties.

In Texas and the Southwest, ranches traditionally had a leatherworker on the premises or nearby to make and repair *vaquero* equipment. This craftsman knew how to make a saddle strong enough to withstand the weight of a one thousand-pound bull roped to the saddle horn. He also knew how to fit the rider on the top and the horse on the bottom, while ensuring comfort for many consecutive hours. As a matter of pride in his work, the saddlemaker also took care to make the saddle pleasing to the eye.

Every stage of the leatherworking process is important to a dedicated craftsman. The process begins with selection of the live animal from which the leather will be made, followed by tanning, removal of hair, and kneading of the rawhide until it is smooth and even. The leather is cut into strips of varying width, depending on the intended purpose. It takes more than one hundred square feet of leather to make one saddle. Tooling or embossing adds art to the craft of leatherworking. Working saddles are more stingy in design than other leather articles, such as belts, boots, knife cases, chair backs, boxes, or parade saddles. These objects are often prized because of their intricate designs and patterns.

Woodworking. Latinos have been active in woodworking and furniture making in the Southwest since Spanish colonial times. Traditional New Mexican furniture was made of pine and red spruce with pegs and dowels of scrub oak. The tools of the trade included the adz, ax, auger, chisel, gouge, awl and froe for splitting planks, as well as the hammer, knife, and handsaw. Families often constructed their own church pews, leading to a great variety of styles and sizes of bench seats in Southwestern churches. With the advent of factory-made furniture, however, Latino craftsmen lost much of their livelihood. By 1925, many furniture makers had moved into other lines of work. Others joined the revival of colonial crafts that was being promoted by Anglo collectors at the time.

One of the most distinctive Latino folk art forms is that of the carved wooden images of saints known as santos (*see* SANTOS AND SANTO ART). Hispanic artisans in present-day New Mexico began using local materials and styles to make religious images in the late 1700's that were modeled on the baroque paintings and carvings brought to the colony from Spain. They continued making sculptures called BULTOS for home or church use well into the 1800's. Gradually, however, imports cut into the local market and the tradition became dormant.

In the early 1900's, Anglo artists and collectors who hoped to revive Spanish colonial decorative arts discovered the carvings of José Dolores LÓPEZ, a farmer from Cordoba in northern New Mexico. He and others were encouraged to carve santos for the Anglo market. The revival of santos making continued in the late twentieth century with various families in Cordoba and a smaller number of self-styled contemporary "traditional" artists. The same woodcarving skills have also been applied to domestic scenes, animals, and humorous subjects by Hispanic craftsmen.

Tinwork and Textiles. The tools of tinwork, such as hammers, nails, snips, and dies, are simple and readily available. Tinworking became popular in the Southwest in the 1840's when food supplies arrived with the U.S. Army in metal tins. Before that time, tins were imported from Mexico and were fairly rare. Many uses for this new, relatively inexpensive material were quickly found. The early tinworkers made elaborate chandeliers, picture frames, mirrors, crosses, niches, and an array of decorative items for homes, churches,

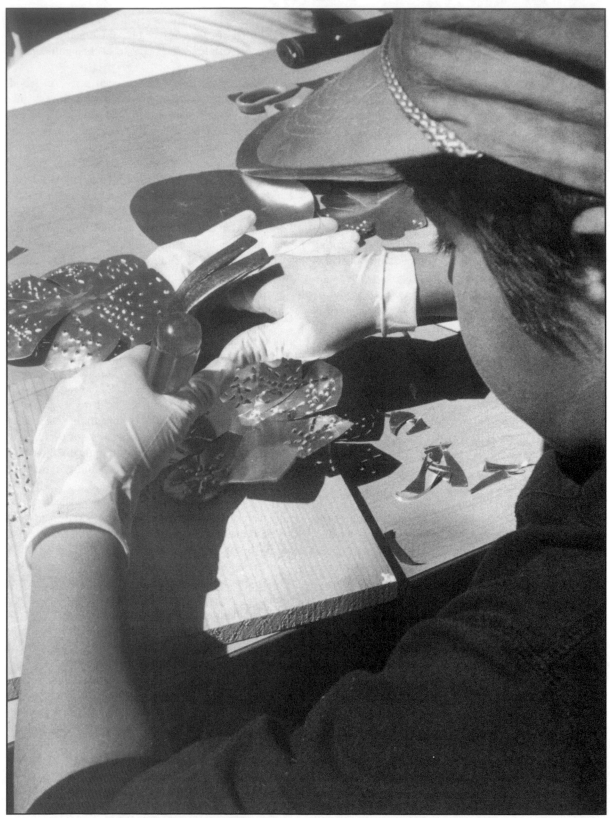

A student in Taos, New Mexico, creates a tin star. (Elaine Querry)

and shrines. They often embellished tin boxes and trays with pieces of wallpaper, greeting cards, or original artwork.

Like Mexican American tinwork, Mexican American weaving resembles its counterparts in Mexico. In the Southwest, weaving is a tradition that has been passed down within families in certain villages. Rich colors are dyed into wool or cotton yarns with blackberries and other organic materials. Then, with an exciting mix of colors, bold, geometric patterns are woven to fit the purpose of the artisan. Blankets known as *colchas* are embellished with intricate embroidery and sometimes pictorial designs. Southwestern rugs, *colchas*, SARAPES, and wall hangings are much prized in international crafts markets.

In other parts of the United States, women from throughout Latin America preserve the traditions of quilting, embroidery, and crochet. Originally, quilts were made from necessity out of scraps of recycled material and handed down within families. Those who practice quilting today do so because it is enjoyable, sociable work, with a greater emphasis on design, particularly in rural areas and small towns. Salvadoran Americans, Cuban Americans, and others make embroidered or crocheted items to decorate their homes or give as gifts. Some Mexican Americans lend their talents to make authentic costumes for folklórico dance groups. A few Guatemalan Americans of Mayan heritage are skilled in traditional backstrap loom weaving but find, like other immigrants, that such work cannot support them in the American economy.

Other Folk Art Forms. Jewelry of the American Southwest has long been noted for its uniqueness both among Latinos and American Indians. Delicate filigree work and silversmithing using precious and semiprecious stones were brought to the region from Mexico and then took on local characteristics.

Latino folk ceramics made of glossy, painted red clay are also related to those found in modern Mexico. They range from decorative cooking and eating ware to popular images of heroes such as Pancho VILLA and Emiliano ZAPATA, bulls and bullfighters, brides and grooms, or animals performing human tasks. Ceramacists are often asked to make images of deceased family members or friends that are kept on display with religious items in the home.

A number of Mexican American folk art forms are ephemeral in nature, especially those intended for special occasions. These include PIÑATAS, paper flowers, *papel picado* (decorative papercuts), Day of the Dead altars, and *coronas* (crowns), made of intricately fash-

Ceramic vessels and cookware cover the top of an adobe stove in the mission of San José y San Miguel de Aguayo, San Antonio, Texas. (Ruben G. Mendoza)

ioned hardened and colored bread dough, for weddings and baptisms. Some families make many of the objects for room-size Southwestern-style nativity scenes called NACIMIENTOS, which became the focus of home Christmas celebrations.

Some types of Latino folk art have links to fine and popular art. For example, the Latino mural movement in the United States was strongly influenced by the bold style of Mexican artist Diego RIVERA and others but went on to become a distinctive urban tradition (*see* MURAL ART). Contemporary murals range from simple depictions of the Virgin of Guadalupe painted on garage doors to ambitious depictions of Latino history conceived by professional artists and executed by teams of students. LOW RIDERS use some of the visual symbolism and style to personalize their cars.

—Beaird Glover

SUGGESTED READINGS:

• Body, Elizabeth. *Popular Arts of Spanish New Mexico.* Santa Fe: Museum of New Mexico Press, 1974. A large volume containing biographies of artists and many color photographs.

• Dickey, Roland F. *New Mexico Village Arts*. Albuquerque: University of New Mexico Press, 1970. A survey of decorative and utilitarian arts in historical Spanish villages of New Mexico.

• Graham, Joe S., ed. *Hecho en Tejas: Texas-Mexican Folk Arts and Crafts*. Denton: University of North Texas Press, 1991. A comprehensive study of Texas-Mexican folklore including historic perspectives, pictures, and statistical research.

• Panyella, August, ed. *Folk Art of the Americas*. New York: Harry N. Abrams, 1981. A large picture book with folk art categorized by the North American or Latin American country of origin.

• Wroth, William. *Hispanic Crafts of the Southwest: An Exhibition Catalogue*. Colorado Springs, Colo.: Taylor Museum of the Colorado Springs Fine Arts Center, 1977. An exhibition catalog of Southwestern arts and crafts, with special attention to historical significance.

Folk medicine: Latino folk medicine is a branch of ethnomedicine and a subdivision of medical anthropology. It can be defined as a set of beliefs and practices among Latinos relating to disease that are derived from indigenous culture and folk custom rather than from the principles of modern medicine. Native American (primarily Aztec) roots, Spanish colonial theories, and Catholic rituals all play an important role in the folk system.

Latino folk medicine is closely related to other aspects of Latino culture such as religion, concepts of death, and even music. Folk medicine implies specific

Latino folk medicine often has a large religious component, with cures sought both through prayer and through the work of human healers. (James Shaffer)

theories and definitions of health and illness that may seem magical, naturalistic, or supernatural but that are rational when viewed in the light of prevailing beliefs.

Folk Theories and Cures. Sometimes referred to as Spanish American folk medicine, Latino folk medicine has been studied by anthropologists in Mexico, Puerto Rico, and Cuba, as well as among Mexican Americans in the Southwest, especially Texas, New Mexico, and Colorado. Researchers have found Latino folk medicine to be an integrated system of theory and therapy. It conforms to an equilibrium model of health in which the human body maintains a balance between "hot" and "cold" qualities; when there is an excess of one or the other, illness results. Medical anthropologists and scholars of ethnomedicine stress the importance of using "emic" approaches to this phenomenon (native ways of describing and categorizing medical beliefs and behaviors) as opposed to the "etic" approaches, which view cultural phenomena from outside the culture.

Latino folk etiologies, or explanations for the causes and origins of illness, frequently involve sorcery known as *brujería*, in which the intrusion of a diseased object or spirit causes the loss of soul or spirit. Both physical and mental illnesses are thought to be a result of witchcraft, punishment from God, or other significant cultural agents. Folk healers in Latino communities, be they *curanderos* or ESPIRITISTAS (spiritualists), combine "clinical" skills in diagnosing problems with a variety of empirical remedies, such as herbs, or ritualistic cures, such as the inducing of emotional catharsis (*see* CURANDERISMO; HERBAL MEDICINE).

The Catholic religion is often a central focus of *curanderos* and other Latino folk health practitioners. For example, they seek the intervention of Christ, the saints, and the Virgin Mary through prayers and rituals. The afflicted person may make a religious vow or promise to do a pilgrimage if the cure is effected.

Folk Illnesses and Treatments. Latinos recognize certain folk illnesses based on culture-bound concepts of health and illness. Some of the most common are *empacho* (clogging of the stomach and upper intestinal tract), *caída de la mollera* (fallen fontanel), *susto* (sickness resulting from fright), *bilis* (a jaundice-like condition, believed to result from anger or fear, which also attacks the digestive system), and *mal de ojo* (evil eye).

Caída de la mollera is very common in the Latino community and corresponds to what has been called "displaced-parts-of-the-body" types of folk etiology. This illness most frequently attacks infants and children, especially very young infants with soft fontanels.

It is said to be caused by a shock to the system, such as fright or a blow to the head, a fall, or the sudden withdrawal of the nipple from a nursing infant. *Mal de ojo* also often attacks infants and children. It is said to be brought about by a look or a glance from a person who has a "strong vision," sometimes deliberately to hurt the child, sometimes unintentionally. Latinos who admire children are careful to touch a child on the head in order to counteract the possible effects of the evil eye. *Susto* (fright), according to folk belief, is brought on by a terrifying experience that releases the soul from the body.

Curanderos and *curanderas* are male and female folk health practitioners who have learned the hot and cold qualities of medicinal plants and herbs. They also use Christian prayers, magico-religious practices, and the physical manipulation and rubbing of the body, as in the case of SOBADORES (specialists in message) and *hueseros* (bone doctors). One of the cures for *susto*, for example, is medicinal herbs that are part of *limpias*, or ritualistic cleansing. *Mal de ojo* is also treated with *limpias* and the rubbing of an unbroken egg over the patient's body. Among the many cures for *caída de la mollera* are pushing of the skull plate upward with the fingers or holding the child upside down and shaking him or her so that the fontanel falls back into place.

Spanish and Indigenous Medicine. One of the most interesting subjects in the study of Latino folk medicine is the issue of syncretism, or the fusion of two different cultural systems, especially with respect to Mexican Americans. Medical syncretism, also known as medical *mestizaje* (mixing), involves the mixing of European/Spanish sixteenth-century medicine and native American (New World) elements. In Central Mexico, this involved the mixing of Aztec medical thought with imported academic medicine from Spain.

Spanish or European medical theory and practice was based on humoral pathology, or "humors" as the cause of disease and illness. In this tradition, treatment was based on the assumption that nature had a strong healing force and that the role of the physician was to assist nature in the healing process. Health was defined as a state of harmonic mixture or balance of the humors, with illness as a faulty mixture. The four fundamental humors were blood, phlegm, yellow bile, and black bile. This theory of humors is associated with the four elements (air, fire, earth, and water) and even the four seasons. These groups of four were further developed by Galen, a Greek physician of the second century, with his theory of four temperaments (melancholic, sanguine, phlegmatic, and choleric). Humoral

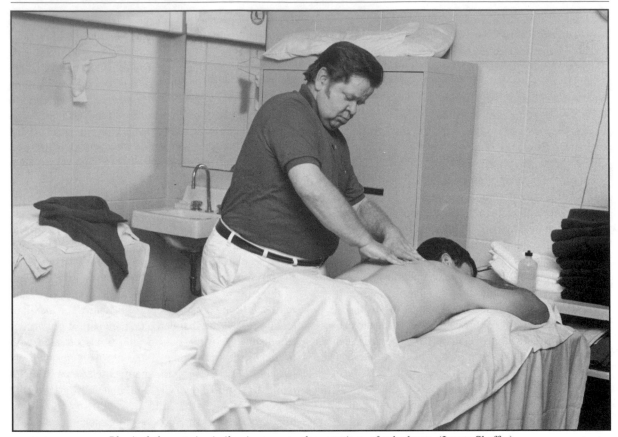

Physical therapy is similar in ways to the practices of sobadores. (James Shaffer)

removal involved bleeding, vomiting, purging, and sweating brought about by medicinal plants and herbs.

The Spanish brought not only their theory and practice of medicine to the Americas but also their system of medical education, based on the curriculum of the University of Salamanca, and their system of licensing and regulating health practitioners (the *Protomedicato*). In the New World, the Spanish excluded native and non-Christian health practitioners from the practice of medicine. Many Spanish health practitioners were university-trained medical professionals, but many had no formal university training. The latter group included folk practitioners such as *algebristas* (bonesetters), *hernistas* (hernia healers), *sacadores de la piedra* (kidney stone removers), *sacamuelas* (tooth pullers), and PARTERAS (midwives, also known as *comadres* or *madrinas*). The Spanish also brought their *curanderos*, magical healers, astrologers, BRUJOS and *brujas*, and *hechiceros* (those who practiced witchcraft).

The Spanish incorporated the use of native drugs into their medical practice. The native population and mestizos subsequently often mixed humoral antece-

dents with Catholic rituals. Aztec explanations of disease were lost because they were thought to be contrary to Christian beliefs.

In Mexico, native *curanderos* continued to accommodate Aztec and Catholic practices by using Christian prayers along with traditional Aztec herbal cures. Scholars are divided over whether "hot" and "cold" qualities were a folk borrowing from the Spanish or existed in pre-Columbian Aztec culture. Whatever the origins of the idea, diseases and their cures continue to be classified as "hot" or "cold" by both modern Mexican folk practitioners and their counterparts in Mexican American and Chicano barrios.

Santería, Espiritismo, and Curanderismo. In Cuba, Puerto Rico, and the Dominican Republic, CURANDERISMO coexists with folk religious practices such as Spiritualism and Santería. An ESPIRITISTA (spiritualist) serves as a medium for the dead to communicate with the living, restoring relationships between people and between people and the supernatural (*see* SPIRITISM AND SPIRITUALISM). In many Puerto Rican spiritist centers in New York, mutual aid and health treatments are offered to members during times of crisis.

SANTERÍA is a set of folk beliefs associated with the cult of *orishas* (gods or deities) who control the forces of nature. Santería mixes elements from West African Yoruba cults and Catholicism in a case of religious syncretism. Some of its practices were originally brought to the Caribbean by African slaves. *Santeros* and *BABALÁOS* are spiritualist healers who combine aspects of Santería and *curanderismo*. Their services are in demand in Latino communities throughout the United States, especially in New York, Tampa, Miami, and Los Angeles. Latinos from the Caribbean, like many Mexican Americans, frequent *BOTÁNICAS* (herb stores), where they can purchase medicinal plants and other magico-religious products recommended by *curanderos* or spiritualist healers. —*Rafael Chabrán*

SUGGESTED READINGS:

• Clark, Margaret. *Health in the Mexican-American Culture: A Community Study*. Berkeley: University of California Press, 1959. Represents some of the first work done on Mexican and Mexican American folk medicine.

• Foster, G. M., and Barbara Gallatin Anderson. *Medical Anthropology*. New York: John Wiley & Sons, 1978. The authors describe the "new" field of medical anthropology and outline basic aspects of ethnomedicine. Foster's work with respect to Mexican Americans is discussed in the section on "Spanish-American" folk medicine. The authors reject the idea that Mexican folk medicine's "hot/cold" aspects have roots in Aztec beliefs.

• Kay, Margarita A. "Health and Illness in a Mexican-American Barrio," In *Ethnic Medicine in the Southwest*, edited by Edward H. Spicer. Tucson: University of Arizona Press, 1977. Much of the health behavior that Kay described stems from humoral assumptions among Mexican Americans that are identical to those found in Mexican communities.

• Kiov, Ari. *Curanderismo: Mexican-American Folk Psychiatry*. New York: Free Press, 1968. A study of prescientific psychiatry, clarifying the therapeutic significance of culture-bound elements. Explores the role of *curanderos* and the therapeutic value of their health practices.

• Madsen, William. *Mexican-Americans of South Texas*. New York: Holt, Rinehart and Winston, 1964. Some of the first work done on the folk medicine of Chicanos.

Botánicas *sell many of the herbs and plants used by practitioners of folk medicine.* (City Lore, Martha Cooper)

• Ortiz de Montellano, Bernard. *Aztec Medicine, Health, and Nutrition*. New Brunswick, N.J.: Rutgers University Press, 1990. In the context of Aztec medicine, the author discusses the subject of syncretism in Mexican folk medicine and concludes that much of modern Mexican folk medicine derives from a mix of European/Spanish concepts and earlier Aztec concepts.

• Ortiz de Montellano, Bernard. "*Caída de mollera:* Aztec Sources for a Mesoamerican Disease of Alleged Spanish Origin." *Ethnohistory* 34 (Fall, 1987): 381-399. Describes fallen fontanels and relates to Aztec beliefs.

• Rubel, Arthur J. *Susto: A Folk Illness*. Berkeley: University of California Press, 1984. Discusses the origins, nature, epidemiology, and treatment of *susto* (fright).

Folklore, Central American: The folklore of Central America represents a unique blend of indigenous and Spanish traditions. Central American refugees and immigrants have brought some traditional beliefs and practices with them to the United States, mingling their customs with those of mainstream culture. Among the types of Central American folk traditions to be found in the contemporary United States are foods such as the savory Salvadoran *pupusa*; crafts such as Honduran woodcarving and Mayan weaving; folk dances such as the Costa Rican *punta*; musical instruments such as the Guatemalan MARIMBA; rituals such as the QUINCEAÑERA celebration for fifteen-year-old girls; and folk beliefs such as healing through the help of a *curandera*.

Villagers may be more likely than urbanites to follow traditional practices such as folk medicine, both in their native land and in the United States. Many Central American refugees have been too preoccupied with basic survival to sustain folklore forms as publicly and visibly as other Latino groups. Whatever their current practice, Central Americans share an ancient heritage of lore and mythology that has shaped their contemporary folklore.

Ancient Mythology and Belief. Pre-Conquest folklore and mythology present some highly developed customs and religious systems, particularly among the Aztec and Mayan Indians. In early manifestations,

The quinceañera *celebrates a girl's fifteenth birthday.* (James Shaffer)

conceptions of the world and of nature appear in very crude form, but in Mexico, the Yucatán, and Guatemala, they were elaborated by a high-ranking priesthood to landmarks of ancient civilization.

By destroying temples and all manifestations of Aztec and Mayan belief and building Catholic churches on traditional religious sites, the Spanish conquistadores threatened to destroy entire cultures in Guatemala and Mexico. Ironically, the rapid conversion and education of many Indians by the missionaries allowed the Indians to preserve many indigenous folk beliefs in written form.

The Spanish Legacy. The Spanish conquerors of the sixteenth century were themselves highly superstitious. Although they rejected the custom of human sacrifice, they absorbed a number of indigenous taboos and beliefs. An elaborate system of taboos, or rules regarding things to avoid, was necessary because life was perceived as perilous. Nature could destroy as well as give life, so respect for it was paramount. Indigenous cultures had well-developed systems regarding the workings of nature.

Among the legacies of the Spanish Conquest were certain beliefs and treatments in what still thrives as Latino folk medicine. Salvadorans, for example, call on the *curandero* or *curandera* (folk healer) to correct imbalances in the body that lead to the loss of the soul and sickness (*see CURANDERISMO; HERBAL MEDICINE*). Folk healing today involves the use of medicinal herbs, magico-religious rituals, and the invocation of the help of the Catholic saints, much as it did in Spanish colonial times.

Spanish Catholicism helped shape many aspects of Central American folklore. Its mark can still be seen in fiestas for patron saints, the making of large-scale *nacimientos* (nativity scenes) in El Salvador, and the raucous celebration of Mardi Gras before Lent by *comparsas* (merrymakers) in the streets of Panama.

Folktales. A variety of influences can be seen in Central American folktales. Many Indian legends use animal characters and have elements of witchcraft. A Costa Rican tale plays on the universal theme of the struggle between a peasant and a rich man, in which the peasant emerges with the gold. A Guatemalan story tells the origins of the *chirimia* reed flute in a suitor's quest to cheer up a sad princess; the Great Spirit shows him how to make an instrument that can imitate the sound of birds. There are also trickster stories, as in Indian, European, and African traditions.

When African peoples came to the New World as slaves, their stories about the clever Brer Rabbit spread through the Caribbean. One version from Panama tells how Brer Rabbit outwits the powerful Brer Tiger by offering him a ball of cheese that is really the moon's reflection in the water. Other examples of African influence on Central American folklore are the use of the MARIMBA xylophone made of wooden slats over gourd resonators and the unique traditions of the Garifuna people of Belize and Honduras, which blend African, Spanish, and Arawak Indian elements. Compared to the impact of African rhythms, folktales, and foodways on North American culture, however, the African influence in Central America is minor.

—*David Laubach*

SUGGESTED READINGS: • Collier, John. *The Indians of the Americas.* New York: W. W. Norton, 1947. • De Onis, Harriet. *The Golden Land.* New York: Alfred A. Knopf, 1948. • Gallenkamp, Charles. *Maya: The Riddle and Rediscovery of a Lost Civilization.* New York: McKay, 1959. • La Farge, Oliver, et al. *The Maya and Their Neighbors.* New York: Appleton-Century, 1940. •Picon-Salas, Mariano. Translated by Irving A. Leonard. *Cultural History of Spanish America: From Conquest to Independence.* Berkeley: University of California Press, 1962. • Redfield, Robert. *The Folk Culture of Yucatan.* Chicago: University of Chicago Press, 1941. • Seeger, Charles, comp. *Music in Latin America.* Washington, D.C.: Pan American Union, 1942.

Folklore, Cuban: When Cubans began to arrive in significant numbers in the United States, in the early 1960's, they brought their customs and adapted them to their new home. Somewhat reluctant to abandon their cultural identity, Cuban Americans have retained a distinctive popular culture wherever they reside in large numbers, as they do in Miami, Florida; northern New Jersey; and New York, New York.

The folkways of Cuban Americans have their origins on the island of Cuba and are basically religious, social, and verbal in nature. They stem from the two dominant cultures in Cuba, the European (mainly Spanish) and the African. Because the native Indian population of Cuba, the Taino, had a rather undeveloped culture and were exterminated, Cuban culture has almost no significant Indian elements aside from some words for native plants and the names of several towns on the island.

Religious Folklore. The most notable element of the religious folklore of Cuban Americans is a Spanish devotion to the Virgin Mary. The story of three men in a canoe in the Bay of Nipe who found a statue of the

This church in Miami, Florida, holds a statue of Our Lady of Charity, with a mural as its backdrop. (Martin Hutner)

Virgin Mary floating on a board bearing the inscription "I am the Virgin of Charity" is central to the history of the Cuban people. The devotion to the Virgin that subsequently developed gave Cubans a sense of identity and destiny. The sanctuary dedicated to Our Lady of Charity became a place of national pilgrimage and a repository for tokens of gratitude from Cubans and even non-Cubans such as Ernest Hemingway, who left there the medal of his Nobel Prize in Literature, won for his Cuban-set novel *The Old Man and the Sea* (1952). In Miami, on the grounds near Mercy Hospital overlooking Biscayne Bay and facing Cuba, Cuban Americans have built a modern sanctuary that houses an exact replica of the original statue of Our Lady of Charity. This is the site of an important manifestation of Cuban folklore, the *romerías*, or outdoor gatherings for social, civic, and religious purposes.

Another religious expression of Cuban popular culture is the worship by some Cubans of the *lucumí* deities (*orishas*). The *lucumí* religion is an African animist religion closely tied to nature and infused with a deep sense of magic. The pantheon of its many deities was originally brought to Cuba by African slaves. With time, a religious syncretism (mixing of different and seemingly irreconcilable religious or cultural elements) took shape, not exclusively among Cubans of African origins. SANTERÍA, a popular form of African animism, became for some Cubans a religion parallel to the official Catholicism professed, at least nominally, by a majority of Cubans before the Cuban Revolution. It identified African deities with Christian saints and martyrs. One of its principal deities is Babalú Ayé, later identified with Lazarus, the Biblical character raised from the dead by Christ.

Other important figures of *lucumí* religion and folklore are Changó (Saint Barbara, an early and obscure Christian martyr), Ochún (Our Lady of Charity at Cobre), and Yemayá (the Black Virgin, patroness of the Havana harbor). Their worship involves passionate, even frenzied, songs and dances, initiation rites, animal sacrifices, medicinal herbs, complex symbols and instruments (drums, sacred rocks, ritual foods, Catholic sacramentals, or religious objects such as medals and rosaries), and ritual clothing (necklaces, masks, white attire). In the United States, *santeros* (Santería priests) set up shops known as BOTÁNICAS selling many of these artifacts and herbs. In Hialeah, near Miami, *santeros* established a temple and found themselves involved, in 1993, in a legal controversy regarding animal sacrifice that reached the United States Supreme Court.

Maxims, Proverbs, and Sayings. The *lucumí* religion has also contributed to Cuban culture many maxims transmitted through the oral tradition. Some examples are "The evil you do comes back to you"; "The eyes speak"; and "Better to have the head of the mouse than the tail of the leopard." Other maxims (*refranes criollos*) do not stem from the ancestral wisdom of Afro-Cubans, coming instead from the rich popular culture of Spain. They were brought to Cuba by Galicians, Andalusians, and *isleños* (immigrants from the Canary Islands), the main Spanish groups to migrate to Cuba. Some of these sayings became part of everyday Cuban speech: "The tree that grows twisted can never be straightened"; "Happiness does not dwell long in the poor man's house"; "A donkey's curse does not reach heaven." This allegorical, metaphoric speech remains a vital part of the conversation of Cubans.

Jokes, Rhymes, and Superstitions. With the modernization of the Cuban American family, legends and tales have been largely lost because the oral tradition is not as vital. Even the old extemporaneous peasant rhymes (*décimas guajiras*), sung narratives that recall love, work, death, and nature in the Cuban countryside, have lost their prominence. The same could be said of the tradition of telling or reading tales in the tobacco factories of Ybor City in Tampa. What remain vital to Cuban folklore are jokes (*chistes*), salacious stories usually reflecting current political situations and personalities, and popular superstitions. Some of the latter are rather colorful: buckets of water should be emptied at midnight on New Year's Eve to expel bad luck during the new year, umbrellas should never be opened indoors lest bad luck follow, and rocking an empty rocking chair foreshadows death. The tradition of political protest through jokes has given rise, in Miami particularly, to a popular theater that dramatizes the exile experience of older Cubans and serves as a medium for social satire and political commentary.

Festivals and Carnivals. The carnivals popular in Havana and Santiago de Cuba have been transported to the United States since the 1960's. They express the Cuban love of music and spectacle. In Miami, for example, there are two such festivals, on the Feast of the Epiphany and around the beginning of Lent. These involve elaborate floats, costumed representations of the Three Magi, ethnic food and music (performed live), competing dance troupes, and the parading of important civic figures and entertainers.

—Robert Carballo

SUGGESTED READINGS: • Cabrera, Lydia. *El monte.* 2d ed. Miami, Fla.: Roma Press, 1968. • Didion, Joan.

Miami. New York: Simon & Schuster, 1987. • Portes, Alejandro, and Robert L. Bach. *Latin Journey: Cuban and Mexican Immigrants in the United States*. Berkeley: University of California Press, 1985. • Rieff, David. *The Exile: Cuba in the Heart of Miami*. New York: Simon & Schuster, 1993. • Shorris, Earl. *Latinos: A Biography of the People*. New York: W. W. Norton, 1992.

Folklore, Mexican American: Folklore is based on oral tradition and develops within a defined group. Folklore includes the songs, stories, legends, superstitions, sayings, games, riddles, beliefs, proverbs, and customs of a people.

Corridos and Other Song Forms. Among Mexicans and Mexican Americans, songs, notably CORRIDOS or ballads, recount the exploits of heroes and villains. The traditional *corrido* begins with the singer informing his audience of the theme of the song as well as its date, place, and characters. Mexican Americans, in their *corridos*, have celebrated the exploits of César CHÁVEZ, Reies López TIJERINA, Gregorio Cortez, and other heroes, as well as the tribulations of migrant life. "El Corrido de Delano," for example, describes the march of farmworkers, led by Chávez, from Delano, California, to the state capital in Sacramento to press their demands for higher wages and better working conditions (*see* MARCH TO SACRAMENTO). Many of the *corridos* that became popular in the United States dealt with poverty and the hardships faced by those leaving Mexico to work in *El Norte*.

Another song form is the CANCIÓN. It also tells a story, but unlike the *corrido*, it is a love song. Many, such as "La Adelita," honor the women soldiers of the Mexican Revolution. There are even comic songs, such as "Mi carrito paseado," that poke fun at people's fascination with cars.

Dichos. Proverbs or DICHOS were common in Mexican American folklore but began to disappear as Mexican Americans became more acculturated and spoke less Spanish. *Dichos*, in a sentence or two, impart advice or wisdom for living and are applicable to anyone. The origins of these sayings generally are unknown. Traditionally, *dichos* were passed on from mother, father, or grandparent to child. By the late twentieth century, *dichos* were no longer commonly passed on from generation to generation, but books of *dichos* could often be found in bookstores, particularly in the Southwest.

A typical *dicho* is "Dime con quien andas y te dire quien eres," literally translated as "Tell me who your friends are and I'll tell you who you are" and comparable to the saying "Birds of a feather flock together." Another is "El amor no obedece rey ni respeta ley," literally "Love neither obeys kings nor respects laws," or loosely, "Love is blind."

Cuentos and Leyendas. *Cuentos* (stories) and *leyendas* (legends) abound in Mexican American communities. La LLORONA (the weeping woman), probably the best known CUENTO among Mexicans and Mexican Americans, is an Aztec story that was transformed into a Mexican story. In one Aztec version, La Llorona foretold the fall of the Aztec empire. Another version has her drowning her children as a sacrifice. In the Southwestern version, she murdered her children because of a failed love affair. In all versions of this story, the woman cries for her lost children and seeks other children. Water, in the form of a lake or river, or even an irrigation ditch or well, is a common setting for the appearance of La Llorona.

Cuentos often are religious in nature, such as the story of the *Santo Niño* (the holy child) who wanders northern New Mexico and southern Colorado helping travelers in need. Each year, the tiny village of Chimayo, New Mexico, has a celebration in honor of the *Santo Niño*. During the celebration, the Christ child is taken from his niche. His old clothes are removed and replaced with new ones. His shoes invariably are scuffed and worn, despite having been replaced the year before. This lends credence to the story of his wandering about helping others.

Other stories are moralistic, with strong messages about proper behavior including honor and respect. In northern New Mexico, stories about Doña Sebastiana abound. She rides through the mountain villages in a cart, gathering souls. These stories do not diminish death but instead explain that death is an inevitable fact.

Creencias. Beliefs, or *creencias*, such as those involving superstitions, witchcraft, and certain illnesses and their cures, are also a part of folklore. Generally, the sources of these beliefs have been lost to history.

Among Mexican Americans, *el mal ojo* (the "evil eye") is a common belief. *El mal ojo* often is believed to be the cause of a child becoming ill. When a baby is brought into a room, almost everyone present may touch the child to prevent *el mal ojo*.

Among Mexican Americans, folk cures may be used when children suffer from *empacho*, or intestinal blockage. One cure involves placing lit candles at the head, foot, and sides of the bed to form the shape of a cross. An egg is then passed over the child's body to remove the item causing the blockage. When the egg is broken, it often is found to have been cooked by the heat generated by the illness, or it has spoiled, another sign that the illness has been removed.

When Mexican American children suffer from *mollera caída* (a sunken soft spot at the crown of the head, the fontanel), the folk treatment is to wrap the child in a blanket and have someone, preferably named Juan, pass water from his mouth to the mouth of the sick child. This cure has a scientific basis—a sunken fontanel is usually a sign of dehydration.

Another common belief is that a pregnant woman should never go out at night because a partial moon will cause the baby to be born with a harelip. Wearing a brass key around her stomach will eliminate this problem. Some Mexican American beliefs are similar to those of other cultures. For example, if salt is spilled, a pinch of salt should be thrown over the shoulder to make the devil flee.

Brujería, or witchcraft, abounds in Mexican and Mexican American folklore (*see* WITCHES AND WITCHCRAFT). Many of the stories regarding witches came to the Southwest with the Spaniards and were later combined with those of the Navajo, Zuni, Hopi, and Pueblo Indian tribes. Spanish documents in the state archives of New Mexico indicate that many women claimed that their straying husbands had been bewitched. The common sentence for those convicted of witchcraft was to be ordered out of the settlement. Native Americans convicted of being witches often were flogged, and in some cases they were executed.

American Indians of the Southwest believed in "skinwalkers," ghosts who roamed the earth because they were unhappy or had died in an unholy manner. The Spanish believed that those who had led an evil life and died as a result of their sinfulness were condemned to roam the earth for eternity. Priests often refused to bury these individuals in the *camposanto*, or sanctified earth of the cemetery, and these sorrowful souls were believed to appear to others who were going astray.

To ward off witches, especially on Friday nights, when they were believed to be most active, clothes were worn inside-out. Because witches were believed to be unable to penetrate any area protected by a cross, another common technique was to place crosses over doors and windows.

Owls or *lechuzas* have played important roles in most beliefs dealing with witchcraft. There are many stories regarding owls and their mystical powers. In Rudolfo ANAYA's *Bless Me, Ultima*, an owl appears and drives away brothers who have accused Ultima of being a *bruja*. Other stories tell of owls being shot by farmers defending their flocks of poultry; the next day a person suspected of being a witch is seen with an arm in a sling. Owls are also often heard when a tragedy is imminent.

Names are important in Mexican and Mexican American folklore. The name Juan or a derivative (Juanita or Juana, for example) is considered to be extremely powerful. People with these names often are called upon to remove curses or to cure those who have had spells cast upon them. Persons named Juan are also called on to cure *mal de ojo* and *mollera caída*.

Adivinanzas, Ritmos, and Versos. Adivinanzas, or riddles, have enjoyed popularity among Mexican Americans, particularly in the time before the advent of radio and television. Many *adivinanzas* involve trying to guess the identity of everyday items, with clues disguised in the form of a poem. By the end of the twentieth century, *adivinanzas* were dying out, but like DICHOS, they have been collected in book form. *Ritmos* and *versos* (rhymes and verses), often nonsensical, are usually passed on from mother to child or are the basis of children's games.

Mexican American folk traditions have changed as certain oral traditions have faded from use, but as long as some communities develop their own traditions outside the mainstream, folklore will remain a part of Latino life experiences. —*Louis Sarabia*

SUGGESTED READINGS:

• *Antología del Saber Popular*. Selected by Frank B. Aguilar et al. Los Angeles: Chicano Studies Center Publications, University of California, 1971. A collection of Mexican and Mexican American folktales, anecdotes, legends, beliefs, prayers, verses, children's games, and proverbs. Compiled by students at UCLA at the height of the Chicano movement.

• Aranda, Charles. *Dichos: Proverbs and Sayings from the Spanish*. Rev. ed. Santa Fe, N.Mex.: Sunstone Press, 1977. A small booklet containing twenty-six pages of *dichos*, six pages of *chiquillados* (comments used in flirting), *adivinanzas*, and some *creencias*.

• Bullock, Alice. *Living Legends of the Santa Fe Country*. 2d ed. Santa Fe, N.Mex.: Sunstone Press, 1972. Twenty-four legends and stories from northern New Mexico. Most of the stories have some type of supernatural flavor.

• Coffin, Tristram, and Hennig Cohen, eds. *Folklore in America: Tales, Songs, Superstitions, Proverbs, Riddles, Games, Folk Drama, and Folk Festivals*. Garden City, N.Y.: Doubleday, 1970. A series of articles previously published in the *Journal of American Folklore*.

• Griego y Maestas, José. *Cuentos: Tales from the Hispanic Southwest*. Translated by Rudolfo A. Anaya. Santa Fe: The Museum of New Mexico Press, 1980. Contains twenty-three folktales originally collected by Juan B. Rael. Has a glossary of archaic and idiomatic words and expressions.

• Limon, Jose E. *Mexican Ballads, Chicano Poems: History and Influence in Mexican-American Social Poetry*. Berkeley: University of California Press, 1992. Limon deals with folklore, literary theory, the social and political theories of Karl Marx, the Chicano movement, and Chicano and American studies.

• Simmons, Marc. *Witchcraft in the Southwest: Spanish and Indian Supernaturalism on the Rio Grande*. Lincoln: University of Nebraska Press, 1974. Simmons, one of New Mexico's leading historians, examines similarities in beliefs in Europe and the New World regarding witchcraft and supernatural occurrences.

Folklore, Puerto Rican: Folklore is a part of everyday life for the people of the island. It is made up of indigenous elements from the Aruacos and Taino, the original inhabitants of the island, along with both Spanish and African cultural influences (resembling those of Cuba, Haiti, and Brazil) that have adjusted to the changing needs and desires of the Puerto Rican people. Thus folklore is a mix of indigenous mythology and Spanish games, dances, songs, fiestas, and legends. Because Spanish is the dominant language, most, if not all, elements of Puerto Rican folklore are in Spanish.

Folklore is found and collected from the homes of the wealthy or from the most humble *bohío* (house or cottage in which the indigenous people live). It is manifested in daily activities such as the stories people narrate, the traditional songs they sing, and the proverbs they use, as well as in language, customs, celebrations, and children's games. Folklore has also left its mark on the fine arts, classical music, and literature. In essence, folklore is present wherever Puerto Rican life is present.

The frequent migrations of mainland Puerto Ricans back and forth from the island help ensure the maintenance of Puerto Rican folklore. For example, NUYORICANS have built numerous *casitas* (small houses) in vacant city lots that are modeled on the traditional wooden houses of rural Puerto Rico; these serve as headquarters for social clubs and community activities. Some Nuyoricans also carry on traditional musical styles such as the *JÍBARO* ensembles of the hillsides,

the old African-derived, percussion-based *BOMBA*, and the more recent Caribbean-influenced *PLENA* of the island barrios. Forms of folk religion, folk medicine, and traditional foodways are an important part of daily life for some mainland Puerto Ricans, along with the more conventional types of oral folklore described below.

Legends and Myths. Legends are stories founded in history that are not necessarily true. Using realistic detail, they re-create the spirit and the psychology of the people of Puerto Rico by bringing a sense of poetry to regional history. The themes of sixteenth and seventeenth century legends range from the religious, such as "Los milagros de San Patricio," "La Virgen de Bélen," and "El Cristo de los Ponce" to the historical, such as "Las garras de la Inquisición." Other legends tell of heroic characters and their adventures, such as "El Capitán Salazar" or "La Mensajera de la Muerte," and supernatural events of fortune or misfortune, such as "El grano de oro," "Una buena espada toledana," "Una buena jugada de naipes," and "La sortija de diamante."

Some Puerto Rican myths originated with the indigenous Taino, who inhabited the island before the Spanish came. These myths and legends are native explications of how the world came to be and other probing questions. They are narrated in Spanish with some indigenous vocabulary.

Folktales. Folktales can be classified in three distinct groups: They have psychological, symbolic, or social themes. Many of the stories can be traced to the Orient and thence to Spain. When the Spanish came to Puerto Rico, the tales were transmitted from parent to child, generation to generation. One of the most famous and beloved types of folktales centers around the character Juan Bobo or Juan the Simpleton. He is recognized as a *bobo*, or a dunce, for his candor, ingenuity, and infantile enthusiasm for the strange and new. Translations of these tales can be found in books by Pura Belpre such as *Juan Bobo and the Queen's Necklace: A Puerto Rican Folk Tale* (1962) and Bernice Chardiet's *Juan Bobo and the Pig: A Puerto Rican Folktale Retold* (1973). Folktales like these are told not only to entertain but also to instruct the young.

Musical Forms. The *DÉCIMA* is a poetic-musical composition with ten eight-syllable lines. *Décimas* are sung at religious ceremonies such as the *velorio cantao*, a rosary Mass given to a patron saint. Musicians and singers sing the *décimas* in antiphonal form; that is, one singer begins to sing and in turn, another singer or a group answers with more verses. *Décimas* are also found in the *jíbaro* folk music of mountainous rural areas as well as in work songs, lullabies, serenades, and other forms. Children's songs and games constitute another important element of folklore.

Proverbs and Riddles. Puerto Rican proverbs are a large part of the culture of the people. They serve as warnings of avoidable circumstances, as in "Nadie sabe el valor del agua, hasta que no se seque el pozo" (nobody knows the value of water until the well runs dry); and as recommendations, as in "Haz bien y no mires a quien" (do good, and don't look to whom) or "El que desea mal a otro, el suyo viene caminando" (he who wishes wrongfully [badly] to another, his is on its way). There are sayings to fit all sorts of situations and occasions.

Puerto Rican riddles may make plays on words, pose mathematical problems, or tell a story; some have no response or answer. Riddles are usually published in formal Spanish, although some versions use dialect to accentuate their folkloric quality. Many are of Spanish origin. Folktales such as those about Juan Bobo often contain riddles, as in the traditional form of the riddle-story.

Puerto Rican folklore is a reflection of the culture as it is found in the present, but it also reflects the essence of its appropriated cultures. The study of folklore helps in reconstructing the past culture as well as in understanding the present one. *—Angélica Jiménez Narain*

SUGGESTED READINGS: • Alegría, Ricardo E., ed. *Cuentos Folklóricos de Puerto Rico.* San Juan, Puerto Rico: Editora Corripio, 1969. • Arroyo Gómez, Alberto. *Bibliografía del folklore de Puerto Rico.* San Juan, Puerto Rico: Instituto de Cultura Puertorriqueña, 1991. • Coll y Toste, Cayetano. *Puerto Rican Tales: Legends of Spanish Colonial Times.* Translated by Jose Ramirez Rivera. Mayagüez, Puerto Rico: Ediciones Libero, 1977. • Mason, J. Alden. *Adivinanzas.* Edited by Aurelio M. Espinosa. San Juan, Puerto Rico: Instituto de Cultura Puertorriqueña, 1960. • Skinner, Charles M. *Myths and Legends of Our New Possessions and Protectorate.* 3d ed. Philadelphia, Pa.: J. B. Lippincott, 1902.

Fomento: Economic development organization. Formed in 1942 as the Puerto Rico Industrial Development Company, this agency was reorganized in 1950 as the Economic Development Administration, popularly known as Fomento. Its programs became popularly known as OPERATION BOOTSTRAP.

Fomento was not intended to further the industrial programs of Puerto Rico but instead to attract foreign investors, primarily from the United States. Domestic industrialization was aided, however, by the government's emphasis on education, which resulted in a well-trained labor force suitable for industrial work. Tax incentives induced foreign businesses to build plants on the island. By 1955, income from manufacturing exceeded that from agriculture.

Foodways, Central American: Central American cuisine and cultural usages surrounding it derive from the American Indian, Spanish, and African roots of the Central American people. Some of those usages have come to the United States with Central American immigrants.

Foodways in Central America. Central American foodways are the fusion of indigenous American Indian cuisine, Spanish cuisine brought with the European conquest, and African cuisine brought by slaves. Cuisines with the greatest African inputs are found along the Atlantic Coast, where slave ownership and contacts with Caribbean islands were the greatest. Spanish-dominated cuisines are most prominent in major cities, especially in countries such as Costa Rica where Indian influences on culture have declined along with the Indian populations. Indian-dominated cuisines are mostly in out-of-the-way places where native enclaves persist.

Central Americans in towns and cities usually follow the Spanish meal pattern, eating their main meal around noon, with smaller meals in the morning and evening. Working hours accommodate this arrangement, with a long noon break. Snacking is common between meals.

The vast majority of people in all Central American countries are poor. Consequently, most people eat inexpensive food most of the time. The most common mainstay is some version of rice and beans, called *gallo pinto* in most southern parts of Central America. This dish is eaten at all times of the day, sometimes alone, sometimes on tortillas. It may be made at home, but street vendors also sell the dish.

Some corn specialties, usually purchased from vendors, also are important as inexpensive mainstays. Guatemala, Honduras, and (to a lesser extent) Belize have corn dishes reminiscent of Mexican TACOS, TAMALES, and TOSTADAS. El Salvador has its distinctive corn dish, the *pupusa:* corn dough filled with beans, cheese, meat, eggs, or some mixture of these, formed into an enclosed pancake and grilled.

There are many options for eating out in Central America. In cities, street vendors sell everything from ice cream, banana chips, and fruits to more substantial fare. They often come into the city from villages, bringing with them village Indian dishes, such as tamales. The next step up in cost is to stalls in open-air markets, where each vendor prepares one or a few hot dishes over a simple and portable stove. A bit more expensive are the small restaurants, variously called *sodas* (Costa Rica), *comedores* (Guatemala and Nicaragua), *pupuserías* (El Salvador), and cafés (everywhere). These places offer seats and tables and a range of items, usually including inexpensive staples and a few more expensive local specialties. Restaurants with international menus are out of the financial reach of all but the wealthiest local diners. These restaurants cater to foreigners.

Regional specialties reflect the historical inputs to cuisine. Coastal Honduras is known for its seafood stews with coconut milk, direct descendants of West African dishes. El Salvador's national dessert, *la semita*, is a pineapple torte, using Spanish cooking concepts with a local fruit. The Nicaraguan *nacatamal* is a pre-Columbian Indian dish.

In addition to everyday cooking, there are special festival dishes, often different in each community. These usually are fancy, requiring expensive ingredients, large amounts of labor in preparation, or both. *Tamales negros*, for example, are steamed corn dough with chile and chocolate, eaten on holidays in the Guatemalan highlands around Quetzaltenango. They take a long time to prepare and use cocoa, a royal prerogative in pre-Columbian times. *Tamales negros* are used variously as part of the celebrations of Christmas and village patron saints' days.

World cuisine has affected Central American foodways to varying extents. American-based fast-food restaurants can be found in every country, although the dishes occasionally show local modifications. For example, Costa Rican McDonald's restaurants invariably sweeten iced tea with apple juice. The greatest outside influences show up in the cities, in the richer countries, and in countries with larger tourist industries. *Comida típica*, or local food, persists everywhere.

Central American Foodways in North America. Extensive migration from Central America to North America occurred in the latter half of the twentieth century, with large numbers of migrants leaving Guatemala, El Salvador, and Nicaragua. This influx took

A Salvadoran American woman prepares pupusas *for a restaurant on Long Island.* (Impact Visuals, Donna DeCesare)

A shop in the Little Managua area of Miami, Florida, offers a mix of Central American and North American food. (UNHCR/L. Solmssen)

certain Central American foodways to North America, but others stayed behind.

The most visible of Central American food institutions in North America is the Salvadoran *pupusería*. Two factors probably played parts in its success: the strong tradition of restaurants in El Salvador and the fact that the *pupusa* is unlike any Mexican dish well known in North America. Although some have become more upscale, most North American *pupuserías* are similar to their modest counterparts in El Salvador. They serve *pupusas* and often a range of other Salvadoran dishes, including tamales, fried and boiled manioc, plantain dishes, and traditional stews. Some *pupuserías*, especially in Latino neighborhoods with small Salvadoran communities, also serve Mexican dishes.

Other Central American foodways have not traveled as well. Most Central Americans have adopted the North American system, necessitated by work schedules, of having the largest meal in the evening. The range of dishes served at home typically has expanded with the economic means of the immigrants. Festival dishes sometimes are prepared at home or at community fiestas, but some have been abandoned. Others are eaten on non-traditional occasions. There are some Guatemalan *panaderías* (bakeries) that continue the traditions of breads and sweet buns, but other Central American businesses serving prepared foods (except *pupuserías*) are rare. There are, however, many supermarkets that stock Central American ingredients and cuts of meat. —*Russell Barber*

SUGGESTED READINGS: • Avila Hernandez, Dolores, et al. *Atlas Cultural de México: Gastronomía.* Mexico City, Mexico: Secretaria de Educacion Publica, 1988. • Marks, Copeland. *False Tongues and Sunday Bread: A Guatemalan and Mayan Cookbook.* New York: M. Evans, 1985. • Ramírez Saizar, J. *Folclor Costarricense.* San José, Costa Rica: J. Ramirez Saizar, 1986. • Ross de Cerdas, Marjorie. *Al Calor del Fogón: 500 Años de Cocina Costarricense.* San José, Costa Rica: Cultur Art, 1986. • Ross de Cerdas, Marjorie. *La Magia de la Cocina Limonense: Rice and Beans y Calalú.* San José, Costa Rica: Editorial de la Universidad de Costa Rica, 1991.

Foodways, Cuban American: The food traditions of Cuba were formed primarily from Native American,

The display case of a market in Miami, Florida, shows a variety of Cuban food items. (Library of Congress)

Spanish, African, and American influences. Cuban Americans retain many of those traditions.

Influences. The cuisine of Cuba is a complex amalgam of diverse cooking traditions. Although the extinction of the natives of the island (the Taino and Siboney) followed in the wake of the entry of the Spanish and their diseases in the early 1500's, native elements persist in Cuban cooking. The Cuban custom of roasting meat and vegetables, often wrapped in leaves, derives directly from the Taino BARBACOA, from which the term "barbecue" is derived. Cassava (yucca), a starchy root, remained a staple of the poor in the twentieth century, just as it was before the arrival of Christopher Columbus. Local fruits included avocados, pineapples, papayas, and coconuts, and all of these were integrated into Cuban cooking.

Spaniards provided a second major influence on Cuban cooking. The Spanish brought their distinctive ideas about taste and preparation methods, often overlaying these on local ingredients. *Ropa vieja*, a braised beef dish, was seasoned with ACHIOTE, a seasoning native to Cuba and added to a dish otherwise squarely in the Spanish tradition. New foodstuffs were brought to Cuba, most particularly rice and pigs, both of which became mainstays of Cuban cuisine.

A third major input to Cuban cooking was African. The decimation of the native population led the Spanish to import vast numbers of slaves into Cuba, especially to work in sugarcane fields. These slaves had been captured in Africa, and they brought with them African techniques of preparing food and particular tastes for its seasoning. Sometimes they smuggled African foods onto the packed slave ships and were able to establish new crops in Cuba and elsewhere. Yams and ackee, a starchy fruit, are African foodstuffs that were carried to Cuba.

The North American influence in Cuba was strong from the late 1800's through the revolution of 1959. During that period, Cubans adopted various North American dishes and ingredients, such as hot dogs, processed cheese, and canned vegetables.

Twentieth Century Cuban Cuisine. Traditionally, Cuban cuisine has been marked by strong flavors that require long cooking times to blend properly. Although rapid frying has been used for fish and some other dishes (often the result of influences from Chinese laborers who came to Cuba in the late 1800's), these are exceptions to the general rule of long cooking. Fruit juices, particularly citrus juices, are commonly used to marinate meat, and the marinade often is used as part of the cooking liquid.

As everywhere, the food of the poor is dominated by starches. In Cuba, typical starches have been cassava, rice, and yams; corn, which is more expensive, has been less significant. Fish are eaten widely, a relic of both the Native American and Spanish traditions. Meat is relatively expensive and so has been eaten primarily by the wealthy. Restaurants in many price ranges have been available; and eating out in Cuba traditionally has not been reserved only for the wealthy.

The traditional Cuban meal pattern was a variant on that of the Spanish. A light breakfast was followed by a mid-morning snack of coffee and sweets. A fairly heavy noontime lunch was followed by a *merienda* in the middle or late afternoon, and an evening dinner completed the day.

Large-scale immigration of Cubans to the United States began in the 1950's and continued through the 1990's. Major Cuban American communities were es- tablished both in southern Florida and in New York City and adjacent New Jersey. There, Cuban home- cooking traditions flourished, and Cuban restaurants of various kinds became common. Elsewhere there were smaller communities, and traditional home cook- ing was less well preserved in many of these. The American pattern of three meals was adopted widely by Cuban Americans.

Festivals and Celebrations. Festival cooking persis- ted in the United States wherever there was a Cuban community. Important festivals include Christmas, the Festival of the Three Kings (in January), and Carnival (July in Cuba but March in Florida). The first two are Catholic holidays, but Cuban Carnival is an outgrowth of SANTERIA, a syncretic religion blending Catholi- cism and African religions that has been prominent in Cuba. Also important were QUINCEAÑERAS, coming-of- age parties for fifteen-year-old girls.

On all these occasions, food plays a crucial role in the celebration. Each event may have particular dishes associated with it, but all include pork, the festival ingredient of Cuba. Most relished is roast suckling pig, but substitutes are made if that expensive dish is im-

Roasted pig is a favorite festival dish. (Envision, Norman Isaacs)

practical. "Moors and Christians" (black beans and rice) is traditional for the Catholic holidays, and multi-tiered cakes are common at *quinceañeras*.

Cuban restaurants in the United States in the 1990's served as gathering places for certain types of celebrations, particularly celebrations of personal success, such as getting a new job or a promotion. Some families had the tradition of eating weekly at a particular restaurant. Most Cuban restaurants primarily serve traditional food, although some in areas with small Cuban communities also served Mexican or American food. Cuban-Chinese restaurants, limited mostly to Florida and New York, served Cuban-style Chinese food with Cuban ingredients and seasonings. In the late 1980's, *nuevo cubano* cooking developed as a fusion between American nouvelle cuisine and traditional Cuban cooking, adopting techniques from the former and ingredients from the latter.

—*Russell Barber*

SUGGESTED READINGS:

• Barer-Stein, Thelma. *You Eat What You Are: A Study of Ethnic Food Traditions*. Toronto, Canada: McClelland and Stewart, 1979. A compendium of food habits around the world, including a section on the Caribbean.

• Creen, Linette. *A Taste of Cuba*. New York: E. P. Dutton, 1991. A cookbook with commentary on Cuban cooking in Florida.

• Mullin, Sue. *Nuevo Cubano Cooking*. Secaucus, N.J.: Chartwell, 1993. Primarily a recipe book, but its introductory sections discuss Cuban cooking in general and the development of *nuevo cubano* cooking.

• Randelmann, Mary Urrutia, and Joan Schwartz. *Memories of a Cuban Kitchen*. New York: Macmillan, 1992. A memoir of Cuba and its cuisine, with recipes included.

Foodways, Dominican: Like other Caribbean countries, the Dominican Republic had its foods and cuisine shaped by Native American, African, and Spanish influences. African influences are especially strong there.

The cuisine of the Dominican Republic, like that of other Caribbean countries, resulted from the intimate mixing of Native American, African, and European cuisines. The local Arawak Indians were agriculturalists who raised cassava (yucca), a starchy root, and MAIZE, obtained in pre-Columbian times from Mexico. They harvested a variety of cultivated and wild fruits, including pineapples, avocados, and papayas. Fish, both from the ocean and from freshwater streams, was an important foodstuff. All these foods, as well as others used before European arrival, have found their ways into modern Dominican cuisine.

Spanish Influence. The coming of the Spanish greatly changed Dominican cuisine. The Arawaks rapidly became extinct as the result of introduced disease and oppressive Spanish policies, including enslavement; with them died most Arawak influences on Dominican cuisine. Spanish cooks adopted local ingredients, supplementing them with foods from Spain, including wheat, rice, beef, and pork. They also introduced foodstuffs they had acquired in other colonies, including tomatoes and various kinds of beans.

Perhaps the most influential introduction, however, was sugar cane. Europe had developed an insatiable taste for sugar, which had been introduced there a few centuries before by the Arabs, but almost no place in Europe could grow this plant. The Caribbean islands, however, were ideal for sugar plantations, and the Spanish set about developing the sugar industry there. Sugar production is labor intensive, and the extinction of the Arawaks meant that another labor source was required.

The Spanish turned to Africa for slaves, and those slaves made significant contributions to Dominican cuisine. The vast majority of the population was slaves, and they prepared their own meals in ways similar to those to which they had been accustomed in Africa. Many slaves became cooks for plantation owners, and their culinary ideas helped shape the elite cooking of the owners. The Dominican emphasis on braised vegetable dishes with small amounts of meat for seasoning probably is directly attributable to African culinary inputs. Slaves also brought foods with them and planted many of them in their new homes. Some foods that made their way to the Dominican Republic on slave boats include yams, ackee (a starchy fruit), and pigeon peas.

Common Foods. Cassava bread has held a special place in the food history of the Caribbean in general and the Dominican Republic in particular. Natives virtually everywhere in the Caribbean made cassava bread by grating the cassava root, soaking it in several changes of water (to remove the toxic prussic acid naturally occurring in the plant), pressing the grated cassava into a thin mat by wringing it out in a cloth, then baking it on a flat stone in a fire until hard. The Spanish found that this hard bread remained fresh better than their ships' biscuits, and they took it on their voyages from the Caribbean. There were two main methods of rejuvenating the bread so that it became edible: soaking it briefly in water, then baking it briefly (for soft bread); or baking it without soaking (for crisp bread). Cassava bread no longer requires leaching because toxins were bred out of the cassava. Coconut, baking powder, flours, and oil have been added in response to European and African tastes, and twentieth century breads are cooked on metal sheets over a fire.

If there has been a national dish of the Dominican Republic, it is *sancocho*. *Sancocho* is a stew with many ingredients, primarily starchy vegetables. *Sancochos* may include meat, but usually in small quantities, more to provide taste than to dominate. Vinegar or citrus juice usually is an important seasoning. Pumpkin is a common ingredient. It is cooked long enough to disintegrate, flavoring and thickening the cooking liquid, and making it into a sauce. The technique for *sancocho* is typically West African, but the ingredients are the Dominican mix.

Food for the poor of the Dominican Republic traditionally has been cassava bread, *panecicos* (baked cassava cakes), and beans and rice. Cassava is weak in vitamins and minerals, and heavy reliance on it as a staple contributed to severe nutritional problems among the poor.

Special Feasts. As in many other parts of the Caribbean, pork has been the favored ingredient for festival use. Christmas and weddings traditionally have featured roast suckling pig; the nineteenth century Dominican custom was to cut out the anal ring of the roasted pig at wedding feasts and award it to the most beautiful single woman or girl present, as an indication that she soon would marry.

Dominican Cuisine in the United States. In the United States, Dominicans settled primarily in cities along the East Coast, particularly New York, and in Chicago. The Dominican Republic never had a strong restaurant tradition, and Dominican restaurants in the United States have not been common. As a result, the maintenance of traditional foodways has been left to the household through home cooking.

—*Russell Barber*

SUGGESTED READINGS:
- Barer-Stein, Thelma. *You Eat What You Are: A Study of Ethnic Food Traditions.* Toronto, Canada: McClelland and Stewart, 1979. A compendium of food habits around the world, including a section on the Caribbean.
- Brown, Cora, Rose Brown, and Bob Brown. *The South American Cook Book: Including Central America, Mexico, and the West Indies.* New York: Doubleday, Doran, 1939. Reprint. New York: Dover, 1971. A rambling book with some interesting commentary wedged between the recipes.
- Ortiz, Elisabeth Lambert. *The Complete Book of Caribbean Cooking.* New York: M. Evans, 1973. There are few published sources on Dominican foodways, but this cookbook includes some commentary on Dominican cookery and recipes.

Foodways, Mexican American: Food plays many different roles in the lives of Mexican Americans. It nourishes, offers opportunities to combine modern with traditional ways, and creates social bonds and obligations.

Regional Variation. Mexican American cooking has many regional variations. For example, *sopaipillas* (fried puffs of dough usually eaten with honey) are far more common in New Mexico and Texas than in California, where *buñuelos* (a similar treat served with anise-flavored syrup or sprinkled with cinnamon and sugar) are preferred. Immigration patterns and the influence of other cultural groups helped to establish these differences. As Mexicans immigrated north to join relatives already there, pockets of people from the same area of Mexico would form. Because each region of Mexico has a different cuisine, certain foods or cooking styles became common in some areas but not in others. Over time, other groups adopted and modified some foods. Recipes were changed to use the ingredients that were readily available, and new hybrid cooking styles developed, such as Tex-Mex.

Common Foods and Ingredients. The TORTILLA (a thin, unleavened, pancakelike bread) and *frijoles* (beans) are staples of the traditional Mexican American diet. There are two basic types of tortillas, wheat and corn. Most cooks purchase ready-made tortillas, but some still make tortillas from scratch, using wheat flour or special corn meal, lard, salt, and water. The most common *frijoles* are the pinto bean (a speckled pink and brown bean), the black bean (especially among those who trace their ancestry to southern Mexico), and the garbanzo bean (or chickpea).

Traditionally, SALSA (a chunky tomato-based sauce), *frijoles*, and tortillas are served at every meal except *desayuno*, the first meal of the day. *Desayuno* is the early breakfast, a light meal of tortillas or *panes dulces* (sweet rolls) and café con leche (coffee with milk). *Almuerzo*, a heartier breakfast of fruit, eggs, *frijoles*, tortillas, salsa, and coffee, is eaten at midmorning. *Comida*, the midafternoon meal, consists of *caldo* (soup) followed by SOPA (a less liquid, more stewlike soup, typically made of pasta or rice with vegetables or seafood), then a main course of meat or fish, with cakes or sweets and coffee to finish. In the late afternoon, *merienda*, a light snack often consisting of sweet bread or Mexican hot chocolate, is eaten. The last meal of the day is *cena*, another hearty meal served around 9 P.M.

Mexican American cooking calls on a wide range of ingredients. Some that help to identify a dish as Mexican American are TOMATILLOS (Mexican green tomatoes), CILANTRO (leaves of the herb coriander), jicama (a firm tuber that can be eaten raw), NOPALES (prickly pear cactus), *tuna* (the fruit of the prickly pear cactus), chayote (a variety of squash), *tamarindo* (a fleshy seed pod with a sweet and sour flavor), *flor de calabaza* (squash blossom), *epazote* (a tealike herb), *huitlacoche* (a mushroomlike fungus that grows on ears of corn),

hoja de elotes (corn husks used in tamale making), pumpkin seeds, CHORIZO (Mexican sausage), CHICHA-RRONES (fried pork rinds), *piloncillo* (Mexican raw sugar), sweet potatoes, fresh coconuts, maguey hearts (the center of the agave plant), and many types of CHILE peppers, including JALAPEÑO, serrano, guero, California green (Anaheim), and pasilla.

Dietary Health. The traditional Mexican American diet has both strengths and weaknesses. Its strengths are the abundance of complex carbohydrates (provided by the tortillas and *frijoles*) and fruit. Because of the popularity of fried foods, sweet beverages, and desserts, the weaknesses are the diet's large amounts of fat and sugar. Compared to the general population, Mexican Americans have high rates of obesity and DIABETES. Studies conducted in the 1980's suggest a correlation between the traditional Mexican American

Most North American Latino families use ready-made tortillas, but some make them from scratch. (Impact Visuals, Donna DeCesare)

Various foods can be part of the celebration of El Día de los Muertos. (Diane C. Lyell)

diet and these conditions. Mexican Americans who eat less fat and more vegetables have lower rates of obesity and heart disease than those who eat more traditional fare.

Food Beliefs and Superstitions. Many Mexican Americans believe that foods, herbs, illnesses, and physical conditions such as pregnancy can be divided into two categories: hot and cold. This has nothing to do with temperature. Instead, this belief system is thought to be derived from the ideas of the ancient Greeks, who believed in four elemental bodily fluids, called humors, which were thought to determine personality and the best treatment for diseases. A variation of the idea was brought to Mexico by the Spanish.

Although not everyone agrees which foods and conditions are "hot" or "cold," these foods are usually considered "hot": chile peppers, garlic, onion, many grains, fruits from temperate climates (such as apples and pears), the most expensive cuts of meat (such as steaks and roasts), oils, and alcoholic beverages. These foods are usually considered "cold": vegetables, tropical fruits (including mangoes and pineapples), dairy products, and the least expensive cuts of meat (such as kidneys and liver).

Hot illnesses such as fevers are often treated with cold foods, and cold illnesses with hot foods. Other illnesses, such as diarrhea, are thought to be created by an imbalance of hot and cold within the body and are treated by avoiding extremely hot foods (such as chile peppers) or extremely cold foods (such as fruit juice, tortillas, and bananas). There are also special rules for women. Those who are nursing should avoid cold foods. Pregnant women should avoid certain foods of both varieties, for example avocado, chile peppers,

Mexican foods familiar in the United States include (clockwise from upper left) tortilla chips, salsa, flan, quesadillas, fajitas, a taco, and an enchilada; the foods are often accompanied by refried beans and Spanish rice. (Dawn Dawson)

fish, and acidic fruits (such as oranges). The folk belief that no one should drink milk and eat avocado at the same time (two cold foods together) is probably also based on the hot-and-cold system.

Chile peppers have their own folklore. They are said to cure ague (alternating attacks of fever and chills), colds, and sore throats. Ground chile pepper supposedly keeps evil away from those who sprinkle it on their shoes. Growing chiles is said to bring good luck, while the hottest peppers are said to be those that were planted by an angry gardener.

Food and Holidays. Sugar skulls, candy skeletons, and specially decorated *panes de muertos* (breads of the dead) are eaten during El Día DE LOS MUERTOS (the Day of the Dead, November 2). Pumpkin cooked in molasses and *mole* (a rich sauce usually containing chocolate and pumpkin seeds) is part of the feast brought to the graves of dead friends and family members to be "shared" with them. The special foods and the feast in the cemetery help to reinforce the beliefs that relationships continue after death and that death is a part of life.

Another holiday connected with food is *Noche Buena*, part of the Christmas season in some areas. Children go from house to house carrying bags to be filled with sweets. They ask for the door to be opened to them, threatening to break it down otherwise. Once the door is opened, they are given *empanditas* (little pies with a sweet filling), *bizcochitos* (little sweet breads), cakes, candies, raisins, and apples or other fruit.

Semana Santa, or Holy Week (the week between Palm Sunday and Easter), has its own food traditions. Some meats are avoided, and special vegetable dishes are prepared. *NOPALITOS* (the green paddles or "leaves" of the prickly pear cactus) are dethorned, chopped, and cooked. When cooked with eggs, they make a dish called *nopalitos con huevos*. The flowers of "God's candlestick" (the yucca plant) are fried or made into a soup. On Good Friday, families eat sparingly—fish, eggs, and fruit—or they fast until evening. On Easter Sunday, *capirotada* (bread pudding) is also traditional, because bread is symbolic of the holiday.

Social Functions of Food. The making of TAMALES shows how food can be used to show affection and to foster mutual interdependency by creating social obligations. Tamales are potent symbols of love and obligation. A wife may make tamales for her husband in order to show that she is a proper wife, or she may give tamales to extended family and outsiders so that they will help her in the future. Homemade tamales are often reserved for special occasions. Tamales are often made at Christmas, for a QUINCEAÑERA (an elaborate celebration held on a girl's fifteenth birthday), for Mother's Day, or to celebrate a crop harvest.

Tamale-making is often a group project, because the process is labor intensive and can be expensive. The first step is to gather or purchase the ingredients: special corn meal (called *masa harina* or *masa nixmital*), which usually comes from a *tortillería* (tortilla factory); corn husks (*hoja de elotes*) for wrapping the tamales; and the filling mixture, which can be savory or sweet. Savory fillings usually consist of some type of meat mixed with chile peppers. Sweet fillings are made of sugar, spices, and fruit or corn kernels. Next, the corn husks must be soaked in water and separated from one another. The MASA is then mixed with fat, such as pork lard or butter, and beaten until it is the right consistency to be spread on the corn husks. Usually the most experienced tamale maker in the group is in charge of the *masa* mixing and beating, because this is the most difficult task. Once the *masa* is ready, it is spread on the corn husks. The filling is added on top of the *masa*, and the tamales are rolled up. If more than one type of tamale is being made, the way that the tamales are tied with the husk may be used to tell the types apart. After all the tamales are assembled, they are steamed. Every tamale maker has a favorite steaming method. Some use pressure cookers, others use a pot and steaming rack or even a large tin can.

Impact. Mexican Americans have profoundly influenced the diet of the United States. Early in the twentieth century, Mexican food was reviled or unknown outside the American Southwest. The advent of standardized Mexican fast-food chains helped put to rest fears that Mexican food was dirty and unfit to eat. These restaurants served reassuring food in which unfamiliar, sharp-tasting, or pungent-smelling ingredients had been removed—for example, by substituting processed cheddar cheese for more authentically Mexican *queso fresco* (fresh cheese). The menus included old Mexican favorites such as tacos as well as some "Mexican" food that had been invented in America, such as enchuritos (a meat, tortilla, and sauce dish) and fajitas (strips of sautéed or grilled beef, pork, or

chicken). By the early 1990's, salsa outsold catsup in the United States.   *—Kelly Fuller*

SUGGESTED READINGS:

• Brown, M. H. De La Peña. "Una Tamalada: The Special Event." *Western Folklore* 40 (January, 1981): 64-71. Describes a communal tamale-making session, with emphasis on the division of labor and the social interactions of the tamale makers.

• Camp, Charles. *American Foodways*. Little Rock, Ark.: August House, 1989. An introduction to the concept of foodways by a major name in the field. Bibliography includes a list of periodicals that publish foodways research.

• Dewey, Kathryn G., Margaret A. Strode, and Yolanda Ruiz Fitch. "Dietary Change Among Migrant and Nonmigrant Mexican-American Families in Northern California." *Ecology of Food and Nutrition* 14, no. 1 (1984): 11-24. Describes the traditional Mexican American diet, the system of hot and cold foods, and common factors that cause dietary change.

• Kennedy, Diana. *The Cuisines of Mexico*. Rev. ed. New York: Harper & Row, 1986. Long considered the most authentic Mexican cookbook available in English. Includes recipes, explanations of ingredients and cooking equipment, and a useful vocabulary and pronunciation guide.

• Levenstein, Harvey A. *Revolution at the Table: The Transformation of the American Diet*. New York: Oxford University Press, 1988. A survey that chronicles the changes in the American diet since the nineteenth century, with special attention given to the effects of immigrants.

• Sewell, Ernestine, and Joyce Gibson Roach. *Eats: A Folk History of Texas Foods*. Fort Worth: Texas Christian University Press, 1989. Contains a long interview that discusses food names, folk beliefs about food, and traditional foods for the holidays among Mexican Americans living in Texas. Includes recipes.

• Stern, Michael. "Knowledge, Attitudes, and Behavior Related to Obesity and Dieting in Mexican Americans and Anglos." *American Journal of Epidemiology* 115 (June, 1982): 917-928. A major study of the link between obesity, certain illnesses, and the traditional Mexican American diet. The article is not easy reading but is useful for its solid statistical evidence.

• Williams, Brett. "Why Migrant Women Feed Their Husbands Tamales." In *Ethnic and Regional Foodways in the United States*, edited by Linda Keller Brown and Kay Mussell. Knoxville: University of Tennessee Press, 1984. A scholarly, well-researched

This Puerto Rican restaurant in Rochester, New York, serves tacos and alcapurrias de yuca *(stuffed yucca).* (Don Franklin)

work that examines the role of food in the lives of Mexican American migrant workers.

Foodways, Puerto Rican: Puerto Rican cuisine followed the general pattern of Caribbean cuisines, deriving jointly from Native American, African, and European roots. It has been one of the more diverse cuisines in the Caribbean, and its New York version saw subtle changes in the latter half of the twentieth century.

Early Influences. In 1511, King Ferdinand of Spain established an experimental farm in Puerto Rico's Toa Valley, the first known agricultural station in the Americas. This farm raised local plants as well as ones imported from the far corners of the Spanish Empire. These products made their way into Puerto Rican cooking soon after. Plantains, a starchy banana with little sweetness, were first raised in the Caribbean on Puerto Rico. From there, they spread to adjacent islands. The same pattern is true for many other foodstuffs.

As with all Caribbean cooking, Puerto Rican cuisine has its roots in Native American, African, and European traditions. Many of its ingredients are native, cultivated or foraged by the Native Americans before Europeans arrived. These include cassava (yucca), MAIZE, peanuts, sweet potatoes, pineapple, papayas, and COCOA. Other ingredients were brought from Spain, including rice, wheat, chicken, pork, beef, and sugar. Still others came from Africa, as slaves were brought to Puerto Rico to labor on the sugar plantations after the extinction of the local natives by diseases introduced by the Spanish. These African imports include yams, bananas, malagueta pepper, okra, and probably pigeon peas (*gandules*). Along with these ingredients came the cooking techniques, taste preferences, and ideas surrounding food that were held by these diverse peoples.

Seasonings. Puerto Rican cooking has been characterized by emphasis on seasonings, including standard mixtures. The three most important of these mixtures are adobo, *sofrito*, and *achiote*. Adobo is a mixture of salt, black pepper, oregano, and garlic, sometimes with oil and either vinegar or citrus juice. This mixture is rubbed onto fish, meat, or poultry as a standard seasoning before cooking. *SOFRITO* is a purée of bell peppers, garlic, onion, cilantro, and oregano; sometimes tomatoes, ham, bacon, or herbs are added. This mixture is sautéed briefly to bring out its flavors, and it is ready to use in seasoning soups, vegetables, and meat dishes.

Achiote technically refers to the seeds of a tropical tree, but the term has been extended to include a col-

ored and slightly flavored fat produced by sautéing the seeds lightly; traditionally, ACHIOTE was made with lard, but other oils have come into wide use. *Achiote* is used to color rice, sauces, and other foods, and it lends a subtle taste of its own. Commercial powders purporting to replace these mixtures have become available, but generally they are considered to be inferior substitutes.

Common Dishes and Ingredients. Puerto Rican cuisine has been one of the more varied cuisines of the Caribbean, and the range of dishes is large. Nevertheless, some ingredients and dishes have appeared with sufficient frequency to warrant special note. Rice has been a mainstay of most Puerto Rican diets, and many people prefer to have it at least once a day. Richer people have been able to make rice merely one of several foods, but poorer people may fill up on rice and other inexpensive starches.

Also important are the fruits and vegetables collectively termed *bianda*. *Bianda* comprises starchy roots (yams, sweet potatoes, potatoes, cassava, taro, and others), as well as similar fruits and vegetables that are not roots (plantains, pumpkins, and CHAYOTES). Most of these are moderately inexpensive, and they have provided dietary variety that appeals to the taste and helps ease nutritional deficiencies. *Bianda* of several types usually are mixed together in a dish, often served boiled with oil-and-vinegar dressing or as part of a hearty soup.

Bacalao or *BACALAITOS*, dried salt codfish, also has been used widely in Puerto Rican cooking. *Bacalao* has been common and popular in the Mediterranean and is part of the Spanish legacy of Puerto Rican cuisine. After soaking for several hours to desalt it, *bacalao* is shredded and used in stews, casseroles, salads, and other dishes.

PASTELES are a Caribbean version of Mexican tamales. A dough is made of mashed *bianda* and spread inside a banana leaf; meat filling is placed in the center of the dough; the leaf is wrapped up and tied with the dough and filling inside it, enclosing the filling inside the dough; and the package is boiled. These have been a favorite item of street vendors, but the large amount of labor required means that they usually have been made at home only for special occasions.

JUEYES (land crabs) once were extremely numerous in sugarcane fields and were a regular part of Puerto Rican diet, especially in rural areas. They were served boiled, stewed with vegetables and seasonings, baked, or as the filling for *EMPANADAS*. They became far less common, and their consumption fell off. In New York,

Rice is a mainstay of Puerto Rican cooking. (Don Franklin)

they were replaced with sea crabs, and the meaning of the term gradually shifted to include crabs of all kinds.

Special Feasts. As elsewhere in the Caribbean, pork has been commonly used as a festive food. *Lechón asado*, roast pork, preferably made from a suckling pig, has been a common and revered dish among Puerto Ricans. The cleaned pig is rubbed with adobo before being roasted over charcoal and basted periodically with *achiote*. *Lechón asado* is a traditional picnic food, typically accompanied by plantains wrapped in leaves and roasted in the coals as the pig cooks. In the 1990's, such dishes generally were reserved for special occasions. A typical old-fashioned Christmas dinner would consist of roast pork, accompanied by *pasteles*, rice, and pigeon peas (a fancier version of the everyday rice and beans).

Other Dishes. In addition to these distinctively Puerto Rican dishes, many classic dishes of Spanish cuisine came to Puerto Rico with little or no modification. Examples include GAZPACHO (bread-thickened, uncooked tomato soup, served cold), TORTILLAS, and PAELLA (a rice dish with chicken, shellfish, and sausages). West African dishes that were incorporated into the Puerto Rican repertoire with almost no change include *coo-coo* (a gruel of corn meal, cassava flour, or other starch with various additions, known as "foo-foo" in West Africa) and *mofongo* (balls made from crushed fried plantains and cracklings, served with a sauce).

Cooking and Meal Patterns. Traditionally, well-to-do Puerto Rican families had servants to do the cooking, and it was considered uncivilized to know much about cooking. Families of more modest means had to cook their own meals, and cooking traditionally was done by the wife. If that was impossible, another female member of the household assumed the duties. The kitchen was dominated by a *fogón*, a built-in stove with four or five grates on its upper surface and an oven below. *Fogóns* were made of bricks or blocks and their exteriors often were decorated with beautiful tiles. Supplementing the *fogón* was an *anafre*, an iron brazier similar to the Japanese hibachi.

With these tools, the cook turned out several meals a day. Following the general Spanish meal plan, Puerto Ricans ate a light breakfast, a late morning snack, a heavy luncheon around noon, another snack (*merienda*) in the mid-afternoon, another full meal in the mid-evening, and a light snack before retiring for the night. The noontime and mid-evening meals had several courses, usually beginning with soup and salad and moving on to several dishes.

Traditional patterns of food preparation in Puerto Rico changed over the years. The *fogón* and *anafre* were replaced by standard gas or electric stoves, and few families could afford servants to cook for them. As women became more involved in the workplace and in social and political affairs, the complexity of meals generally diminished. Many Puerto Ricans continued to have five meals a day, but others reduced the number to the three meals common in North America.

Puerto Rican Cuisine in New York. There was a limited Puerto Rican immigration to New York in the 1920's and 1930's, giving rise to the SPANISH HARLEM section. In the 1950's, however, greater employment opportunity and less expensive means of travel encouraged larger numbers of Puerto Ricans to immigrate to the United States, particularly New York City. The New York Puerto Rican—sometimes known as "Nuyorican"—community swelled and established the institutions necessary to maintain Puerto Rican foodways.

An important institution was *la marqueta*, a partially open-air market dealing in Puerto Rican foodstuffs. Open every day except Sunday, it was most heavily patronized on Saturday, the traditional market day. Haggling over prices was encouraged, and the many stalls and vendors ensured that the diligent shopper could find whatever was needed. By the 1980's, *la marqueta* had declined, largely as a result of competition from major supermarkets. A plan to revitalize *la marqueta* was beginning to be implemented in the early 1990's.

Equally important to sustaining Puerto Rican cuisine in New York were restaurants and food stalls. These establishments ranged from simple catering carts selling *piragua* (fruit-flavored shaved ice), to market stalls selling TOSTONES or PASTELES, to elegant restaurants serving *comidas criollas*, traditional Puerto Rican cooking.

Nuyorican cuisine remained quite similar to its ancestral cuisine in Puerto Rico. The major differences were a greater usage of meat (in part the result of higher incomes and lower meat prices), a tendency to season somewhat less heavily, and an eclecticism that took advantage of the foods of other ethnic groups in New York. Dishes such as lasagna, prepared foods such as bagels, and ingredients such as daikon (Chinese radishes) all made their way into Nuyorican cuisine. As Puerto Ricans adapted to job schedules in New York, most adopted the American pattern of three meals per day.

To an extent, these changes influenced foodways in Puerto Rico. As some Puerto Ricans returned from

Stores in New York City specialize in selling ingredients commonly used in Puerto Rican cooking. (Frances M. Roberts)

New York to Puerto Rico, and as others communicated with their relatives there, Nuyorican ideas became more prominent in Puerto Rico. For example, some Puerto Ricans developed a family tradition of serving spaghetti on Wednesday, an Italian custom in the northeastern United States, and bagel shops opened in San Juan.   —*Russell Barber*

SUGGESTED READINGS:

• Barer-Stein, Thelma. *You Eat What You Are: A Study of Ethnic Food Traditions.* Toronto, Canada: McClelland and Stewart, 1979. A compendium of food habits around the world, including a section on the Caribbean.

•Cabanillas de Rodriguez, Berta, and Carmen Ginorio. *Puerto-Rican Dishes.* 4th ed. Rio Piedras, Puerto Rico: Editorial de la Universidad de Puerto Rico, 1974. Primarily a recipe book. Includes useful discussion of the history of dishes and their social context in Puerto Rico.

• Ortiz, Yvonne. *A Taste of Puerto Rico.* New York: Dutton, 1994. A cookbook with a brief but excellent history of the development of Puerto Rican cuisine. Includes commentary on most recipes.

• Rivera, Oswald. *Puerto Rican Cuisine in America.* New York: Four Walls Eight Windows, 1993. An excellent source for Nuyorican cooking and foodways. Includes introductory essays, recipes, and brief discussions of the cultural or culinary place of most dishes. The best single source on this subject.

• Valldejuli, Carmen Aboy. *Puerto Rican Cookery.* Gretna, La.: Pelican, 1991. English translation of *Cocina Criolla*, the most successful Puerto Rican cookbook. Contains almost no food history or foodways information, but the roster of recipes is extensive and representative of Puerto Rican cooking.

Foodways, Spanish American: Spanish American foods and foodways owe much to the Spanish tradition, although local Native American cuisines and foodstuffs also had an influence. The diverse cuisines of Latin America all were derived from the interaction of Spanish cooking with local Native American food traditions; in some cases, African or other traditions also made significant contributions. Much of the commonality of Spanish American foodways can be traced to the Spanish influence.

Colonial Cuisine. The conquistadores and the first wave of Spanish colonists came primarily from the Extremadura region of Spain, and it is there that one must look for the Spanish roots of Spanish American cuisine. The Estremadura lies along the mountainous border between Spain and central Portugal, a region forested with oaks and chestnuts. In the sixteenth century it suffered from serious environmental degradation, brought on by overuse of the land. This degradation encouraged adventuresome young people to consider leaving for the newfound Americas, and many did. With them came their foodways, forged by the influences of native Iberian cooking, the Roman occupation, and the Moorish occupation.

Spanish cuisine of this period had several characteristics distinguishing it from other European cuisines, many of which derived from the Moorish influence. Some of these characteristics were passed on to Spanish America.

Southern Europe, and Spain most of all, was known for its heavily seasoned dishes. The Moors had popularized strong flavorings during their occupation of Spain, and their links to the rest of the Arab world made spices relatively inexpensive in Spain. The Iberians pioneered voyages to establish the oceanic spice trade, perpetuating the relative ease with which they procured exotic seasonings. Many of the culinary traditions encountered by the Spanish colonists, especially the Mexican tradition, also featured heavy spicing, and these inclinations encouraged one another. Even in parts of the Americas where the native cuisine was sparing with spices, such as Louisiana, Spanish influence encouraged generous use of seasonings.

Ingredients, Dishes, and Implements. Certain ingredients common to the Spanish kitchen were transported to the Americas, often to be grown there. Olives, capers, onions, garlic, almonds, citrus fruit, and saffron all were distinctive Iberian ingredients brought to the Americas and incorporated into various Spanish American cuisines. Certain staples, particularly rice, became important in Spanish American cooking, partly because of the Spaniards' established taste for it and partly because it could be grown in wetlands otherwise of little use for crops. Other Spanish ingredients, such as *bacalao* (dried salt codfish) in Puerto Rico, became important in one or more Spanish American cuisines.

Patterns of using these ingredients sometimes have transferred from Spain to the Americas. For example, adobo, a spice mixture the Spanish rubbed on meat before cooking it, was transferred to many Spanish American traditions without modification. SOFRITO, on the other hand, was a vegetable mixture used for seasoning in Spain that came to the Americas as a concept and word. Tomatoes and bell peppers were substituted for European vegetables, and *sofrito* became part of Caribbean cooking. Curiously, it was transmitted back to Spain in its modified form, and later Spanish *sofrito* included those American ingredients.

Some Spanish dishes were transmitted to Spanish America directly. FLAN, *PAELLA*, *HORCHATA*, and dozens of other dishes have been essentially the same in the Americas as they were in their original Spanish forms; some saw minor modifications, especially to take advantage of locally available ingredients. Others, such as *GAZPACHO*, were modified considerably in parts of Spanish America.

Some dishes and ingredients transported to the Americas maintained the cultural associations they had in Spain. Pork, for example, was the favorite meat of the Extremadura, and the pork sausages of that region were famous. The pig retained its festival character in most of Spanish America, especially the Caribbean, and the tradition of eating roast suckling pig (*cochinillo asado*) at Christmas dinner persisted in both the Extremadura and the Spanish Caribbean. The importance of sausage (*CHORIZO*) throughout Latin America has been part of the same phenomenon.

Implements for food preparation throughout Spanish America include Spanish forms. Some pot types, such as *ollas*, were present in pre-Columbian America nearly everywhere. Other Spanish forms that became part of the American tradition had no local antecedents, such as the *cazuela*, used in parts of Central America, and the bread ovens of New Mexico, used by both Pueblo Indians and Latinos.

Patterns and Rituals. Everyday patterns of food consumption in most of Spanish America mirrored the common patterns of Spain. The meal pattern of Spain, for example, had from five to seven meals per day, starting with a light breakfast, followed by a late morning snack, a heavy lunch, a *MERIENDA* in the mid-afternoon, and a heavy dinner in the mid-evening; two additional *tapas* snacks sometimes were incorporated. That pattern or some variant on it was adopted throughout Spanish America, although in some places it had broken down by the 1990's under the influence of non-Latino culture. Multicourse meals were virtually unknown in Native American foodways, restricted essentially to the Aztec imperial household; in reflection of the Spanish standard, they became widespread in Spanish America.

A shop in New York City displays its offerings. (Hazel Hankin)

Special ritual uses of food were carried by the Spanish to the Americas. The use of wheat bread and wine as Catholic sacraments is one example; others come from folk culture. The celebration of El Día de los Muertos in Spain involved the making of *huesos de santo* (holy bones), bone-shaped cookies to be used in cemetery rituals; it also included marzipan candies for children. Both of these traditions were adopted in parts of Spanish America, particularly Mexico.

Conclusion. Spanish American foodways are more than a mere copy of Spanish foodways, but the Spanish input has been considerable. This was especially true in places where Native Americans became extinct early (such as Costa Rica) and in larger communities where a Spanish-oriented elite made these practices fashionable. —*Russell Barber*

Suggested Readings:

• Casas, Penelope. *The Foods and Wines of Spain.* New York: Alfred A. Knopf, 1982. A widely available cookbook with a good introductory section.

• Emery, William H. *The Flavor of Spain.* Boston: CBI, 1983. Mostly recipes, but a good introductory essay on regional cuisine.

• Feibleman, Peter S. *The Cooking of Spain and Portugal.* New York: Time-Life Books, 1969. Widely available. Historical material is limited.

• Manjón, Maite. *The Gastronomy of Spain and Portugal.* New York: Prentice Hall, 1990. An encyclopedia of food of Iberia. Mostly text but includes a few recipes.

• Martínez, Llopis, Manuel. *Historia de la gastronomía española.* Madrid: Alianza Editorial, 1989. Excellent treatment of the history of Spanish food, geared especially to elite cooking. In Spanish.

• Pohren, D. E. *Adventures in Taste: The Wines and Folk Food of Spain.* Morón de la Frontera, Spain: Society of Spanish Studies, 1972. Mostly devoted to wine, but some good treatment of Spanish food.

Foraker Act (1900): In order to establish a system of government for Puerto Rico after it was acquired at the end of the Spanish-American War, the Foraker Act set up a classic "crown colony" government for the island.

When Puerto Rico became a ward of the United States in 1898, there was no comprehensive colonial policy. Other territories that had been acquired were contiguous and had not been colonized extensively. The Caribbean territories and the Philippines, by contrast, were enormously populated. On the basis of the specious argument that the Puerto Ricans had no governmental skills, the island was designated "unorganized," in contrast to the Hawaiian Islands and Alaska, which were considered potential new states.

The Foraker Act was named for Senator Joseph Forest Foraker of Ohio, a member of a "power bloc" of senators who formed the nucleus of the government at the end of the nineteenth century. Because senators were appointed by the various state legislatures, few reached the Senate without the financial assistance of the industrial and commodity interests. This practice endured until the ratification of the Seventeenth Amendment in May, 1913. As a result of the selection process of U.S. senators, the colonial policy of the United States was securely in the hands of a self-serving plutocracy. Although the economic potential of the new territories was not yet evident, it was considered good business to keep them under strict colonial control.

At the time, the pattern for expansion of U.S. territory had been defined by President Woodrow Wilson as more concerned with "human rights, national integrity, and opportunity" than "material conquests." Despite this liberal philosophy, colonial rule extended in Puerto Rico until 1917, when modification through the JONES ACT allowed the Puerto Rican people citizenship in the United States and greater representation in government. It was not until 1947, however, that the territory became completely democratic.

Patterned after the British "crown colony" concept, the Foraker Act set up a bicameral legislature. The lower house was elected by the governed people, and the upper house was an executive council consisting of six department heads and five other Puerto Ricans, all appointed by the president of the United States, as was the governor.

In addition to establishing the structure of government, the act established tariffs on goods shipped between Puerto Rico and the United States in both directions. These provisions remained in force in Puerto Rico until mitigated by the JONES ACT, which gave a greater measure of self-government to the people.

The control given to the Senate and the interests supporting it extended to commerce in sugar and other tropical products that were to grow enormously in importance during the early twentieth century. As was the case in many other Latin American countries, the importance to United States and European companies of the economic potential of the region was the force driving nearly every political decision. A positive consequence of Puerto Rico being an "unorganized" possession is its complete freedom from federal taxes, which was to facilitate economic growth.

Foreign Miners' Tax Law (1850): California law passed to restrict mining activities to white Americans only. Mexican Americans and other foreign miners were harassed by vigilantes and evicted from their claims. The state legislature enacted a license fee of $20 per month on all foreign miners, but the tax collectors could not protect the claims of those who paid the tax. Many Mexican American miners refused to pay the tax and faced vigilante violence. Many were murdered or lynched to eliminate them from staking claims. Others chose to abandon their mining claims to avoid such an end. Although the tax was repealed in 1851, the law had already achieved its objective. Mexican Americans became more convinced that their guaranteed rights as citizens of California would fail to be honored by the white-majority government.

Forty-eighters: Miners. Although the term "Forty-niner" has been associated with miners who traveled to California during the GOLD RUSH, a significant number of people began migrating to the gold country prior to 1849. On January 24, 1848, John Marshall discovered gold at Sutter's Mill, and soon thereafter, many people migrated to the Sierra Nevadas in search of riches. In the fall of 1848, thousands of Mexicano, Peruvian, and Chilean miners joined some of the initial arrivals in Northern California. For a short time, these skilled Latino miners worked alongside Anglo and Chinese miners in the goldfields. By 1850, however, Anglo violence and foreign miners' taxes against Latino and Chinese "Forty-eighters" and Sonoran miners ensured white miners of exclusive rights to California's gold.

Four, Los: Group of artists and collective art exhibition. The "Los Four" exhibition toured various California sites including the Los Angeles County Museum of Art. It featured artists Carlos Almaraz, Roberto "Beto" de la Rocha, Gilbert Sánchez LUJÁN, and Frank ROMERO, together known as Los Four.

The exhibition "Los Four," featuring young artists from Los Angeles, demonstrated a strong sense of Chicano style in art. This style was not invented but seemingly grew naturally as an expression of the many Chicanos living in the Southwest. It can be called an urban folk style. The works were exhibited without name labels, so as not to feature only one artist or artistic style. The intent was to give an overall appreciation of the style and content. Some of the pieces in the exhibition were produced by all the artists working as a team.

The works of art incorporated many themes of Mexican culture, such as altars, mural painting, and folk art techniques. A popular Chicano icon, the "low rider" car, and graffiti-painted walls were also featured.

Carlos Almaraz was born in Mexico City in 1941. His work is reminiscent of the large-scale works painted by the Mexican muralists Diego RIVERA (1886-1957) and José Clemente OROZCO (1883-1949). The subject matter is political, and the figures are involved in the struggle for social justice.

Roberto de la Rocha uses colored felt-tip pens and ballpoint pens to give his drawings a graffiti-like quality. His scribbled, rapid markings, piling color upon color, give his drawings a vibrant texture, splintering the colors across the page.

Gilbert Sánchez Luján was born in 1940 in Stockton, California. He constructed a multitiered "Pyramid Altar." This piece incorporated two historically relevant features in Chicano art, the ancient Mayan pyramids and the altars for personal devotion. A statue of the Blessed Virgin is the central figure in Luján's construction, surrounded by paper flowers and brightly colored glasses. Other significant artifacts decorate the altar, such as a book on pre-Columbian art, an empty wine bottle, and clay figurines. Another work of interest by Luján is a carefully matte-painted front end of a 1952 Chevy low-rider. His other contributions were six watercolor portraits done on spiral notebook sheets and a series of painted tortillas.

Frank Romero was born in 1941 in East Los Angeles, California. In addition to drawings and paintings using a graffiti-like technique, he also produced colored cut-paper constructions. Protected under plexiglass boxes, these pieces are reminiscent of the Mexican folk art technique of cut tin.

The "Los Four" exhibition was not without its critics. Some of the critical reviews faulted the artists for being college educated, thereby losing their status as true folk artists. Others doubted their viability as artists of any type. Still others were critical of the Los Angeles County Museum for attempting to "museum-ize" the Chicano art form for the mainstream art community.

The group show originated at the University of California, Irvine, in 1973, then traveled to the Los Angeles County Museum of Art in 1974. A 16 millimeter film was produced by Eduardo Moreno to document the exhibition, the first time Chicano art was shown at the museum.

The group took on other members, including Judithe Hernández. In addition to the group shows, Los Four painted several street murals in Los Angeles, La Puente, and Long Beach, California. In 1977, the members collaborated on a comic book, *Tales from the Barrio*. The group disbanded in 1983, though individually the artists continued with successful careers.

Fourteenth Amendment (1868): The Fourteenth Amendment to the United States Constitution provides, for all citizens, safeguards from action by states. These safeguards are the same as from actions of the federal government. Of particular importance to Latinos, the amendment established that any person born in the United States is a U.S. citizen. Many Latinas have crossed the U.S.-Mexico border to give birth in the United States, ensuring U.S. citizenship for the child.

The Fourteenth Amendment, ratified on July 28, 1868, was a legalistic ploy to punish the former political leaders of the Confederate states by excluding them from any future political power. The amendment is known best for the assurance it provides that the states would have no power to disenfranchise citizens who were already allowed participation in the government by the U.S. Constitution.

The amendment guarantees that no state may infringe in the legal rights of a citizen to life, liberty, and property without due process. The protection of the law cannot be withheld by the states from any citizen. This clause was included to provide protection for black people recently freed from slavery. Finally, the amendment includes guidelines for apportionment of representatives. Pivotal to the well-being of the Latino population of the United States is the equal protection concept.

At the time of the amendment's ratification, there was no popular concern over whether Latinos were protected because they were present in small numbers and had virtually no political power. During the railroad expansion of the late nineteenth century, however, Hispanic people found themselves scattered across the country. In addition, expansion of agricultural exports and the transition of American farming from the family farm to the managed agribusiness created a growing need for low-paid agricultural workers. A ready source of cheap labor was found in Latin America, particularly Mexico and, later, Puerto Rico.

The Fourteenth Amendment helps to protect workers, but only if it is enforced; this woman must cover her face to protect herself from pesticides as she picks grapes. (Impact Visuals, Kathleen Foster)

Not aware of their right to redress, many Latinos were forced into an essentially feudal system. Large tracts of land were assembled from small farms, and stark housing was provided to accommodate permanent or seasonal workers. The owners created banks where the workers' wages were "deposited" and from which they could withdraw only for use in the owners' stores.

Nearby communities found themselves suddenly "invaded" by people with a foreign culture and language. Public pressure on lawmakers to discourage immigration spawned many abuses. Property owners and lenders rather than lawmakers were the primary force restricting Latinos' freedom to change jobs, patronize the "free" stores, or move to "better" neighborhoods when their fortunes allowed. Because legislative restrictions on specific ethnic groups were unconstitutional, the legal system merely cooperated by closing its collective eyes to harassment.

Worse than harassment for the individual was the lack of legal protection from the excesses of the agribusiness owners. Workers were required to use dangerous machinery and chemicals, living conditions were substandard, and competent medical support was unavailable. Despite these known abuses, law enforcement agencies at the local level seldom intervened.

It remained for advocates to arise who had the education to understand the provisions of law. Eventually legal actions were brought to bear on employers to improve working and living conditions. The Fourteenth Amendment provided access to protection through landmark cases that gave notice to offenders that equal rights were available to Latinos and that these rights would be enforced. No longer did instances of harassment and denial of right have to be fought on a case-by-case basis.

Franciscan missionaries: Important figures in the religious, economic, and cultural development of New Spain during the Spanish colonial era. Franciscan missionaries first arrived in the Americas with Christopher Columbus on his second voyage in 1494. Over the next three centuries, they accompanied almost every important French and Spanish expedition to what became the continental United States. They were the principal missionaries in Florida and Georgia, and in

1598 they were a part of the Juan de OÑATE expedition into New Mexico. As the frontier pushed northward, Franciscans ventured into the northern and northeastern regions of New Spain. After expulsion of the Jesuits in 1767, the Franciscans extended their labors to California (*see* MISSIONARY IMPULSE).

Franciscans, like other Spaniards, believed that religious conversion was a broadly civilizing process that required a complete social and cultural reorientation of native life. They actively promoted the *congregación* (community life), considering it necessary for religious conversion. These missionaries were impelled to create new societies to further their goals, notably the extensive MISSION SYSTEMS in Florida, Louisiana, California, and New Mexico.

Franciscan friars employed the standard physical form for missions that the Jesuits had developed for their missions in northern Mexico. Indian houses were grouped together in an orderly pattern within the mission confines. The largest building was the church. A blacksmith's shop, workshops, granary, tannery, and stables surrounded the central quadrangle. In New Mexico, however, missionaries retained the existing Indian communities and built their churches on the edges of these settlements.

In California, the Franciscans developed elaborate economic complexes. They directed native inhabitants to build aqueducts, dams, and reservoirs, and to cultivate gardens, orchards, vineyards, and grain fields. The friars also taught the Indians construction, operation of grain mills, stock raising, and crafts. Even in areas such as Texas and New Mexico, where the missions were less economically developed, the friars taught stock raising and crafts and introduced the

Mission Santa Barbara in California remained in use by Franciscans into the twentieth century. (Security Pacific Bank Collection, Los Angeles Public Library)

plow, European plants and seeds, and new agricultural techniques. The teaching of the Spanish language on the northern frontier, as a means of facilitating communication with and among the Indians, also became an important part of the missionaries' religious program.

Missionaries faced strife both within and beyond their communities. Conflicts between them and the political authorities were common. They accused royal administrators and civilian colonists of exploiting native labor and harsh treatment of the Indians, only to find themselves also accused of the same by the administrators and civilians. Within the *congregación*, the Franciscans imposed European standards on non-European peoples by varying degrees of force.

There were many outstanding friars among the Franciscan missionaries in New Spain. Peter de Gante, a Flemish Franciscan lay brother, set the pattern for the theory and method of missionary work generally followed in Mexico, insisting that Indians were rational beings innately and spiritually equal to Europeans. Junípero SERRA arrived in New Spain in 1749 and became one of the leaders in California missionary activity during its first fifteen years. Appointed to accompany the early Spanish settlers into California after the expulsion of the Jesuits, he was the founder of the overall California mission system as well as many of the individual missions.

Franco, Julio (Julio César Robles y Franco, b. Aug. 23, 1961, San Pedro de Macoris, Dominican Republic): Baseball player. Franco began his major league career as an infielder with the Philadelphia Phillies in 1982. After only sixteen games with Philadelphia, he was traded to the Cleveland Indians, and he quickly became the Indians' starting shortstop. In six seasons in Cleveland, Franco established himself as a solid major league hitter, but he had defensive problems at shortstop and was eventually moved to second base.

In 1989, Franco was sent to the Texas Rangers, and in 1991 he captured the American League batting title with a .341 average. A three-time All-Star with the Rangers, Franco became a free agent after the 1993 season and signed a one-year, $1 million contract as a designated hitter for the Chicago White Sox.

Freedom Airlift (Dec. 1, 1965—Apr. 6, 1973): On December 1, 1965, the United States and Cuba entered into an agreement establishing an airlift between Havana and Miami. An estimated 297,318 Cubans immigrated to the United States during the operation.

Julio Franco hits a home run in a 1994 game against the Milwaukee Brewers. (AP/Wide World Photos)

After Fidel CASTRO took over Cuba in 1959, thousands of Cubans, mostly wealthy and professional, began immigrating to other countries, including the United States. They were often forced to leave quickly, without their relatives or capital. Castro's government made it difficult to emigrate, and legal migration was halted completely in 1962 following the CUBAN MISSILE CRISIS. On September 28, 1965, however, Castro announced that Cubans with relatives in the United States could begin emigration on October 10.

The first departees left by boat from Camarioca, many of them in poorly equipped boats crewed by their relatives from Florida. Disorganization and the ignoring of safety precautions resulted in accidents and the deaths of many people.

Nearly 300,000 Cubans took Freedom Airlift flights to the United States. (AP/Wide World Photos)

In response to this situation, the United States and Cuba agreed to establish an airlift between Havana and Miami. The flights under this agreement (also known as the Freedom Flights and Family Reunification Flights) were handled through the Swiss embassy in Havana. Two airplanes departed from Cuba daily, five days a week, carrying between three and four thousand Cubans per month to Miami and the New York City area. Seats on the planes were limited in number, creating long waiting periods before space became available.

Most refugees came from the Havana and Las Villas provinces, with only a small number from rural areas. An estimated 93 percent of Cubans who went to West New York and 99 percent of those going to Miami had some family members living in the United States before they arrived. Participation was restricted to close relatives of the family member residing in the United States, with spouses and their children given highest priority. Males of draft age (seventeen to twenty-six) were not allowed to emigrate.

CASTRO stopped accepting applications for visas in May, 1969, leading to interruptions of the Freedom Airlifts in August, 1971. In September, 1971, Castro announced that requests for exit permits were decreasing and that flights would end. The last airlift took place on April 6, 1973.

Generally, emigrants taking part in the airlift had a higher socioeconomic and educational status than those who stayed behind. Thus, the impact was more negative for Cuban society than for the United States. The airlift resulted in a large influx of professional, educated Cubans to the United States. Many initially had to work for much lower pay than they had in Cuba but eventually became successful.

Freighters, Mexican: Operators of transportation systems. Spanish colonists in Mexico developed the country's first major transportation systems. After the independence of Mexico in 1821, these systems were linked to the United States. Mexican independence in 1821 led to the opening of the Santa Fe trading system. After the TREATY OF GUADALUPE HIDALGO in 1848 and the GADSDEN PURCHASE in 1854, Mexican freight-

ers continued to ply their trade, until railways replaced the teamsters around 1880.

In a handbook for the *Prairie Traveler* published in 1859, Captain Randolph B. Marcy wrote, "The mule and the donkey are to them (Mexicans) as the camel to the Arab." In this statement, he confirmed two hundred sixty years of experience in Mexico. The frontier of New Mexico required a caravan system from Chihuahua, and Texas settlements in the interior required supply through an overland system.

By 1824, New Mexico's markets were saturated with manufactured goods, and Santa Fe had become a port of entry into the Mexican interior. Annual trade fairs at places such as San Juan de los Lagos allowed merchants to market their goods. Mexican merchants

A mule team hitched to a freight wagon, photographed around 1900 in Wickensburg, Arizona. (University Libraries, Arizona State University, Tempe)

This cart was used to haul water along the Texas-Mexico border. (Library of Congress)

dominated trade in both directions on the SANTA FE TRAIL by 1843. The Chávez, Otero, Armijo, Delgado, and Perea families were influential in freighting efforts, expanding their business in New Mexico. They often used the Spanish firm in New York of Peter Harmony, Nephews and Company. Esteban OCHOA dominated the Gila Trail until it was made obsolete by the railroad. Mexicans were employed in every aspect of the freighting business, as proprietors, teamsters, *arrieros* (muleteers), guides, translators, animal tenders, hunters, and skinners.

Trade spread in numerous directions, with Santa Fe as the hub from 1821 until 1848. Merchandise traveled

from Santa Fe along the Camino Real to El Paso del Norte and numerous interior destinations. The Gila Trail connected California to the system. In 1829, Antonio Armijo opened the OLD SPANISH TRAIL, an overland route from northern New Mexico to Chávez Ravine in California. The Old Spanish Trail was primarily a livestock route, but the Gila Trail saw heavy wagon freighting of goods. An attempt by American and Chihuahua merchants to bypass Santa Fe and transport wares via San Antonio showed promise in 1830.

Goods arriving in Santa Fe after 1824 were usually taken from wagons and transferred to mule trains for the southern route. After 1848, wagon freighting became common all the way to El Paso del Norte. Railroads later penetrated the area, but the mule train also continued in use.

American freighters adopted Spanish and Mexican methods as well as language. Fifty loads could be managed by six *arrieros*, who began the day's journey by enticing the mule herd with the *madrina* (bellmare). A *riata* (lariat) held the mule. The animal was loaded with a pack saddle and the cargo.

With the American conquest came a need to supply Indian reservations. Military installations led to extensive use of government contracts, and the nature of freighting changed. Racial conflict between Mexican freighters and Anglo-Americans sometimes led to armed conflict such as the Gunnysacker War in Texas.

Freire, Paulo (b. 1921, Recife, Brazil): Educator. Freire is known for his theories of education and work using visual aids to teach illiterate peasants. He has written several books on education, particularly on education as a means to obtain freedom, including *Education for Critical Consciousness* (1973). His work earned him the 1980 UNESCO Prize for Peace Education, among other awards.

Freire was a professor of history and the philosophy of education at the University of Recife until 1964. In 1963, the Ministry of Education committed to a national literacy campaign that would employ his teaching methods. At the time, the law forbade illiterate people from voting. The educational program threatened the power elite, and Freire was placed under arrest in April, 1964. He was allowed to go into exile several months later.

Freire then served as a consultant to the UNESCO Institute of Research and Training in Agrarian Reform as well as working with the Office of Education of the World Council of Churches from 1974 to 1981. In 1981, he returned to Brazil, taking a post as professor of education at the Catholic University of São Paulo. His career has also included service as general coordinator of Brazil's National Plan of Adult Literacy and as the country's secretary of education.

Fresquez, Carlos (b. 1956, Denver, Colo.): Painter. Fresquez is a figurative painter whose work deals with the urban life of working-class Mexican Americans. After graduating from Abraham Lincoln High School in Denver, Colorado, Fresquez earned his bachelor's degree in fine arts from Metropolitan State College in the same city.

Fresquez is known for vibrantly colored works that often feature painted figures cut from wood and then mounted on a separate background or installation. His acrylic-on-wood *Zoot Suit en los Rockies* (1984) is one such work. In it, the figure of a young man clad in the wide-brimmed hat, thin tie, and stylishly loose suit popularized by Mexican American youth in the 1940's is set against a mountainous backdrop. In Fresquez's other works, city silhouettes and curtains often form backgrounds to painted figures. Fresquez's work has been included in numerous group exhibits across the United States.

Frigerio, Ismael (b. 1955, Santiago, Chile): Painter. Frigerio's reputation rests on expressionistic paintings that explore such issues as identity, loss, and conquest. Many of his paintings focus on the post-Conquest period and the confrontation of Aztec and European cultures.

Frigerio is the oldest of five children born to a Chilean mother and an Italian father who left Europe before World War II. As a child, Frigerio wondered about his father's past, and the long journey and sense of mystery he associated with the man surfaced in his paintings as an adult.

The content and the titles of many of Frigerio's works—*The First Opportunity of Pain* (1985), *Division of Souls* (1987), and *The Lurking Place* (1985), for example—reveal a dark, sometimes haunting view of life. In the paintings, fragments of Frigerio's personal history mix with snakes, fish, and other images of ancient Hispanic legends.

Frigerio studied fine arts and philosophy at the University of Chile and was influenced by the work of German and American expressionist painters. Wishing to avoid the political struggles in Chile that he thought would distract him from art, he moved to the United States in 1981. Frigerio settled in New York, New York, and worked as a dishwasher, carpenter, and furniture designer as he continued to paint and exhibit his work.

Frijoles refritos: Refried beans. *Frijoles refritos* are eaten throughout Mexico, especially in rural regions and in the north. Diced onion, and perhaps some garlic is sautéed in lard with cumin or other spices. When the onion is soft, already-boiled beans are added and mashed in the pan as they cook further in the lard. When the beans are a relatively smooth and shiny mush, they are ready. *Frijoles refritos* can be eaten plain or as a filling for ANTOJITOS. "Refried beans," the

Carlos Fuentes delivers a commencement address at Harvard University in 1983. (AP/Wide World Photos)

usual English rendition of the Spanish name, is misleading to many, since the dish is neither fried in the conventional sense nor fried twice; the "re" in the name indicates merely that the beans are thoroughly cooked.

Fuentes, Carlos (b. Nov. 11, 1928, Mexico City, Mexico): Writer and diplomat. Fuentes, the child of a diplomat, is of cosmopolitan background. He learned English beginning at the age of four in Washington, D.C., studied at schools throughout the Americas, and traveled on his own from a young age before returning to Mexico. In Mexico City, he obtained a degree in law, and, for a short time, was a member of the Mexican diplomatic service. He has taught or lectured at institutions in Mexico, Chile, France, and the United States.

Fuentes is one of Latin America's foremost cultural figures. A novelist, short-story writer, playwright, and essayist, he has received such encomiums as an honorary degree from Harvard University, an ambassadorship in Paris (in Latin America, writers are often awarded diplomatic posts), a banning from entry into the United States as an "undesirable alien" (resulting from his criticism of the United States' military and economic involvement in Latin America), and a rescinding of that ban as a result of public outcry. As an exponent of cultural diversity, he has advocated causes on behalf of the preservation and incorporation of different cultures into his country's heritage and consciousness.

Fuentes' first book, *Los días enmascarados* (1954), a collection of short stories, heralds Fuentes' forging of an understanding of the psyche of modern Mexico. Fuentes is preoccupied with how history floods the perceptions of the present and how its constancy, at odds with the present's constant change, brings suffering and conflict.

The blurring between past and present is both a common theme in Fuentes' works and a literary device. Well versed in modernist literary theory, Fuentes frequently appropriates its devices of fragmentation, imitation of cinema, and the blurring of past and present (often mixing, for example, the historical past and a fictional depiction of the present). In *Terra Nostra* (1975; English translation, 1976), for example, the narrative shifts from twentieth century Paris to the Spain of Philip II.

One of Fuentes' better-known books, *El gringo viejo* (1985; *The Old Gringo*, 1985), also mixes history and fiction in a masterful demonstration of the painful complications that result from denials of cultural and historical imperatives in favor of adherence to an ideology and resistance to change. Set in Mexico in 1913, with two main characters from the United States, the novel uses the historical facts of the disappearance of Ambrose Bierce (the old gringo of the title) and the MEXICAN REVOLUTION together with the fictional portrayals of Bierce as a character; of Tomás Arroyo, leader of a battalion on the side of Pancho VILLA; and of Harriet Winslow, an American schoolteacher who finds herself in the middle of the revolution.

Fuentes has also been influenced by the cinema. In *La muerte de Artemio Cruz* (1962; *The Death of Artemio Cruz*, 1964), narrative techniques of flashback, fragmentation, symbolic motifs, and cross-cutting imitate films. Other notable novels include *Cambio de piel* (1967; *A Change of Skin*, 1968) and *Cristóbal nonato* (1987; *Christopher Unborn*, 1989).

Fuentes, Juan R. (b. 1950): Artist. Although he is an accomplished independent artist, Fuentes is best known for the key role he played in popularizing Hispanic art. Fuentes and a colleague helped bring a Cuban poster exhibition to the California Palace of the Legion of Honor, a major mainstream museum in San Francisco, California.

The exhibition, which highlighted the social and political content of poster art, fueled the Chicano poster movement of the late 1970's. Chicanos who felt a closer alignment with artists of the Third World began to use posters to stimulate cultural identity and make political statements about the treatment of Latinos, and postermaking was taught in Hispanic centers in working-class and powerless communities.

Fuentes taught postermaking at La Raza Graphic Center of San Francisco, an independent, nonprofit organization founded by Latinos as a center of art and culture. In the 1970's, Fuentes' artwork was reproduced and popularized in several versions of *The Chicano Calendar*, copublished by La Causa Publications and Southwest Network.

Fuerzas Armadas de Liberación Nacional (FALN): Militant Puerto Rican political organization. The Civil Rights movement in the United States during the 1960's created splinter groups of left-wing radicals who believed that revolution was imminent and that members of minority groups would lead the revolution. Some underground organizations espousing a Marxist-Leninist ideology were dedicated to armed struggle.

Some Hispanic students, believing in the historic nature of the movement, later became involved in such groups as the FALN (the name of which translates as "armed forces for national liberation"), formed in 1975. It was dedicated to gaining independence from the United States for Puerto Rico and took credit for various acts of violence in the United States. In 1976, the FALN assaulted business and police targets in Chicago and Manhattan. In 1983, Mexican authorities arrested a Puerto Rican man who was operating a terrorist training camp out of a house in Mexico.

Fur trade: Trade in animal skins and furs. The fur trade included the skins of elk, deer, and *cíbolo* (buffalo) as well as trade pelts such as those from the beaver, muskrat, and raccoon. Trappers in the Spanish era emphasized the softer animal skins for clothing, but fashion items became profitable and interest in pelts shaped the trapping and trading system.

During the Spanish colonial period, *cíboleros* (buffalo hunters) provided materials for colonial settlers who were isolated from manufacturing industries. The experience improved the Spanish colonists' skill at horsemanship, and they became known for their skill in hunting buffalo with lances.

A Spanish/French connection led to cultural amalgamation in the Louisiana region as well as in New Mexico. In 1699, Elena Gallegos married Santiago (Jacques) Grolé; two years earlier, Jean L'Archeveque had married Antonia Gutiérrez. Exploration and furs took these two men and many others to the Louisiana region; love caused them to stay.

The Louisiana Purchase of 1803 opened new worlds to several generations of fur traders. The first expeditions led to increased knowledge of the region and its people, resulting in more efficient production and trade.

The earliest licensed trappers in American Louisiana included Benito Vásquez, August Chouteau, Jean Cabanne, Jacques Clamorgan, and Bernard Pratte. The most important pioneer of the fur trade was probably Manuel LISA, who envisioned a network of fur traders from the upper Missouri River through Santa Fe and to the Gila River. This initial dream faltered as Euro-Americans began to realize the size of the country. In the spring of 1807, Lisa established Fort Raymond on the upper Missouri. He also developed the Missouri Fur Company, and as the government's subagent for Indian affairs he kept American Indian tribes on the American side during the War of 1812.

After Mexico declared independence in 1821, American trappers and traders were welcomed into the territory and were allowed to purchase trapping licenses. Spanish policies had prohibited American trade throughout the region; Mexicans wished to regulate it. Mexican guides, translators, and trappers contributed to every phase. By the mid-1820's, a fur trade based on beaver pelts, *estranjero* (American) trappers, and an overland supply route enveloped the frontiers of two nations, Mexico and the United States.

The Santa Fe trading system, which began at about the same time, often was part of the overland supply routes essential to the trapping system. Pelts, skins, and robes became commercial items shipped internationally. By 1824, Taos was the center of the beaver trade.

The *cambalache*, or trading fair, was supplanted by a fort system on the eastern slope of the Rocky Mountains. William Bent, Ceran St. Vrain, and Charles Bent developed a partnership with William's Fort (Bent's Fort) on the American side of the Arkansas River. Charles Bent located his interest in Taos, where Mexican labor could be recruited. Numerous other communities located along river drainage basins followed the same pattern, employing Mexicans to construct buildings and perform other labor as well as to work as specialized skinners and hunters.

Furniture: Skills of furniture crafting among Latinos have been carried to the present through numerous generations, all the way from craft workers of the Spanish colonial period.

Functionalism. Furniture in the northern frontier of New Spain was sparse and limited to essentials. Poverty, geographic isolation, and natural resources all played parts in development of a style later called Spanish Colonial.

The sparse furniture in common use consisted of tables, chests, boxes, and benches; beds and chairs were far from universal. Isolation from major cities forced most households to construct their own furniture with basic tools.

Tables were used to hold things, not as places at which to sit. Chairs were usually small, box shaped, and built low to the ground. Few settlers had tables, chairs, or beds, relying instead on *bancos* (benches) for sitting and on mats and hides piled on the floor for sleeping. Storage consisted of *cajones* (boxes) and *trasteros* (armoires). Most settlers were relatively poor and had few possessions to store. The tables, chairs, *trasteros*, *cajones*, and *camaltas* (beds) of the wealthy could be quite elaborate; decoration was more important than function.

Distinguishing Features. Spanish Colonial furniture has unique features dictated by the wood used. Most

This bookcase from a Texas mission is far more ornate than most furniture of the Spanish colonial period. (Ruben G. Mendoza)

furniture of the Southwest from this period is made of pine. Local craft workers had no access to the hardwoods common to Mexico and other Spanish colonies. Pine was available, but it has deficiencies when used for furniture and required certain adaptations in design and joinery.

Because pine is soft, it splinters easily and can be damaged when exposed to hard usage. Spanish Colonial furniture features rounded edges to avoid splintering. Pine is hard to season, and in the arid climate of the Southwest, shrinkage is common. Furniture designers developed a system of full mortise and tenon joints, rather than the partial mortises and tenons used with harder woods. Mortises were cut with chisels, rather than with augers, and were square. Tenons were sawed off flush with the surface and held in place by square or hexagonal pegs. These pegs could be driven more tightly and were less likely to split the surface. Full tenons allowed wedges to be driven into mortises should the wood shrink.

Tables. Tables were of simple design, generally small, and not intended as places at which to sit. The top, a series of planks, was set into a rectangular frame, which was pegged and mortised into legs. A wooden apron was mortised into the legs below the top for stability; the apron also kept one's legs from fitting under the table while sitting. Table aprons, four to twelve inches in height, were often decorated with carving. Stringers, located a foot or so from the floor, ran from one leg to another and provided more bracing. The stringers, like the apron, could be carved or shaped. Cutouts in rectangular, round, or diamond shapes were used to decorate these portions of the table.

The area between the apron and the stringers might be filled with slats or spindles. The use of spindles denoted wealth because they required a lathe to manufacture, and most villagers did not have access to that tool. Most tables with spindles were imported. Slats were hewn, cut in zigzag or stairstep shapes, and mortised into the stringers and aprons.

Trasteros. The *trastero* was used to store food items, dishes, utensils, and other items. A typical *trastero* was about six feet tall and twelve to sixteen inches deep. The width varied but was usually about two-thirds of the height. *Trasteros* had short legs and three or four shelves with scalloped edges and lath to keep items from sliding off. The top of the *trastero* usually featured a decorative cornice that was carved and shaped. Doors of the *trastero* were divided into an oblong lower panel and a square upper panel. The upper panel featured lath, spindles, leather, cloth, or tin inserts. The most common inserts were shaped lath.

Cajones. Wooden boxes were used for all manner of storage. These boxes, with the addition of lids, carving, and paint, became chests. Construction consisted of planed boards pegged and dovetailed to form a rectangular box with a hinged lid. Often the *cajón* was placed on a small platform, or legs would be attached to the corners. Carving or painting could be extensive because of the many large flat surfaces.

Decoration. Paint, which is a common decorative item today, was virtually unused on Spanish Colonial furniture. Painting required time and money that the average settler did not have.

As preparation for painting, a wood surface would be covered with a number of thin coats of a paste made of gypsum cooked with wheat flour. Each layer was sanded, then powdered color would be mixed and applied. Earth colors, yellow, rust, and brown predominated, as well as white, black, and gray. Varnish for protection was made using amber colored pine resin diluted with grain alcohol. Common designs included flowers, vines, and geometric forms.

Pine requires incision rather than raised forms of carving. Rosettes, half moons, and sunbursts were common design themes. More common than carving was cutwork. The simplest cutwork resembled stairs or scallops. Cutting completely through a piece of wood in the shape of diamonds, rectangles, or circles also provided simple decorative touches.

Straw inlays were popular for *trasteros*, chests, and other items. This artform began with cutting a shallow indentation in a wooden surface. Wheat straws were split, flattened, and cut to various lengths. The indentation was smeared with pine pitch. Straw was then laid into the pitch, creating an inlay as simple or as complex as the artist's creativity allowed. The contrast between the light-colored straw and the deeper hue of the pitch and wood created a pleasing effect.

Hardware used for hinges and hasps on *trasteros* and chests was often decorative and featured heraldic or floral designs that artists then sometimes carved into the *trastero* or chest. Most fancy ironwork was imported into the Southwest rather than manufactured there; furniture with ironwork therefore denoted wealth.

Today, Spanish Colonial furniture is popular because its simplicity, comfort, and durability make it suitable for use with many styles of decor. The traditions of incised carving, slat inserts, and cutwork decoration continue. Painted decoration, as in the Spanish Colonial period, is very limited.   *—Louis Sarabia*

SUGGESTED READINGS: • Brown, Lorin W. *Hispano Folklife of New Mexico: The Lorin W. Brown Federal Writers' Project Manuscripts.* Albuquerque: University of New Mexico Press, 1978. • Dickey, Roland F. *New Mexico Village Arts.* Albuquerque: University of New Mexico Press, 1970. • Federal Art Project of New Mexico. *Portfolio of Spanish Colonial Design in New Mexico.* Santa Fe: Works Progress Administration, 1938. • Hall, Elizabeth Boyd White. *Popular Arts of Colonial New Mexico.* Santa Fe: Museum of International Folk Art, 1959. • New Mexico. State Board for Vocational Education. *Spanish Colonial Furniture Bulletin.* Santa Fe: Author, 1933.

Fusco, Coco: Performance artist and writer. Fusco emerged as a major theorist and writer on Latino art and culture during the 1980's. Her writings have appeared regularly in *Art in America*, *The Nation*, *The Drama Review*, and *The Village Voice*. Having written extensively on Cuban art and its development under the Fidel CASTRO regime, she was curator for the exhibition "Signs of Transition: Eighties Art from Cuba." She has also become well known for her performance art pieces examining the Latino experience in the United States, including *Norte/Sur* (1989, with Guillermo GÓMEZ-PEÑA) and *The New World (B)order* (1993, with Gómez-Peña and Robert Sifuentes).

Among Fusco's most controversial works has been *Two Undiscovered Aborigines Visit Irvine* (1992), in which she and Gómez-Peña, posing as Caribbean islanders, put themselves on display inside a cage in California for an uninterrupted three-day performance that invited audience curiosity and interaction. They presented similar performances in London's Covent Garden, Madrid's Plaza de Colón, the Smithsonian Institution's Museum of Natural History in Washington, D.C., and the Whitney Museum in New York.

G

Gabacho: An ANGLO. *Gabacho* is a derogatory term used by some Chicanos to describe Anglos and their culture. The term was created by PACHUCOS in the United States during the 1940's and remained in use, mostly among Chicanos, through the late twentieth century.

Gachupín: Pejorative name for Spaniards. *Gachupín* is a pejorative term used for the Spanish conquistadores (and their descendants) who invaded Mexico and ruled for four centuries. It comes from a Nahuatl word meaning "men who wear spurs." During the Mexican Revolution of 1810, the term commonly was used in reference to the Spanish ruling class.

Gadsden Purchase (Apr. 25, 1854): Treaty allowing the United States to purchase from Mexico the territory that became the southern portions of Arizona and New Mexico, completing what later became the forty-eight contiguous states. The purchase was controversial in the United States; the Senate greatly weakened the original purchase proposal and barely passed the treaty.

Soon after the Mexican American War ended with the TREATY OF GUADALUPE HIDALGO (1848), disputes concerning boundaries and protection rights flared up between the United States and Mexico. President Franklin Pierce was concerned because, although the treaty gave the United States almost half of Mexico, it did not include access to the Gulf of California or the territory that included the best route for a southern transcontinental railroad.

Pierce appointed, as minister to Mexico, James Gadsden, a South Carolina railroad executive who had long promoted a railroad route from the South to the Pacific. Pierce ordered Gadsden to negotiate a new treaty with Mexican dictator Antonio López de Santa Anna. Pierce hoped this treaty would settle the disputes and allow the United States to purchase new territory from Mexico. Gadsden was authorized to offer Santa Anna as much as $50 million for Lower California, land for a transcontinental railroad, and a port on the Gulf of California.

Complications over private speculators' land rights and Santa Anna's growing suspicions of the intentions of the United States (fueled by William Walker's invasion of Lower California and his creation of a "republic" there) resulted in a treaty of far lesser scope—the

right to purchase thirty-nine million acres for $15 million. Gadsden probably succeeded in negotiating any treaty at all only because Santa Anna's government was in desperate financial trouble.

The U.S. Senate hotly debated the treaty terms, especially the controversial claim of speculator Albert G. Sloo for rights to a railroad crossing the Isthmus of Tehuantepec. In the end, the Senate rejected the purchase. Many Northern senators believed that it would expand the nation's slave territory, and other senators did not want to give financial aid to Santa Anna. Eventually a compromise treaty did pass the Senate, one that reduced the purchase by nine thousand square miles and the payment by $5 million. After the treaty was ratified on April 25, 1854, Mexico sold the United States what is now southern New Mexico and Arizona for $10 million. This purchase included land for the southern railroad route to the Pacific but did not include Lower California or a port on the Gulf of California.

The Gadsden Purchase ended immediate threats of war between the United States and Mexico but did little to reduce sectional conflicts in the United States, which by now were so great that they had resulted in the U.S. Senate's first-ever rejection of an opportunity for continental expansion.

Galarraga, Andres (b. June 18, 1961, Caracas, Venezuela): Baseball player. Signed by the Montreal Expos at the age of seventeen upon the recommendation of Felipe Alou, Galarraga served a four-year apprenticeship in the minor leagues before reaching the majors in 1985. The huge first baseman emerged as a star in 1988, when he hit twenty-nine home runs, batted .302, led the National League in hits and doubles, and was named to the National League All-Star Team.

Despite his size, Galarraga proved to be an exceptionally agile first baseman, and he won Gold Glove Awards for defensive excellence in 1989 and 1990. Troubled by a series of injuries, however, he struggled in 1991, and a trade to the St. Louis Cardinals failed to help. Granted free agency after the 1992 season, he signed with the expansion Colorado Rockies. Although injuries limited him to only 120 games, he won the National League batting title with a .370 mark, was named to the All-Star Team again, and was selected as the league's Comeback Player of the Year by *The Sporting News*.

Andres Galarraga, shown in a spring training game in 1988, emerged as a star that year. (AP/Wide World Photos)

Galarza, Ernesto (Aug. 15, 1905, Jalcocotán, Nayarit, Mexico—June 22, 1984, San Jose, Calif.): Labor organizer, scholar, and writer. Along with his mother, aunt, and uncles, Galarza migrated to the United States during the Mexican Revolution (1910-1921). His family settled in Sacramento, California. Galarza worked during the harvest season as a farmworker while attending Lincoln Elementary School and Sacramento High School. He studied at Occidental College in Los Angeles as an undergraduate and obtained a master's degree in history and political science from Stanford University in 1929. After his graduation, he married Mae Taylor, with whom he had two children. He received his Ph.D. in political science and history from Columbia University in 1947.

Between 1932 and 1936, Galarza and his wife served as co-principals and then owners of Gardner School, a private school in Jamaica, Long Island, devoted to progressive education. In 1936, he was hired by the Pan American Union (an organization created in the 1900's to promote unity, peace, and economic trade among the various American nations) as a research associate in education. In 1940, the Pan American Union created a Division of Labor and Social Information with Galarza as its chief.

Between 1947 and 1959, Galarza organized agricultural workers in California with the NATIONAL FARM LABOR UNION (the predecessor to the United Farm Workers) as union secretary and vice president. During his later years, Galarza taught at the University of Notre Dame, San Jose State University, and the University of California at San Diego and at Santa Cruz. He worked with BILINGUAL EDUCATION programs and wrote a collection of short stories for children he called the *Colección mini libros*. A prolific writer, he produced hundreds of publications on the topics of Latin America, farm labor, literature, bilingual education, urban sociology, and Chicano studies. Among his more important books are the scathing critique of the BRACERO PROGRAM *Merchants of Labor* (1964), *Mexican Americans in the Southwest* (1969), *Spiders in the House and Workers in the Field* (1970), his autobiography *Barrio Boy* (1971), and *Farmworkers and Agribusiness* (1977). He was the first U.S. Latino to be nominated for the Nobel Prize in Literature.

Galleries and museums: Latin American art has been featured in museums of the United States for most of the twentieth century. Art by Latinos who live in the United States has become increasingly visible since the 1960's. (*See* ART, CUBAN AMERICAN; ART, LATIN AMERICAN; ART, MEXICAN AMERICAN; ART, PUERTO RICAN; ART, SPANISH AMERICAN.)

Galleries. With the civil rights movements of the 1960's, Hispanic art, as well as that of other minority groups, became popular in the United States. Art of the barrios and of the Southwest was in great demand. Older galleries soon incorporated Latino drawing, PAINTING, and SCULPTURE, and newer galleries began to specialize in art by Spanish-speaking people.

Galleries often carry new works or works by local artists, while museums are more likely to have landmarks of cultural heritage. Some Latino galleries are outgrowths of community activism, such as Self-Help Graphics in East Los Angeles, which offers printmaking workshops and celebrations of the Day of the Dead in addition to art exhibits. Other well-known galleries that show Latino and Latin American work include Brockman Gallery Productions (Los Angeles), Galeria de la Raza/Studio 24 (San Francisco), Fondo del Sol (Washington, D.C.), and Oller/Campache Gallery (New York), as well as many sites in New Mexico such as Stables Art Center (Taos), The Little Gallery (Albuquerque), and New Mexico State University Art Gallery (Las Cruces). The Wight Gallery at the University of California, Los Angeles, organized a massive touring exhibit of Chicano art in the 1980's.

Museums. An important function of Latino art museums is to provide a sense of cultural identity to people of the Latino community. Schools often rely on museum programs to strengthen their curricula and to give minority children a link with their unique history.

Museums also function as a source for cultural interchange. Latinos use the museum as a voice and outlet; people of other cultures expand their own range of experience by seeing Latino work.

One of the greatest problems faced by Latino museums, like most museums, is that of insufficient funding. The result is that museums are not adequately staffed and are unable to expand their collections. Security is often insufficient, and maintenance of building and art treasures difficult. Museums survive on grants from the government and private contributions.

Latino museums often offer workshops in art, theater, and dance. Public cultural events and summer classes for youth are available from larger museums. These programs help maintain community awareness of and interest in the museum while expanding on the significance of the art displayed.

Major Museums. The Museum of Modern Art of Latin America in Washington, D.C., has ongoing exhibitions featuring contemporary work from the entire

MUSEUMS FEATURING ARTWORKS BY LATINOS

Albuquerque Museum
  (Albuquerque, New Mexico)
Antonio Sanchez Cultural Center
  (Las Vegas, New Mexico)
Artes Latinos Mejorando Arkansas
  (Little Rock, Arkansas)
Bond House Museum (Española, New Mexico)
Branigan Cultural Center
  (Las Cruces, New Mexico)
Bronx Museum (New York, New York)
Centro Cultural de la Raza (San Diego, California)
Los Colores (Corrales, New Mexico)
Cuban Museum of Arts and Culture
  (Miami, Florida)
Florence Hawley Ellis Museum of Anthropology
  (Abiquiú, New Mexico)
Fondo del Sol (Washington, D.C.)
Galeria Ortega (Chimayó, New Mexico)
Harwood Foundation of the University of New Mexico
  (Taos, New Mexico)
Maxwell Museum of Anthropology
  (Albuquerque, New Mexico)
Mexican Museum (San Francisco, California)
Millicent Rogers Museum (Taos, New Mexico)
Museo de Antropologia, Historia y Arte
  (Rio Piedras, Puerto Rico)

Museo de Arte de Ponce (Ponce, Puerto Rico)
El Museo del Barrio (New York, New York)
El Museo y Centro Cultural (Taos, New Mexico)
Museum of Fine Arts (Santa Fe, New Mexico)
Museum of International Folk Art
  (Santa Fe, New Mexico)
Museum of Modern Art of Latin America
  (Washington, D.C.)
Museum of New Mexico System
  (Santa Fe, New Mexico)
Old Cienega Village Museum
  (La Cienega, New Mexico)
The Palace of the Governors
  (Santa Fe, New Mexico)
Rancho El Gavilan
  (Ojo Caliente, New Mexico)
Rough Riders Memorial and City Museum
  (Las Vegas, New Mexico)
South Broadway Cultural Center
  (Albuquerque, New Mexico)
Spanish History Museum
  (Albuquerque, New Mexico)
Tomé Parish Museum
  (Tomé, New Mexico)
University of New Mexico Art Museum
  (Albuquerque, New Mexico)

spectrum of Latin American and Caribbean countries. The Mexican Museum in San Francisco has exhibited a variety of artists from Diego RIVERA and Frida KAHLO to prominent Mexican folk artists. In a relatively short time, it has become an important asset to the Mexican American community. Its permanent collections include works from five principal areas: pre-Conquest, colonial, folk, Mexican, and Mexican American fine arts. Elsewhere in California, community cultural centers such as Centro Cultural de la Raza in San Diego and Plaza de la Raza in East Los Angeles exhibit works by Mexican and Mexican American artists. A number of cultural organizations in Los Angeles also sponsor tours of the many Latino murals that make the entire city a virtual Latino art museum.

El Museo del Barrio in New York is the foremost Hispanic visual arts organization in New York City and is one of the most renowned such institutions in the United States. Its collections include a wide array of prints, drawings, and photographs from Puerto Rico and Latin America. It has the largest public collection of Puerto Rican SANTOS and more than six hundred PAINTINGS by Puerto Rican painter Eloy Blanco. It

also has a large collection of pre-Columbian artifacts, miscellaneous items of FOLK ART, and about five hundred historic photographs, as well as contemporary work by NUYORICANS.

The Museum of International Folk Art in Santa Fe holds the nation's most important repository of Hispanic folk art, with an emphasis on Hispanic folk art of New Mexico and the Spanish colonial world. There are also a gallery and public programs devoted to contemporary traditions. Also in New Mexico are dozens of other museums focusing on Hispanic art, such as the Albuquerque Museum, the Millicent Rogers Museum in Taos, and the Palace of the Governors and Museum of Fine Arts in Santa Fe.

In other parts of the country, Chicago has the Mexican Fine Arts Center-Museum in the Pilsen barrio, presenting both historical and contemporary art by Mexicans and Mexican Americans. A unique institution for Cuban and exile art is the Cuban Museum of Arts and Culture in Miami.

Latin American and Latino art can also be seen in many university art galleries, anthropological collections, and historical museums in areas with large Latino populations. Municipal museums such as the Bronx Museum in New York and the San Antonio Museum of Art in Texas have sponsored notable exhibits of Latino art.

Latino art can be found in unexpected places, such as Artes Latinos Mejorando Arkansas in Little Rock. As Latinos gain in numbers, income, and political clout, the number of Latino galleries and museums throughout the United States will surely grow.

—Beaird Glover

SUGGESTED READINGS: • Amy, Mary Montaño, Carol Guzman, and Juanita Wolff, eds. *The New Mexico Directory of Hispanic Culture.* Albuquerque, N.Mex.: Hispanic Culture Foundation, 1990. • Ardali, Azade. *Black and Hispanic Art Museums: A Vibrant Cultural Resource.* New York: Ford Foundation, 1989. • *Directory of Minority Arts Organizations.* Washington, D.C.: Civil Rights Division, National Endowment for the Arts, 1982. • Espejel, Carlos, et al. *The Nelson A. Rockefeller Collection of Mexican Folk Art: A Gift to the Mexican Museum.* San Francisco: Chronicle Books/The Mexican Museum, 1986. • Grove, Richard. *Mexican Popular Arts Today.* Colorado Springs, Colo.: The Taylor Museum of the Colorado Springs Fine Arts Center, 1954. • Mexican Museum. *The Mexican Museum: Catalog of Selections from Its Collection with Introductions to Mexican and Mexican American Art.* San Francisco: Author, 1981. • Nuevo LA Chicano Arts. *First Annual Nuevo Chicano Arts: An Exhibition of Works by Newly Recognized Los Angeles Chicano Artists.* Los Angeles: Plaza de la Raza, 1988. • *Plaza de la Raza Folklife Festival.* Los Angeles: Plaza de la Raza Cultural Center for the Arts and Education, 1984.

Gallinas de la tierra: Female turkey. *Gallinas de la tierra* is the name given in Mexico to the female *guajolote*, or turkey. The word *guajolote* derives from the Aztec *huexolotl* (rooster) and designates both the native domestic and wild varieties of the bird. *Guajolotes* are also called *gallos de papada*, or double-chinned roosters; females are known as *gallinas de papada*, or double-chinned hens. Another common Mexican name for *gallinas de la tierra* is *pípila. Mole de guajolote* or *mole de pípila*, turkey stewed in a hot spicy sauce, is a festive native Mexican dish.

Gallup incident (1935): Riot and subsequent trial. Beginning in 1933, the National Miners Union (NMU) represented the largely Mexican American miners of the coalfields near Gallup, New Mexico. The NMU led a successful strike that year and was active in working with the unemployed persons of the community. The NMU activities were disrupted, however, by the Gallup incident.

A large landowner in the area had secured control of one of the towns controlled by a coal company. He attempted to force the miners and others who lived there to buy the houses at high prices or face eviction. The NMU organized resistance. Tensions ran high during the evictions, and a member of one crowd shot and killed the sheriff.

In the aftermath of the shooting, members of veterans' groups were deputized. They went through the Mexican American community making arrests. More than one hundred workers were arrested in the first twenty-four hours, many of them NMU leaders and others believed to be "radical." About one hundred deportations of Mexicans followed, as did the trial of ten persons for the murder of the sheriff.

Events in Gallup attracted attention across the United States. Of the ten defendants, seven were acquitted and three were found guilty of second-degree murder. The incident gutted union influence in the area.

Gálvez, Bernardo de (July 23, 1746, Macharaviaya, Spain—Nov. 30, 1786, Mexico City, Mexico): Soldier and administrator. Gálvez served as an officer in the 1762 Spanish-Portuguese war. He then migrated to Mexico with his uncle, José de Gálvez, that country's viceroy. Ever a successful military officer, Gálvez led several forays against the Apaches ravaging Chihuahua between 1769 and 1771. In 1772, Gálvez was transferred back to the Spanish army in Europe, where he served well but was wounded in battle. Returning to North America as a colonel, Gálvez became the governor of Louisiana in 1777.

In this office, Gálvez supported the American colonists in their revolution. To this end, he supplied arms and provisions to colonial forces and seized British ships entering Louisiana. When Spain and Great Britain went to war in 1779, his forces drove the British out of Louisiana and surrounding areas, taking Baton Rouge, Louisiana; Natchez, Mississippi; Mobile, Alabama; and Pensacola, Florida. Appreciative King Charles III renamed Pensacola Bay as Santa Maria de Gálvez Bay and made Gálvez both a count and a lieutenant general. Galveston, Texas, is also named for him. Gálvez became the captain general of Louisiana, Florida, and Cuba (1784) and viceroy of New Spain (1785). A caring administrator, Gálvez made peace with many Indian tribes and attempted to relieve fam-

O.V.EX.^{MO}.D.D.BERNARDO DE GALVES, PRO GRATIT.MON.D.O.C.

Bernardo de Gálvez served as a military officer and government official for Spain during the period of the American Revolution. (Library of Congress)

ine and an epidemic in Mexico. He died as a victim of that epidemic.

Gálvez, Daniel (b. 1953): Artist. Photorealist Gálvez usually works in pastels, doing portraits that capture the essence of BARRIOS AND BARRIO LIFE. Critically, his work is viewed as part of the facet of Chicano art that subverts rather than confronts authority, often in an irreverent and witty style. Along with John VALADEZ and César MARTÍNEZ, he is cited as an outstanding painter of barrio characters.

Gamboa, Diane (b. 1957, Los Angeles, Calif.): Artist. Often considered to be one of the brightest of a new generation of Chicanas who were too young to be influenced by the sociocultural protest years of the 1960's and early 1970's, Gamboa shows in her anguished portraits a more personal issue. Gamboa was deeply affected by the experience of rape. From her perspective, being on the receiving end of macho brutality is a part of Mexican heritage, older even than the Virgin of GUADALUPE.

In lighter moods, Gamboa creates startling paper fashions. She acquired an interest in fashion as a child, watching her aunt sell things at swap meets. She became interested in hippie fashions and bought vintage clothes at thrift shops in East Los Angeles, collecting accessories, jewelry, and hats. She particularly admired the pachuca and chola looks (*see CHOLO*; PACHUCO). She started doing paper fashions in 1982 for a Día de los Muertos (Day of the Dead) show at Self-Help Graphics. She later developed several lines of custom handmade paper dresses.

Gamboa, Harry, Jr. (b. 1951): Artist and photographer. Gamboa attended Garfield High in East Los Angeles, California. The school had a dropout rate of 60 percent. Gamboa helped organize mass walkouts of students protesting the state of education in the area.

At the age of twenty-one, as a college student, he found himself editing and designing a magazine called *Regeneration* with friends. This activity evolved into a performing ensemble dedicated to humorous, nihilistic, and mocking outbursts that often disgusted unwitting spectators. The group named itself ASCO, which can be translated as "nausea."

Gamboa became one of the founding members of LACE Gallery. He received a fellowship from the U.S. National Endowment for the Arts to work on intermedia pieces, and he wrote a play titled *Jetter's Jinx*. He is the older brother of artist Diane GAMBOA.

Games and toys: Many games that are played in Latin America were brought by the Spaniards. The Spaniards learned some of the games from the Romans who invaded and conquered Spain in the second century B.C.E. The games that Spaniards learned from Romans and later brought to the Americas include forms of handball, an early form of croquet, obelisks (an early form of bowling), and horseshoes.

Spaniards also learned games from the civilizations of the Americas and took them back to Europe. Among the American games that became popular in Europe were those employing rubber balls. Rubber was abundant in the Americas and was used to make objects such as balls and to protect the body from insect bites.

Rubber Ball Games. The rubber ball games that Spaniards learned in the Americas include bamboula, tlachtli, tlatlico, and hulama. Bamboula was played with two opposing teams composed of between five and twelve players. Each player had two rackets, one for scooping up, and another for throwing, a ball smaller than a tennis ball. The objective of the game was to hit the goal boards at the ends of the field. The ball was tossed up at a center pole, called a bamboula, to start the game. One point was scored whenever a player hit the boards at his or her team's end of the field with the ball.

Tlachtli, tlatlico, and hulama were similar games in which players would wear leather devices on the hips, thighs, and lower back. These devices were used to strike a ball. The objective was for the players to stroke the ball through a ring using these devices.

Of all the games shared between the Americas and Europe, soccer is by far the most popular. Baseball and basketball are increasing in popularity. Many baseball and basketball teams in the United States are attempting to reach the Latino and Latin American market through such means as broadcasting games in Spanish.

Sports and Games Participation. Latino participation in many sports surpasses the U.S. average. Latinos surpass the U.S. average in participation in aerobics, basketball, bicycling, hiking, racquetball, running, skiing, soccer, softball, swimming, tennis, and weight training. In contrast, a survey conducted by the Department of Education in the early 1990's indicated that among eighth graders, Latino children spent the least time per week on outside reading and homework. In addition, they spent 22.6 hours per week watching television.

Computer games are popular among American youth. Access to a home computer expands the possibilities for engaging in this form of play. One survey in

Although Latino athletes are best known in soccer and boxing, Latinos participate more than other Americans in a wide variety of sports. (Robert Fried)

the early 1990's found that 14.3 percent of Latino children had computers at home. That was lower than the percentages for white and African American children. Latino youth, however, have been very creative in artistic areas that have elements of play but do not require sophisticated equipment. These include the creation of graffiti, murals, and rap music.

Toys. The economic impact of the toy industry is important to highlight. About 60 percent of all toy sales are made during the Christmas season. In the early 1990's, these sales amounted to approximately $7 billion. Clearly, the choices children make concerning toys are important to the economy. Because Latino children are a large and growing proportion of the market for toys, their choices are particularly important.

At the 1991 Toy Fair, manufacturers introduced a line of ethnic dolls with African American, Latina, Asian, and Caucasian versions. The manufacturers chose to target children in minority groups because those children represented 31 percent of all children in the United States.

To date, marketers have not been able to discover the toy preferences of particular ethnic groups. Latino children may prefer dolls with Latino coloring and facial characteristics. It is also possible that on Christmas Day, even while their parents listen to their favor-ite Christmas music from Latin America or their native countries, Latino children would be happiest playing with replicas of Ninja Turtles, Power Rangers, Batman, or the latest popular figures from mainstream culture. —*Carlos I. Ramos*

SUGGESTED READINGS: • Arnold, Serena. "The Dilemma of Meaning." In *Recreation and Leisure: Issues in an Era of Change*, edited by Thomas Goodale. State College, Pa.: Venture, 1991. • Cooper, Paulette, ed. *Growing Up Puerto Rican*. New York: Arbor House, 1972. • Cordasco, Francesco, and Eugene Bucchioni, comps. *The Puerto Rican Experience: A Sociological Sourcebook*. Totowa, N.J.: Rowman and Littlefield, 1973. • Kate, Nancy. "Hispanics Hit the Hoops." *American Demographics* 15 (June, 1993): 22. • List, S. K. "Ethnic Babies Come to Toyland." *American Demographics* 13 (June, 1991): 10. • Panati, Charles. *Extraordinary Origins of Everyday Things*. New York: Perennial Library, 1987. • Sutton-Smith, Brian. *Toys as Culture*. New York: Gardner Press, 1986. • Vinton, Iris. *The Folkways Omnibus of Children's Games*. Harrisburg, Pa.: Stackpole, 1970.

Gamio, Manuel (Mar. 2, 1883, Distrito Federal, Mexico—July 16, 1960, Mexico City, Mexico): Anthropologist and sociologist. Gamio was a noted sociologist and authority on Mexican labor migration. He is

Manuel Gamio receives an honorary doctorate from Columbia University. (AP/Wide World Photos)

considered to be the founder of modern indigenist studies in the Western Hemisphere and was one of the first to study Mexican migration to the United States. Gamio believed that emigration harmed Mexico because the most talented people left the country in search of greater opportunities. He favored Mexican workers going to the United States seasonally and under government supervision. His work was considered in the decision to implement the BRACERO PROGRAM in 1942.

Gamio earned his bachelor's degree at the National Preparatory School of San Ildefonso and began working in the field of archaeology. He studied at Columbia University from 1909 to 1911. From 1917 to 1924, he was director of anthropology for Mexico, serving under the secretary of agriculture. His studies of Mexican immigration in the 1920's were supported by the Social Science Research Council. From 1942 to 1960, he was director of the Instituto Indigenista Interamericano. Among his publications is *Mexican Immigration to the United States: A Study of Human Migration and Adjustment* (1930).

Gandert, Miguel Adrian (b. Jan. 12, 1956, Española, N.Mex.): Photographer. Gandert studied at the University of Mexico, where he received his undergraduate degree in 1977 and his master's degree in 1983. He has worked throughout New Mexico, and his exhibitions have reached as far as Norway. He has taught photography at the University of New Mexico at Albuquerque.

Gandules: Pigeon peas. *Gandules* were domesticated in Africa and brought to the Americas by slaves. As a consequence, they are prominent in Latin American cuisine only in areas where there were many African slaves, particularly the Caribbean islands and the mainland Atlantic coasts from Belize south to Costa Rica. *Gandules* are similar to common peas, though a bit stronger in taste. They can be used fresh but more commonly are stored dry and reconstituted in cooking. They can be stewed, added to rice, or used in Puerto Rican *ASOPAOS*. Along the mainland coast, they often are called gungo beans.

Gangs and gang activity: Research on gangs and gang activity dates to the 1920's. The 1980's saw a renewed interest in the subject because of the proliferation of gang activity and increased violence in schools. Many gangs of the late twentieth century were organized along racial and ethnic lines, and Latino gangs proliferated.

Unlike research on criminology, which focuses on quantitative approaches and government statistical data, research on gang activity has been primarily qualitative and has relied on in-depth, face-to-face interviews and observation. Delinquent subculture was a prevalent theme in the early studies of gangs and gang activity. Causal theories for gang behavior promulgated in the 1960's came to be replaced by the notion of the urban underclass. Some researchers believe that gangs are not part of a counterculture but instead are a microcosm of American society within a subculture of poverty and crime.

Definitions. Street gangs are primarily American products: Although they exist in other countries, they take a unique form in the United States. The term "gang" has been difficult to define because of various assumptions made by researchers, the police, the media, and community members. Criteria often used to define or identify gangs include community attribution, recognition within the group, and activities, usually illegal, that elicit negative responses from police officers and the community. Members of gangs are not necessarily juveniles, as is sometimes believed; some gangs have memberships across three generations.

Usually a gang is an organized, self-formed group of people who share similar interests and wish to establish territorial control within a community. Youths who join gangs are often drawn by a need for belonging and protection, as well as by a sense of adventure. Solidarity within the group is achieved by the members' dependence on the group and the group's ability to control its members. Societal pressures that lead to gang behavior include socioeconomic, cultural, and psychological deprivation. Gang members often adopt specific styles of clothing and language; some adopt a tattoo associated with the gang. Gang activity often includes painting GRAFFITI in public places (also known as tagging) and other criminal behavior. Gang members are perceived by the mainstream society as marginalized individuals. Some gangs, however, operate social clubs that provide recreational activities for neighborhood residents.

Perceptions of the Problem. A 1990 survey of national police chiefs revealed that more than 80 percent reported gangs as a law enforcement problem, with about 10 percent of all crimes related to gang activity. More than 80 percent of the respondents believed that some street gangs were involved in organized crime. The majority of police chiefs believed that families, community agencies including churches and businesses, and correctional facilities should cooperate in

Lou Rivera (front) coaches youth sports teams in Brooklyn, New York, offering an alternative to involvement in gangs. (Hazel Hankin)

finding ways to counteract gang affiliation. Half of the respondents indicated that the gangs in their jurisdiction were ethnically homogeneous.

Historical Perspective. Some of the organizations that became gangs associated with criminal activity started out as noncriminal fraternal associations. For example, acculturation of immigrants in the United States was often facilitated by membership in ethnically organized groups. Ethnic, cultural, and linguistic traits of these organizations led to suspicion of them on the part of the majority culture.

Negative STEREOTYPES concerning various cultural groups is not a twentieth century phenomenon. In colonial America, women of non-European different ethnic backgrounds often were accused of witchcraft, and Catholics, slaves, and Native Americans were viewed in a suspicious manner by Southerners. In response to the emancipation of slaves, the Ku Klux Klan emerged as a secretive organization engaging in criminal activity. New York City witnessed gang activity in the 1800's.

As American society evolved, criminal activity became prevalent in major American cities. During Prohibition, many illegal activities were carried out by secret organizations. Gangs became associated with bootlegging of liquor, drug trafficking, and other forms of crime.

At times, the media appeared to glamorize gang activity and elevate it to an almost legitimate status. Negative stereotyping of some groups by the media, however, has also led to misunderstandings and injustices in U.S. society. Such was the case with the internment of Japanese Americans during World War II: Racial identification was the only motive for that social injustice. During the 1980's and 1990's, Latinos became identified with problems related to illegal immigration, gangs, and abuses of the social welfare system. Such identifications, although not limited to Latinos, led to stereotyped views of Latinos. These views encouraged positive responses in the form of political activism; they also caused some Latinos to feel marginalized and to turn to gangs and gang activity as a means of identification.

Gang Diversity. Gang activity reaches beyond urban areas to suburban and even rural communities, and gangs include both male and female members. Although gangs have various ethnic affiliations (or no such affiliation), Latino gangs have gained wide recognition in certain parts of the United States, particularly in California, Florida, and New York. African Americans, Asian Americans, Filipino Americans, and European Americans have not been immune to gang activity. Irish gangs, for example, were well established in New York in the early 1800's. Gang activity has also been reported among Jews, Italians, and other ethnic groups.

Lower socioeconomic status has long been a characteristic of gang affiliation; however, ethnic composition has changed over the years. In the 1950's, most gang members were white, but by the 1990's, gangs were disproportionately composed of minorities, particularly African Americans, Latinos, and Asian Americans. By some estimates, half the gang members in New York City were Puerto Rican and 35 percent were African American. Youths who joined gangs were primarily in their late teens or early twenties, were doing poorly in school or had dropped out, and were usually involved in drug use. Lack of education and poor English-language skills contributed to low self-esteem and cultural marginalization of gang members.

At times, gang members attempt to bring about peace in their communities. For example, after the 1992 Los Angeles riots, rival African American gangs, the Bloods and the Crips, agreed to a truce and symbolically tied together their gang bandannas.

Female Gang Members. Women became involved in gangs in New York in the early 1800's, in annexes to male gangs. In urban areas, female members of minority groups, primarily Latinas and African Americans, have been active in gangs since the 1950's. Many of these women dream of having a happy home in a life away from the danger and poverty of the streets. Various forces, however, push them toward the very different life of gang membership.

Gangs can provide a sense of community or family that may be lacking in a girl's or woman's life. Female gang members often address one another as "sister" or "homegirl" and view the gang as a family. In interviews conducted by sociologists, many have referred to themselves as loners, without connections to school or community prior to joining gangs. The future of female gang members in the early 1990's was bleak. About one-third could expect to be arrested, and the majority were on welfare. Gang membership is both a response to and a partial cause of these conditions.

Latino Gangs. Cultural marginalization of impoverished Latino immigrants has put many young people at risk of joining gangs. Racism, as exemplified in the zoot-suit riots of 1943, was influential in the development of Latino youth gangs (*see* SLEEPY LAGOON CASE). Schools were seen as having failed Latino youths. Young Latinos, who have the highest dropout rates in many communities, found comfort and safety in joining gangs.

MACHISMO, or a sense of "manly" behavior, plays an important role in male gangs: Engaging in gang activity shows courage. Fighting with rival gangs and establishing a territory promotes a sense of group pride and community as well as providing a sense of control. Some gangs promoted the same ideals through more socially accepted means, acting more as social organizations than as the stereotypical type of criminal gang. LOW RIDER car clubs, for example, could be classified as gangs even though many or most do not engage in criminal activity. Gangs do promote some positive so-cial values, such as respect for leadership, but those values are warped by criminal activity.

Because of the nature of gang activity and the motivations behind it, efforts to combat gang activity and membership must involve the whole community. Schools, churches, businesses, and other community agencies need to become more active in developing effective, proactive programs for impoverished and disillusioned youths. —*Maria A. Pacino*

SUGGESTED READINGS:

• Campbell, Anne. *The Girls in the Gang.* 2d ed. Cambridge, Mass.: Basil Blackwell, 1991. Intimate and dynamic ethnographic portrayal of female gang

Girls increasingly are drawn into gang membership. (Impact Visuals, Jim Tynan)

members. Through interviews and analysis, the author dispels myths and describes the role of women in both male and female gangs. Includes black-and-white photographs and extensive notes.

• Huff, C. Ronald, ed. *Gangs in America*. Newbury Park, Calif.: Sage Publications, 1990. Summaries of ethnographic studies by researchers in the field. Attempts to explain the role of ethnicity in gang membership and activity. Contains informative statistical data and theoretical assumptions concerning the United States' apparent inability to deal effectively with gang activity. Includes a bibliography.

• Jankowski, Martin Sanchez. *Islands in the Street: Gangs and American Urban Society*. Berkeley: University of California Press, 1991. A study based on ten years of fieldwork (1978-1988) with more than thirty gangs in Massachusetts, California, and New York. The author relates his experiences and makes generalizations about gang membership and activity.

• Klein, Malcolm W., ed. *Juvenile Gangs in Context: Theory, Research, and Action*. Englewood Cliffs, N.J.: Prentice Hall, 1967. Experts in the field survey developments in gang membership and activity and suggest proactive ways of controlling juvenile delinquency by examining the roles of religious, judicial, and economic agencies, as well as family and school.

• Knox, George W. *An Introduction to Gangs*. Barrien Springs, Mich.: Vande Vere Publishing, 1991. Reviews and summarizes the extensive literature in the field and reports new national research findings. Practical, comprehensive, and interdisciplinary. Extensive bibliographies.

• Rodriguez, Luis J. *Always Running: La Vida Loca, Gang Days in L.A.* Willimantic, Conn.: Curbstone Press, 1993. Autobiographical account of a former gang member. Remarks on the growing genocidal destruction of poor, young, marginalized Latinos in contemporary society. Urges collective responsibility and planning in preventing gang membership and activity.

• Vigil, James Diego. *Barrio Gangs: Street Life and Identity in Southern California*. Austin: University of Texas Press, 1988. Drawing on years of experience working in barrios, the author identifies the complex elements of gang membership and suggests a holistic approach to the study of gangs. Includes a glossary of gang terminology.

Garbanzo: Chick pea. A native of the Middle East, the garbanzo is one of the many Latin American foodstuffs that came to America from the Arab world via Spain. Although neither a true bean nor a true pea, the garbanzo is similar to both, with high protein content and good storage properties when dried. Garbanzos are used primarily in soups and a few stewlike dishes. Although used regularly in Latin America, especially in Puerto Rico and parts of Mexico, garbanzos never attained the importance of beans, probably because they are similar to beans, which were culturally established in Latin America thousands of years before garbanzos arrived.

Garcés, Francisco Tomás (Apr. 12, 1738, Aragon, Spain—July 18, 1781, near the Gila River, Ariz.): Missionary and explorer. Garcés was born at Villa Morata del Condé in the Spanish kingdom of Aragon. He joined the Franciscan order and was sent in the mid 1760's to Mexico, where he became a missionary and explorer. His explorations, with Juan Bautista de ANZA and Father Juan Díaz, were carried out in efforts both to settle the country and to find a route from the Mexican province of Sonora to California. These explorations resulted in thorough examination of the Colorado and Gila rivers of Arizona and the founding of several Franciscan missions among Pima, Yuma, and Opa tribes, which at first venerated him.

Eventually, Garcés identified a route from Sonora to California. It was longer and more arduous than that discovered by another expedition under Anza and therefore was used less often. Today, both routes are components of California highways. During Garcés' exploration of Yuma lands at the mouth of the Gila River—and efforts to found settlements at Purísima Concepción and San Pedro y San Pablo De Bicuner there—Garcés and Juan Díaz were killed by Yumas. This occurred during an uprising called the Yuma Massacre. Two other priests and thirty Spanish soldiers also were killed.

García, Cristina (b. July 4, 1958, Havana, Cuba): Writer. When she was two years old, García moved with her family to the United States, where she grew up among English-speaking friends with English as her primary language. She did her undergraduate work at Barnard College and received a master's degree from the Johns Hopkins University School of Advanced International Studies, specializing in Latin American studies.

García began her career in journalism, working as a reporter and researcher for *Time* magazine; she later became a bureau chief and correspondent for the magazine. In 1990, she began to write poetry and to work on a novel, *Dreaming in Cuban* (1992), which

Cristina García wrote the popular novel Dreaming in Cuban. (AP/Wide World Photos)

explores the reactions of three generations of Cuban women to the CUBAN REVOLUTION. García credits writing the novel with helping her to understand better the generation of Cubans who fled the Fidel Castro regime.

García, Enrique Gay (b. 1928, Santiago de Cuba, Cuba): Sculptor and muralist. García left Cuba via Rome in 1963. In Italy, he studied at the University of Perugia and the Art Institute of Venice. He later moved to Miami, Florida. His murals can be found in Puerto Rico and Florida (*see* MURAL ART). García began showing his work in solo and group exhibitions in the 1950's and continued to exhibit through the 1980's.

García's mother encouraged him to finish high school and go to college rather than pursuing a career as an artist. He took refuge in art school, where he felt more comfortable and was encouraged by teachers.

When García finished school, he went to Mexico to study muralist technique. He worked with David Alfaro SIQUEIROS in the execution of murals.

Although García's passion for sculpture originated in Cuba, where he had done some preliminary work in casting, he did little sculpting until he left the country. In Italy, he worked with casting, and when he arrived in the United States, he had significant experience.

García, Gus C. (1916, Laredo, Tex.—June 3, 1964, San Antonio, Tex.): Lawyer. García is best known for his role as chief counsel in the Supreme Court case *HERNÁNDEZ V. TEXAS* (1954). That case, decided fourteen days before the historic *BROWN V. BOARD OF EDUCATION* desegregation case, found that exclusion of Mexican Americans from trial juries was illegal. Although the Brown case received far more attention, *Hernández v. Texas* was an important step in breaking down racial barriers.

Earlier in his career, García had served as an assistant district attorney for Bexar County, Texas, and as an assistant city attorney for San Antonio. Following the unanimous decision in *Hernández v. Texas*, he returned to San Antonio, where he fought for better jobs and working conditions for Mexican Americans. The value of his work, however, was not recognized, even by his Latino peers, and he died penniless on a park bench.

García, Héctor Pérez (b. Jan. 17, 1914, Llera, Tamaulipas, Mexico): Political figure. García completed his undergraduate studies in 1936 at the University of Texas. Four years later, he earned his medical degree. During World War II, García served in the U.S. Army

Medical Corps and was awarded the Bronze Star. In 1948, he founded the AMERICAN G.I. FORUM to organize Latino veterans around issues of civil rights and education.

García, a member of the Texas State Democratic Committee, also served on the Democratic National Committee in 1954. He was a founding member of the POLITICAL ASSOCIATION OF SPANISH SPEAKING ORGANIZATIONS and served as national coordinator of the VIVA KENNEDY CLUBS.

In 1964, García served as an alternate ambassador to the United Nations. He was appointed four years later to the U.S. Commission on Civil Rights. President Ronald Reagan bestowed the U.S. Medal of Freedom on García in 1984.

Garcia, Jerome John "Jerry" (Aug. 1, 1942, San Francisco, Calif.—Aug. 9, 1995, Novato, Calif.): Singer, songwriter, and guitarist. Garcia's parents were José Garcia, a bandleader, and Ruth Garcia, a nurse. When he was a child, Garcia took piano lessons. He learned how to play the guitar at the age of fifteen and the banjo sometime later. In 1959, he dropped out of high school and joined the U.S. Army. As a nonconformist, Garcia was not suited for military life and was discharged in the same year. After his discharge, Garcia played folk and bluegrass music in coffeehouses. In 1965, he formed the Warlocks, a rock group; it became the Grateful Dead in 1966. In addition to Garcia, the original members of the band included Bob Weir as singer and guitarist, Phil Lesh as singer and bass guitarist, Ron "Pigpen" McKernan as singer, keyboardist, and harmonica player, and Bill Kreutzmann as drummer.

The Grateful Dead signed a recording contract with Warner Brothers in 1967. The group mixed a number of musical styles, including blues, jazz, and country. It was one of the first bands from San Francisco to popularize the psychedelic sound. The band proved to be a popular live act because of its penchant for adding long improvisational sections to songs. The album *Live/Dead* (1969) captured the feeling of a live performance. In 1970, the group released two tightly constructed studio albums, *Workingman's Dead* and *American Beauty*, that contained a strong country music feel.

Garcia recorded his first solo album, *Hooteroll*, in 1971. The Grateful Dead had some professional and personal problems during the early 1970's, and various members decided to concentrate on solo projects. In 1973, Pigpen McKernan died of liver disease. Garcia continued to release solo albums, including *Garcia* (1972), *Compliments of Garcia* (1974), *Old and In the*

Jerry Garcia celebrates his fiftieth birthday by performing a concert with his band, the Garcia Band. (AP/Wide World Photos)

Way (1975), and *Reflections* (1976). In addition to his work with the Grateful Dead and his solo music projects, he became a successful visual artist.

García, Roberto (b. Jan. 9, 1933, Bronx, N.Y.): Public official. García, a businessman, was elected to the New York State Assembly in 1966. The following year, he became the first Puerto Rican state senator in New York. When Congressman Herman Badillo resigned from the U.S. House of Representatives in 1978, García received his endorsement and subsequently won the special election to Congress. During his first campaign, García paid an unprecedented visit to Puerto Rico, illustrating the strong ties between the two communities.

García rose quickly in the nation's capital, serving on the House Banking, Finance, and Urban Affairs committee and chairing the subcommittee on Census and Population. This subcommittee oversaw the 1980 Census. He also served on the House Post Office and Civil Service committee and as chairman of the Congressional Hispanic Caucus. He left office in 1990 under indictment for receiving illegal gratuities. The charges were later dropped.

García, Rupert (b. Sept. 29, 1941, French Camp, Calif.): Artist. In the late 1960's and early 1970's, artists of Mexican descent consciously began to integrate their Chicano identity into their work. As Chicanos, they discarded the terms "Spanish American" and "Mexican American" as inappropriate, because those terms did not adequately represent the critical stance of CHICANISMO.

García reached maturity in the 1960's and was at first influenced by early and late modernism. He received an A.A. in painting in 1962 from Stockton College. He then studied painting and printmaking at San Francisco State University, earning a B.A. (1968) and an M.A. (1970). He earned an M.A. (1981) in art history from the University of California, Berkeley. Eventually, he became fully involved in various social movements including the Chicano art movement, in which the Latin American phenomenon of intertwining political and artistic thought remained alive.

García was among the best of the graphic and poster artists of the movement. His work combined contemporary art forms, aesthetics and images from the mass media and consumer culture, and expressions of social conscience. His prolonged and substantial professional career as an artist in the United States has included solo and group exhibitions. He has also taught at San

Artist Rupert García. (David Bacon)

Francisco State University, San Francisco Art Institute, the University of California, Berkeley, San Jose State University, and the Mexican Museum in San Francisco.

García Diego y Moreno, Francisco (Sept. 17, 1785, Lagos de Moreno, Jalisco, Mexico—Apr. 30, 1845, Santa Barbara, Calif.): Catholic bishop and educator. Born in Mexico, García Diego received his education in Guadalajara, where he attended St. Joseph's Conciliar Seminary. After joining the Franciscan order in Guadalupe in 1801, García Diego continued his studies at Our Lady of Guadalupe College in Zacatecas before being ordained to the priesthood in 1808. He became a teacher at the college and advanced in his career to be named a superior of the college in 1832. That same year, he traveled to California with ten other friars from Zacatecas after the Mexican government decided to give control of the missions to Mexican-

born clergy and expelled all Spanish friars. After his arrival in California in 1833, García Diego began to work from his headquarters at the mission in Santa Clara. He worked diligently to restore many of the missions that had fallen into disrepair.

García Diego returned to Mexico after the Mexican government decided to reorganize the church in California by converting the mission churches to parishes that were placed directly under the control of the secular government. García Diego used his influence to overturn the new decree and managed to suspend the imposition of secular control until the pope could establish a new diocese in California. This new diocese of Ambas Californias, overseeing the churches in Alta (upper) and Baja (lower) California, was established in 1840. García Diego was ordained as the first bishop of this new diocese, and he established the seat of his bishopric in San Diego. In 1842, he relocated religious offices to the mission at Santa Barbara and held the first ordination services in California there. Later, he established the first Catholic seminary in California at the mission of Santa Inés in 1844. After Mexican president Antonio López de Santa Anna confiscated the primary source of income that supported the bishopric, García Diego struggled to keep the diocese in order until his death in 1845.

García Márquez, Gabriel (b. Mar. 6, 1928, Aracataca, Colombia): Writer. The oldest of twelve children of Luisa Santiaga Márquez Iguarán and Gabriel Eligio García, García Márquez was reared by his grandparents in Aracataca, the model for his fictionalized Macondo. He has credited his grandparents and aunts for instilling in him a love of storytelling and history.

García Márquez began to write poetry and short stories around 1946. In 1947, he began to study law; as he once said, law was the only subject he could study at university in the mornings, leaving him with time in the afternoon and evening to work. In that year he published for the first time. In 1948, Jorge Eliécer Gaitán, a liberal candidate for the presidency, was assassinated, setting off a wave of violent civil unrest in Bogotá and elsewhere in the country. This event politicized García Márquez, who began working as a journalist for a newspaper in Cartagena. He moved to Baranquilla in 1950 but relocated to Bogotá in 1954. The controversy generated by his reports caused his newspaper to send him to Geneva as a foreign correspondent. Eventually he established residency in Paris, where he continued his writing. His two novels from this time are *La mala hora* (1962; revised, 1966; *In*

Gabriel García Márquez displays his medal shortly after presentation of his Nobel Prize in Literature. (AP/Wide World Photos)

Evil Hour, 1979) and *El coronel no tiene quien le escriba* (1961; *No One Writes to the Colonel and Other Stories*, 1968).

García Márquez continued his journalistic career in Caracas, Venezuela; New York, New York; and Mexico. In 1965, he began a year and a half of secluded writing that produced *Cien años de soledad* (1967; *One Hundred Years of Solitude*, 1970), one of the major novels of the twentieth century. It was instrumental in García Márquez's winning such prizes as the Neustadt International Prize for Literature in 1972 and the Nobel Prize for Literature in 1982. Critics invented the memorable oxymoron Magical Realism to categorize the narrative technique of this novel and other similar works.

After the success of *One Hundred Years of Solitude*, García Márquez was able to devote himself to writing and to journalism on behalf of political and social issues. In addition to his journalism, García Márquez has written numerous novels, among the best-known of which are *El otoño del patriarca* (1975, *The Autumn of the Patriarch*, 1975), *Crónica de una muerte anunciada* (1981; *Chronicle of a Death Foretold*, 1982), *El amor en los tiempos de cólera* (1985; *Love in the Time of Cholera*, 1987), and *El general en su laberinto* (1989; *The General in His Labyrinth*, 1990). With these works, García Márquez continued masterfully to explore the themes of antirationality, solitude, love, and power.

García-Ramis, Magali (b. Sept. 20, 1946, Santurce, Puerto Rico): Writer. García-Ramis was born into a privileged Puerto Rican family of Spanish heritage. She began her college education at the University of Puerto Rico at Rio Piedras, and she was graduated from Columbia University in New York City in 1968.

While in New York, García-Ramis won the coveted Ateneo Puertorriqueño prize for a short story, "Todos los domingos." Returning to Puerto Rico in 1971, she worked in journalism and taught, and she had a story, "La viuda de Chencho el Loco," accepted for publication. Later, while García-Ramis was living in Mexico, the Institute of Puerto Rican Culture published a collection of her short stories, *La familia de todos nosotros* (1976). In 1977, she resettled in Puerto Rico and took a position at the School of Public Communications of Puerto Rico. She has also published *Felices días, Tio Sergio* (1986).

García Rivera, Oscar: Politician. García Rivera was elected to represent East Harlem in the New York State Assembly in 1937. He was the state's first Puerto Rican assemblyman. An attorney by training, he was concerned with social reforms.

Because of his support from labor, the Republicans refused to endorse García Rivera in 1938. He ran on the American Labor Party ticket and defeated the Republican candidate. García Rivera was assisted in his campaigns by the community organizing skills of his wife, Eloísa García Rivera. She organized door-to-door canvassing, voter registration drives, escort service to the polls, and childcare.

As a state legislator, García Rivera championed reforms for migrant agricultural workers as well as for tenement dwellers. After leaving office, he provided legal representation for Puerto Rican small business owners and citizens.

Gardel, Carlos (Charles Romauld Gardes; Dec. 11, 1890, Toulouse, France—July 6, 1935, Medellín, Colombia): Actor and singer. Gardel moved with his mother from France to Buenos Aires, Argentina, at the age of three. As a teenager, he learned how to dance TANGOS and developed his singing and performance skills. Gardel began his recording career in 1913. Through the rest of the decade, he toured as a singer and dancer through Argentina, Brazil, and Uruguay with his own group. In 1934, he arrived in New York, where he performed on radio and made his film debut in *Cuesta abajo*. He followed that feature with *El Tango en Broadway* (1934), *El día que me quieras* (1935), and *Tango Bar* (1935), all Paramount Pictures Spanish-language films made in New York.

By virtue of his first few films, Gardel became a major film star in the Spanish-speaking world. To establish himself further, he embarked on a grand publicity tour of Latin America. He was killed in a plane crash.

Garifuna (also known as Garinagu or Black Caribs): Culturally distinct ethnic minority group. The Garifuna settled along the Caribbean coast of Central America from Belize City, Belize, to Pearl Lagoon, Nicaragua, primarily in Belize and Honduras. African cultural survivals can be found in the unique Garifuna language as well as music and dance.

Traditionally assumed to be the product of African slaves and Carib Indians, the Garifuna first emerged on St. Vincent, in the eastern Caribbean. They were transported by the British to the Bay Islands in 1797 and eventually spread along the Caribbean coast. A Black Carib reservation existed in Belize for about fifty years.

684 — *Garriga, Mariano Simon*

Major strides were made toward recognition and integration of the Garifuna between 1940 and 1970, including establishment of Garifuna Settlement Day on November 19 to mark their arrival in Belize. In Belize, a former leader of the United Democratic Party, the first native Roman Catholic bishop, and a number of priests have been Garifuna. The Garinagu were recognized as a separate and important group by Honduras in the 1970's. The Nicaraguan settlements suffered losses during the early years of the Sandinista government.

The Garifuna have a tradition of short-term and seasonal migration in search of employment. Many worked on the construction of the Panama Canal and even more responded to the need for merchant mariners during World War II. Affiliation with the National Maritime Union helped these Garifuna gain U.S. citizenship and establish an economic base. Most do not return to their country of origin after retirement, with the exception being Garifuna from Honduras. Illegal migration tends to be overland, through Belize and Mexico, or as stowaways on merchant ships.

Scholars and cultural leaders have estimated that about 100,000 Garifuna lived in the United States in the early 1990's, with more than half of them in the New York City area, particularly Brooklyn and the Bronx. Smaller groups were found in Los Angeles, New Orleans, Chicago, and Miami. Most Garifuna immigrants are from Honduras or Belize.

Garifuna in the United States are represented in every major occupation, from menial jobs to the professions. The better-educated Garifuna have used their diaspora to foster cultural traditions, the Garifuna language (recognized for instruction in Bronx schools), and attempts at pan-Garifuna cooperation in the United States and their home countries. There is much participation in volunteer activities, particularly the brotherhoods of the Roman Catholic church. The United Garifuna Cultural Association of Greater New York appears to be the largest of the Garifuna groups, but student groups such as Lumalali Garifuna in New York and the Walagante Dance Group in Los Angeles also promote cultural preservation.

Garifuna Day was proclaimed in New York in 1991, and Garifuna in Los Angeles celebrate Garifuna Settlement Day annually with a Mass and a festival. *Punta* rock, a modernized version of traditional Garifuna music, has become popular even among non-Garifuna Caribbean Americans and fans of reggae music through bands such as Chatuye. Some radio stations regularly carried Garifuna programming in the early 1990's.

Garinagu. *See* **Garifuna**

Garriga, Mariano Simon (1886, Point Isabel, Tex.—Feb. 21, 1965, Corpus Christi, Tex.): Catholic bishop. Educated at St. Mary's College in Kansas City, Kansas, before attending St. Francis Seminary in Milwaukee, Wisconsin, Garriga was ordained to the priesthood in 1911. He first worked as a missionary in western Texas. Between 1916 and 1919, Garriga served as a chaplain during World War I. After his stint as chaplain ended, he served as a pastor at St. Cecelia's Church in San Antonio, Texas. In 1934, Garriga was selected to be a papal chamberlain, and he advanced to become a domestic prelate in 1935. The following year, Garriga became the first native Texan to be consecrated as a titular bishop and as coadjutor bishop of the diocese of Corpus Christi, Texas. With this appointment, Garriga was the first American of Mexican descent to be named as a bishop in the Catholic church. He officially succeeded to the episcopal see in 1949. In 1959, he was given the honorary title of "Mr. South Texas" in recognition of his work as a bishop and his contributions as a historian of local Texas lore and culture. Garriga was active in Catholic affairs and traveled to Rome in 1962 to attend the historic Second Vatican Council (VATICAN II).

Garza, Catarino (Nov. 25, 1859, near Matamoros, Tamaulipas, Mexico—1902, Panama): Journalist and revolutionary. Garza's family moved to Brownsville, Texas, while he was a child. Despite having a limited formal education, he developed an interest in writing and journalism. He founded several newspapers during the 1880's. His editorials provided leadership and guidance in the fight for Mexican American civil rights, and he helped organize mutual aid societies in the Rio Grande Valley.

Garza also became an important border rebel who opposed Mexican president Porfirio Díaz. In Corpus Christi, Texas, Garza accused a United States customs officer, Victor Sebree, of assassinating Mexican prisoners who actively opposed Díaz. Sebree shot and wounded Garza when the two met during an election at Rio Grande City in 1888. Garza recovered and prepared to invade Mexico with approximately one thousand followers. He launched three separate expeditions in 1891 and twice reached Nuevo León, Tamaulipas, but he was turned back by the Mexican army.

Garza's guerrilla activities ended in 1893, but his actions rekindled fears of a Mexican revolt in the border region. To prevent such an occurrence, United States authorities stationed large numbers of troops in the area. Garza fled to Cuba and later traveled to the isthmus of Panama, where he died fighting in that Colombian province's fight for independence.

Garza, Reynaldo (b. July 7, 1915, Brownsville, Tex.): Federal judge. President John F. Kennedy appointed Garza as a U.S. district court judge in Brownsville, Texas, in 1961. He was appointed as the senior judge of the U.S. Court of Appeals, Fifth Circuit, by President Jimmy Carter in 1979. Garza was appointed in 1987 to the Emergency Court of Appeals of the United States, later becoming its chief judge.

Garza received his B.A. and his LL.B. from the University of Texas. After passing the Texas bar in 1939, he established his own law practice. In 1942, he enlisted in the United States Air Force, serving until 1945. He then returned to private practice until 1950.

Garza has been a prominent member of many boards and committees and has received recognition for his contributions as an active community leader. For his work with the Knights of Columbus, he was the recipient of the Pro Ecclesi et Pontifice medal in 1952,

Reynaldo Garza became a U.S. district court judge in 1961. (AP/Wide World Photos)

and in 1954 he was decorated a knight in the Order of St. Gregory the Great by Pope Pius XII. Garza also has the distinction of having the Reynaldo G. Garza School of Law in Edinburg, Texas, named for him. While serving as the chief judge of the U.S. Emergency Court of Appeals, Garza declined the cabinet post of attorney general of the United States rather than resign his lifetime appointment as a federal judge.

Garza v. County of Los Angeles, California Board of Supervisors (June 4, 1990, as corrected May 14, 1991): Political redistricting case. This decision of the United States District Court for the Central District of California bears numbers CV 88-5143 KN (EX) and CV 88 5135 KN (EX). Garza, who enjoyed the support of the United States of America as a coplaintiff, challenged the apportionment of the Los Angeles County Board of Supervisors as racially discriminatory against Hispanics and in violation of the VOTING RIGHTS ACT OF 1965. District Judge Kenyon ruled in favor of Garza's complaint.

In this decision, the court found that the Los Angeles County Board of Supervisors violated section 2 of the Voting Rights Act of 1965 and the equal protection clause of the FOURTEENTH AMENDMENT to the Constitution by failing to draw a redistricting plan in 1981 that created a Hispanic majority in one of five supervisorial districts. The court ordered the Board of Supervisors to redraw its redistricting plan to conform with this decision. There were some partisan implications to this decision, since Hispanics in Los Angeles County were a Democratic voting bloc and the changing demographics caused by a rapidly increasing Hispanic population were clearly threatening Republican control of Los Angeles County.

In its decision, the court found that the Hispanic community of Los Angeles County was large enough and geographically compact enough so that REAPPORTIONMENT could create a supervisorial district in which Hispanics were a majority of the voting age population. The court also found that Hispanics in Los Angeles County were a politically cohesive group and that their political behavior was polarized in opposition to that of non-Hispanic voters.

According to the decision, the following factors should be considered in redistricting plans. An unusually large election district is a relevant factor in a claim of violation of the Voting Rights Act. The overriding objective of a proper legislative districting plan is substantial equality of population among various districts, and this goal applies to county legislative bodies as

The court decision in Garza v. County of Los Angeles, California Board of Supervisors *aided Gloria Molina in becoming the first Latino member of that board since the 1870's.* (AP/Wide World Photos)

well as to statewide legislative bodies. The number of residents ineligible to vote because of alien status or past criminal convictions should be included in the apportionment base by which legislators are distributed. Finally, the task of reapportionment is properly a legislative function that should be performed by the legislature and not by the courts where at all possible. The court ruled that the Board of Supervisors had conducted reapportionment with the intent of protecting incumbents and fragmenting the Hispanic vote.

In addition to its impact on the distribution of political power between parties and voting groups in Los Angeles County, California, this decision had broader effects on the development of voting rights principles. The United States has moved beyond merely implementing the Fifteenth Amendment to guarantee minorities the right to vote. Many courts are now increasingly seeking all possible means to maximize minority voting strength, although the United States Supreme Court remains divided on this issue. This redistricting decision was important in Gloria MOLINA's election to the Board of Supervisors.

Gaston, Cito (Clarence Edwin Gaston; b. Mar. 17, 1944, San Antonio, Tex.): Baseball player and manager. Gaston began his major league playing career in 1967 as an outfielder with the Atlanta Braves. After a trade to the San Diego Padres, he briefly emerged as a star, hitting .318 with 29 home runs and 93 runs batted in and earning All-Star selection in 1970. He never approached that level again, however, and he retired with a .256 lifetime average after an eleven-year career with the Padres, Braves, and Pittsburgh Pirates.

In 1981, after a brief stint as a player in the Mexican League, Gaston became a batting coach in the Braves' minor league organization. A year later, he was offered a coaching job with the Toronto Blue Jays, a position he held for the next seven years. Early in the 1989 season, with the talented Blue Jays off to a disappointing 12-24 start, Toronto manager Jimy Williams was fired, and Gaston was named as his temporary replacement. Under Gaston, the team streaked to a 77-49 finish and won the American League Eastern Division title, and the managing job was his to keep. The first black Latino to manage in the majors, Gaston led the

Toronto Blue Jays manager Cito Gaston led his team to a second consecutive World Series championship in 1993. (AP/Wide World Photos)

Blue Jays to another division title in 1991 and to consecutive World Series championships in 1992 and 1993.

Gaston, Mauricio (Sept. 10, 1947, Havana, Cuba—Sept. 13, 1986, Boston, Mass.): Political activist and educator. Gaston's family moved to the United States shortly after the Cuban Revolution in 1959. Gaston completed his undergraduate studies with high honors in the field of architecture at Princeton University in 1968. He began what became a lifelong pursuit of social justice when he cofounded a tenant organizing group called City Life/Vida Urbana in Boston.

Gaston became an organizer and strategist for the Puerto Rican Socialist Party, working for the cause of Puerto Rican independence. He linked such local community issues as tenants' rights and BILINGUAL EDUCATION to a broader definition of social justice. Gaston also worked to develop bridges between the United States and Cuba.

In 1980, with a master's degree in urban planning from the Massachusetts Institute of Technology, Gaston began working on urban redevelopment. He died suddenly in 1986. The University of Massachusetts honored him by establishing the MAURICIO GASTON INSTITUTE FOR LATINO COMMUNITY DEVELOPMENT AND PUBLIC POLICY.

Gazpacho: Spanish soup of tomatoes, cucumbers, green peppers, onions, and seasonings. *Gazpacho* is an old Andalusian dish, transported to the Americas by the Spanish. It took root in the Americas most strongly in Puerto Rico, where it is made essentially in the Spanish manner. Tomatoes, cucumbers, green peppers, and onions form a vegetable purée, which is thickened with bread and seasoned with garlic, olive oil, and vinegar. It is served cold, sometimes with croutons for garnish or a shot of lemon vodka for zest. *Gazpacho de aguacate* is a Puerto Rican creation consisting of a pitted avocado half filled with cold diced tomato, cucumber, green pepper, and onion, then seasoned with olive oil, vinegar, garlic, and herbs.

Gender roles: Specific behaviors, attitudes, values, and motives are considered appropriate or typical for each gender in a given society or culture. From birth, a person's gender is the most salient characteristic used to classify that individual. Gender concerns both biological sex (chromosomal and hormonal makeup) and the process by which children are shaped by their environment into patterns of behaviors, attitudes, values, and motives deemed appropriate according to societal norms. Throughout infancy, childhood, and adolescence, and even into adulthood, individuals are encouraged and rewarded for engaging in behaviors and values that are considered gender "appropriate" while being discouraged or punished for exhibiting gender inappropriateness.

In many Western societies, attributes such as nurturance, cooperativeness, kindness, and sensitivity have been characterized as feminine. Attributes such as dominance, assertiveness, independence, and competitiveness are seen as appropriate or typical characteristics of males. (*See* STEREOTYPES OF LATINAS; STEREOTYPES OF LATINOS.)

Traditionally, gender roles in Latin American cultures have been clearly defined. Male and female children are socialized differently from an early age. There are certain jobs and tasks that are part of women's activities that men will not do, as well as jobs that men perform that are not considered appropriate for women. People of both sexes accept these delineations, which increase the gender role rigidity found in traditional Latin American countries. Latino communities in the United States exhibit these distinctions to a lesser, but still large, degree. Latino men are seen as dominant, authoritarian figures, and Latinas are perceived as caregivers and nurturers who take care of everyone else before themselves.

The cultural expectations surrounding the concepts of MACHISMO and *MARIANISMO* also act to increase gender role rigidity among Latinos. Machismo ideals portray men as having the need to be strong, in control, and good providers for their families. It calls for men to defend the strength and honor of their families, particularly the virtue of women. *Marianismo* ideals are based on having the Virgin Mary as a model for women. Women are expected to be submissive, self-sacrificing, and stoic.

The rigidity of gender role expectations held by a Latino depends in part on the length of time spent in the United States, socioeconomic level, and country of origin or descent. Newly arrived Mexican natives from rural areas, for example, tend to subscribe to more rigid gender roles than do second-generation Cuban American professionals. As immigrants, Latinos must learn to live in a culture that can be very different from their own. This acculturation process has often eroded strict traditional gender role differences. Roles and expectations for males and females in the Latino culture appear to be undergoing important changes. Although these changes may bring about additional gen-

Gender roles such as those governing division of household tasks tend to fade as Latino families assimilate. (James Shaffer)

der role flexibility, they may also affect the manner in which traditional gender roles have served as stabilizing factors in the Latino culture.

Gente de razón: Term used in colonial Spanish America to refer to people other than Indians. Originally intended to refer to the upper classes, *gente de razón* (people of reason) was used to refer to all non-Indian people in Spanish colonial societies. It was used particularly in reference to Spaniards, MESTIZOS (people of Spanish and Indian ancestry), and mulattoes (people of Spanish and African ancestry). The term was reserved for people who had adopted Spanish culture and religion. Although it pretended to make a clear distinction between Indians and non-Indians, reality

was often too complex for such a distinction. Some people qualified as *gente de razón* in some respects but remained attached to Indian ways in others. This term illustrates the social divisions of Spanish colonial society, divisions that in many ways remained in independent Latin America.

Gentrification: Gentrification is the process of change that takes place in deteriorated city neighborhoods when relatively affluent people move in and extensively improve the local housing. Gentrification became a significant trend in the United States in the 1970's. There are many widely publicized examples, such as the Adams Morgan area of Washington, D.C., Ansley Park in Atlanta, Georgia, and the MISSION DIS-

TRICT of San Francisco, California. Gentrification also occurred in many other Western nations in the 1970's in such cities as Toronto, Canada; Amsterdam, The Netherlands; London, England; Munich, Germany; Paris, France; and Copenhagen, Denmark.

The extent and cost of such renovation varies. Architecturally unique details and fixtures of old dwellings, such as marble fireplaces and leaded-glass windows, are often retained. Gentrification usually involves residential properties converted for continued residential use, but nonresidential buildings are sometimes converted to use as dwellings. Examples are old warehouses, schools, churches, and industrial lofts. Once residential restoration occurs in a neighborhood, there is often renovation of buildings for such commercial ventures as private art galleries, antique shops, and gourmet restaurants.

Gentrification happens only in certain types of neighborhoods and buildings. The typical neighborhood lies within two miles of the city center and has good access to transportation. It consists of only a few blocks and has a natural boundary such as a waterfront. The area contains single-family dwellings or townhouses, but not large apartment buildings. Selected buildings have a distinctive architecture (often Victorian) and some historical significance.

The typical person who becomes a gentrifier is a young white adult. The typical gentrifier is college-educated, works in a white-collar occupation, and earns a middle-class or upper-middle-class income. The gentrifying household is often childless. Contrary to popular belief, gentrifiers usually move from another area of the city, not from the suburbs. Factors in deciding to move include the short commute to work, the availability of cultural activities in the city, and an appreciation for the workmanship and charm of old dwellings. Gentrification can be a good investment, because property values typically rise in gentrified areas.

A negative consequence of gentrification is that it displaces poor residents who cannot afford higher rent and increased property taxes. Because low-income housing is in short supply, the poor may take lower-quality housing, pay more for housing, or become homeless. The displaced poor are often members of racial and ethnic minorities.

Research is neither consistent nor complete on the impact of gentrification on Latinos. For example, studies of gentrified areas of Washington, D.C., found both African Americans and Latinos displaced in Adams Morgan; in Dupont Circle, on the other hand, African Americans were displaced, but the Latino population grew during gentrification. Changes in the U.S. Census classification system between 1970 and 1980 complicate research. (Latinos were classified as "white" in 1970 and as "other" in 1980.) Furthermore, gentrification has not been as extensive in the South and Southwest (where many Latinos live) as in other regions of the country.

Geronimo, Cesar (Cesar Francisco Geronimo y Zorrilla; b. Mar. 11, 1948, El Seibo, Dominican Republic): Baseball player. First signed by the New York Yankees, Geronimo rose to stardom as the center fielder for the Cincinnati "Big Red Machine" of the mid-1970's. He made his major league debut with Houston in 1969 but did not become a regular until a 1972 trade took him to the Cincinnati organization.

A fleet defensive outfielder who won Gold Glove honors every year from 1974 to 1977, Geronimo was a major contributor to Reds teams that captured five divisional championships, three National League pennants, and two World Series titles. Although he was primarily renowned for his defensive skills, he hit for a respectable .258 average, with a high of .307 in 1976. He remained with the Reds through the 1980 season. After a 1981 trade, he spent three seasons as a part-time player with the Kansas City Royals before retiring in 1983.

Cesar Geronimo. (AP/Wide World Photos)

Gerrymandering: Changing the boundaries of an electoral district with the intent of creating an advantage for a particular group. The term was coined in response to the actions of Elbridge Gerry, a nineteenth century governor of Massachusetts who was instrumental in redrawing an electoral district in a salamander shape to favor the candidate of the Republican Party. During the late twentieth century, gerrymandering was used to dilute the voting strength of minority groups, including Latinos.

The U.S. Constitution requires that seats in the House of Representatives be redistributed every ten years, following the U.S. Census. Redistribution of congressional seats among states ensures that states are represented in proportion to their populations; within each state, congressional districts are redrawn if the state's number of representatives changes or if population changes within the state have changed the relative sizes of congressional districts. Redistricting, with potential gerrymandering, also occurs for districts used in elections for other offices.

The redistricting process is complex because of the need to consider demographic variables while establishing districts almost exactly equal in population size. Moreover, each political party sees REAPPORTIONMENT as a way of improving its position. In traditional gerrymandering, the party in control draws electoral districts to its advantage.

Beyond partisan politics, gerrymandering has occurred along racial and ethnic lines. Partly because of gerrymandering, minority groups historically have been underrepresented in Congress, in state legislatures, and in some local positions. Latino communities have been divided among different electoral districts to reduce their political power and to benefit non-Latino candidates.

Congress moved to remedy the practice of diminishing minority representation through redistricting with the passage of the VOTING RIGHTS ACT OF 1970. That law prohibits changing district boundaries if the effect is to dilute the voting strength of minority groups. In 1982, Congress extended the act to prohibit voting practices that result in discrimination.

The Voting Rights Act of 1970 gave Latinos the tools to correct gerrymandering and traditional representational imbalances through the legal process. Latinos and African Americans have used the act to challenge redistricting plans that diluted their voting power. The Supreme Court, in *Thornburg v. Gingles* (1986), established a test for determining when districts must be created in which members of minority groups would constitute the majority of the electorate. The minority group must be able to show that it is sufficiently large and geographically compact enough to constitute a majority in one or more districts. It must also be able to demonstrate that under current apportionment members of a geographically cohesive minority group face substantial difficulty in electing a candidate of their choice. The decision came close to declaring that the number of representatives from each minority group should reflect the proportions of each group in the population.

During the 1980's, Latinos dramatically increased their representation in Congress through the redistricting process. In 1980, there were only five Latino members of Congress. After the 1982 reapportionment, this number increased to eleven. After the 1992 redistricting, the number climbed to eighteen.

Gold and silver rushes, Colorado: Discoveries of precious metals in Colorado from 1859 to 1880 that led to Euro-American migration. Early techniques of MINING had been developed in northern Mexico, and much of that historical experience contributed to the North American mining industry. Early gold panning by grub-staked miners was followed by large-scale mining employing modern techniques as an industrial capitalist economy enveloped the region.

Spaniards looked for gold in their earliest explorations, and Antonio de Espejo returned with ore samples in 1582. Other explorers justified their missions with searches for precious metals. Spanish mining technology underwent a rebirth during the sixteenth century. Various techniques of Spanish mining influenced extraction into the nineteenth century. For example, the system of pan amalgamation employed in the Colorado gold fields was used because there was no better method at the time. Spaniards used the stair-step separator, sometimes called a sluice box. The pan was essential to early placer mining. Mexican mining also taught the methods of dragging to crush ore. The basic philosophy employed in Mexico was to use whatever technology best suited the environment.

Zebulon Pike found samples of mineral wealth in Colorado in 1807, but the potential could not even be imagined. During the Mexican American War (1846-1848), William Gilpin, who campaigned through Colorado, found signs of this wealth that inspired him during his term as the first territorial governor of Colorado in 1861.

The first Colorado gold rush occurred before Colorado became a state. William Green Russell of Georgia found gold in July, 1858, at the mouth of Dry Creek. His discovery set off an intensifying rush of miners; the "Fifty-Niners" who entered the area in 1859 numbered more than a hundred thousand. "Pikes Peak or Bust" signs covered many of the wagons crossing the SANTA FE TRAIL through Kansas. By November of 1859, residents proposed the creation of the Jefferson Territory.

In 1861, Colorado was created out of several jurisdictions: northern New Mexico, eastern Utah, and western Kansas. The first rush saw miners using the panning method of extracting minerals from streams and rivers, but the more modern techniques of placer mining and milling soon supplanted older techniques. The initial rush for gold was later replaced by a search for other metals. California Gulch of 1863 eventually became Leadville, and silver instead of gold would favor the community in the 1870's.

Mines of different types were used. Deep pit mines were connected by narrow gauge railroads; small-scale miners often used the "rat-hole" technique. The miner would dig a hole into the side of a mountain, following a vein as far as possible, then dig another hole above the last, continuing until the vein was exhausted. The washes below silver lodes could be scavenged for silver chlorides. Such scavenging was often a sign that an area had been worked clean. The "chloriders" were often Mexicans.

Gold rush, California (1848): After gold was discovered in California, thousands of fortune seekers poured in. Boomtowns and mining camps sprang up overnight. Most prospectors did not become rich, but many personal fortunes were made, and the gold industry provided impetus for economic development. Because of the gold rush, California was settled much faster than it would have been otherwise.

Gold was discovered by James W. Marshall at Sutter's Mill on January 24, 1848, a few days before California was signed over by Mexico to the United States. The California mountains soon became the site of the first major gold rush. For the first year after the discovery, residents, both U.S. entrepreneurs and CALIFORNIOS, worked claims with little conflict. There seemed to be plenty of land and gold for everyone.

By the fall, newspapers had spread word throughout the United States and beyond of easy riches to be had in California. By the spring of 1849, tens of thousands of fortune seekers from around the world had set out for the goldfields.

Great waves of immigrants poured in, and Califor-

nia's population mushroomed. The territory's economy boomed, but the rapid growth was devastating to the Native Americans, whose extermination was hastened, and the Californios, who suffered from suppression and violence as victims of nationalism and racism. By the end of 1849, there was already talk of expelling "foreigners" from the goldfields. The non-Hispanic settlers included Californios in this category, making no distinctions between them and the thousands of newly arrived Mexicans, Chileans, and other Latinos.

Mexicans from the northern regions were more successful than most Latinos at finding a niche in the rapidly changing economic structure. Many successfully mined in the Sonora region, where they introduced techniques later adapted throughout the goldfields; others regularly supplied mules and transported provisions to prospectors.

Soon, however, race crimes, purges, and legislation made the lives of the Mexican miners hazardous. The 1850 FOREIGN MINERS' TAX LAW mandated a tax of $20 per month on foreigners' mining permits. The law was rarely enforced for Northern European miners but was used to drive Mexicans from their claims. By the fall of that year, between five thousand and fifteen thousand foreign prospectors, mostly Mexican, had left their claims.

Social distinctions collapsed as all Latinos, including Californios, were labeled "GREASERS" by many non-Hispanic settlers. In 1851, Chinese immigrants began replacing Latinos at the bottom rung of the social ladder. Nevertheless, Latinos, especially Mexicans, suffered from hate crimes (often violent), legal injustices, and discrimination throughout the 1850's. The gold boom continued for the next several decades.

The legacy of the gold rush is mixed. It catapulted CALIFORNIA into statehood (in 1850), prosperity, and national and international prominence. It brought to California a cultural diversity never before achieved so quickly; San Francisco quickly became a major port and an international city. It also damaged the area ecologically and hastened the extermination of its Native American population. Gold, therefore, not only shaped much of California's early economic history but also left an environmental and social legacy still evident in the state.

Golf: Very few Latinos have achieved prominence in golf. Reasons include the expense of playing, ethnic discrimination, and golf not occupying a central place in Latinos' sports priorities. Nevertheless, two Latinos,

Individual miners used a variety of methods to find gold; this illustration shows a miner using a device called a cradle. (Library of Congress)

Nancy Lopez was the first Mexican American to achieve a large degree of success on the women's professional golf tour. (AP/Wide World Photos)

Nancy Lopez and Lee Trevino, overcame obstacles to become established superstars.

Obstacles to Golf. In contrast to BOXING, BASEBALL, SOCCER, and other sports, the number of Latinos who have achieved prominence in golf is small. Reasons for this relate to how golf developed in the United States. Golf was brought from Scotland in 1887 by two upper-class white businessmen, Robert Lockhart and John Reid. When the first golf courses were built shortly thereafter, their memberships consisted of upper-class whites with sufficient wealth to afford the expense of maintaining a golf course and clubhouse and to buy the expensive equipment necessary to play the game. Public courses (there were more than a thousand by 1900) made the game accessible to the masses, but primarily to the white masses rather than Latinos and other ethnic minorities, who still could not afford the expense of equipment and the cost of greens fees.

Another factor that effectively barred Latinos and other ethnic minorities was an attitude that characterized golf from the beginning. Golf in the United States was perceived to be an aristocratic game, drawing the

Lee Trevino had a successful professional golf career that extended into play on the seniors' tour. (AP/Wide World Photos)

upper classes as both participants and spectators. From the beginning, golf was effectively controlled by the upper classes and white society members.

Overt and covert racial and ethnic DISCRIMINATION were commonly practiced. Cases arose even as late as the end of the twentieth century, particularly at private clubs reluctant to abandon their exclusivity and open their doors to anyone wishing to join. It was not until September 17, 1956, that Ann Gregory became the first black woman to play in a national championship (U.S. Women's Amateur) sponsored by the United States Golf Association. Lee Elder became the first African American to play in the Masters tournament in 1975. The rather explicit "Caucasian only" clause in the bylaws of the Professional Golfers' Association (PGA) was not removed until 1961.

Aside from the economic and ethnic restrictions golf has imposed on Latinos, a third factor that has limited the number of successful Latino golfers is that golf has never been central to the Latino sport experience. The sport is not popular among Latinos and is not played widely in Latin America. In one bibliography concerning Latin American sport containing more than thirteen hundred entries, only six referred to golf.

Lopez and Trevino. Nancy LOPEZ, the first Mexican American female golfer to achieve success and fame, recalled an incident of discrimination early in her career. Lopez golfed at the municipal course in Roswell, New Mexico. There was a private club in Roswell, but her parents could not have afforded the membership fees for her, even if she had been welcomed. Lopez recalled after playing a city tournament at the private club that she was afforded a "polite frostiness" by the members and was glad to leave and return to her municipal course.

Lee Buck TREVINO, the first Mexican American male golfer to achieve fame and success, had his first exposure to golf doing maintenance work at the country club located near his home in Dallas, Texas. Trevino worked for four years, from the age of twenty-one to the age of twenty-five, at a par-three course and driving range in Dallas as an assistant pro. He saw the job as a way to get his PGA Tour card, which otherwise would have been difficult to earn because he could not get a job at a country club. Even after he became successful, he suffered personal slights that he never forgot. At his first Masters tournament, he was not allowed inside the clubhouse at the Augusta National course. For the next decade, he changed his shoes in the parking lot to avoid entering the locker room.

Other Prominent Latino Golfers. Over the years, Latinos have been exposed to golf through the media. As the sport has filtered through to the middle and lower classes, with less expensive equipment and greater availability of inexpensive public courses, more Latinos have taken up the game. Public recognition afforded to the first two Latino superstars in the sport, Nancy Lopez and Lee Trevino, encouraged participation and spectatorship, if not in person then through the increasing number of televised tournaments. Additionally, Spaniards Seve Ballesteros, Jose-Maria Olazabal, and Marta Figueres-Dotti, along with Puerto Rican Juan "Chi Chi" RODRÍGUEZ, achieved significant fame and popularity in the United States. Robert Gamez showed early promise in his career, winning the 1990 Bay Hill Classic. Perhaps their examples will encourage other Latino golfers to emerge as future Latino golf superstars.   —*Laurence Miller*

SUGGESTED READINGS: • Boswell, Thomas. *Strokes of Genius*. New York: Doubleday, 1987. • Campbell, Malcolm. *The Random House International Encyclopedia of Golf*. New York: Random House, 1991. • Emery, David. *Who's Who in International Golf*. New York: Facts on File, 1983. • Glenn, Rhonda. *The Illustrated History of Women's Golf*. Dallas: Taylor, 1991. • Peper, George. *Golf in America: The First Hundred Years*. New York: Harry N. Abrams, 1988.

Gomes, Lloyd H. (b. Feb. 8, 1913, Turlock, Calif.): Military figure. Gomes reached the rank of major general in the U.S. Army in August, 1967. He retired on August 31, 1969.

Gomes joined the Army Reserve Corps in May, 1937. He was commissioned as a second lieutenant in July, 1938. He saw combat during World War II and the Korean War, earning the Purple Heart, Bronze Star, Silver Star, and Distinguished Service Cross, among other commendations and decorations.

During World War II, Gomes earned promotion to the rank of full colonel. Like many officers who stayed in the Army following the war, his rank was lowered, to lieutenant colonel. He was promoted back to full colonel in December, 1952.

In 1958, Gomes was named chief of staff for the Eighty-second Airborne Division at Fort Bragg. In 1965, he was promoted to brigadier general and assigned as a senior adviser to the First Republic Korean Army and as commander of a U.S. Army advisory group. His final assignment was as chief of the Joint United States Military Advisory Group to the Philippines.

Lefty Gomez in 1942, shortly before his retirement. (AP/Wide World Photos)

Gomez, Lefty (Vernon Louis Gomez; Nov. 26, 1908, Rodeo, Calif.—Feb. 17, 1989, Greenbrae, Calif.): Baseball player. A tall, thin, left-handed pitcher, Gomez spent two seasons in the minor leagues before making his major league debut in 1930 with the powerful New York Yankees. After a brief return to the minors, he became a Yankee regular the following season, winning twenty-one games and losing nine while posting an excellent 2.63 earned run average. He was a fixture of the great Yankee teams of the decade, leading the American League in victories and earned run average in 1934 and 1937, in winning percentage in 1934 and 1941, and in strikeouts in 1933, 1934, and 1937. He won more than twenty games in a season four times and compiled a brilliant 6-0 record in five World Series. A seven-time All-Star, Gomez, a weak hitter, drove in the first run in All-Star Game history.

After thirteen seasons with the Yankees, Gomez pitched in one game for the Washington Senators before retiring in 1943 with a lifetime 189-102 record. During his playing career, he had become well known for his outgoing, affable nature, his sense of humor, and his eccentricities, and he established a reputation as a popular banquet speaker and comic after his playing days were over. In 1972, he was elected to the National Baseball Hall of Fame.

Gomez, Preston (Pedro Gomez y Martinez; b. Apr. 20, 1923, Central Preston, Cuba): Baseball player and manager. Gomez's major league playing career consisted of eight games as a reserve infielder with the 1944 Washington Senators; he earned his U.S. baseball fame during a long career as a coach and manager. After a long stint as a minor league coach, Gomez was named the manager of the San Diego Padres in 1969, guiding the newly formed team to three consecutive last-place finishes. In 1974, he led the Houston Astros to a fourth-place finish in the National League Western Division with an 81-81 record, but he was replaced in the middle of the 1975 season after the club had

Preston Gomez. (AP/Wide World Photos)

slipped to last place. The Chicago Cubs hired Gomez for the 1980 season, but he was again replaced in midyear after the team performed poorly. Gomez compiled an overall 346-529 record as a manager in the majors.

Gómez-Peña, Guillermo (b. September, 1955, Mexico City, Mexico): Performance artist. Gómez-Peña attended Jesuit schools before entering the Universidad Nacional Autonoma de Mexico, where he created performance pieces with his fellow students. In 1978, he moved to the United States to study at the California Institute of the Arts. In 1980, Gómez-Peña cofounded the Poyesis Genetica, a performance group focused on cultural and border issues. In 1983, he relocated to San Diego, where he cohosted a radio show titled *Border Dialogues*, worked with the Centro Cultural de la Raza, and published the journal *The Broken Line/La Línea Quebrada*. In 1985, he cofounded the Border Arts Workshop/El Taller de Arte Fronterizo.

Through his work, Gómez-Peña has confronted racism on both sides of the Mexican-U.S. border. His "performance actions" have been presented at such politically sensitive sites as the Federal Building in San Diego. In 1988, he married fellow artist and collaborator Emily Hicks through a fence on the border. Gómez-Peña's performances and writings include *Border Brujo* (1988), *Border Axis* (1989), *Warrior for Gringostroika* (1993), *The Shame-Man Meets El Mexican't at the Smithsonian Hotel and Country Club* (1993), and *The New World (B)order* (1993). In 1991, he was named recipient of a MacArthur Foundation fellowship.

Gómez-Quiñones, Juan (b. Jan. 28, 1942, Parral, Chihuahua, Mexico): Historian, poet, and activist. An activist who cofounded UNITED MEXICAN AMERICAN STUDENTS and who cofounded and directed Chicano Legal Defense, Gómez-Quiñones is also highly regarded as a historian. His historical studies examine Chicano history as composed of several periods, with evolution occurring through them. He sees class divisions and different interests among Chicanos, with attitudes about assimilation into Anglo society linked to class status. The role of intellectuals, in his opinion, is to clarify cultural values and introduce new ideas to bring about progressive change. This perspective links his scholarly work with his activism. His most important contribution to Chicano studies, other than his writing, is his directorship of the Chicano Studies Re-

search Center at the University of California, Los Angeles (UCLA), from 1975 to 1985.

Gómez-Quiñones' best-known work is the pioneering *Sembradores, Ricardo Flores Magón y el Partido Liberal Mexicano: A Eulogy and Critique* (1973). His poetry is collected in *Fifth and Grande Vista: Poems, 1960-1973* (1974). He grew up in the Los Angeles area, attending local parochial schools before enrolling at UCLA. After earning a B.A. in English in 1962, he continued his education there, getting an M.A. in Latin American studies in 1964 and a Ph.D. in history, specializing in Latin America, in 1972. After teaching at San Diego State University for a year, Gómez-Quiñones joined the faculty of UCLA in 1969.

Gonsalves, Paul (July 12, 1920, Boston, Mass.—May 14, 1974, London, England): Tenor saxophonist. As a boy, Gonsalves listened to the music of Duke Ellington and Jimmie Lunceford. By the time he was sixteen, he could play the guitar. He also began playing tenor saxophone at local clubs in Boston.

After serving in the United States Army during World War II, Gonsalves joined Count Basie's band. He remained with Basie for four years and earned a reputation as an expressive saxophone player in the big band style. During 1949 and 1950, Gonsalves played in Dizzy Gillespie's big band. After his short stay with Gillespie's bop-oriented band, he joined the Duke Ellington Orchestra, taking over for the legendary Ben Webster. He would remain with Ellington for the rest of his career.

In addition to Gonsalves' exciting playing with Ellington, he was active as a soloist with various groups. He is remembered for both his frenetic solos at fast tempos as well as numerous memorable performances of ballads. Although Gonsalves could not always be counted on to show up for a performance on time, Ellington forgave him because of his remarkable musical talent. Gonsalves died less than two weeks before Ellington.

Gonzales, Pancho (Richard Alonzo Gonzalez; May 9, 1928, Los Angeles, Calif.—July 3, 1995, Las Vegas, Nev.): Tennis player. Introduced to the sport with a fifty-cent drugstore racket, Gonzales became a world-class player without a single professional lesson. His precocity caused him occasional problems; in 1943, although ranked number one among boys in Southern California, he was disqualified from tournament play for truancy.

After a stint in the Navy, Gonzales returned to tennis

Pancho Gonzales defeated Charles Pasarell in a 1969 Wimbledon match that lasted a record 112 games. (AP/Wide World Photos)

in 1947. A year later, he won the U.S. Championship by downing Eric Sturgess in straight sets (6-2, 6-3, 14-12). He defended his title in 1949, rallying from two sets down—including a loss in a thirty-four-game first-set marathon—to defeat Ted Schroeder (16-18, 2-6, 6-1, 6-2, 6-4). That year, Gonzales joined with Frank Parker to capture doubles titles at Wimbledon and the French Championship and also helped the U.S. team to defend its Davis Cup title.

In October, 1949, Gonzales turned professional, signing to play a series of matches against Jack Kramer, the professional world champion. In his first year as a professional, however, Gonzales played poorly and was dropped from the tour. He soon returned and proved himself a top-flight player, capturing numerous professional titles throughout the 1950's and 1960's. In 1953, he won the U.S. Professional Championship for the first of a record eight times.

A well-rounded player, Gonzales overwhelmed opponents with a strong serve and an arsenal of drop volleys and overhead smashes. He remained a leading player even into his mid-forties, retaining a top-ten U.S. ranking as late as 1972. In 1968, he was elected to the National Lawn Tennis Hall of Fame.

Gonzáles, Rodolfo "Corky" (b. June 18, 1928, Denver, Colo.): Chicano activist and poet. Gonzáles was born into a migrant-worker family. He was graduated from high school in Denver at the age of sixteen. His love of boxing earned for him a Golden Gloves title; as a professional boxer, he became a contender for the world featherweight title.

Gonzáles left boxing in 1955 to pursue business and politics. He was involved in the John F. Kennedy presidential campaign, and he became active in programs to improve the life of Chicano youth, including Los Voluntarios (The Volunteers) and the CRUSADE FOR JUSTICE. The Crusade for Justice headquarters became an activist center. Gonzáles published a newspaper, and the center sponsored a school that included classes on Chicano awareness and pride.

In 1967, Gonzáles published an epic poem, *I Am Joaquín/Yo Soy Joaquín*. Basically a social statement, *I Am Joaquín* had more than one hundred thousand copies printed.

González, Adalberto Elías (b. Altar, Sonora, Mexico): Playwright and actor. González was one of the most prolific, versatile, and respected figures in early Los Angeles Hispanic theater. He attended the Escuela Normal in Hermosillo, Mexico, then moved to Los Angeles in 1920. His *Los amores de Ramona* (the loves of Ramona), adapted from the Helen Hunt Jackson novel, broke Los Angeles box-office records by playing to some fifteen thousand people in its first week. In 1924, González became a film critic for *El Heraldo de México*, and in 1926 he won a playwriting contest sponsored by the Teatro Hidalgo.

Other plays by González include *Los misioneros* and *Los expatriados*, based on Mexican American life in California; *La asesina del martillo o la mujer tigresa* (1922), a popular thriller; *Sangre yaqui* (1924), a three-act melodrama with a military setting; *El enemigo de las mujeres*, about a boxer in love; *La casa de misterio*, a detective yarn; *La desgracia del pobre* (1926); and *La flor del fandango* (1928), a melodrama about marital politics. González's plays were performed throughout the southwestern United States and Mexico.

González, Genaro (b. Dec. 28, 1949, McAllen, Tex.): Writer. González was born to a family of migrant farmworkers. While he was a youth, his mother was hospitalized with tuberculosis, and financial hardships plagued the family. González was a top student, winning a scholarship to Pan American University in Edinburg, Texas. He also attended Pomona College, the University of California at Riverside, and the University of California at Santa Cruz, completing a master's degree and a doctorate in social psychology. He has taught at Pan American University and at the Universidad de las Americas in Mexico.

González won recognition as a promising writer with the short story "Un hijo del sol" (1971; child of the sun), written while he was a college student. His 1988 novel *Rainbow's End* was nominated for the American Book Award.

González, Henry Barbosa (b. May 3, 1916, San Antonio, Tex.): Public official. Born to Mexican parents who had fled the Mexican Revolution, González dedicated his life to public service. He was educated in San Antonio and in Austin, earning his law degree in 1943.

González prepared for federal government service by serving in the Texas State Senate. His election in 1956 earned for him the distinction of being the first Mexican American to serve in that legislative body in more than one hundred years. González had already gained national attention for his antisegregation and civil rights efforts by the time he launched the historic campaign in 1960 that ended with him becoming the first Mexican American to be elected to Congress from Texas.

Henry González signals victory in his first campaign for Congress. (AP/Wide World Photos)

As chairman of the House Banking Committee, González played a key role in reducing the financial consequences caused by government bailouts of the savings and loan industry during the 1980's. He has earned respect for his willingness to take on powerful interests without regard to partisan considerations.

González, José Luis (José Luis González Coiscou; b. Mar. 8, 1926, Santo Domingo, Dominican Republic): Writer. González's mother came from one of the most prestigious families in letters in the Dominican Republic. The family migrated to Puerto Rico when José Luis was four, and he spent his childhood in Guaynabo. As a youth, he lived in San Juan, and he was graduated from the University of Puerto Rico in 1946.

Before his graduation, González had published two collections of short stories exploring the condition of the Puerto Rican poor. While doing postgraduate work in political science at the New York School for Social Research in 1947, he observed the unfavorable living conditions of Puerto Rican immigrants. On returning to Puerto Rico in 1948, he presided over an activist group seeking to implement socialism in Puerto Rico. His short-story collection *El hombre de la calle* (1948; man in the street) concerns social and economic oppression of Puerto Ricans. Later, he moved to Mexico and published *En este lado* (1954; on this side), considered by many to be his best short-story collection.

González, Juan (Jan. 12, 1945, Camagüey, Cuba—December, 1993, New York, N.Y.): Artist. González left Cuba in 1961. He studied art at the University of Miami in Florida for seven years, graduating with both bachelor's and master's degrees in fine arts. His work has appeared in one-man shows and group shows across the United States. Formerly a member of the radical Hispanic group YOUNG LORDS, he lived his later life in New York City.

González saw his work as a dialogue of symbols, with different kinds of dialogues and associations occurring in different levels of work. His early exposure to art was in the churches of Cuba, and as a teenager he sometimes speculated about becoming a priest. Later, he said in interviews, art came to replace religion in his life, although he always considered himself to be a religious person.

González, Myrtle (Sept. 28, 1891, Los Angeles, Calif.—1919, Los Angeles, Calif.): Actress. González descended from an early California Mexican family. She grew up in Los Angeles, where she started acting in plays at an early age. As a teenager, she began performing professionally with the Los Angeles Belasco Theater Company. In 1911, González made her film debut in *Ghosts*, and over the next six years she performed in more than forty films produced by Vitagraph and Universal Pictures.

González was the first Mexican American actress to become a leading lady in feature films in the United States. She generally played hearty, adventurous heroines. Her most famous role was in *The Chalice of Courage* in 1916. A horseback-riding injury she received while shooting a film contributed to a bad case of influenza that caused her death at the age of twenty-seven. Her last film was *Captain Alvarez* (1917).

González, Pedro J. (1895, northern Mexico—Mar. 17, 1995, Lodi, Calif.): Radio personality. González was the first Spanish-speaking radio announcer in Los Angeles, California, and was a defender of Mexican American rights during the Depression. A film, *Break of Dawn*, was made about his life in 1988.

After serving with Pancho VILLA's forces in the Mexican Revolution, González relocated to Los Angeles in 1923 with his wife. In Los Angeles, he eventually found work making announcements in Spanish on a radio station. In time, he obtained his own radio program named *Los Madrugadores* (meaning "early risers").

González became an influential figure for the Mexican and Mexican American people in Los Angeles. In 1929, he played an important role in speaking out against human rights violations and the massive deportations of Mexicans. His attitude annoyed many politicians, particularly those who aired political campaign messages on his program. His enemies first attempted to take away his announcer's license. When that failed,

they fabricated evidence to accuse him of raping a sixteen-year-old girl. González was found guilty in 1934 and was sentenced to fifty years in prison. He was freed after serving six years when the girl he was accused of raping recanted her story. González was deported, and he settled in Tijuana, Mexico, where he formed a band, resumed radio broadcasting, and became a folk hero with his activism against social injustice.

González, Ray (b. Sept. 20, 1952, El Paso, Tex.): Editor and poet. González grew up in El Paso, Texas, and received a bachelor's degree in creative writing from the University of Texas at El Paso in 1975. Following his graduation from college, he went to Colorado, where he taught writing. González served as editor of *La Voz* (the voice), a Latino newspaper, and was poetry editor for the *Bloomsbury Review*. His own press, Mesilla, promoted the work of other poets and gained him respect among the Colorado arts community.

In 1988, González received the Four Corners Book Award for Poetry as well as the Colorado Governor's Award for Excellence in the Arts. In 1989, he became head of the Guadalupe Cultural Arts Center in San Antonio, Texas.

González-Irizarry, Aníbal (b. Puerto Pico): Broadcast journalist. González-Irizarry appeared on the television show *El Show Hispano*, which aired in New York from 1952 to 1954. The show was cohosted by González-Irizarry and Don Mendez. González-Irizarry was responsible for the fifteen-minute news segment, making him the first Hispanic television newscaster in the United States.

González-Irizarry was also a well-known disc jockey and a newscaster on two of the early Spanish-language radio stations in New York City. After returning to Puerto Rico in 1955, González-Irizarry became the most prominent and respected anchorman on Puerto Rican television, appearing on news shows for more than twenty years.

González Parsons, Lucía (c. 1852, near Fort Worth, Tex.—1942): Labor leader. An important socialist reformer and feminist for seven decades, González Parsons began her activism in the last quarter of the nineteenth century. With her husband, journalist Albert Parsons, she rose to prominence in the Chicago labor movement and in the socialist party. She joined the Chicago Working Women's Union, organizing demonstrations for women's rights. After the May 4, 1886,

Haymarket Riot, Albert was convicted and executed as one of eight leaders. Lucy, as she was known, led a public movement in support of the convicted men but failed to save their lives. After Albert's death, Lucy became a founder of the Industrial Workers of the World and of the International Labor Defense, an organization she was still serving in her eighties. She traveled throughout the Southwest, recruiting supporters of women's and workers' rights.

Good Neighbor Policy: Policy of Franklin D. Roosevelt. In an effort to secure the loyalty of Latin American countries against the growing threat of fascism, Roosevelt established the Good Neighbor Policy in 1933. The policy firmly stated the United States' commitment to assist in the development and protection of all Latin American people and countries. The Mexican government, Mexican Americans, and Mexican immigrants interpreted this policy to include Latin Americans living within, as well as outside, U.S. national boundaries. Therefore, by the late 1930's and the 1940's, the Mexican consulate and Mexican Americans began to demand civil rights for their people, using the Good Neighbor Policy as leverage against the U.S. government. In 1943, a Good Neighbor Commission formed in Texas to hear discrimination complaints and publicize state policies that did not adhere to the spirit of the Good Neighbor Policy.

Gorme, Edith "Eydie" (b. Aug. 16, 1932, Bronx, N.Y.): Singer. Gorme is the daughter of Nessim Gorme, a tailor, and Fortune Gorme. Her father, born in Turkey, was of Spanish descent. Until Gorme was five years old, Spanish was the only language spoken in her home. When Gorme was three years old, she sang on the radio.

During Gorme's high school years, she starred in a number of school musicals. After graduation from William Taft High School, Gorme worked as a Spanish interpreter. Eventually, she decided to focus on establishing her singing career.

In 1953, Gorme signed a recording contract with Coral. She had become a regular by 1954 on *The Tonight Show*, hosted by Steve Allen. Gorme met Steve Lawrence on the show, and they were married on December 29, 1957. After their marriage, they became a popular club act. In 1963, Gorme released the popular single "Blame It on the Bossa Nova," with a Latin rhythm. Gorme and Lawrence received Emmy Awards for their television specials. In 1967, Gorme won a Grammy Award as Best Female Vocalist for the song "If He Walked into My Life." She has been active in charitable work, and she and Lawrence continued to be popular concert and television attractions into the 1990's.

Gorras Blancas: Militant organization. In the late nineteenth and early twentieth centuries, Mexican American property owners came under siege in parts of New Mexico, and their rightful titles to land were not honored. Under the terms of the TREATY OF GUADALUPE HIDALGO (1848), the U.S. government agreed to honor titles to land in the Southwest that had been granted either by the Spanish government or the Mexican government. When this provision of the treaty was violated, such groups as the Gorras Blancas and the Mano Negras led the Mexican American resistance.

The Gorras Blancas organized a political arm in 1890. The short-lived United People's Party fielded candidates that year for local elections in New Mexico. The Gorras Blancas also protected themselves from extreme violence in these land disputes. Such violence took the life in 1904 of Colonel Francisco J. Chaves, Jr., a surgeon and Civil War veteran who was a leading spokesman for Mexican Americans.

Gou Bourgell, José (b. Cataluña, Spain): Playwright and journalist. Gou Bourgell established his career in Los Angeles and the Calexico area near the California/Mexico border from 1924 to 1937. His plays include *La mancha roja* (1924); *El crimen de la virtud* (1924), a comedy about Mexican customs; *El parricida* (1926) and *El suicida* (1927), two social dramas; and *Virginidades* (1928). As a journalist, Gou Bourgell worked for *El Heraldo de México* in Los Angeles and served as editor of *La Voz* and *El Mundo al Día* in Calexico.

Graffiti: Words and symbols written in public places. Graffiti is a form of written expression used primarily by young people, mostly gang members, to identify themselves and their gangs (*see* TAGGING AND TAGGERS). Graffiti is written on walls of buildings and other public spaces, usually without permission. It is characterized by highly stylized lettering created with markers or spray paint. Each individual has his or her own style of writing, developed from traditional styles of graffiti alphabets. Individuals write their names, gang symbols and slogans, and names of boyfriends and girlfriends. The symbols used in some graffiti may be undecipherable to an outsider but are fully understood by the writers' peers and rivals. Graffiti is often

Graffiti can have social meaning, as illustrated by this rock proclaiming "don't sell the land" in New Mexico. (Lou DeMatteis)

viewed as defacement of property, though it can also be understood as an artistic form of communicating personal identity and making oneself visible to others in the community.

Graham v. Richardson (decided June 14, 1971): Welfare rights case. This U.S. Supreme Court case (403 U.S. 365) was a consolidation of two cases, one brought by alien residents of Arizona and the other brought by Pennsylvania aliens. In each case, the noncitizens alleged the unconstitutionality of state laws denying welfare payments to them because of their alien status. The Court agreed that such laws were unconstitutional.

In Arizona, alien residents protested a law that denied state welfare payments to noncitizens unless they had resided in the state for at least fifteen years. Several aliens brought suit in the U.S. District Court for Arizona, charging that the state law violated the U.S. Constitution, in particular, the FOURTEENTH AMENDMENT's proviso that no state may deny any person the equal protection of the law. The district court ruled in favor of the resident aliens, and the state took an appeal to the nation's highest court.

Meanwhile, in Pennsylvania, alien residents brought a similar case, contesting that state's law that no noncitizen could receive welfare payments. As in the Arizona case, the lower federal court ruled in the non-citizens' favor. The state of Pennsylvania took an appeal to the U.S. Supreme Court. Attorneys agreed to consolidate the two essentially similar cases to allow a single hearing and a single judgment.

The U.S. Supreme Court upheld the lower federal courts' rulings. The Court held first that the Fourteenth Amendment's promise of equal protection to all "persons" applies to aliens as well as to citizens. The Court went on to rule that any state law that made distinctions based on race, nationality, or alienage was immediately suspect, and that courts must give such laws close scrutiny.

After giving the Arizona and Pennsylvania laws this close scrutiny, the Court ruled that the laws in question violated the Fourteenth Amendment's equal protection clause. The Court also held that state laws denying certain rights or privileges to resident aliens conflicted with the federal government's exclusive power to regulate aliens and, more generally, immigration issues.

The Court refused to give credence to the states' argument that their need to aid their own citizens justified the discrimination against aliens in the matter of welfare payments. The attorneys for Arizona and Pennsylvania also claimed that welfare payments were not a right, but a privilege, and that therefore the Fourteenth Amendment was not applicable to the case. The Court disagreed with this argument. Its decision was unanimous, although Justice John Marshall Harlan II did not agree that the two state laws interfered with any exclusive federal powers over aliens and immigration.

This case is arguably the U.S. Supreme Court's strongest statement that all noncitizens who are in the United States legally have equal rights under the law. The case struck down existing state laws that denied certain rights and privileges to resident aliens, as well as working to prevent passage of similar laws in the future.

Gran Círculo de Obreros de México: Labor union. This union was established in Mexico in the early 1870's. In 1872, thirty-two thousand textile workers joined the organization. They organized the "Gran Círculo" conference in 1876 to inform workers of their rights. Continuous strikes were organized against the textile industry in Mexico, but the efforts were suppressed when union leaders were arrested in 1906.

Gran Liga Mexicanista de Beneficiencia y Protección, La: Antidiscrimination organization. The Liga Mexicanista, along with the Liga Femenil, emerged from the PRIMER CONGRESO MEXICANISTA in 1911. Amid a climate of intense discrimination in Texas, its goals were to find solutions to Anglo-Mexican race relations difficulties, unlawful treatment of Mexican Americans by authorities, and exclusion of Mexican American children from Anglo schools. The Liga Mexicanista also sought to promote culture and moral instruction among its members. Its president was Nicasio Idar, who hoped to establish chapters throughout Texas. The Liga Mexicanista lasted less than a year but was important in the history of Chicano organizing. Members of this group went on to participate in later organizations such as the LEAGUE OF UNITED LATIN AMERICAN CITIZENS and the AMERICAN G.I. FORUM.

Gran Quivira: Archaeological site. Located about twenty-six miles south of the town of Mountainair, New Mexico, Gran Quivira is a site that combines Indian structures with Spanish ruins. It contains seventeen house mounds and nine *kivas*, or circular underground structures used for kin group meetings. In addition, it contains the ruins of the chapel of San Isidro and the mission of San Buenaventura.

The Indian structures date from as early as the fourteenth century or even earlier. The Spanish chapel and mission were built between 1629 and 1631. Because it combines Indian and Spanish ruins, the Gran Quivira site sheds light on the period of first contact between Europeans and Native Americans.

Grape boycotts: The California grape boycotts of the UNITED FARM WORKERS OF AMERICA attempted to improve living and working conditions for migrant farm laborers.

By 1972, the United Farm Workers of America (UFWA) had grown from a small and rather ineffective coalition of Mexican and Filipino farmworkers to a solid segment of the American Federation of Labor-Congress of Industrial Organizations (AFL-CIO) with 147 contracts. These contracts only partially atoned for the omission of farm laborers from the NATIONAL LABOR RELATIONS ACT of 1935. The rationale for the omission of farmworkers was that if they became involved in a strike, crops might rot in the fields.

From 1965 to 1972, one of the country's most interesting unionization struggles was orchestrated by César CHÁVEZ. The DELANO GRAPE STRIKE of 1965 involved major attempts to urge consumers not to purchase grapes picked by non-UFWA laborers. In addition to picketing growers and boycotting markets, farmworkers encouraged teamsters and longshoremen to refuse to work with nonunion grape shipments.

Among the first boycott targets were the DI GIORGIO FRUIT CORPORATION's wines, Schenley Industries' liquor labels, Treesweet Juices, and S and W Fine Foods. The boycott was supported by AFL-CIO president

Walter Reuther, the National Council of Churches, and several student groups. The boycott eventually spread throughout the United States. Boycott houses, the residents of which helped organize boycotts in various urban areas, were established in more than forty American cities.

During 1972, a separate UFWA-sponsored grape boycott was directed against the E. and J. Gallo Wineries, the largest in the United States. After a contract with the UFWA expired, the Gallo Corporation elected to engage in a labor contract with the Teamster's Union, precipitating the boycott. Ultimately, the issue was resolved with a statement of agreement between the Teamsters and the UFWA.

The early boycotts were concerned with the right of migrant farmworkers to bargain collectively with growers. Later boycotts of grapes and other crops protested poor working conditions. One major concern related to health problems encountered by migrant farm laborers because of their exposure to pesticides over long periods of time. DDT-type chlorinated hydrocarbons were eventually banned, but the substitutes were phosphate-based poisons that can harm the central nervous system. In 1969, boycotters in Washington, D.C., purchased table grapes from a grocery store and had them tested for residues. The grapes were found to contain concentrations of Aldrin, which has been linked to cancer.

During the 1980's and early 1990's, boycotts centered on health issues and working conditions. A boycott in the state of Washington during the 1990's addressed the poor working conditions at some wineries, including lack of shade stations and field toilets. The state legislature required growers to provide these items.

Grassroots organizations: During the late twentieth century, Latinos in the United States formed several

Marchers in Modesto, California, called for boycotts on grapes and Gallo products. (Lou DeMatteis)

Through grassroots organizations, people become involved in issues on a personal level. (Hazel Hankin)

hundred grassroots (self-help) organizations to resolve problems encountered in immigration, farm work, and the transition from rural to urban life. These groups are of several types, but almost all were formed by Latinos with common economic and political problems.

Latin Americans in the United States have formed several hundred groups, most with specialized agendas. Lists of such organizations appear in Darren L. Smith's *Hispanic Americans Information Directory* (Gale Research, updated periodically), Alan Edward Schorr's *Hispanic Resource Directory* (Denali Press, 1988), and Sylvia Alicia Gonzales' *Hispanic American Voluntary Organizations* (Greenwood Press, 1985). Gonzales' work alone lists more than five hundred groups.

Permanent grassroots organizations have formed in both rural and urban areas. Rural organizations usually address the low pay and hazardous conditions of migrant farm labor. The UNITED FARM WORKERS OF AMERICA, organized in the 1960's by César CHÁVEZ, used a combination of grassroots organizing tactics of the type pioneered by Saul Alinsky and traditional union-organizing strategies, such as strikes and boycotts. By the 1990's, farmworker unions had formed in various states and regions of the United States, including Texas, Washington, Ohio, and Florida.

Other grassroots organizations address problems of immigration that arose with the rapid influx of Latin Americans into the United States after World War II. Some groups formed permanent structures, with offices, boards of directors, and substantial budgets; others faced a single issue in a single place.

Late in 1992, for example, Latino citizens in Omaha, Nebraska, formed an ad hoc effort after two Mexican teenagers, Ambrosio López and Agustin Antunez, were arrested on November 6, 1992. They were arrested at their high school and deported to Mexico by the IMMIGRATION AND NATURALIZATION SERVICE (INS). These arrests differed from most INS raids in that they occurred in a public school and in that the INS deported children whose parents were United States citizens.

This effort brought together clergy in churches with Latino congregations, school officials, the editors of Omaha's bilingual newspaper *Nuestro Mundo*, Latino business owners, immigration-rights lawyers, and eventually Nebraska's governor, Ben Nelson. The organizers even brought the time of the year—the weeks before Christmas—into the struggle. After considerable haggling on a national level, Governor Nelson announced the return of the two boys at a press conference on Christmas Eve.

Some urban grassroots organizations formed during the CHICANO MOVEMENT of the late 1960's and 1970's had achieved substantial size and permanence by the 1990's. In many urban areas, especially in the western United States, grassroots groups formed to bring together Latinos who had migrated to urban areas as farmwork became mechanized. By 1980, more than 85 percent of the Latinos in the United States lived in urban areas. These urban residents organized to gain political power and to solve problems specific to urban life.

One example from the city of Seattle, Washington, illustrates the role of grassroots groups. Chicanos and supporters from other ethnic groups occupied an abandoned school and gradually began to renovate it with their own labor. Twenty years later, El CENTRO DE LA RAZA had become a large social-service organization with an annual budget of several million dollars, worldwide activities, and several dozen salaried employees.

Greaser: Pejorative term used to describe Mexican and other Spanish-speaking people. This derogatory term was created by Anglos during a period of their expansion into the American Southwest in the mid-1800's. It was used in reference to all Spanish-speaking persons, many of whom were Mexican. The GOLD RUSH of 1849 brought many Anglos to the California area, and the pre-existing Mexican population became a minority. Anglos instigated so-called greaser laws that made certain Mexican cultural practices illegal and excluded Mexicans from participating fully in the economy. The term continued to be used into the early twentieth

century. Greaser films were a genre of film stereotypically portraying Mexicans as lazy and greedy.

Great Depression. *See* **Depression, Great**

Great Society programs: President Lyndon B. Johnson's multifaceted War on Poverty program began in 1964. Various Great Society agencies promoted community action, job training, education, legal aid, and services for seasonal farmworkers. Poverty was not vanquished, but some programs continued into the 1990's. Mexican Americans and Puerto Ricans were affected by many of the Great Society programs.

History. In the early 1960's, the U.S. economy was thriving and most Americans were comfortably within the middle class. There were, however, substantial pockets of POVERTY in the midst of prosperity. About one-fifth of the population lived below the poverty line in 1959, according to census studies. The television documentary *Harvest of Shame* (1960) publicized the plight of migrant workers, most of them Latino, and Michael Harrington's *The Other America* (1962) brought attention to unacceptable living conditions in both rural and urban areas. The Civil Rights movement, mounting unrest in the cities, and the formation of the UNITED FARM WORKERS union in 1962 were further signs of the link between poverty and social injustice. The Johnson Administration came to see the eradication of poverty as the first step in its liberal social agenda.

In his 1964 State of the Union address, President Johnson declared "unconditional war on poverty in America." He proposed a series of programs that would build a "Great Society" in which all Americans could contribute and prosper. The Economic Opportunity Act, which was passed by Congress in August of 1964, created the Office of Economic Opportunity (OEO) with a first-year budget of $1.5 billion. The OEO targeted four populations with high poverty rates for special emphasis: rural families, American Indians, the elderly, and seasonal farmworkers. Under Director Sargent Shriver, the War on Poverty employed a mix of conventional and experimental approaches in a multifaceted attack on poverty's many causes.

The War on Poverty was an uphill battle from the start. By 1966, some of its programs were already unpopular. The Johnson Administration eliminated some programs and transferred others to different departments. When Richard M. Nixon became president in 1969, he continued to dismantle the OEO and move some of its operations to the states. The Ronald Rea-

Lyndon B. Johnson's Great Society programs attempted to alleviate the poverty illustrated by this home in the Rio Grande Valley and to increase opportunities for the poor. (AP/Wide World Photos)

gan Administration hastened this process in the 1980's with severe budget cuts to social programs. Few Great Society programs continued into the 1990's.

Historians and social scientists remain divided on the effectiveness of Great Society programs. From 1959 to 1969, a period that included the most vigorous OEO programs, the overall poverty rate decreased from 22 percent to 12 percent. From 1969 to 1990, however, the poverty rate remained essentially the same, fluctuating between 11 and 13 percent. Meanwhile, poverty actually increased among Latinos, from 21 percent in 1973 (or 10 percent of the nation's poor) to 29 percent in 1990 (18 percent of the nation's poor).

The War on Poverty brought improvements to some people's lives but failed to eliminate poverty for many reasons, including inadequate funding in a period when the Vietnam War competed for federal dollars.

Among those who benefited from Great Society programs were some poor African Americans, Mexican Americans, and Puerto Ricans in both rural and urban areas.

Community Action Agencies. Unlike loans to students and small businesses, Community Action Agencies were one of the newer aspects of the Great Society. OEO funding established neighborhood service centers where poor people could obtain many kinds of help, such as medical care and childcare. A unique feature of the legislation was that it required "maximum feasible participation" of the poor in Community Action Agencies. The clients the agencies served were supposed to be represented in planning and operations. After some controversy over how much power the poor should have, a later amendment required that they constitute one-third of board members. Community members were also employed in the agencies as paraprofessionals such as teachers' aides, health aides, and community organizers.

The agencies often served as a springboard for community organizing among members of racial or ethnic minorities. In New York City, for example, Puerto Ricans formed antipoverty agencies such as the Puerto Rican Forum, the Massive Economic Neighborhood Program, and the PUERTO RICAN COMMUNITY DEVELOPMENT PROJECT. These organizations provided leadership training for future politicians and became important in the growth of political power in the Puerto Rican community. Mexican Americans were active in antipoverty agencies in the Southwest. Many leaders capitalized on poverty issues and their community action experience when they later established other organizations, such as the CRUSADE FOR JUSTICE and the BROWN BERETS.

Programs for Youth and Children. The Job Corps targeted poor high-school dropouts for counseling, health care, and education at eighty-two rural residential centers and twenty-four urban centers. In 1967, enrollees were 59 percent African American, 32 percent Caucasian, and 9 percent "other" (a category that included Latinos). The costly program provided insufficient urban job training, and many graduates were unable to find good jobs. Job Corps was discontinued in 1972.

Head Start, initiated in 1965, was both more popular and of longer duration. Its goal was to enrich the learning experiences of poor preschool-age children so that they would not be disadvantaged upon entering first grade. Three- to five-year-olds received nutritious meals and medical care, took field trips, and learned vocabulary while their mothers were trained in nutrition and parenting skills. Head Start was transferred to the Department of Health, Education, and Welfare in 1969. It continued into the 1990's but was never funded sufficiently to reach all poor children. Studies of Head Start families in the 1970's and 1980's found that Latino families constituted between 9 and 22 percent of the total. Latino immigrant children especially benefited from the program as an orientation to American culture and education.

Designed as a "Head Start for teenagers," Upward Bound helped poor youths prepare for college. Colleges were given grants for projects to generate motivation and develop study skills in disadvantaged high school students. The students attended residential summer programs and received tutoring and other services during the school year. In 1967, 8 percent of Upward Bound enrollees were Latino. The program was later transferred to the Office of Education.

Legal Services. A 1965 amendment to the Economic Opportunity Act established a program to provide legal assistance to the poor and to promote legal reform favoring their interests. By 1967, there were two thousand attorneys working in 850 neighborhood law offices. Staff attorneys handled a variety of legal problems, including divorces and landlord-tenant disputes. Appeals established important legal precedents, such as the successful challenge to rules denying welfare eligibility to female householders if there was a man in the house.

In a case benefiting some Latinos and hurting others, California Legal Assistance sued the Department of Labor for being too permissive in admitting large numbers of Mexican laborers to harvest tomatoes. Migrant workers arriving from Mexico were lowering wages and employment opportunities for farmworkers already in the United States. The Labor Department settled out of court, agreeing to more careful screening of jobs in the future.

When the OEO was dismantled, Legal Services became the Legal Services Corporation, a nonprofit organization that continued in the early 1990's. The OEO had set an important pattern of free or low-cost legal aid that made legal services accessible to poor Latinos for the first time.

Vista. VOLUNTEERS IN SERVICE TO AMERICA (VISTA) was a domestic Peace Corps program that sent trained volunteers to live and work in American slums, mining camps, barrios, Indian reservations, and other economically depressed areas. Volunteers set up programs in adult literacy, day care, and recreation, according to community need. They sometimes helped the poor to organize tenant unions to protest against slum landlords. Similar to the Community Action Agencies, a major goal of VISTA was the empowerment of poor people and the shaping of social programs to meet what the people thought were their greatest needs. Records were not kept on the ethnic or racial affiliation of volunteers. In 1971 VISTA became part of ACTION, an agency that also oversaw the Peace Corps. VISTA was still active in the early 1990's in all states as well as the Virgin Islands and Puerto Rico.

Seasonal Farm Labor Program. Many Latinos were affected by the OEO's program for seasonal agricultural laborers, as they were heavily represented in the streams of migrants originating in California, Texas, and Puerto Rico. This Great Society program reinforced other new programs and legislation such as the Migrant Children's Assistance Act of 1960 in bringing aid to a particularly impoverished and isolated population. Among the program's projects were improvements in sanitation and housing, remedial education for adults, and a High School Equivalency Program for youth. —*Nancy Conn Terjesen*

SUGGESTED READINGS: • Acuña, Rodolfo. *Occupied America: A History of Chicanos.* 3d ed. New York: Harper & Row, 1988. • Jennings, James, and Monte Rivera, eds. *Puerto Rican Politics in Urban America.* Westport, Conn.: Greenwood Press, 1984. • Levitan, Sar A. *The Great Society's Poor Law.* Baltimore: The Johns Hopkins University Press, 1969. • Moynihan, Daniel P. *Maximum Feasible Misunderstanding.* New York: Free Press, 1969. • Waxman, Chaim I., comp. *Poverty: Power and Politics.* New York: Grosset & Dunlap, 1968.

Green card: Slang term for the Alien Registration Receipt Card (Form I-151 or Form I-551). Many versions of these forms are not green in color; however, the media and general public have accepted this term. This card is given to persons who have been granted lawful temporary residency status under the first stage of amnesty or the Special Agricultural Worker Program. The "green card" became increasingly significant after the IMMIGRATION REFORM AND CONTROL ACT OF 1986 passed. This legislation prohibited employers from hiring undocumented immigrants by implementing employer sanctions against those who chose to employ UNAUTHORIZED WORKERS. The "green card" served as an indicator of an immigrant's legal status.

Gringo: Pejorative term. "Gringo," as used by Latinos, is a pejorative term for an ANGLO. The word may have its origin in an Anglo song that contained the phrase "green grows" and was popular during the time of the Mexican American War (1846-1848). During this time, the word was used as a counter to "GREASER," a pejorative term applied to Mexicans. "Gringo" can also describe a person unfamiliar with or intolerant of Latin culture.

Grito de Dolores, El (Sept. 16, 1810): Call for rebellion. Father Miguel HIDALGO Y COSTILLA issued a stirring address to his largely Indian parishioners, calling them to rebel against Mexico's colonial government. This *grito* (shout or cry) is considered to be the earliest document of Mexico's independence movement.

Early in his career, Father Hidalgo developed a reputation as a freethinker. He found himself in trouble with colonial authorities and the Spanish Inquisition. He was stripped of his job as a college rector, being assigned instead to the sleepy village of Dolores, north of Mexico City. Even as a village priest, however, he read forbidden literature of the Enlightenment and attracted a circle of Creoles (persons of European ancestry born in the New World). Like Creoles in other areas of Latin America, this group began to dream of independence from Spain. When King Ferdinand VII was toppled in 1808 during the Napoleonic Wars and a pretender arose in his place, many Creoles considered using the disruption in Europe as a cover for their own desires for self-determination.

On September 16, 1810, Father Hidalgo addressed his Indian parishioners in what became known as El Grito de Dolores. No transcript of his words that day has survived, but it is generally agreed that he did not actually call for Mexican independence. Instead, Hidalgo called for loyalty to the deposed King Ferdinand VII and for the establishment of a Creole-led colonial government. To attract the Indian masses to the revolt, Hidalgo promised redress of their ancient grievances.

The priest's *grito* succeeded immediately in winning the energetic support of about six hundred Indians. The number of Indian participants in his campaign increased daily. Hidalgo's ragtag, poorly equipped army swept across the countryside, destroying the hated plantations and killing any Europeans who got in their way.

When the group arrived at the edge of Mexico City Hidalgo ordered his followers back. He may have feared that his army was no match for the well-trained soldiers within the capital. He may also have feared uncontrollable killings and plunder by his undisciplined followers. It is clear that the order to fall back destroyed Hidalgo's reputation among the Indians. Spanish soldiers soon captured and killed Hidalgo.

For a time, José María Morelos successfully carried on the rebellion in southern Mexico, but he too was captured and shot. Mexican independence finally came in 1820. Mexican conservatives, fearing loss of their own power and prerogatives as a new regime came to power in Spain, forcibly seized control and proclaimed Mexican independence.

The rebellion launched by Father Hidalgo's *grito* was one of very few Latin American independence struggles that called for truly revolutionary change and that invited the participation of the Indian masses. Hidalgo's efforts were not successful, however, and

Father Miguel Hidalgo y Costilla led Indian parishioners in a revolt against the government of Mexico. (Institute of Texan Cultures)

Mexico's first independent government was made up of members of the conservative elite. Not until the MEXICAN REVOLUTION (1910-1921) would the mass of Mexico's population participate successfully in government.

Grito de Lares, El (Sept. 23, 1868): Revolt against Spanish rule. Puerto Rican patriots revolted against Spanish domination in Lares, in northwestern Puerto Rico. Within three days the revolt was defeated, but the event remains a symbol of unity and resistance for both island and mainland Puerto Ricans.

In the mid-nineteenth century, Puerto Ricans suffered under SLAVERY and the excessive taxes of Spanish rule. The *libreta* system required that day laborers have a passbook that contained their work schedule, wages, debt owed, and work conduct. The *peninsulares* (Spaniards) had advantages over Creoles (those born in the New World) with respect to employment, economic opportunities, and political affairs. It was in this atmosphere that Ramón Emeterio BETANCES, exiled in St. Thomas for his leadership in the abolitionist movement, issued the Ten Commandments of Free Men in 1867. This declaration demanded, among other things, the abolition of slavery, the right to vote for taxes and elect representatives, freedom of speech, and freedom of the press. It became the platform for Puerto Rican separatists who wanted independence from Spain.

Betances organized the revolt with Manuel Rojas, American Matías Bruckman, revolutionary poet Rodríguez de Tío (who wrote the lyrics to the Puerto Rican national anthem), and Ana María (Mariana) Bracetti Cuevas, known as Brazo de Oro or Arm of Gold, who sewed the revolutionary flag of Lares that has come to symbolize the struggle for independence. Betances had contracted a steamship to transport people and arms from Santo Domingo and St. Thomas to Puerto Rico. The plot was discovered, and Betances and his ship were captured by Spanish authorities.

The revolt took place with between six hundred and one thousand poorly armed Puerto Rican patriots shouting "Death to Spain! Long live liberty! Long live free Puerto Rico!" They took control of the town of Lares, declared the Republic of Puerto Rico, abolished slavery and the *libreta* system, and set up a provisional government under Francisco Ramírez Medina as president.

The rebels headed to the neighboring town of Pepino to obtain weapons but were unsuccessful. The Republic was overtaken within three days, but it took more than a month to capture all the patriots. Some were killed in the struggle; others were jailed, sentenced to death, or exiled. After pleas for mercy by the clergy and women of the island, the death sentences were commuted. Accused persons not previously sentenced to death were granted amnesty by the new Spanish government.

El Grito de Lares is seen by many as the first occasion for a national identification among Puerto Ricans. Some believe that the revolt hastened the abolition of slavery and the *libreta* system, granted in 1873, and the institution of freedom of the press, granted in 1874.

Since 1930, the *independentistas* (who want separation from the United States) have commemorated September 23 as the Day of the Martyrs of Independence. In 1969, that date was declared a national holiday in Puerto Rico.

Grito de Yara, El (Oct. 10, 1868): Proclamation of Cuba's independence. The speech launched the first of two protracted revolutionary struggles to free Cuba from Spanish colonial rule.

A combination of geographic, political, and social factors prevented the Caribbean islands of Cuba and Puerto Rico from breaking with Spanish rule, as did the rest of Latin America, in the early nineteenth century. Later efforts to obtain independence failed as a result, in part, of white racial fears of the large percentage of black people in the island's population. By the 1860's, Cuba was producing nearly one-third of the world's sugarcane, with nearly all the work done by African slaves. As an alternative to either independence or the prospect of abolition, some planters favored annexation to the United States, where slavery still flourished.

Between 1865 and 1868, internal dissent and political difficulties at home prompted the Spanish government to offer conciliation and reform in an attempt to head off independence movements in both Cuba and Puerto Rico. Excitement and hopes that this promise stirred soon turned to bitter resentment after failure of the reform effort. Instead of seeing reform, Cuba was subjected to higher taxes, political repression, and a severe economic recession. Planters in the eastern half of Cuba, hardest hit by economic losses, became more willing to join with other social groups favoring revolt.

After planning an uprising for Christmas Eve of 1868, Cuban conspirators were forced to strike instead on October 10. The conspirators learned that Spanish military and political authorities had discovered their activities. On this date, wealthy lawyer and landowner Carlos Manuel de Cespedes, accompanied by thirty-seven other sugar and coffee growers from Oriente Province, issued the historic Grito de Yara from his plantation, "La Demajagua," near the community of Yara and the city of Manzanillo. Cespedes, the co-author of this proclamation issued in the name of the Cuban Revolutionary Junta, freed his slaves and incorporated them into his small amateur army.

The leaders organized a provisional government of the Republic of Cuba at Bayamo. Their ranks were soon joined by other planters, many students, free black people, and newly emancipated slaves. A long, painful struggle for freedom known as the Ten Years' War engulfed Cuba.

Although initially successful, the revolutionary guerrilla fighters and patriots known as Mambises did not triumph. After the loss of 200,000 lives, the revolt ended with acceptance of Spanish assurances of social and political reform. Nevertheless, the desire for freedom survived. The movement resurfaced under the inspired leadership of exiled poet and intellectual José MARTÍ. The ultimate triumph of this renewed struggle justified the efforts of the masses who answered the Grito de Yara, perhaps the most important event in Cuban history up to that time.

Gronk (Glugio Gronk Nicandro; b. 1954, Los Angeles, Calif.): Artist. In labor, Gronk's mother chose his middle name from a *National Geographic* magazine. *Gronk* is a Brazilian word meaning "to fly." Living sometimes with his mother, sometimes with her various relatives, Gronk knew at an early age that he wanted to be an artist. Art was an escape, and drawing was a way of creating new worlds for himself.

In school, Gronk was encouraged to take auto shop more seriously than art. A few teachers, however, noted his talent and encouraged him. After dropping out of school, Gronk became one of the founding members of the street performance group ASCO. ASCO became known for protest antics, theater works, and videos.

Improvisation and physicalness punctuate the internationally recognized work of this painter. Gronk has been described as an archaeologist who digs deep into the imagination. Gronk once commented that to him, the measure of success is not being in the public eye or becoming wealthy; it is the ability to do what is exciting and meaningful for oneself.

Guacamole: Seasoned avocado paste eaten as a salad, appetizer, and condiment. A dish favored by the Aztecs and their predecessors, guacamole is eaten most often in Mexico and adjacent areas. Guacamole at its simplest is no more than ripe avocados mashed with onion, chile, and salt. Fancier versions can include garlic, CILANTRO, tomatoes, TOMATILLOS, or citrus juice. Traditional recipes never include the sour cream often added by restaurants catering to non-Latino tastes. Modern urbanites typically make guacamole with a blender or food processor, but the traditional technique has all the ingredients pulverized in a *MOLCAJETE*. Guacamole can be eaten plain, with tortillas, or as a filling in tacos or other dishes.

Guadalupe, Virgin of: In 1531, the VIRGIN MARY is said to have appeared to the Indian Juan DIEGO outside the colonial capital of Mexico. According to legend, Diego was on his way to find a doctor to treat his uncle, who had been bitten by a poisonous snake. Diego had abandoned his Indian religion and was a Catholic, but he had not attended Mass that Sunday as a result of his uncle's condition. The Virgin appeared and scolded him for not attending Mass. When Diego told her of his uncle's illness, she told him that he had been cured; this was the Virgin's first miracle. The Virgin also instructed Diego to go to the bishop of the viceroyalty of Mexico and ask that a church be built for her on the spot of her appearance. Diego did this, but the bishop did not believe that the Virgin had visited an Indian.

Because he had failed, Diego tried to avoid the place where the Virgin had appeared. When she found him again, Diego told her that the bishop had asked for proof of her appearance. Although it was winter, a bush of roses of Castile sprung from the ground; this was considered a second miracle. When Diego told the bishop about the roses, the bishop did not believe him. As Diego traveled toward his home again, the Virgin appeared for the third and last time and told him to take the roses to the bishop wrapped in his *tilma* (an outer white apronlike garment worn by the Indians in the colonial era). Diego followed her instructions and opened the *tilma* before the bishop.

Instead of roses, the *tilma* bore the image of the Virgin as she appeared to Diego—in a cloak of blue filled with stars of gold. As a result of this miraculous event, the bishop ordered the construction of a temple to the Virgin on the site of her appearances. This became the Basilica of Guadalupe, which still stands in the suburbs of present-day Mexico City. A second, modern basilica has been built next to the original basilica. The location has become a pilgrimage shrine

Images of the Virgin of Guadalupe appear in Catholic Latino churches and homes. (James Shaffer)

to Catholics from all of Latin America and from the entire world.

The Virgin appeared to an Indian, a member of one of the lowest classes of Mexican colonial society. She told Diego that she would be the protector of the poor and oppressed. Latinos continue to be devoted to the Virgin of Guadalupe and ask for her assistance because they remain among the lowest socioeconomic groups and often suffer from discrimination.

The image of the Virgin on the *tilma* of Diego is of a brown-skinned woman. Latinos consider her to be their virgin—a virgin for the non-Anglo-Saxon peoples of the world. Latino Catholics typically feel closer to the Virgin of Guadalupe than to the fair-skinned Virgin Mary. Many Latinos do not consider the Virgin of Guadalupe to be a manifestation of the Virgin Mary but rather to be a separate virgin. In December, Latino

Catholics celebrate the festival of the Virgin of Guadalupe rather than the Festival of the Immaculate Conception of the Virgin Mary. Many Latino families name daughters Guadalupe (often shortened to Lupe or Lupita) in honor of the Virgin of Guadalupe.

Guadalupe Hidalgo, Treaty of. *See* **Treaty of Guadalupe Hidalgo**

Guajira: Cuban narrative song and dance form. Spanish in origin but with more Cuban characteristics than the HABANERA, the *guajira* resembles in style the folk dances of Spain, with rhythmic patterns of African origin. The music, in three-four and six-eight time, is performed mainly by stringed instruments such as guitars, with maracas or claves providing rhythmic accompaniment. Other dances associated with the *gua-*

jira are the *zapateo*, a derivation of FLAMENCO dance with similar heel- and toe-beating steps, and the *punto*, a form stressing a graceful movement rather than stamping of feet. *Guajiras* were popular during the nineteenth century but have almost disappeared.

Guaracha: Afro-Cuban song and dance form. The *guaracha* is a Cuban solo theater dance performed to lively, cheerful songs in three-four, six-eight, or two-four meter, with humorous, ingenuous lyrics that poke fun at famous people or subjects. It is performed by a soloist, with a chorus repeating the *estribillo* (refrain), accompanied by the guitar, the *tres* (small three-string guitar), and *güiro* (gourd scraper). The dance bears close resemblance to the *zapateado*. Its origin can be traced to 1875, with a number of *cantos aguarachados* (songs in a similar form) stemming from it in the following decades.

Guatemalan Americans: Guatemalan Americans were one of the fastest-growing Latino groups in the United States in the 1980's and 1990's. At that time, Guatemalan immigrants were fleeing to the United States to escape political repression and human rights abuses in their homeland.

History. Most Guatemalans who immigrated to the United States by the end of the twentieth century did so in the 1980's and 1990's to escape repressive political regimes in Guatemala. The Guatemalan population includes native Maya and ladinos (or MESTIZOS). Sharp racial and socioeconomic divisions have relegated most indigenous people and even many ladinos to a powerless underclass. These inequities have created a social situation in which political stability has become nearly impossible to achieve. The precarious political situation there has driven many Guatemalans north in search of a new life. The history of Guatemalan Americans, therefore, begins with the history of political instability in Guatemala.

Political instability in Guatemala began in 1944 after longtime dictator General Jorge Ubico retired. The regime that succeeded Ubico was toppled by a reform-

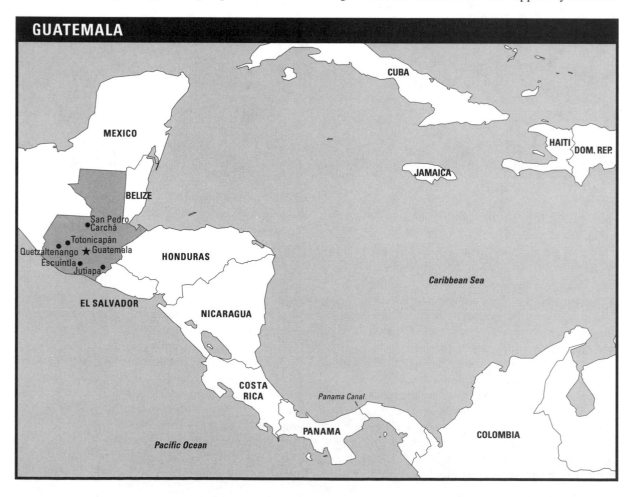

STATISTICAL PROFILE OF GUATEMALAN AMERICANS, 1990

Total population based on sample: 268,779

Percentage foreign-born: 80%

Median age: 27 years

Percentage 25+ years old with at least a high school diploma or equivalent: 38%

Occupation (employed persons 16+ years old)

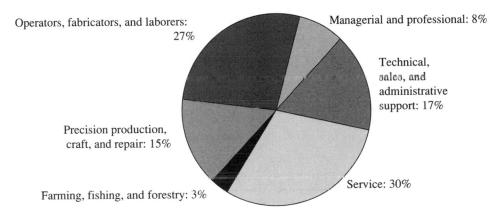

Operators, fabricators, and laborers: 27%

Managerial and professional: 8%

Technical, sales, and administrative support: 17%

Precision production, craft, and repair: 15%

Farming, fishing, and forestry: 3%

Service: 30%

Percentage unemployed: 10.2%

Median household income, 1989: $24,569

Percentage of families in poverty, 1989: 21.1%

Source: Data are from Bureau of the Census, *Census of 1990: Persons of Hispanic Origin in the United States* (Washington, D.C.: Bureau of the Census, 1993), Tables 1, 3, 4, and 5.

ist alliance of Guatemalans spearheaded by Juan Jose Arevalo. Guatemala began experimenting with democratic forms of government, but democracy failed within ten years of the revolution.

In 1954, a military coup headed by Colonel Carlos Castillo Armas and supported by the country's right wing, its elite agricultural businesspeople, and the U.S. Central Intelligence Agency (CIA) took control of the fledgling democracy. The new government reinstalled oligarchic and military rule.

The new oligarchic government gained strength after the 1954 coup. The military's power, which during previous regimes had been minimal, was augmented immensely as a result of the government's policy of using force to extinguish opposition. Most of this opposition came from leftist organizations such as political parties, labor unions, student groups, and indigenous rights advocacy groups. In order to quell sparks of rebellion, the government began systematic coun-

terinsurgency campaigns. These campaigns resulted in the death or disappearance of countless Guatemalans, most of whom were innocent victims.

A democratic government was reinstituted in 1986 with the election of Vinicio Cerezo, the leader of the Christian Democrat party. His five-year stint, however, did not effectively change the Guatemalan social dynamic. The military retained its power and continued its policies of favoring the elite upper class and marginalizing leftist political activists and the poor.

In 1993, a coup by former president Jorge Serrano Elias proved unsuccessful after the United States condemned the act and cut off economic aid. Serrano's new government fell within a month. The Guatemalan congress then elected Ramiro de Leon Carpio as president.

During Guatemala's history of human rights violations, civil rights leaders in Guatemala and human rights activists worldwide challenged the repressive policies of the government. Nobel Peace Prize winner Rigoberta Menchu, a Guatemalan Indian woman, became the most notable leader of this movement. Despite such efforts to end human rights abuses, the military continued its brutal practices. Many Guatemalans fled from their native land to the United States for asylum (*see* ASYLUM POLICIES).

Immigrating. Guatemalans wishing to flee their country have faced the choice of traveling through Mexico to the United States as undocumented immigrants or applying for political asylum. Traveling north through Mexico entails many risks. Not only must emigrants cross the Guatemala-Mexico border, but they also must avoid apprehension by Mexican patrols, which send immigrants back to border camps. Once through Mexico, they face the Mexico-United States border and the U.S. Immigration and Naturalization Service patrols.

Nevertheless, most Guatemalan emigrants have believed that trekking through Mexico to the United States as undocumented aliens was the most viable method for obtaining freedom. The other option, applying to the United States for political asylum, has proved unsuccessful for most Guatemalans. Despite the political situation in Guatemala, the United States granted political asylum to only 0.9 percent of the Guatemalan applicants during the height of political turmoil between 1983 and 1986. The class action lawsuit AMERICAN BAPTIST CHURCHES IN THE UNITED STATES V. THORNBURGH successfully gained sixty-nine thousand unsuccessful Guatemalan applicants for asylum a new review. In 1992, the approval rate for Guatemalans climbed to 7 percent.

Settling. The United States admitted 120,000 legal Guatemalan immigrants between 1982 and 1992. The U.S. government estimated that another 120,000 Guatemalans were residing in the United States as undocumented immigrants, and this number continued to rise. During times of political instability, such as the coup in 1993, the number of Guatemalans immigrating to the United States increased.

Undocumented Guatemalan immigrants have tended to settle in areas with large Latino populations, such as California, Texas, New York, and Florida. Washington, D.C., and its surrounding areas have been a magnet for legally admitted immigrants from Guatemala.

Guatemalan Americans became one of the more rapidly growing immigrant groups during the 1990's. As members of a relatively new immigrant community, their cultural contributions were still minimal. Most Guatemalans are descended from the rich Mayan culture, some of which has been mixed with Spanish colonial culture. Guatemalan Americans can be expected to add their cultural heritage to many American institutions, including the Catholic church and college campuses, as their numbers grow.   —*Jaime Pelayo*
SUGGESTED READINGS:

- Amnesty International. *Guatemala: The Human Rights Record.* London: Amnesty International, 1987. Amnesty International's investigation of human rights abuses in Guatemala.
- Barry, Tom. *Guatemala: A Country Guide.* Albuquerque, N.Mex.: Inter-Hemispheric Education Resource Center, 1989. A comprehensive guide to the political situation in Guatemala.
- Dunkerley, James. *Power in the Isthmus.* New York: Verso, 1988. A political history of modern Central America.
- Menchu, Rigoberta. *I, Rigoberta Menchu.* Edited by Elisabeth Burgos-Debray, translated by Ann Wright. London: Verso, 1984. Rigoberta Menchu's account of the Guatemalan human rights struggle.
- Simon, Jean-Marie. *Guatemala: Eternal Spring, Eternal Tyranny.* New York: Norton, 1987. Photographic guide to Guatemala and its people during the civil war.

Guava: Tropical American fruit. There are more than one hundred species of guava, all from tropical America. Most are eaten, at least locally. The fruit is acid and has a strong smell, but it is relished by many. Although it can be eaten raw, it more frequently is eaten cooked or rendered into juice. It also is known as *guayaba.*

Guayabera: Traditional shirt style from Cuba. The *guayabera* is a four-pocket, long shirt adorned with vertical pleats both in front and in back. It is worn over the pants, not tucked in. The shirt was originally part of the traditional clothes worn by men in the rural zone of Sancti Spiritus, Cuba. Its use extended to the rest of Cuba, other islands of the Caribbean (particularly Puerto Rico), Mexico, and Central America. Made of cotton or silk, this style of shirt is deemed ideal for warm climates. *Guayaberas* are worn as part of casual wear or on semiformal occasions, without a jacket and tie.

Guerrero, Pedro (b. June 29, 1956, San Pedro de Macoris, Dominican Republic): Baseball player. Originally signed by the Cleveland Indians, Guerrero came to the Los Angeles Dodgers in a 1974 trade of

Pedro Guerrero connects for one of his several hits in the sixth game of the 1981 World Series. (AP/Wide World Photos)

minor leaguers. After brief major league trials in 1978 and 1979, he batted .322 in seventy-five games in 1980. Promoted to regular status in 1981, he hit an even .300 to help Los Angeles capture the National League pennant, and he was named a cowinner of the World Series Most Valuable Player Award in the Dodgers' triumph over the New York Yankees.

A power-hitting outfielder who was sometimes used at third base, Guerrero was a five-time National League All-Star. He enjoyed his best season in 1985, when he led the National League in slugging percentage, hit 33 home runs in only 137 games, batted .320, and led

the Dodgers into the National League playoffs. A serious knee injury cost him most of the 1986 season, but he returned in 1987 to hit .338 with 27 home runs, totals that won for him the United Press International Comeback Player of the Year Award. Traded to the St. Louis Cardinals in the middle of the 1988 season, Guerrero began to be used primarily as a first baseman. In 1989, he drove in 117 runs for the Cardinals and led the National League with 42 doubles, but injuries soon diminished his effectiveness. After several seasons in St. Louis, he began playing professionally in Mexico.

Guevara, Che (Ernesto Guevara de la Serna; June 14, 1928, Rosario, Argentina—Oct. 9, 1967, La Higuera, Bolivia): Revolutionary. Guevara was born to middle-class parents in Argentina in 1928. According to his extensive diaries, which have been discovered and published, even as a child he felt sympathy for the poorer classes. After earning a medical degree in 1953, Guevara began touring South America in an attempt to understand the people. In 1954, he found himself in Guatemala, where the government was attempting socialist land reforms, breaking up large holdings and distributing them to peasants. Guevara likely began to form his socialist leanings at this time.

The socialist government of Guatemala was overthrown by rebels, backed by the United States, and Guevara left for Mexico. In July, 1955, he met Fidel CASTRO, who had left Cuba after a failed revolution and was planning a second attempt. Guevara joined the revolution immediately and provided strategic as well as medical skills when Castro's forces invaded Cuba. The revolution was to last more than three years and end with the overthrow of Fulgencio Batista, Cuba's dictator.

By the time of the CUBAN REVOLUTION, Guevara was clearly a socialist; Fidel Castro had not yet declared himself to be such. Guevara's skills were appreciated by the new Cuban leader, and he was, in effect, second in command. He initiated a number of economic programs that were not generally successful. His skill lay in spreading the word of revolution in other nations. He visited many other countries in attempts to get the people to form revolutionary socialist governments. In July, 1959, when Castro declared himself a Communist, Guevara's place in the government seemed secure.

There were, however, differences between the two leaders. The most crucial involved relationships with the Soviet Union. Castro actively sought Soviet help, especially military help, but Guevara distrusted economically advanced nations. He was particularly distressed when the Soviets backed down during the CUBAN MISSILE CRISIS of 1962. He openly denounced the Soviet Union, a position Castro found difficult to tolerate.

In November, 1966, Guevara led a small group of Cubans into Bolivia in an unsuccessful attempt to foment revolution there. Support, even among Bolivian Communists, was not forthcoming, and the Bolivian government was heavily supported by the United States. On October 8, 1967, Guevara was shot; he is believed to have died the following day.

Guevara had a lasting impact on revolutionaries throughout the world. In the United States, a country Guevara soundly denounced many times, protesters against the Vietnam War dressed in jungle fatigues and carried posters reading "Che Lives!" His policy of encouraging revolution in other parts of the world was continued by the Cuban government.

Guillén, Nicolás (Cristobal Guillén y Batista; July 10, 1902, Camagüey, Cuba—July 16, 1989, Havana, Cuba): Poet. Guillén, who was of mixed African and European descent, wrote his poetry on behalf of the Afro-Cubans, the poor, and the oppressed. He attended the University of Havana in 1920 but was forced by economic hardship to abandon the study of law. He read widely in literature in Spanish, combining in his work an awareness of traditional poetic forms and a use of the speech and song of Afro-Cubans. The *son*, or popular dance song, is of particular influence on his poetry. Guillén has credited the North American poet Langston Hughes with influencing his work.

In the 1920's, Guillén began to work as a journalist and founded the literary magazine *Lis*. In 1930 he published *Motivos de son* (motifs of *son*), a book of poetry widely recognized as a masterpiece of poetic representation of Afro-Cuban language. It has been set to music; much of Guillén's poetry is rhythmic and lyrical. *West Indies, Ltd., Poemas* (1934) is, as are other books by Guillén, a deliberate and direct effort to acknowledge and celebrate the African heritage in Cuban culture. In 1937, Guillén published *Cantos para soldados y sones para turistas* (songs for soldiers and *sones* for tourists), which signaled an increasingly politicized understanding of the marginalized. That same year, he went to Spain to involve himself in the republican cause, as did many writers and intellectuals of the time. Guillén then published *España: Poema en cuatro angustias y una esperanza* (1937; Spain: a poem in four anguishes and one hope), a tribute in mourning to the country that was losing its struggle against fascism and to Federico García Lorca, a martyr of the war and one of the greatest lyric poets of the century.

On his return to Cuba, Guillén became a communist and, later, a laureate of the revolution. On behalf of the revolution, he worked as a journalist and helped found the National Union of Cuban Writers and Artists. His books from 1959 on reflect his enthusiastic support of Fidel CASTRO and of the revolution; he also denounced United States politics, racism, and imperialism. Titles from this period include *Che comandante* (1967; Che

Nicolás Guillén accepts the 1954 International Stalin Peace Prize. (AP/Wide World Photos)

commander) and *La rueda dentada* (1972; the gear or sprocket). His depiction of slum life and his affirmation of the black role in the creation of Cuban culture have earned for him an enduring place in literature.

Guineos: Green bananas. *Guineos* are slightly sweeter than plantains, but they are used in much the same way in Caribbean cooking. In Puerto Rico, they are considered a kind of *bianda* (starchy root vegetable). They can be used in the various soups, casseroles, and other dishes that use *bianda*. In Puerto Rico and elsewhere, *guineitos* are finger bananas, often sautéed when ripe and dusted with grated parmesan cheese to create a sweet contrast to other dishes in a meal.

Güiro: Percussion instrument of pre-Columbian origin. The *güiro* is a hollowed, notched gourd scraped with a stick, also known as the *rascador* or scraper. The instrument is made of an elongated gourd, on the sides of which marks or frets have been made. When rubbed with the scraper, the frets produce penetrating rhythms. The *güiro* is an integral percussion instrument of Latin American folk ensembles, most particularly those performing Puerto Rican folk and popular music. They customarily form part of the accompaniment for traditional songs such as the DÉCIMA and Cuban folk dances such as the GUARACHA.

Guitarrista: Solo guitar performer of considerable virtuosity. A skillful accompanist for both song and dance, the *guitarrista* emerged during the *café cantante* period that reigned in Spain during the second half of the nineteenth century. *Guitarristas* showed excellent technique and an accurate sense of tempo; they also possessed a gift for accompaniment, and as the famous guitarist Melchor de Marchen (1908-1980) said, the ability to play from the soul. The term was originally associated with FLAMENCO players but soon spread to encompass all classical guitarists.

Gutiérrez, Horacio Tomás (b. Aug. 28, 1948, Havana, Cuba): Pianist. When Gutiérrez was eleven years

Horacio Tomás Gutiérrez. (AP/Wide World Photos)

old, he had the privilege of being a guest soloist with the Havana Symphony. He was forced to leave Cuba after Fidel Castro came to power in Cuba in 1959. In 1967, Gutiérrez became a United States citizen. He studied music at the prestigious Juilliard School.

In 1970, Gutiérrez received the Silver Medal at the Tchaikovsky Competition in Moscow. He made his professional debut with the Los Angeles Philharmonic Orchestra the same year. Gutiérrez later performed with many of the world's most respected orchestras, including the San Francisco Symphony, the Orchestre National de France, and the Berlin Philharmonic. In 1982, he was awarded the Avery Fisher Prize. Among his numerous other honors is an Emmy Award. He has recorded several albums for Telarc Records.

Gutiérrez, José Ángel (b. Oct. 25, 1944, Crystal City, Tex.): Activist and educator. In 1970, Gutiérrez and his associates founded La RAZA UNIDA PARTY, a Chicano political organization. He became the executive director of the Greater Texas Legal Foundation in 1986 and the city of Dallas administrative law judge in 1990.

At the age of twelve, Gutiérrez, along with other members of his family, was forced into farmwork after

his father died. Despite this hardship, Gutiérrez earned his B.S. in political science from Texas Arts and Industries University at Kingsville in 1966. After briefly studying law at the University of Houston, in 1968 he earned a master's degree in political science at St. Mary's University in San Antonio, Texas.

While a student at St. Mary's, Gutiérrez helped to organize the MEXICAN AMERICAN YOUTH ORGANIZATION. Gutiérrez was elected its first president and was also a cofounder of the MEXICAN AMERICAN UNITY COUNCIL in 1968. After serving in the U.S. Army, he received his Ph.D. in political science from the University of Texas at Austin.

After a Chicano student walkout in CRYSTAL CITY, TEXAS, in 1970, Gutiérrez led a group in founding La Raza Unida Party. As a result, Gutiérrez and two other Hispanic candidates were elected to the city council. Gutiérrez then won a place on the school board and was later elected its chairman. Under Gutiérrez's leadership, the school board introduced innovative bilingual and bicultural educational programs.

Gutiérrez was elected judge of Zavala County but resigned in 1981 to teach at Colegio César Chávez in Mount Angel, Oregon. In 1982, he became associate professor in social sciences at Western Oregon State College in Monmouth.

Gutierrez, Sidney (b. June 27, 1951, Albuquerque, N.Mex.): Astronaut. By 1994, Gutierrez had attained the rank of colonel in the U.S. Air Force and had participated in several space missions for the National Aeronautics and Space Administration (NASA). He received his B.S. in aeronautical engineering from the U.S. Air Force Academy in 1973 and his M.A. in management from Webster College in 1977. Upon graduation from the Air Force Academy, he began to train as a test pilot. He attended the USAF Test Pilot School in 1981 and served as a test pilot for various aircraft.

In May, 1984, Gutierrez was selected for astronaut training. He became an astronaut for NASA in 1985. Among many duties for NASA, he served as commander for the Shuttle Avionics Integration Laboratory and as a pilot on the crew of the STS-40 Spacelab Life Sciences craft on a nine-day mission launched on June 5, 1991. Gutierrez also served as commander of the STS-59 Space Radar Laboratory in April, 1994. Gutierrez has received the NASA Exceptional Achievement Medal, the NASA Space Flight Medal, the Congressional Hispanic Caucus Award, and the 1992 Hispanic Engineer of the Year Achievement Award.

Astronaut Sidney Gutierrez. (AP/Wide World Photos)

Ralph C. Guzmán served as Jimmy Carter's deputy assistant secretary of state. (AP/Wide World Photos)

Guzmán, Nuño Beltrán de (?, Spain—1544, Spain): Explorer. Guzmán was Hernán CORTÉS' bitter rival in the conquest of Mexico. Their rivalry dated to Cortés' attempt to annex the colony of Pánuco with the rest of New Spain. Guzmán was named governor of that colony in 1527 as a way to thwart Cortés' progress.

In 1527, Cortés had to return to Spain to secure his holdings. The king left Guzmán in charge of the colony by creating the first audiencia, a council of magistrates who were to administer the king's justice and authority.

When Guzmán was relieved of his duties as president of the audiencia, he embarked on the colonization of the northern frontier, again in direct competition with Cortés. Guzmán was a brutal conqueror. In 1530, he killed thousands of Indians while securing what he turned into the colony of New Galicia.

Guzmán was governor of New Galicia until 1537. Reports of Guzmán's illegal slave trade and harsh treatment of Indians led to an investigation and imprisonment. After several months, Guzmán was sent to Spain. Guzmán spent the rest of his days in Spain trying to vindicate his name. He died in poverty.

Guzmán, Ralph C. (Oct. 24, 1924, Mexico—Oct. 10, 1985, Santa Cruz, Calif.): Public official and scholar. Guzmán spent a lifetime detailing the Mexican American experience. He was considered one of the foremost Hispanic educators in the United States. Guzmán recognized early the connection between education and the path out of poverty. His knowledge of Latin American affairs was exhibited through several books, including *The Political Socialization of the Mexican Ameri-can People* (1976). He also collaborated on the Mexican-American Study Project at UCLA that culminated in publication of *The Mexican-American People: The Nation's Second Largest Minority* (1970).

In 1978, Guzmán answered the call of public service and took a leave of absence from his beloved teaching to serve President Jimmy Carter as deputy assistant secretary of state. For the next two years, he was responsible for much of U.S. policy toward Central and South America. When Ronald Reagan became president in 1980, Guzmán returned to teaching.

Guzmán Aguilera, Antonio (b. Mar. 21, 1894, San Miguel de Mesquital, Mexico): Playwright. During the 1920's, Guzmán Aguilera established himself as a master of the *REVISTA* form of short comedic theater. He was based in Los Angeles but also saw his work produced in San Antonio and Mexico City. Among his more than 450 works, few of which were saved, are plays such as *Oro, seda, sangre y sol* (1924) and *María del Pilar Moreno o la pequeña vengadora* (1924). His most popular *revistas* include *Alma tricolor*, *La huerta de don Adolfo*, *Exploración presidenciál*, *Evite peligro*, and *Pierrot mexicano*.

Through his *revistas*, Guzmán Aguilera examined Mexican American culture, topical events in Los Angeles, and U.S. politics. He was critical of U.S.-Mexican relations in *México para los mexicanos* and *Los Angeles vacilador*, and he poked fun at the Mexican theaters of Los Angeles in *Los cuatro asas de la calle Main*. He established the Compañía Guzmán Aguilera and in 1927 returned to Mexico City before touring Mexico and the southwestern United States.

H

H-2 provision: Immigration provision. The H-2 provision was part of the IMMIGRATION AND NATIONALITY ACT OF 1952. This provision allowed Mexican workers to enter the United States legally in search of employment. In the wake of discontinuation of the BRACERO PROGRAM, the H-2 program provided a significant means of recruiting Mexican laborers.

Habanera: Cuban song and dance form. Habaneras derived from Creole and black *totónes* around 1850. In slow to moderate tempo and in duple meter, they consist of a short introduction followed by two sections of eight or sixteen bars that alternate from a major key to a minor one, relying largely on the *tresillo*, a two-beat bar divided into three notes. Singing is in the FLAMENCO style. Dancers use voluptuous bodily motion and gestures, with minimal foot movement. When danced by multiple couples, the habanera is called *contradanza criolla*. Habaneras became popular in Spain and Europe. They strongly influenced the DANZÓN, the Mexican DANZA, and the Argentine TANGO.

Habichuelas: Puerto Rican word for common beans. *Habichuelas* are a staple of Puerto Rican cuisine. Basic Puerto Rican *habichuelas* are boiled until nearly ready, then augmented with SOFRITO, seasonings, and vegetables or starchy roots. The mixture is simmered until everything is cooked and the sauce has thickened somewhat. *Habichuelas* also are used in hundreds of other dishes and form an inexpensive mainstay of the diet.

Hacendado: Owner of a large property on the Spanish/Mexican northern frontier. An *hacendado* typically owned an hacienda (a large ranch) on which he employed Mexican *rancheros* (ranch hands) or used enslaved Indian people to raise and care for livestock. *Hacendado* families were considered to be the GENTE DE RAZÓN (people of reason), or the most privileged class of people in the society of the Spanish/Mexican northern frontier. The noble position depended on the subordination and loyalty of laborers, and therefore a reciprocal relationship developed between the *hacendados* and their workers. Frequently, *hacendados* held large celebrations in the pueblo plaza where these various social classes mixed, but the social hierarchy remained rigid.

Hacienda system: The hacienda, which in Spanish means "estate" or "wealth," in Mexico came to mean a very large landed estate. Haciendas, which flourished in central New Spain and were present in some areas of the northern frontier, constituted a limited socioeconomic system.

Haciendas tended to be self-sufficient, with many having their own churches, stores, and primitive factories. In a sense, they continued the old custom of land assignment. Faced with vast amounts of land to manage, the HACENDADO (landowner) would assign the Indians plots to work; all surplus produced belonged to him. The *hacendado* had title to his property, and this ownership deprived the Indians of any communal or collective rights to it. The Indian workers were free men who, under the law, should be paid wages, but this same law barred them from almost all occupations except primitive labor. Minimum wages were established, and limits were placed on the amounts that Indians could borrow, thus denying them the opportunity to purchase land.

Hacendados kept their workers eternally in debt by giving them small wage advances, a custom still prevalent in the twentieth century. Debt peonage was created by preventing an employee from leaving his master while in debt to him and by making debts hereditary. *Hacendados*, like *encomenderos* (landowners under the ENCOMIENDA SYSTEM of royal land grants) before, became masters of hundreds or thousands of Indians, but whereas the *encomenderos* had certain moral and legal obligations to the natives, the *hacendado* was free of governmental regulation. Under the class system of the hacienda, *indio* or mestizo (mixed Spanish-Indian blood) *peónes* received the same treatment and had the same prospects.

The hacienda system flourished in the fertile Central Valley of New Spain. As a form of plantation agriculture, it should have produced surpluses, but neither the system of taxation (based on use rather than value) nor the social system encouraged efficient use of the land. Hacienda workers produced little for export, but the vast size of the hacienda allowed the landowner to live in luxury.

In northern New Spain, haciendas were more efficient. In the sixteenth and seventeenth centuries, individuals became great *hacendados* in Nueva Vizcaya, wielding enormous political, economic, and social power. On the northeastern frontier, Spanish society was largely pastoral and agricultural. The large haciendas devoted to raising livestock in Coahuila were also sizable communities of Spaniards, mestizos, and Indians. The haciendas usually exceeded twenty-five hundred acres in size, but few of these were ever established along the northern frontier that is now the American Southwest. In New Mexico, for the most part, Spanish settlers were small farmers rather than rich *patrones*. The consolidation of settlement in Texas in 1721 was the result of the great wealth and power of *hacendado* Marqués de Aguayo. No haciendas existed in Texas, however, where the *RANCHO*, or stock farm, was prevalent.

Haitian Americans: Despite origins in the Caribbean region and the fact that Haiti shares the island of Hispaniola (*see* ESPAÑOLA, LA) with the Dominican Republic, Haitian Americans are very different in some ways from most Latinos. Haitian Americans are rarely classified as Latinos. They represent a unique culture and have faced a series of unique problems.

Haitian Culture. Haitian culture is unique in the Americas. Haitians speak a language, Creole, virtually unknown outside their country. Almost all Haitians are black, as descendants of African slaves. Although an estimated 90 percent are Roman Catholics, a majority practice VODUN (voodoo), a religion that has been misrepresented grossly in the popular media of the United States. Because of the differences between Haitian culture and the cultures of the Caribbean and the United States, Haitians and people of Haitian descent have been targets of prejudice. Haitians became associated with the ACQUIRED IMMUNE DEFICIENCY SYNDROME (AIDS) epidemic in the 1980's, making them less welcome in the United States.

Haitian Americans are among the most recent arrivals in the United States. Although there have been people from Haiti on the mainland of North America since before the United States became a nation, the vast majority of Haitians migrated to the United States after the rise to power of François Duvalier in 1957. More than half of all Haitian immigrants to the United States by 1993 arrived after 1980.

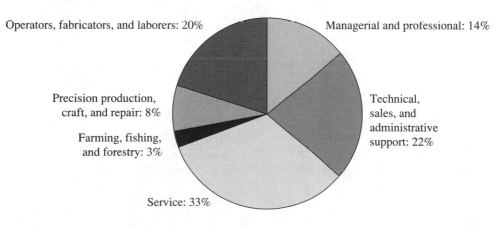

STATISTICAL PROFILE OF HAITIAN AMERICANS, 1990

Total population based on sample: 280,874

Percentage foreign-born: 71%

Median age: 29.5 years

Percentage 25+ years old with at least a high school diploma or equivalent: 58%

Occupation (employed persons 16+ years old)

Operators, fabricators, and laborers: 20%
Managerial and professional: 14%
Precision production, craft, and repair: 8%
Farming, fishing, and forestry: 3%
Technical, sales, and administrative support: 22%
Service: 33%

Percentage unemployed: 12.1%

Median household income, 1989: $25,547

Percentage of families in poverty, 1989: 20.7%

Source: Data are from Bureau of the Census, *Census of 1990: Ancestry of the Population in the United States* (Washington, D.C.: Bureau of the Census, 1993), Tables 1, 3, 4, and 5.

Historical Background. The island of Hispaniola was originally inhabited by Arawak Indians. The island was named La Española by Christopher Columbus, who visited the island in 1492. He claimed the island for Spain and returned in 1493 with a much larger fleet. After a number of voyages, the island was finally secured as Spanish territory, but not without a fight. During the Spanish colonial period, the island was often called Santo Domingo.

By the middle of the sixteenth century, the native population was almost entirely decimated. Hispaniola is therefore unique as the only Caribbean island on which the people have almost no American Indian ancestry. Black slaves were imported at that time to replace the Indians, who had never been cooperative as a labor force.

The Spanish lost interest in Santo Domingo as Mexico and Peru were discovered and exploited; they had greater riches than could be found on Hispaniola. The French developed a nation called Saint-Domingue on the western end of the island. In 1697, Saint-Domingue was recognized by the Spanish government.

Haiti is almost entirely covered by steep mountains, making agricultural work difficult. The French colonists imported many African slaves, who eventually composed 90 percent of the population. In 1795, the slaves revolted. In 1804, the French withdrew, and Haiti became an independent nation. The revolutionary leader, Jean-Jacques Dessalines, declared himself emperor of Haiti.

When Napoleon lost Haiti, he decided that his holdings in North America were useless without a Caribbean stronghold and sold the Louisiana Territory to the United States. Before this time, there was regular migration between Louisiana and Haiti. The new independent nation of Haiti was populated almost entirely by black former slaves, who expelled or massacred the remaining whites. Louisiana, as part of the southern United States, relied on slavery as an economic mainstay. In 1862, President Abraham Lincoln finally recognized Haiti as an independent nation.

Haiti went through a series of emperors and dictators without a stable government. It was occupied by American troops from 1915 to 1934, during which time a representative government of sorts was imposed. Haiti signed a treaty putting itself under U.S. control until 1934. After the Americans withdrew, Haiti returned to its former situation. In 1938, Dominicans, enemies of Haitians since the nineteenth century, killed thousands of Haitian laborers living near the border.

Christopher Columbus landing at Navidad on the island of Hispaniola, December 12, 1492. (Institute of Texan Cultures)

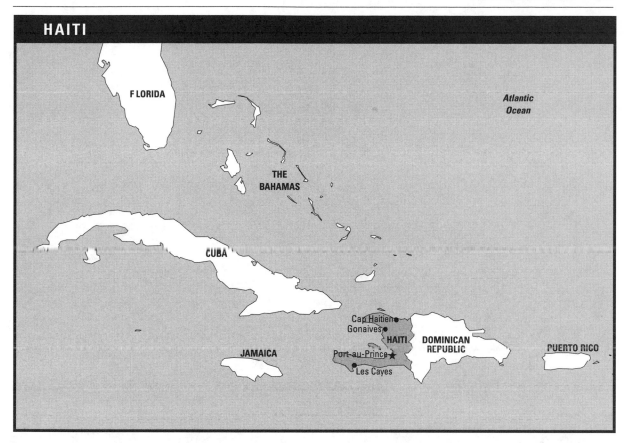

HAITI

In September, 1957, after a long period of unrest and the rise and fall of several presidents, François "Papa Doc" Duvalier was elected president. He had himself elected president for life in 1964. He was ruthless, the economy worsened, and Haitians began to leave.

The neighboring island of Cuba underwent its own revolution in 1959. This was at the height of Cold War fears, and a Communist nation in the Caribbean was considered to be a major threat to United States security. For this reason, despite the dictatorship of Papa Doc and his son, Jean-Claude "Baby Doc" Duvalier, Haiti was considered an ally of the United States.

Haitians nevertheless were not particularly welcomed as immigrants to the United States. Cubans were considered to be political refugees, as they were from a Communist country. Haitians, on the other hand, were considered to be economic refugees, who have never been as welcome in the United States. The situation worsened in the 1980's, when AIDS became a major source of fear in the United States. Haiti and its citizens suffered in extreme from the epidemic, and the United States feared admitting Haitian immigrants who might be infected.

Jean-Baptiste Aristide became Haiti's first demo-

cratically elected president in 1990. On September 30, 1991, however, he was ousted in a military coup led by Lieutenant General Raoul Cedras. Leaders of the military government installed Emile Jonassaint as a figurehead president, but control of the government was maintained by Cedras; Lieutenant Colonel Michel-Joseph François, the police chief in Port-au-Prince; and Brigadier General Philippe Biamby, the army chief of staff who had led an unsuccessful coup in 1989 against then-president Prosper Avril.

The United States and other countries protested the ouster of Aristide and demanded that the military government cede power. The issue came to a head in September, 1994, when U.S. President Bill Clinton demanded under threat of military invasion that the three military commanders surrender control of the government. The three agreed to relinquish power by October 15, 1994, or when the Haitian parliament passed an amnesty provision protecting them from prosecution. Aristide, for his part, promised not to run in the next scheduled election, in 1995, and to relinquish power in 1996.

In the years of the military government, the United States rescued more than twenty thousand Haitian refugees from the repressive government. By the

The Haitian Catholic Center in Miami, Florida, is one of many places where Haitian immigrants obtain aid in learning English, finding homes and jobs, and otherwise adapting to life in the United States. (Impact Visuals, Jack Kurtz)

time the military leaders agreed to surrender power, more than fourteen thousand refugees were living in a refugee camp in Guantánamo Bay in Cuba.

Language and Culture. One of the most pervasive misconceptions that Americans have about Haitians is that they speak French. Although French is the official language of Haiti, it is spoken by less than 10 percent of the population. French speakers primarily are members of the upper class. Many are mulattoes, though color lines are not drawn strongly in Haiti. The vast majority of Haitians, and of Haitian Americans, speak Creole.

Creole is a general term used to describe a number of languages in the Caribbean. In the case of Haiti, Creole is a language based both on the vocabulary of a number of French dialects of the fifteenth and sixteenth centuries and on the languages of western Africa. The grammar is almost entirely African. Haitian

Creole and the French language are not mutually intelligible. The closest relative to Haitian Creole is the French spoken in Louisiana, particularly New Orleans, called Cajun.

Approximately 90 percent of Haitians were Catholic by the late twentieth century, but a large proportion also practiced VODUN. The practice continues among Haitian Americans. Vodun has been distorted by American portrayals in horror fiction and films. Stories of human sacrifices, "voodoo dolls," and cannibalism have never been substantiated. Vodun as a religion is a mixture of Christianity and African religions practiced by the original slave population. The SANTERÍA practices of Puerto Ricans, Cubans, and other Hispanic peoples are similar.

Vodun accepts the existence of many gods. To many Haitians, Jesus Christ is the supreme God but is not concerned with the daily affairs of human beings. The lesser gods, the gods of vodun, are evoked to cure sickness, solve personal problems, and deal with other personal situations.

The Haitian American Population. According to the 1990 census, there were approximately 281,000 Haitian Americans. There were probably tens of thousands more undocumented residents. Some estimates suggest that there are as many undocumented residents as legal immigrants and Haitian Americans born in the United States.

Approximately half of the Haitian American population lived in or near NEW YORK CITY. Many lived in predominantly black neighborhoods, but many did not fit in with the mass of black New Yorkers. Most of New York's black people are the descendants of southern slaves who migrated north during or after the Civil War. Haitian Americans tend to form small neighborhoods of their own within black enclaves of urban areas.

Vodun temples in the United States are hidden from the general public. In New York City, the closest relative to vodun is Santería, another religion based on African rituals influenced by Christianity. Santería is practiced by many Puerto Ricans, who make up the vast majority of the city's population with ties to the Caribbean. Links between Haitian Americans and Puerto Ricans are sometimes strong, despite differences in language. There is also a large Dominican population in New York City, but the Dominican Republic and Haiti have long had a strained relationship.

Despite the fact that Haitian Americans generally have found homes in neighborhoods dominated by black Americans, intergroup relations have in some cases been strained. The Baptist, fundamentalist Christianity prominent among black North American populations is at odds with the Haitian acceptance and tolerance of two different religious heritages.

Conclusion. Haitian Americans are among the U.S. racial and ethnic groups experiencing the most difficulty adjusting to American society. They speak a variant language and practice a religion often associated with violence, human sacrifice, and even cannibalism. They come from a country that has experienced domination by two European cultures, the United States government, and a series of ruthless dictators.

By the end of the twentieth century, Haitian Americans represented a significant minority in the United States but were still newcomers to the country. They faced a series of prejudices against them involving race, religion, and language. Their numbers were impossible to know accurately. The HAITIAN BOAT PEO-

PLE, fleeing from a repressive regime, officially were turned away, but many got past the Coast Guard and entered the United States.

Despite their problems, Haitian immigrants continued to arrive. Many Haitian Americans hoped to return eventually to Haiti, but the political situation in Haiti made emigration a relatively unappealing prospect in the 1990's. —*Marc Goldstein*

SUGGESTED READINGS:

• Desmangles, Leslie G. *The Faces of the Gods: Voudu and Roman Catholicism in Haiti*. Chapel Hill: University of North Carolina Press, 1992. A sociological study of vodun. Includes a history of the religion as well as current practices.

• Foner, Nancy, ed. *New Immigrants in New York*. New York: Columbia University Press, 1987. A series

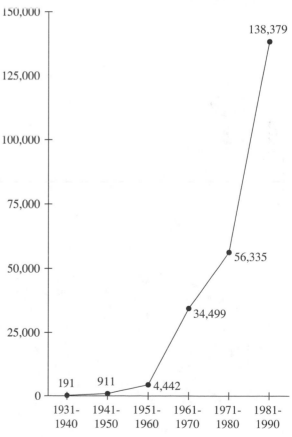

HAITIAN IMMIGRATION TO THE UNITED STATES, 1931-1990

Source: Data are from Marlita A. Reddy, ed., *Statistical Record of Hispanic Americans* (Detroit: Gale Research, 1993), Tables 25 and 26.

of essays by a variety of authors, discussing recent immigrant arrivals in New York City. Included are various Caribbean groups as well as those from Eastern Europe and the former Soviet Union.

• Laguerre, Michel S. *American Odyssey: Haitians in New York City*. Ithaca, N.Y.: Cornell University Press, 1984. A study of Haitian communities in three boroughs of New York City. Covers sociological factors, politics, religion, and family organizations.

• Plummer, Brenda Gayle. *Haiti and the United States: The Psychological Moment*. Athens: University of Georgia Press, 1992. A history of United States relations with Haiti since Haiti's founding in 1804.

Also discussed are the relations of Haiti with other Caribbean nations through the end of the Duvalier regimes.

• Wilentz, Amy. *The Rainy Season: Haiti Since Duvalier*. New York: Simon & Schuster, 1989. An eyewitness account of life in Haiti, written by an American citizen who arrived in Haiti in 1986. The author recounts her experiences in a variety of settings, including the capital, Port-au-Prince, and various countryside settings, where she observed vodun ceremonies.

Haitian boat people: The impetus for flight must be large if one is willing to abandon family, friends, and

Earlier immigrants have proved valuable as resources for new arrivals, offering instruction in English as a Second Language and other services. (Impact Visuals, Donna DeCesare)

homeland, and even risk life, to seek better social and living conditions. Such was the impetus for the Haitian boat people of the 1970's.

The year 1957 was the beginning of the Duvalier regime, starting with François Duvalier, as well as the first year of a significant influx of Haitian refugees onto nearby shores. The first groups of refugees to flee were mostly upper-class Haitians who feared that their political opposition to the Duvalier regime would result in retribution. After 1964, the middle class began to leave Haiti because their participation in government and the economic mainstream, which the Duvalier regime had promised, had not materialized.

Haitian boat people, so named for the overcrowded, often unsafe craft on which they arrived, first arrived on the shores of Florida in 1963. Their requests for asylum, however, were rejected and all were repatriated. Over the next two decades, Haitian refugees continued to flock to the south Florida shore en masse.

This migrational activity throughout the 1970's and into the 1980's, to Florida and also to the region of the Bahamas, was spurred by horrendous economic conditions and an unstable political climate. The lack of scientific farming techniques to avoid soil erosion appears to have contributed to low productivity and low incomes. This lack of income led to Haitian migration to cities or abroad. Further social and economic erosion took place as rural Haitians moved into urban centers at a rate disproportionate to the number of employment opportunities created.

Following the death of François Duvalier in 1971, his son, Jean-Claude Duvalier, came to office and announced that his term would be marked indelibly as an era of "economic revolution." Human rights concessions, coupled with government reformation, attracted foreign aid from the United States, France, and Canada. Those three nations resumed economic and military aid to Haiti in the early 1970's. By the late 1970's, more than two hundred foreign companies, mostly from the United States, had been established in Haiti, mainly engaged in assembly-for-export industries.

In reality, the much-needed foreign aid, investment, and creation of assembly-for-export jobs did not reach the vast majority of the Haitian populace. Most Haitians remained at the subsistence level. This de facto lack of aid to the masses forced Haitians to seek other means of relief. During the 1970's and 1980's, tens of thousands of refugees in homemade "junks" fled to the shores of southern Florida. Many made the trip successfully, but at the same time many corpses drifted ashore.

During this era, the Jimmy Carter Administration (1977-1981) promised to continue U.S. aid to Haiti as long as Haiti organized human rights programs and programs of social reform. The Ronald Reagan Administration, however, in 1981 agreed to support the Haitian populace further only if Haitian efforts were made to limit the departure of refugees.

Hanigan trials (1977, 1980, and 1981): Civil rights litigation. In a federal court in Arizona, a jury convicted a rancher of kidnapping, robbing, and beating three Mexican men who had recently entered the United States illegally. The U.S. Justice Department was unable to prosecute under the nation's civil rights laws because such laws were interpreted as not applying to illegal immigrants. The federal prosecutors did, however, win a conviction against rancher Patrick Hanigan for interfering with interstate commerce, on the grounds that the three victims were seeking work at a farm that raised food for interstate shipment.

In 1976, three Mexican citizens crossed into the United States illegally, near Douglas, Arizona. According to their testimony, they were soon kidnapped by three ranchers, the owner of the land they were crossing and his two sons. The Mexican men complained that ranchers Thomas, Patrick, and George Hanigan took their clothes, beat and robbed them, tormented them with a hot poker, and finally released them, firing shotgun blasts at them as they fled.

On the complaint of the Mexican men, the three Hanigans were indicted on a number of state charges, including kidnapping, robbery, and assault. The father (George) died before trial. Upon trial in 1977 of the two Hanigan brothers in an Arizona court, the jury acquitted on all counts. The case became a *cause célèbre* in the Latino community, pressuring the U.S. Justice Department to enter the case.

The Justice Department originally held that the Hanigans had broken no federal law. Its attorneys pointed out that U.S. civil rights laws were not applicable because such laws did not specifically apply to persons who were in the United States illegally. Federal attorneys instead brought prosecution under the Hobbs Act, a law prohibiting interference with interstate commerce. The law was used most often to punish those involved in organized crime.

In a 1980 federal trial in Tucson, Arizona, the jury reported itself hopelessly deadlocked (eight to four), despite testimony that the Hanigans had bragged about their exploits after the kidnapping. Federal prosecutors renewed the charges in 1981, and a federal judge moved the trial to Phoenix, Arizona, in the hope of finding jurors who had not yet formed an opinion on the case.

In Phoenix, each brother was tried separately. One jury acquitted Thomas Hanigan of all charges, but a second jury convicted Patrick Hanigan of violating the Hobbs Act. The judge sentenced Patrick to three years in prison. His appeal in 1982 failed.

The Hanigan trials came at a time when the national press was full of accounts of the brutal treatment of Latino migrant farmworkers. In some cases, these alien workers were held in peonage; in a few cases, they apparently were held in a condition of slavery. Many workers were severely beaten, yet local juries composed primarily of Anglos often refused to convict. Federal prosecutions for violation of the migrant workers' civil rights were successful only if the workers were U.S. citizens.

The Hanigan case received wide publicity and put the nation on notice that brutality against impoverished immigrant workers could result in imprisonment. This one successful prosecution, however, did not end the appalling treatment of Latino workers.

Harlem riots (July 26, l926): Disturbances that began when a large contingent of young Puerto Ricans entered a neighborhood of older Puerto Rican residents in Spanish Harlem. The police had been informed in advance and were able to disperse the invaders successfully.

East Harlem, in the Manhattan borough of New York City, covers about two square miles, from the East River to Central Park, and roughly from East 96th Street to East 130th Street. By the end of World War I, the European immigrants who had settled in East Harlem had largely left. They were replaced by large numbers of newly arrived Puerto Ricans. The Puerto Ricans settled in the southern end of East Harlem, an area that came to be known as El Barrio or SPANISH HARLEM.

By l926, tension had developed between the more established older residents and the newer, younger residents. The older Puerto Ricans believed that the young people were disrupting the tranquility and order of daily life, engaging in criminal activity, and causing a general decline in the neighborhood. In the week preceding July 26, there were street fights and arguments between the older and newer residents, with incidents of bottle throwing from roofs.

Matters came to a head on the evening of July 26, when a large force of younger Puerto Ricans planned to invade one of the older districts around 115th Street and Lenox Avenue. They intended to incite a riot. An advance guard armed with cudgels marched toward Lenox Avenue from the east. Police Inspector Thomas Ryan, having been forewarned, stationed police reserves from four precincts on all sides of the area to be invaded.

When the police converged on the young Puerto Ricans, the invaders broke rank and fled. The police followed through the streets, into apartments, and over roofs. The commotion prompted a crowd of residents to swarm into the streets. The crowd quickly grew into a milling mass of thousands. This impeded the efforts of the police, who were only able to capture three of the perpetrators. Three sixteen-year-olds were arrested and charged with disorderly conduct. After dispersing the crowd, the police patrolled the scene throughout the night to ensure order.

Harrison, Gloria Macías (b. San Bernardino, Calif.): Educational administrator and publisher. Harrison founded *El Chicano Community Newspaper* in 1969 and became a co-owner and copublisher of the *Colton Courier* and *Rialto Records* newspapers in 1987. She became dean of the humanities division of San Bernardino Valley College in 1991, with previous service as chair of the department of foreign languages (1988-1990) and associate professor (1966-1990).

Harrison holds an A.A. in foreign languages from San Bernardino Valley College (1962). She went on to earn a B.A. in Spanish language (1964) and an M.A. in Spanish literature (1966), both from the University of California, Riverside. Among her civic activities, Harrison has been a member of the Hispanic Chamber of Commerce, the California State Council for the Humanities, and the California State Commission on the Status of Women. She also served as a delegate to the 1984 Democratic National Convention.

Hawaii: Chain of 122 islands extending 1,610 miles in the Pacific Ocean. Hawaii was the fiftieth state to be added to the United States, in 1959. Oahu has the largest population among its islands.

Most of Hawaii's Hispanic influence comes directly from Spain. Because the Hawaiian Islands are not contiguous with Mexico or Central America, there is little migration to the islands. A small Latino influence is present.

Legend attributes the discovery of Hawaii by Europeans to Juan Gaetano in 1555. Careful study does not support this claim. Intermittent contact with Spanish explorers existed by the late 1700's. Business entrepreneurs in Hawaii began importing longhorn cattle from

California in the 1790's. Without proper control, the cattle ran wild, ravaging the fields and forests. By 1830, a Hawaiian chief visiting California induced several Spanish VAQUEROS to come to Hawaii and teach Hawaiian men how to ride horses and herd cattle. The Hawaiian word for cowboy, *paniolo*, derives from *Español* (Spanish).

Documented evidence shows that one of the earliest foreign citizens of Honolulu was a former resident of Andalusia, Spain. Francisco de Paula Marín arrived in the islands sometime before 1813. Some sources cite his arrival as "accidental": He was enticed on board a ship bound for Hawaii and given an alcoholic beverage. He fell asleep and woke up to find himself on his way. Whatever his situation, once in Hawaii he took up residency. He eventually met King Kamehameha, for whom he worked as interpreter, business manager, and occasionally tailor. Marín also set up gardens in Hawaii and introduced numerous varieties of plants from various areas of the world. Marín married at least three wives and had twenty-three documented children.

The current Latino population in Hawaii comes from several sources. Sugar and pineapple plantation owners of the 1800's preferred to diversify their field workers, not wanting to depend on any single ethnic group. Between 1878 and 1887, almost twelve thousand Portuguese people were brought to Hawaii as field workers. Portuguese families were appreciated for their thrift, honesty, and industry. After Hawaii became a United States territory in 1900, the Hawaiian Board of Immigration preferred immigrants who were eligible for U.S. citizenship. Families from Spain and Portugal were offered good working conditions, along with a house and an acre of land in Hawaii. In 1901, a second wave of Portuguese immigrants came. Almost concurrently, fifty-two hundred Puerto Ricans left their island, which had been devastated by a hurricane, and went to Hawaii to work. Between 1907 and 1913, about eight thousand Spanish people were brought in to work the fields. Most of the Spaniards, however, emigrated to California, where other large Spanish populations were already established. The 1920 census of Hawaii recorded 2,430 Spanish people. This number had declined by the 1930 census.

Much of Hawaii's income is now generated from tourism, but agriculture is still important. Many of the Portuguese people became foremen and later, either through industry or marriage, became landowners. The 1990 U.S. Census gave the percentage of Hispanic population in Hawaii as 7.3 percent. The largest subgroup of Latinos (25,778 persons) are those of Puerto Rican descent. More than fourteen thousand Hawaiians were of Mexican ancestry, and those of Cuban descent numbered 558. The remainder of the Hispanic population (40,687 persons) had other backgrounds.

LATINO POPULATION OF HAWAII, 1990

Total number of Latinos = 81,390; 7% of population

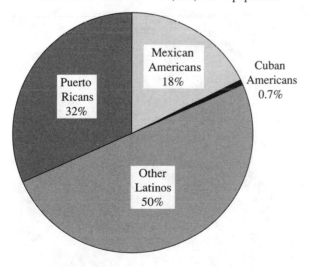

Source: Data are from Marlita A. Reddy, ed., *Statistical Record of Hispanic Americans* (Detroit: Gale Research, 1993), Table 106.
Note: Percentages are rounded to the nearest whole number except for Cuban Americans, for whom rounding is to the nearest 0.1%.

Hayworth, Rita (Margarita Carmen Cansino; Oct. 17, 1918, Brooklyn, N.Y.—May 14, 1987, New York, N.Y.): Actress. Hayworth, an actress of Spanish descent, began dancing at her father's nightclub at the age of twelve. She began her film career, which would include more than forty films over the next four decades, in 1935 under the name Rita Cansino. She soon changed it, however, and dyed her hair auburn to open more casting opportunities. Her early films include *Only Angels Have Wings* (1939), *Strawberry Blonde* (1941), and *My Gal Sal* (1942). *You'll Never Get Rich* (1941) and *You Were Never Lovelier* (1942), both featuring Hayworth dancing opposite Fred Astaire, established her as a major star.

During World War II, Hayworth was the classic pinup girl, and she soon became known by such titles as the "Great American Love Goddess." Her 1946 film *Gilda* featured a controversial striptease and garnered attention. Hayworth's long list of credits includes the thriller *The Lady from Shanghai* (1949), *Salome* (1953),

Rita Hayworth in costume for Salome. (AP/Wide World Photos)

Miss Sadie Thompson (1953), *Pal Joey* (1957), *They Came to Corduna* (1959), *The Money Trap* (1966), and *The Wrath of God* (1972). Hayworth was married five times; her second husband was film director Orson Welles.

Health and illness: A clear understanding of health and illness among Hispanics is still unfolding. National censuses and statistics before the 1980's classified Hispanics as part of the white population, so it was not possible to understand the health status of Hispanics as a group, much less that of the various Latino subpopulations. This situation changed in the early 1980's, when the National Center of Health Statistics undertook the HISPANIC HEALTH AND NUTRITION EXAMINATION SURVEY (HHANES).

Survey Results. The HHANES studied 7,462 Mexican Americans, 2,834 Puerto Ricans, and 1,357 Cuban Americans between 1982 and 1984. This was the largest and most comprehensive Latino health survey ever carried out in the United States up to that time. The HHANES provides a baseline from which one can measure Hispanic health status. Another major survey was conducted in the early 1990's, but its results were not expected to be available until 1998.

The HHANES focused on major conditions such as diabetes, hypertension, heart disease, otitis media and other hearing problems, kidney and liver disease, and depression. It surveyed the prevalence of immunization, consumption of alcohol and cigarettes, and drug abuse. The HHANES also looked at iron status, anemia, and diet in relation to various health conditions.

The HHANES has some shortcomings. It included only the three largest Latino subpopulations. It focused on selected chronic conditions rather than developing a comprehensive understanding of Latino health status. It focused only on conditions recognized as diseases by the dominant biomedical tradition and ignored conditions that some Latinos consider to be diseases. It did not deal adequately with the issue of the impact of migration on health. Thus, it excluded a large segment of the Mexican American population, the group that most actively participates in migratory farm labor. In their defense, however, the HHANES researchers thought that asking questions about migratory labor would discourage people from participating in the survey. Moreover, the migratory lifestyle of farm laborers makes it difficult to study this segment of the Mexican American population.

The HHANES revealed that Cuban Americans, Mexican Americans, and Puerto Ricans had different health profiles. Cuban Americans were similar to non-Hispanic whites in socioeconomic status and health conditions, while Puerto Ricans were similar to African Americans. Nonmigrant Mexican Americans were between these two. The study also showed that diseases affected the different groups at different rates. Scholars attribute these differences to genetic background and lifestyle.

Concepts of Health and Illness. Because lifestyle has an impact on health, the terms "health," "illness," and "disease" must be defined. Health refers to a physical and mental state in which the body and mind function as they should. Illness refers to a single incident of being sick or not functioning properly. Disease refers to a process that suggests a biological or psychological dysfunction in a particular situation. It is a label that suggests the nature of the condition, its cause, and its treatment.

This definition of disease implies that a dysfunction in one context may not be in another. Just as carpal tunnel syndrome was not considered to be a disease in the United States until the 1980's, when it became better understood, two cultures may differ in whether a condition is a disease. For example, Mexican Americans recognize *susto* (described below) as a disease, but modern Western biomedical practitioners and other Hispanic groups may not.

The classification of conditions as diseases raises the question of what causes illness. According to modern Western medicine, germs cause illness. Many Mexican Americans, Puerto Ricans, and Cuban Americans, however, believe spirits or witchcraft cause illness. These ideas are not as unorthodox as they first appear.

The Effects of Cultural Values. A group's understanding of the causes of illness will influence how its members respond to illness. The Western biomedical tradition, with its emphasis on germs, focuses on the individual. Thus, patients typically undergo treatment alone. The traditional Hispanic system, however, considers the individual as part of a community and believes the community is responsible for its members' health. Thus, the larger community takes an active role in the healing process, and it is common for many people to accompany a patient to a clinic or hospital.

The presence of such outsiders can pose problems for modern hospital procedures. In the Hispanic system, however, no procedure would be believed to be effective unless community members were there. Some biomedical practitioners' insensitivity to this belief reduces some Latinos' desire to use biomedical facilities and may impede their recovery when they do.

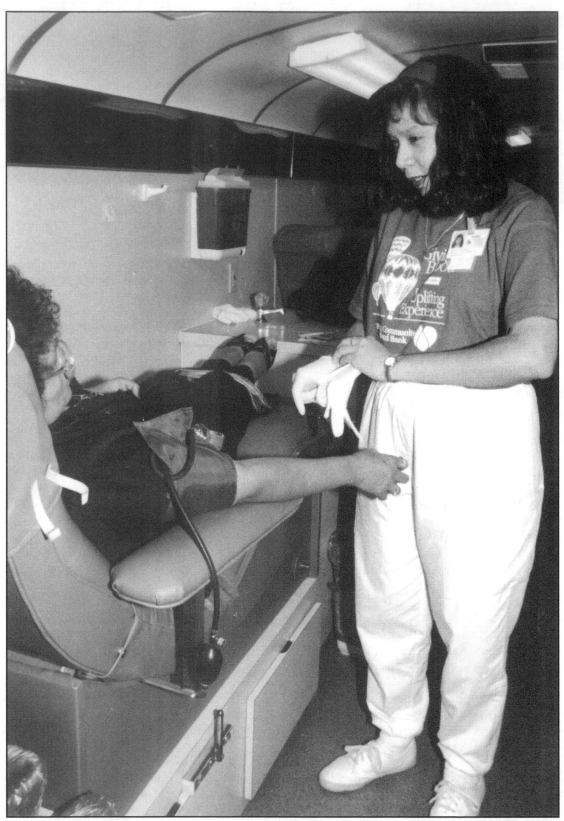

A Latino woman prepares to give blood as a service to her community. (Diane C. Lyell)

The focus on the individual or on the larger social network relates to another difference between the two medical systems. Some Hispanics believe in the concept of limited good. According to this idea, there is only a certain amount of good in the world. If a family has "too much" good luck, wealth, or health, its good fortune will result in another family's misfortune. This perception can result in social tensions among members of a community and lead to bewitching and casting of the evil eye. This may account for the research observation that some Mexican Americans and Puerto Ricans underreport their health; that is, they report their health as "fair" or "poor" while Western physicians regard it as "excellent" or "very good." Researchers report that those Hispanics who underreport their health status are also more likely to consult traditional healers.

Comparison of Medical Systems. Some Hispanic health systems, such as those of Mexican Americans and Puerto Ricans, classify diseases, medicines, and food (because food can be a medicine) as "hot," "warm," or "cold." The underlying idea is that a person will become ill if too hot or too cold. The cures for these diseases attempt to restore the individual to a balanced position. Thus, someone with a "cold" disease should consume "hot" or "warm" foods and medicines.

The origin of this idea is disputed. Some scholars believe it was part of indigenous healing systems, and others believe the Spaniards introduced it. Scholars also have had difficulty understanding this system of classification because it rarely relates to whether the food or medicine is hot or cold in temperature or spiciness. Another difficulty is that two communities may classify the same disease in different ways. There is, however, a logic in the system. A study in one Mexican community suggested that those foods classified as "warm" or "hot" contained the B-vitamin, niacin. Eating this vitamin can cause a person to feel warm. Scholars are uncertain to what extent this logic applies to other communities.

The Western biomedical system and the traditional Hispanic medical system also differ in the way they view the relationship between the body and the mind. The Western biomedical system has traditionally considered the two as distinct entities. Thus, it classifies illnesses into two broad groups, somatic (body) and psychological, and has two categories of healers. Westerners go to physicians when they have something wrong with their bodies and they go to psychiatrists or psychologists when they have something wrong with their minds.

Although Hispanics differentiate between somatic and psychological illnesses, they also acknowledge conditions that Western science calls psychosomatic, in which the disease is a psychological condition that also affects the body. The Western biomedical tradition does not know how to respond to these diseases. Hispanics may go to Western biomedical practitioners for the diseases they believe to be somatic but not for psychosomatic diseases, because the Western physicians do not know how to treat such problems and may ridicule the patient.

As a result, the incidence of these diseases is underreported. One study found that culturally sensitive physicians were more likely to report the incidence of psychosomatic diseases than were those physicians who were not culturally sensitive. In addition, generalists rather than specialists, and Hispanic rather than Anglo physicians, were more likely to report these conditions. Anglo physicians who spoke Spanish were more likely to report psychosomatic diseases than were monolingual physicians. Indeed, many studies report that the inability of many physicians to speak Spanish is one of the most important factors keeping Hispanics from using biomedical facilities. Thus, awareness of and sensitivity to cultural differences will have an impact on whether a Hispanic patient will report these illnesses.

The different classification of diseases has two important results. First, Hispanics may go to practitioners of both systems when they do not know the cause of a disease. There are many reports of Hispanics traveling from the United States to Mexico to consult traditional healers. Second, a Latino patient may use traditional and modern medicines that compete or interact adversely with one another. Further complicating the patient's recovery, the patient may feel embarrassed and therefore not tell physicians they are consulting traditional healers. One study found that many women readily reported that their families had used traditional healers, but said they, themselves, did not use the healer.

Users of Different Systems. Not all Hispanics believe in traditional medical systems. Research has shown that Latinos are more likely to believe in the traditional FOLK MEDICINE system if they have lived in the United States for only a short time, have little formal education, or come from lower socioeconomic or rural backgrounds.

Researchers report that Hispanics in the United States who prefer to speak Spanish tend to be fatalists. That is, they attribute illness to luck, supernatural powers (such as spirits), and God, rather than to their own actions and activities. These Hispanics also emphasize the extended family and give much authority to the family patriarch. They show respect for authority by avoiding eye contact, by acting deferentially, and by being quiet and subservient. Some scholars report that Western physicians may confuse such behaviors with psychopathology. By contrast, those societies that rely on the germ theory emphasize the individual over the community. Higher socioeconomic level, more formal education, and longer exposure to the United States' focus on the individual can erode the traditional focus on the community for healing. The presence of well-educated Puerto Ricans and Cuban Americans who participate in *espiritismo* (*see* ESPIRITISTA) and SANTERÍA, however, indicates that there are exceptions to this pattern.

Another feature that has contributed to the retention of traditional medical systems is the extent to which a group has been permitted to retain its cultural identity and not been forced to assimilate. Cuban Americans, for example, are fairly cohesive, have not been forced to assimilate, and have retained many of their traditional values. By contrast, Mexican Americans are less cohesive as a group, are subject to greater discrimination from Anglos, and are under greater pressure to assimilate. Thus, the erosion of traditional medical systems within this group is more pronounced, especially the longer its members live in the United States.

Mexican Americans. Although there may be similarities in traditional Latino medical systems, there are important differences among subgroups. The Mexican American system is called *CURANDERISMO*. It is a mixture of beliefs derived from Aztec, Spanish, Spiritist, homeopathic, and biomedical traditions. Diseases can be caused by intense emotional states or imbalances between the individual and the natural or social environment. Additionally, the patient may be a victim of malevolent forces or suffer from soul loss.

Several illnesses are reported by Mexican Americans in particular. *Susto* is sometimes called magical fright or soul loss. According to one view, *susto* occurs when an apparition or a frightening event causes the soul to leave the body. Symptoms include sleepiness, anorexia, insomnia, loss of appetite, palpitations, and depression. *Susto* is the most-studied psychosomatic illness.

Bilis is the result of excessive bile in one's system. A person can become ill with *bilis* if he or she becomes angry or frightened.

Caida de la mollera or *mollera caida* (fallen fontanel) occurs only in infants, especially those under six months of age. It occurs when the anterior fontanel (a diamond-shaped soft spot at the top of the head) is believed to fall and block the oral passageway, thus preventing ingestion of food and liquids. The anterior fontanel can fall when the nipple is removed forcefully from the mouth of a nursing infant. Symptoms include an infant's inability to grasp the nipple to feed, slurping sounds, crying, diarrhea, sunken eyes, and vomiting. Many of these symptoms are also characteristic of dehydration, a disease recognized by Western biomedical practitioners but treated in a different way.

Embrujamiento or *mal puesto* (witchcraft) refers to an evil willfully put upon another by a hex. Symptoms include strange and incomprehensible behavior, attacks of screaming, crying, seizure, exposure, convulsions, and uncontrolled urination.

Empacho is an illness caused by food that sticks to the stomach lining. This occurs most frequently when a person consumes a "hot" food instead of a "cold" food or vice versa. An enemy can cause *empacho* by contaminating the food someone eats. Symptoms include stomachaches, diarrhea, vomiting, and fever.

Envidia (envy) is set off when a person is envious of another. Harm can occur to the object or person admired. Touching the object or person after admiring it is thought to remove the harmful force.

Mal de ojo (evil eye) is caused by envy, or by a person staring or gazing at another person for a long time, as in many traditional cultures. It particularly afflicts infants and young children. Symptoms include fever, excessive crying, malaise, and headaches.

Mal aire (bad air) is caused by an evil wind or by the air being at a different temperature from the individual, such as a cool breeze or draft passing over a warm or hot person. This disease can affect both adults and children. Symptoms can range from a common cold or flu to pains in a joint or in the eyes and ears. The most severe cases can include facial twitching and paralysis.

Tirisia has been reported only in Colorado and Arizona. It is caused by depression, disruption of routine, or homesickness. It occurs most commonly when children become separated from their mothers. Symptoms include anxiety, depression, a sallow look, bad skin color, dead and strawlike hair, split nails, excessive crying, and sleepiness.

Puerto Ricans. Puerto Ricans have a medical-religious system called *espiritismo*. It is a combination of the belief systems of the indigenous Taino, African slaves, and nineteenth century Europeans. The Taino used *buhuitihu*, men who conversed with ancestor spirits. Most of the Taino died out after the Spaniards arrived, and the colonists brought Yoruba peoples from West Africa to serve as slaves. These people also worshipped ancestor spirits. The two belief systems later merged into one. A third root of *espiritismo* came from French Kardecian Spiritism as a reaction against Spanish domination.

ESPIRITISTAS believe in an eternal good God, emphasize the spiritual over material goods, and consider the Golden Rule to be the highest ethical teaching. They believe the universe consists of two planes: a visible material plane inhabited by incarnated spirits and an invisible spiritual plane where disembodied spirits live. Spirits are ranked hierarchically. The relationship between one's guardian spirit and the others is critical because some spirits can cause harm and danger, while others offer help and protection.

The structural organization of *espiritismo* reflects the strong patriarchal system of Puerto Rican culture. Puerto Rican society regards men as materially motivated and women as spiritually motivated. Thus men are politically and economically dominant over women, and women's roles are limited to the symbolic realm. Because participation in *espiritista* activities gives women power, they may threaten their husbands with sorcery. Those Puerto Rican men who are more traditional fear women who can engage in revengeful sorcery.

The social structure of *espiritista centros* (churches) reflects these principles. The central authority figure is the godfather, who oversees the mediums. The mediums are generally female and do not challenge his leadership. Women encourage their daughters to become active in the organization, while their sons receive less encouragement to participate in the rituals.

People go to *espiritista* mediums suffering from emotional, interpersonal, and social problems, as well as psychosomatic symptoms such as fatigue, vague aches, skin rashes, and nervousness. Mediums design treatment strategies that identify the problem's cause, provide prescriptions and advice, remove spiritual influences, and help to develop the patient's spiritual abilities. Healing these disorders helps to reintegrate the individual into the society.

Spiritualist mediums can help people by exorcising evil spirits and contacting enlightened ones. *Espiritistas* serve as folk psychiatrists for the poor, and *espiritista centros* serve many psychological and social functions in the community. Because they serve important roles, some scholars believe *espiritistas* and other medical and mental health services should work together. The biomedical and the *espiritista* healers

could then see patients or clients according to whether the syndromes were natural/supernatural or material/spiritual.

Cuban Americans. SANTERÍA is a belief system found primarily in Cuba and among Cuban Americans. Like *espiritismo*, it has some elements derived from Yoruba tradition, to which elements of folk Catholicism have been added. Moreover, local priests interpret beliefs and introduce variations according to their knowledge and experience, as well as their followers' needs. Despite local variations, SANTERÍA has an overarching belief system involving the *orisha-santo*. This is a supernatural being who blends some characteristics of Yoruba spirits with those of Catholic saints. There are many such figures, according to tradition.

Unlike the situation for Mexican Americans, in which the adherents of traditional medicine tend to be poor and uneducated, Santería has believers from all walks of life and in all levels of the socioeconomic ladder. One reason for its popularity is that the manipulation of supernatural forces gives an individual a sense of control. For the poor, it may serve as a hedge against uncertainty in societies with endemic unemployment and poverty. Members of the upper classes would also go to *santeros* (priests) when they faced uncertainty, in hopes of manipulating events in their favor.

In Santería, both natural and supernatural factors can cause diseases. *Santeros* recognize the effects of some microorganisms and degenerative processes. Thus, they will frequently recommend that their patients consult a physician. They also believe that supernatural spirits can interfere with the physician's treatment or be responsible for putting the illness in the patient in the first place. Therefore, a patient needs the *orishas* as allies to overcome the illness.

According to anthropologist Mercedes Sandoval, *orishas* can cause six types of disease. In the case of witchcraft, someone casts an evil spell (*bilongo*) on a person, and the *santero* must perform an *ebbo* (protective spell) to undo the harm. In diseases caused by imitative or contagious magic, an enemy can harm a person by using pictures of or objects associated with an individual. Diseases also can be the result of soul loss, in which an enemy or witch buys a person's guardian spirit and then uses the spirit to harm the individual. A fourth cause of diseases is spirit intrusion, as when the spirits of the dead become angry with the living because the latter have neglected them or wronged them in some way. Likewise, the *orishas* can

Practitioners of the Yoruba religion such as this santero *ask orishas to intervene in curing illnesses.* (Impact Visuals, Allan Clear)

cause illnesses when they believe they have been neglected by an individual, or they can turn against an individual for some unknown reason. Finally, the evil eye can bring on fever, diarrhea, nervous tension, confusion, depression, and headaches, especially in children and pregnant women. People usually recover spontaneously within three to seven days.

Divination is a key feature in all Santería rituals and occurs at the beginning of the ceremonies. Divination is necessary to determine which *orisha* is responsible

for a condition and what is necessary to alleviate it. The advice from the *orishas* focuses on the problems the believers bring to them: health or illness, financial problems, interpersonal relations, misfortune, fears, and anxieties.

One study concluded that Santería provides effective mental health care for Cuban Americans who have become separated from family members who have remained in Cuba. Separation can result in increased feelings of anonymity, loneliness, and anxiety in the absence of close family and strong patriarchal authority, which are important to traditional Cubans. The *santero*'s counseling style appeals to those who come from an authoritarian family structure.

—*Walter Randolph Adams*

SUGGESTED READINGS: • Clark, Margaret. *Health in the Mexican-American Culture: A Community Study*. 2d ed. Berkeley: University of California Press, 1970. • Harwood, Alan. *Rx—Spiritist As Needed: A Study of a Puerto Rican Community Mental Health Resource*. New York: John Wiley & Sons, 1977. • Kiev, Ari. *Curanderismo: Mexican-American Folk Psychiatry*. New York: Free Press, 1968. • Perez y Mena, Andres Isidoro. *Speaking with the Dead: Development of Afro-Latin Religion Among Puerto Ricans in the United States*. New York: AMS Press, 1991. • Rubel, Arthur J., Carl W. O'Nell, and Rolando Collado-Ardon. *Susto, a Folk Illness*. Berkeley: University of California Press, 1984. • Sandoval, Mercedes S. "Santeria." *Journal of the Florida Medical Association* 78 (August, 1983): 620-628.

Health care policy: Health care expenditures in the United States increased from less than $50 billion in 1965 to more than $666 billion in 1990. Despite the tremendous resources devoted to health care, many people do not receive adequate services. Latinos are overrepresented among the "medically indigent." Because the issue of cost containment has dominated public discussion of health care, other issues such as access and equity have received relatively little attention.

Policies. As of the early 1990's, no national policy had been implemented that directly named Latinos as the primary targets of health care services. One early federal program granted matching funds to states, authorizing them to designate an agency responsible for maternal and infant care. The program targeted low-income mothers and children, providing for preventive services in the form of grants to states for well-baby clinics, prenatal care, special services for crippled children, and migrant and Appalachian health care programs. Large numbers of minority families were covered by the program. Services were neither comprehensive nor uniform, and few children received diagnostic or treatment services. Screening services for children were added in 1967, but problems of treatment were not resolved.

Many programs were designed or expanded in the government's effort to assume major responsibility for the health care of the poor and disadvantaged during the GREAT SOCIETY PROGRAMS of the 1960's. These programs included Medicaid, Medicare, the Community Health Centers Program, and the amended Maternal and Child Health Program. These programs made health care more accessible to the poor and eased the financial burden of health care costs for the elderly. Although specific minority groups were not designated as recipients of health care services, many of their members became eligible for services as a result of the legislation. The forces toward increasing insurance coverage to some of those unable to pay included a liberal Congress, accessibility of data documenting the health status of the poor and disadvantaged, and the pressures of the Civil Rights movement.

In 1971, grant funds were specifically designated for the comprehensive health care needs of minority children. These included preventive, diagnostic, and treatment services.

The neighborhood health center program that came into existence as a pilot program of the Office of Economic Opportunity in 1965 was hailed as a new approach to health care delivery. A major feature of the program allowed clients both access to services and participation in operating health care facilities.

One policy that targeted health care for members of minority groups was the MIGRANT HEALTH ACT of 1962, which authorized family service clinics. The first funds were appropriated in 1963 to provide health care services to migrants and their families, most of whom were African Americans and Chicanos.

In 1989, the Border Health Education Centers Program was authorized by the Omnibus Reconciliation Act. It provided funds for contracting with schools of medicine to create health care centers along the U.S.-Mexico border.

Implementation of Policies and Programs. Because states are allowed to determine eligibility, benefit ranges and levels, and reimbursement of health care providers, the Medicaid program varies from state to state. Medicare, administered by the Health Care Financing Administration, was enacted along with Medicaid in 1965. Persons aged sixty-five and over, railroad retirees, persons with chronic renal disease, and disabled persons who have received benefits for two years were eligible to participate.

The Tax Equity and Fiscal Responsibility Act of 1982 created a new system of compensation based on 467 diagnosis-related groups. The system was designed to contain costs by restricting reimbursements to hospitals, based on a formula that takes into account the diagnosis and average cost of care within a geographic area.

Full-time Latino Workers Without Health Insurance, 1989

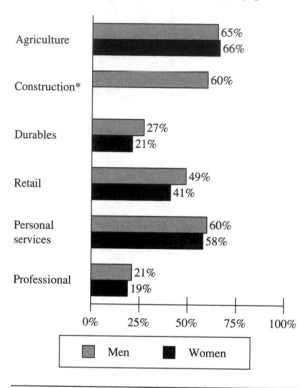

Agriculture — 65% / 66%
Construction* — 60%
Durables — 27% / 21%
Retail — 49% / 41%
Personal services — 60% / 58%
Professional — 21% / 19%

0%   25%   50%   75%   100%

■ Men   ■ Women

Source: Data are from Marlita A. Reddy, ed., *Statistical Record of Hispanic Americans* (Detroit: Gale Research, 1993), Table 469. Original data are from the March, 1990, Current Population Survey.
*Data not reported for women employed in construction.

Impact on Latinos. Before Medicaid and Medicare were implemented, the poor and elderly had little access to comprehensive health services. A small percentage of the poor received care through maternal and child health services or through health services sponsored by private charitable or nonprofit organizations. Latinos were overrepresented among the recipients of care from such programs, reflecting their overrepresentation among the poor.

Studies revealed that patient use of services offered at the Community Health Centers was comparable to that of the general population. Furthermore, a reduction of inpatient hospitalization was documented. At least 20 percent of the recipients of care from these centers were Latino.

Problems and Issues. A number of problems and issues affecting health care delivery and minorities in particular have arisen. Systemic problems refer to issues that arise from the structure of the health care delivery system. These include new and expensive developments in medical technology, inflation of health care costs, policy changes that pass more of the cost of health care to the consumer, and the privatization of the health care system. Societal issues reflect changes in society. These include an aging population, rising MORBIDITY AND MORTALITY rates, cultural and environmental demands, politics, and inflation and other economic conditions.

Despite the availability of both Medicare and Medicaid, members of ethnic minorities have experienced a greater incidence of various health problems, including certain infectious diseases, problems related to alcohol or drug abuse, teenage pregnancy, and mortality resulting from behavioral or social factors, such as family violence that could be reduced through adequate mental health services. HYPERTENSION, DIABETES, INFANT MORTALITY, accidents, homicides, cirrhosis of the liver, and ACQUIRED IMMUNE DEFICIENCY SYNDROME (AIDS) are major health problems among Latinos.

Health care utilization rates have been found to be lower for Latinos than for the U.S. population as a whole. Latinos have fewer physician contacts, fewer office visits, and more hospital outpatient visits. Members of ethnic minorities, including Latinos, spent less time with their physicians during office visits, were less likely to return for follow-up care, and were referred less often to specialists. The average length of stay in a hospital was slightly longer than for non-Hispanic whites. The quality of health care for minorities also has been questioned. Latinos of all groups are less likely to be insured, even when employed, than are members of the U.S. population as a whole. Lack of insurance surely contributes to lower utilization rates of health care services.   —*Marian Angela Aguilar*

SUGGESTED READINGS: • Budrys, Grace. *Planning for the Nation's Health.* New York: Greenwood Press, 1986. • Davis, Karen, and Cathy Schoen. *Health and the War on Poverty.* Washington, D.C.: Brookings Institution, 1978. • Estrada, A., F. Trevino, and L. Ray. "Health Care Utilization." *American Journal of Public Health* 80 (December, 1990): 27-31. • Health Administration Press. "Committee Finds Racial and Ethnic Disparities in Health Care." *Medical Care Review* 39, no. 1 (1982): 48. • National Center for Health Statistics. *Visits to Office-Based Physicians by Hispanic Persons: United States, 1980-81.* Advance Data from Vital and Health Statistics, PHS Number 129. Washington, D.C.: Government Printing Office. • Nickens, H. W. "Health Promotion and Disease Prevention

Among Minorities." *Health Affairs* 9 (Summer, 1990): 133-143. • Shenkin, Budd. *Health Care for Migrant Workers: Policies and Politics.* Cambridge, Mass.: Ballinger, 1974. • U.S. Congress. Office of Technology Assessment. *Health Care in Rural America.* Washington, D.C.: Government Printing Office.

Herbal medicine: The botanical science of the study and use of medicinal plants and herbs. Herbal medicine consists of medical materials made from herbs or medicinal plants, trees, or shrubs.

Herbal medicine, frequently associated with traditional medicine and FOLK MEDICINE, uses vegetable products or herbs for medicinal purposes. Since ancient times, herbs have been used in the treatment of wounds. The administration of herbal drugs and remedies by mouth was accompanied by incantations, dancing, and other magico-religious rituals. The study of medicinal plant lore and the uses of healing plants has overlapped natural history, medical botany, economic botany, ethnobotany, and a branch of ethnomedicine and anthropology called botanical ethnography. Remedies and information on medicinal plants come from both oral and written sources.

Herbs and other plants useful in medicine are often described in "herbals," ancient books or manuals used to facilitate the identification of plants for medical uses. Such knowledge began to be generated in ancient times and continues to be found. Botanical interests were fostered by the herbal tradition and by the empirical knowledge of native plants, trees, and shrubs. During the Renaissance, the revival of ancient texts, notably the works of Pliny and Dioscorides, was spread by the advent of printing. From the fifteenth century on, continuing travel, exploration, and colonial expansion of Europe, especially in Asia, Africa, and the Americas, recast medical botany.

The Aztecs had a highly developed system of and use of medicinal plants. Aztecs saw plants as having both religious and medicinal values. An Aztec illustrated herbal, the *Codex Badianus-Cruz*, was written by Martín de la Cruz, an Aztec doctor, in 1552. It was translated into Latin by Juan Badiano, an Aztec scholar associated with the Colegio de Tlatelolco. Another Spaniard, Fray Bernardo de Sahagún, wrote the *Florentine Codex* and the *Historia General*, which also contain much information on Aztec health practices, especially herbal medicine.

Another important source for the study of New World herbal medicine is found in the work of Francisco Hernández, the personal physician to King Philip II of Spain. His work contains descriptions of and medicinal uses of Mexican herbal plants. His findings are recorded in what was later called *Quatro libros de la naturaleza* (1615; four books of nature) and in *Rerum medicarum Novae Hispaniae thesaurus* (1651; treasury of medicinal things of New Spain).

Mexican and Mexican American folk medicine have continued traditions of herbal medicine, but not all herbs and plants used by *curanderos* (healers) are of American origin. *Curanderos* use both American and European medicinal plants and herbs (*see* CURANDERISMO).

Heredia, José María (Dec. 31, 1803, Santiago, Cuba—May 7, 1839, Mexico City, Mexico): Poet. The son of a government official, Heredia obtained a law degree from the University of Havana, but in 1823 he had to flee Cuba for political reasons. He went to the United States, where he wrote some of his best poetry. *Poesías* (poems) was published in 1825. As a poet, he mastered the techniques of Romanticism, earning for him the epithets "the first Hispanic-American romantic" and "the firstborn of Hispanic Romanticism." His most celebrated poem, "Meditación en el teocalli de Cholula" (1820), written at the age of seventeen, is considered among the highest achievements of early Spanish-American Romanticism.

Hermanas, Las: Catholic women's group. This national association was established in 1971. Its 1994 membership exceeded five hundred, with twelve regional affiliates and forty state affiliates. The membership is restricted to Catholic women of Hispanic origin. The interests of its members center on ministering to the needs of the Hispanic population, assisting in the spread of cultural values held by constituents, and general advocacy for equal treatment for Hispanics in the United States.

The organization offers workshops and gives scholarships targeting both the Catholic church audience and the general population. Specific goals involving the Catholic constituents are to engage Hispanic women in active ministry among Hispanics and to encourage and help one another in the task of cultural identification. The agency also helps locally by means of providing placement information services and sponsoring awareness workshops for those in the Spanish-speaking apostolate. The agency also conducts leadership training, workshops, and retreats.

The group as a whole promotes justice by providing supporting evidence of injustice when necessary. This

Antonia Hernández speaks at a 1982 news conference, in opposition to a Senate bill concerning illegal immigrants that she believed would cause undue hardship to Latinos, both citizens and noncitizens. (AP/Wide World Photos)

is done before federal, state, and local governments and agencies. Las Hermanas conducts semiannual conferences and publishes *Informes* quarterly.

Hermandades: Mutual aid societies of Puerto Rican immigrants. *Hermandades* (literally, "brotherhoods") were associations of Puerto Rican immigrants in the United States. Many of these groups appeared in the 1920's and were accompanied by the creation of trade unions and special interest organizations. The function of the *hermandades* was to provide basic services to the Puerto Rican community to help immigrants cope in a new environment. Two of the largest groups were the Hermandad Puertorriqueño (Puerto Rican Brotherhood) and the Club Democrática Puertorriqueno (Democratic Puerto Rican Club). *Hermandades* were an important force in unifying Puerto Rican immigrants and retaining ethnic nationalism.

Hernández, Antonia (b. May 30, 1948, Torreon, Coahuila, Mexico): Lawyer. Hernández emigrated from Mexico to East Los Angeles with her family when she was eight years old. She received her B.A. and teaching credential from the University of California, Los Angeles (UCLA); in 1974 she received her law degree from UCLA's school of law. While at UCLA, she served in Chicano student organizations and on the admissions committee. She began her career as a staff attorney with the Los Angeles Center for Law and Justice, and in 1977 she became the Legal Aid Foundation's directing attorney in Lincoln Heights.

An expert in immigration issues and civil rights, Hernández worked with the U.S. Senate Committee on the Judiciary and with Senator Edward M. Kennedy. As a prominent national advocate for Hispanics in the United States, Hernández's concerns have included immigrant rights, inequities in education, employment discrimination, U.S. Census figures and redistricting, and language and voting rights.

Hernández became associate counsel of the MEXICAN AMERICAN LEGAL DEFENSE AND EDUCATION FUND (MALDEF) in Washington, D.C., in 1981. As president and general counsel of MALDEF beginning in 1985, Hernández directed all litigation, advocacy programs, and long-range planning. Hernández strove for affirmative action in the public and private sectors and for better opportunities in federal government for Hispanics. Her efforts were critical in defeating legislation in the mid-1980's that would have required people to carry identification cards to prove citizenship status. Through MALDEF, she helped create single-member

election districts and challenged district boundaries in Los Angeles County. After the 1992 Los Angeles riots, Mayor Tom Bradley appointed Hernández to the Rebuild L.A. commission. She actively called for the involvement of Hispanics and immigrants in the rebuilding process.

Hernández, Ester (b. 1944, Dinuba, Calif.): Artist. Hernández, once employed as a farmworker, cofounded Mujeres Muralistas, an art collective. She is also known as a social critic.

Influenced heavily by family, particularly her parents and grandmother, Hernández combines Native American (Yaqui) and Chicano ancestry. She lived the experience of the farmworkers' struggle and creates powerful images of social critique. Her classic piece *Sun Mad* translates a box from the Sun Maid brand of raisins into a disturbing symbol of death. Early experiences of the festivities of the local Guadalupana society coupled with her role models of mother and grandmother affected the devotion to the female image so important in her work.

Hernández has worked in many media but considers herself to be a printmaker. Her images, as she says, are always those of *la mujer Chicana* (the Chicana woman). Her ideas and inspiration come from life itself; as she says, from "the beautiful as well as the gross." The print *Sun Mad*, was a personal reaction to her shock when she discovered that the water in her hometown, Dinuba, had been contaminated with pesticides for decades.

Hernández, Guillermo "Willie" (Guillermo Hernández y Villanueva; b. Nov. 14, 1954, Aguada, Puerto Rico): Baseball player. A tall left-handed pitcher with a good fastball and an even better split-fingered pitch, Hernández made his major league debut in 1977 with the Chicago Cubs. Traded to the Detroit Tigers after six seasons of relative anonymity with the Cubs and the Philadelphia Phillies, he emerged as one of the game's top relievers in 1984, posting a 1.92 earned run average, leading the American League in games pitched, converting 32 of 33 save opportunities in the regular season, and saving two more games in the Tigers' World Series triumph over the San Diego Padres. That season, he was named to his first All-Star team, and he also won the American League's Cy Young and Most Valuable Player awards, making him only the second reliever to win both honors.

Hernández remained an effective pitcher for several more seasons, saving 31 games in 1985 and winning

Willie Hernández saved two games to contribute to the Detroit Tigers' 1984 World Series victory. (AP/Wide World Photos)

additional All-Star selections in 1985 and 1986, but he never recaptured his 1984 form. He retired following the 1988 season.

Hernández, Juano (1896, San Juan, Puerto Rico— July 17, 1970, San Juan, Puerto Rico): Actor. The son of a Puerto Rican fisherman, Hernández was orphaned as a small child and went to live with an aunt in Rio de Janeiro, Brazil. As a young man, he toured South America and the Caribbean with carnivals, circuses, and minstrel shows before arriving in the United States in 1915. Hernández perfected his English and began appearing on New York stages in such plays as *Strange Fruit*, *Set My People Free*, and a one-man version of *Othello*. In 1933, he embarked on a career in radio as "John Henry."

His success on stage and over the airwaves attracted attention in Hollywood, where directors were impressed with Hernández's Afro-Caribbean looks and his imposing physical presence. In 1948, he made his screen debut in *Intruder in the Dust*, a film that explored racial conflict. He played the role of Lucas Beauchamp in a performance hailed as one of the first cinematic portrayals of an African American standing in defiance of racism.

Hernández's numerous other film credits include *Stars in My Crown* (1949), *Young Man with a Horn* (1950), *The Breaking Point* (1950), *Kiss Me Deadly* (1955), *Trial* (1955), *Ransom* (1956), *Something of Value* (1957), *The Pawnbroker* (1964), and *The Extraordinary Seaman* (1968). In 1950, he received an honorary degree from the University of Puerto Rico.

Hernandez, Keith (b. Oct. 20, 1953, San Francisco, Calif.): Baseball player. A left-handed hitter and thrower of Mexican descent, Hernandez made his major league debut in 1974 with the St. Louis Cardinals and became the team's regular first baseman in 1976.

Keith Hernandez hits a home run against the Philadelphia Phillies' Don Carman in 1989; his homer followed those by Darryl Strawberry and Kevin McReynolds, marking the first time three consecutive home runs had been hit at Shea Stadium. (AP/Wide World Photos)

A consistent line-drive hitter with medium-range power and good strike-zone judgment, Hernandez captured the 1979 National League batting title with a .344 average. That season, he also led the league with 48 doubles and 116 runs scored and shared the league's Most Valuable Player Award with the Pittsburgh Pirates' Willie Stargell. The following season, Hernandez again led the league in runs scored with 111. He was also a graceful fielder with exceptional mobility for a first baseman, and he won the National League Gold Glove Award for the position for eleven consecutive years beginning in 1978.

In 1982, Hernandez was a key member of the Cardinals' World Series champions, but he was traded to the New York Mets the following season amid rumors of cocaine use. The drug rumors proved true, but he rid himself of his addiction and became one of the cornerstones of the outstanding Mets teams of the mid-1980's. In 1986, he helped the Mets to a National League pennant and World Series title, batting .310 and leading the league with 94 walks. A five-time All-Star, Hernandez finished his seventeen-year career in 1990 with the Cleveland Indians.

Hernández Cruz, Victor. *See* **Cruz, Victor Hernández**

Hernández de Córdoba, Francisco (?—1517, Havana, Cuba): Spanish explorer. In February of 1517, Hernández de Córdoba sailed from Havana with three ships and 110 men. His intentions were to capture slaves and explore new lands. He sailed west, but violent storms pushed the ships off their course, and they landed in the Yucatán Peninsula. In a battle with natives, Hernández de Córdoba lost nearly half his crew, so he decided to return to Cuba.

On the trip back, another storm drove his ships off their course. The pilot, Antón de Alaminos, decided that it was easier to reach the Florida coast, which he had previously explored with Juan PONCE DE LEÓN. Hernández de Córdoba's ships arrived near the harbor where Ponce de León had anchored.

While the Spaniards searched for drinking water, Indians attacked and wounded Hernández de Córdoba. The expedition returned to Cuba, where Hernández de Córdoba died of his wounds. Although he reached the Florida coast, Hernández de Córdoba is remembered more for the accounts he gave of the Yucatán Peninsula. These inspired future explorers and conquistadores, including Hernán CORTÉS, who later conquered the Aztec empire.

Hernández v. New York (May 28, 1991): Supreme Court case involving jury selection. In this Supreme Court opinion (case number 89-7645) the Court rejected a claim by a Hispanic defendant, Dionosio Hernández, who had been convicted by New York courts of two counts of attempted murder and two counts of possession of a weapon. Speaking for the court, Justice Antony Kennedy concluded that the prosecutor's challenges to Spanish-speaking potential jurors were not discriminatory.

This case applied the jury selection principles of *Batson v. Kentucky* (476 U.S. 79, 106) to a New York criminal trial. Although the Spanish-speaking defendant was unsuccessful in pursuing his claim that the prosecutor had used preemptory challenges against two potential Spanish-speaking jurors to practice racial discrimination, the case illustrated the applicability to Hispanic needs of court victories won by black litigants and the close ties between the legal concerns of the two groups.

Justice Kennedy based his decision on several basic points. First, the trial court had ruled against Hernández on his claim of intentional discrimination, and thus the issue was moot. Second, the prosecutor offered a racially neutral explanation of his decision to strike two potential Spanish-speaking jurors during voir dire. The prosecutor contended that Spanish-speaking jurors would not accept the official court translation of testimony delivered in Spanish. Third, proof of racially discriminatory intent is necessary to find a violation of the equal protection clause. Finally, the trial court did not commit clear error in determining that the prosecutor did not discriminate against potential jurors based on their ethnicity.

Although Justice Kennedy refused to extend the reach of *Batson*, Justice John Paul Stevens wrote a significant dissent supported by Justice Harry Blackmun and Justice Thurgood Marshall. Differing with Justice Kennedy on the standard of proof that should be required of defendants seeking to prove discriminatory jury selection, Justice Stevens wrote, "the Court has imposed on the defendant the added requirement that he generate evidence of the prosecutor's actual subjective intent to discriminate. Neither *Batson* nor any other equal protection holdings demand such a heightened quantum of proof."

Justice Stevens objected to the prosecutor's exclusion of Spanish-speaking potential jurors for three reasons. First, he was troubled by the disproportionate exclusion of Spanish-speaking jurors. Second, he thought that the prosecutor's concern could have been alleviated through less drastic means. Third, Justice Stevens held that if the prosecutor had a valid concern that Spanish-speaking jurors would not accept official translations of court testimony, this concern would have supported a challenge for cause.

This decision imposed a high standard of proof on defendants seeking to use *Batson* to contend that members of their racial group were unfairly excluded from jury service. The trial court was left with almost untrammeled discretion in determining whether the prosecution was attempting to exclude minority jurors for a discriminatory purpose. For Hispanics, the only positive part of this decision was Justice Kennedy's recognition that the exclusion of bilinguals was neither wise nor constitutional in all cases.

Hernández v. Texas (May 3, 1954): (347 U.S. 475); Supreme Court case. In this Supreme Court decision Chief Justice Earl Warren overturned the murder conviction of the Mexican American plaintiff. The grounds for Pete Hernández's successful appeal were the systematic exclusion of fully qualified persons of Mexican descent from service as jury commissioners, grand jurors, and petit jurors in Jackson County, Texas.

Hernández was indicted and convicted for the murder of Joe Espinosa and was sentenced to life imprisonment. His conviction was upheld by the Texas Court of Criminal Appeals, and he was granted certiorari by the Supreme Court.

Even at the trial court level, Hernández moved to quash the indictment against him on the grounds that Mexican Americans did not serve as jury commissioners, grand jurors, or petit jurors. He made this claim before the trial, at the trial, and before the Texas Court of Criminal Appeals.

Hernández provided impressive statistics to support his claim that Mexican Americans were systematically excluded from jury selection and service. Although Hernández admitted that the Texas statute governing jury selection was neutral, he noted that 14 percent of the population of Jackson County had Mexican or Latin American surnames and 11 percent of men over the age of twenty-one had such surnames, but no individual with a Mexican or Latin American surname had served as a juror or jury commissioner within the preceding twenty-five years.

The Supreme Court applied the rule of exclusion to accept Hernández's statistics as proof of a pattern of discrimination violating FOURTEENTH AMENDMENT standards. The rule of exclusion applied in this case was first enunciated in *Norris v. Alabama* (294 U.S.

587). The Norris case concerned the systematic exclusion of African Americans from Alabama jury service. In that case, statistical evidence that no member of a substantial black population, which included some qualified jurors, had been called to jury service over a significant period of time provided persuasive proof of a pattern of discrimination.

In this case, the state of Texas argued that the Fourteenth Amendment defined only claims to equal protection of white and black persons, defined as two separate groups that included the entire population. In his opinion, Chief Justice Warren refused to accept this view. He pointed to other cases in which the state of Texas had recognized that Mexican Americans were a distinct racial group not part of either the white or the black category.

Among the citizens of Jackson County, Mexican Americans were clearly separate from the general population. The county had a record of providing segregated schools for Mexican American children in the primary grades and segregated toilets for Hispanic men at the county courthouse.

Chief Justice Warren stressed that he was not making a quota-based decision and that Hernández had not requested one. The significance of this case is its guarantee that criminal defendants belonging to distinct racial groups will not have members of their group systematically excluded from jury selection and service. This guarantee aided in making the trial system closer to the ideal of having a defendant judged by a jury of peers. The case is also significant for being the first Supreme Court case briefed and argued by Mexican American attorneys, Carlos Cadena and Gus C. GARCÍA.

Herrera, Efren (b. July 30, 1951, Guadalajara, Jalisco, Mexico): Football player. Herrera began his athletic career as a soccer player in his native Mexico. After moving to California during his high school years, he translated his kicking skills to the football field, becoming one of the first and most effective soccer-style kickers.

At the University of California, Los Angeles, Herrera broke ten school records in 1970 and was named an All-American in 1973. Drafted by the Detroit Lions in 1974, Herrera was cut from the team after only a few weeks, but he was picked up by the Dallas Cowboys. He soon emerged as one of the game's top kickers, and his 69.7 field-goal percentage for the 1970's was the decade's best. Herrera was a vital factor in the Cowboys' 1977 Super Bowl championships, but con-

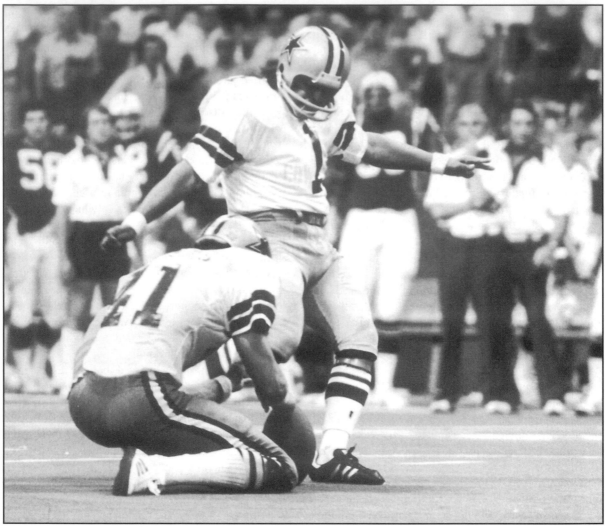

Efren Herrera's fourth-quarter field goal gives the Dallas Cowboys a victory over the Baltimore Colts during the 1977 exhibition season. (AP/Wide World Photos)

tract disputes with Dallas management led to his trade to the Seattle Seahawks in 1978. A year later, he kicked a career-high 100 points. He finished his career with the Buffalo Bills in 1982.

Herrera, Juan Felipe (b. Dec. 27, 1948, Fowler, Calif.): Poet. Herrera, the only child of a Chicano migrant-worker family, received a bachelor's degree in social anthropology from the University of California, Los Angeles, in 1972. He began doctoral work at Stanford University but did not complete his dissertation; however, he earned a master's degree from the prestigious Iowa Writers Workshop.

By the late 1960's, Herrera's poetry was being published. In the early 1970's, he experimented with a book, *Rebozos of Love*, which has no formal beginning or end, no pagination, no titles, and no conventional cover. In 1968, he formed a theater group, Teatro Tolteca. His other works include *Exiles of Desire* (1985).

Herrera, Miguel (1835-1905): Artist. Herrera, a Mexican American, worked and lived in Taos County, New Mexico. Most of his SANTOS are from the 1870's and 1880's. It is possible that he produced *BULTOS* later.

Much of Herrera's work was for the Brotherhood of Penitentes. His religious figures are recognizable for the unusual apparent height of the characters and for their ears, usually made of seashells and set lower on the head than those of real people. Herrera paid significant attention to the heads and hands of his figures, which were meant to be dressed in fabric clothing.

Herrera-Sobek, María (b. Mexico): Folklorist. Herrera-Sobek received her education in the United States. After completing her undergraduate work in chemistry at California State University at Northridge in 1974, she received her master's degree in Latin American studies from the University of California, Irvine, and her Ph.D. from the University of California, Los Angeles. Her books *The Bracero Experience: Elitelore Versus Folklore* (1979), *Beyond Stereotypes: The Critical Analysis of Chicana Literature* (1985), *The Mexican Corrido: A Feminist Analysis* (1990), and *Northward Bound: The Mexican Immigrant Experience in Ballad and Song* (1993) provide cultural insights about Mexican Americans.

Hidalgo, Hilda (b. Sept. 1, 1928, Puerto Rico): Educator and activist. Hidalgo has been pivotal in organizing regional and national organizations for the promotion of higher education among Hispanics. She began her experience as an educator at the Colegio de Nuestra Señora de Valvanera in Coamo, Puerto Rico. She earned her bachelor's degree from the University of Puerto Rico in 1957 and her master's degree from the Catholic University of America in 1959. She received her master's degree in social work from Smith College in Massachusetts in 1966 and her Ph.D. from Union Graduate School in Ohio in 1971.

Hidalgo empowered New Jersey's Hispanic community through her active participation in political, educational, and social arenas. In 1975, she was a founding member and the first president of the Puerto Rican Congress of New Jersey, a group with a mission of coordinating leadership statewide, creating agendas that addressed the concerns of Hispanic communities. The Puerto Rican Congress secures funding and grants for programs that aid Hispanics, covering such issues as education, child welfare, housing, migrant labor, and health care.

In 1977, Hidalgo began teaching at Rutgers University. She was the chair of undergraduate social work, coordinator of Puerto Rican studies, and a full professor in public administration and social work. Before retiring in 1992, Hidalgo was a driving force in creating an experimental and innovative master's program in social work for Hispanics. Under her tutelage, the number of Latinos graduating from Rutgers with master's degrees in social work jumped from fewer than eight in twenty-five years to fifty within four years.

Hidalgo y Costilla, Miguel (May 8, 1753, Corralejos, Guanajuato, Mexico—Aug. 1, 1811, Chihuahua, Mexico): Priest and revolutionary. Hidalgo received his priestly education in Valladolid and Mexico City, at San Francisco and San Nicolas colleges. Ordained in 1778, he soon headed San Nicolas' theology department and became its rector. For most of his life, Hidalgo was a priest who promoted piety and agriculture in the town of Dolores. There he set up brickyards and vineyards as well as introducing silk making to Mexico.

In 1808, Spain's European defeat by Napoleon led Mexicans to revolutionary activity. Secret societies sprang up, and Hidalgo planned a revolt. Betrayal of his plot led to action beginning sooner than planned, on September 16, 1808. Spurred on by his GRITO DE DOLORES, an impassioned speech, Hidalgo's parishioners seized a prison and captured Guanajuato.

Hidalgo used the banner of the Virgin of GUADALUPE, the patroness of Mexican Indians, as his battle standard. After capturing several cities, Hidalgo advanced against Mexico City with almost 100,000 men. Defeated, captured on January 17, 1811, and defrocked, he was executed by firing squad. Many view him as the father of Mexican independence.

Miguel Hidalgo y Costilla. (Institute of Texan Cultures)

Higher education: In the two decades from 1969 to 1989, Latinos and members of other minority groups enrolled in predominantly white colleges and universities in increasing numbers. During this period, student demands for a culturally diverse curriculum led to the development of Latino studies programs in higher education. Despite some modest gains in enrollment, however, Latino Americans continued to be underrepresented in postsecondary education.

Latino Studies Programs. Since the 1960's, colleges and universities have developed and expanded Latino studies programs at the undergraduate and graduate levels. Examples of program titles include Chicano studies, ethnic studies, Hispanic American studies, Mexican American studies, and Puerto Rican studies. Many of these programs are offered by institutions located in California, Texas, New York, and other states with large Latino populations. The *College Blue Book* provides detailed information on degree programs offered at colleges and universities throughout the United States and Canada.

Latino Enrollments. Although the public perception is that Latino enrollments in higher education increased significantly beginning in the 1970's, the reality is different. Although many Latino students can be found in all levels of postsecondary education—two-year colleges, four-year colleges, and universities—Latinos are differentially concentrated in the nation's two-year colleges. *The Almanac of Higher Education* provides information on the enrollment patterns of several racial and ethnic groups for more than three thousand postsecondary institutions.

Some representative two-year institutions and their percentages of Latino enrollment include South Mountain Community College, Arizona (28.7); East Los Angeles Community College, California (66.0); King River Community College, California (34.2); Trinidad State Junior College, Colorado (41.6); Miami- Dade Community College, Florida (53.0); Santa Fe Community College, New Mexico (49.0); Bronx Community College, New York (42.3); and San Antonio Community College, Texas (42.9). Some representative four-year institutions and their percentages of Latino enrollment include Arizona State University (5.3); the University of Arizona (7.5); the University of California, Berkeley (9.4); the University of California, Los

Robert Cruz, president of National Hispanic University in San Jose, California, explains a mural of the history of the campus. (AP/Wide World Photos)

Angeles (11.9); the University of Colorado-Boulder (3.9); the University of Florida (5.1); the University of New Mexico (21.3), and the University of Texas-Austin (9.9).

Latinos in Higher Education. The Latino population of the United States is heterogeneous. Chicanos, Cubans, and Puerto Ricans are the three largest subgroups of Latinos. Together they constitute approximately four out of every five Latino Americans. They are concentrated in different geographic locations, and the motives and circumstances surrounding their arrival in the United States have been different historically. Many Chicanos and Puerto Ricans were forcibly incorporated into the United States by military conquest, but many Cuban immigrants came voluntarily because of their dissatisfaction with the communist regime in Cuba. Although all three groups have shared the status of racial and ethnic minority, with accompanying discrimination, the experiences of Cuban Americans are sufficiently different to have important consequences for college attendance and graduation.

Cuban Americans tend to be more trusting of the educational system because their immigration was voluntary. Moreover, the initial waves of immigrants were predominantly from the middle class. Cubans quickly acquired considerable political clout in the Miami, Florida, area, and they received help and financial support from federal and private sources.

When Cuban Americans are compared to the total Latino population, on average they are found to complete more years of education than are persons of either Mexican or Puerto Rican origin. Cuban Americans are also three times more likely to complete four years or more of college than are Chicanos and Puerto Ricans. Cuban Americans are more similar to non-Latinos in their educational achievement than they are to other Latinos. It is worth noting, however, that persons of Cuban descent have not achieved education levels as high as those who are not of Latino origin.

Beginning in the late 1960's and early 1970's, many colleges and universities developed compensatory programs along with progressive admissions and financial aid policies to encourage the enrollment of Latinos and other ethnic minorities. In part as a result of the easier access afforded by these programs, Latino enrollment in higher education grew. The representation of Latinos in postsecondary education, however, remains disproportionately low in comparison to the Latino representation in the United States.

Latinos have neither entered a broad range of institutions nor dramatically increased their numbers

---

SELECTED INSTITUTIONS OFFERING DEGREES IN LATINO STUDIES PROGRAMS

Chicano Studies
California State University-Sacramento (B)
Scripps College, California (B)
University of California-Los Angeles (B)
University of California-San Diego (B)
University of Texas-El Paso (B)

Ethnic Studies
University of California-Berkeley (B, M, D)
Bard College, New York (B)
University of Texas-Austin (D)
University of Washington (B)
University of Wisconsin-Milwaukee (B)

Hispanic American Studies
University of California-Berkeley (B)
University of Miami, Florida (B)
University of Illinois-Chicago (M)
Smith College, Massachusetts (B)
Bryn Mawr College, Pennsylvania (B)

Mexican American Studies
University of Arizona (B)
California State University-Long Beach (B)
California State University-Los Angeles (B, M)
California State University-Northridge (B, M)
San Jose State University, California (M)
University of California-Davis (B)

Puerto Rican Studies
Rutgers, The State University of New Jersey (B)
Brooklyn College of the City University of New York (B)
Fordham University, New York (B)
State University of New York at Albany (B)

Source: Data are taken from *College Blue Book: Degrees Offered by College and Subject*, 23d ed. (New York: Macmillan, 1991).
Note: (B) = bachelor's program, (M) = master's program, (D) = doctoral program.

---

throughout the system. For example, from 1970 to 1984, full-time Latino undergraduates increased only from 2.1 percent of the total to 3.5 percent. The Latino presence in higher education has not shown the growth one might have expected from affirmative action, governmental, or institutional programs and efforts to increase enrollment of minority-group students.

Latino entry into postsecondary institutions has been neither large nor widespread. Latinos are concentrated in the less prestigious and less well-funded colleges. In 1984, only 23 percent of white full-time students attended two-year colleges, but 46 percent of Latino students attended such institutions.

Two-year colleges have increased Latino access, but students suffer from the inherent problems associated with part-time faculty, commuter programs, transfer to four-year institutions, and funding patterns. Moreover, unlike African American students, who benefit from historically black institutions, Latino students do not

EDUCATIONAL ATTAINMENT FOR SELECTED LATINO GROUPS, 1990
(persons 25 years of age or older)

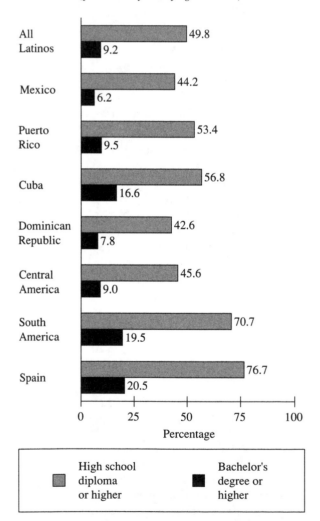

Source: We the American . . . Hispanics (Washington, D.C.: U.S. Bureau of the Census, 1993), Figure 8, p. 5.
Note: Groups are identified by country or region of background.

have access to a network of traditionally Latino colleges. Therefore, Latino students are disproportionately concentrated in fewer than 2 percent of the more than three thousand colleges and universities in the United States and in institutions that lack historical missions to serve Latino students.

Achievement Standards. Almost all selective four-year institutions rely heavily on high school grades and college aptitude test scores as primary evidence of candidates' preparation for the academic demands of college. Consequently, high school grades and college admissions test scores are frequently cited as factors influencing undergraduate achievement in selective colleges. Research findings suggest that these indicators do not do as good a job of predicting Latinos' college grades as they do for white students.

Achievement information alone, based on high school grades, is incapable of indicating whether students' performance has been moderated by the quality of schooling and students' opportunity to learn in classroom settings. Nor are grades capable of capturing students' personal and background characteristics that influence opportunities to learn. There is substantial agreement among social scientists that social background is the most significant factor determining individuals' educational success.

Like high school grades, college admission tests have severe limitations. An admissions score results from an isolated encounter with a test. The scores do not have a cumulative history of repeated assessment over the high school years. Moreover, admissions scores are influenced by background and school factors. These factors do not invalidate the use of high school grades and admissions test scores for Latinos, but they do suggest the need to understand how differences between Latino and white students should affect the interpretation of admissions information.

An examination of the factors influencing Latino enrollment in higher education can be grouped into four general categories: family background, ethnic/cultural, school, and community variables. Latinos and members of other groups predominantly from low socioeconomic backgrounds exhibit generally depressed rates of enrollment and persistence in colleges and universities. The fact that Latinos face considerable educational difficulties is well documented. Attempts to find solutions to these problems have been less than satisfying because the problem has been identified as Latinos themselves rather than the educational system.

There has been a failure to understand fully the relationship between the educational system and rac-

ACADEMIC DEGREES CONFERRED TO HISPANIC STUDENTS, 1990-1991

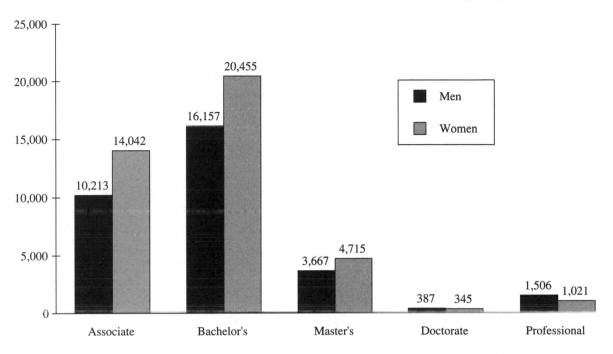

Source: Data are from the U.S. Department of Education.

ism. RACISM and DISCRIMINATION have in some cases provided justifications for the differential treatment of Latinos, such as SEGREGATION, tracking, and a hierarchy of postsecondary educational institutions that separate Latinos from their more privileged counterparts. The effect of such mechanisms is to perpetuate and reinforce stereotypes and to label Latino students negatively.

The diversity of higher education in the United States ensures that those who graduate from high school with reasonable academic preparation, regardless of race, age, or sex, will be accepted for admission at some institution. There is evidence, however, that a student's choice of college is shaped not only by academic preparation but also by ethnic group membership. The call to increase opportunities for Latinos will remain a recurring theme on university and college campuses across the United States as long as Latinos are retained in higher education at a rate significantly lower than that of their white counterparts.

—*Michael Delucchi*

SUGGESTED READINGS:

• Altbach, Philip G., and Kofi Lomotey, eds. *The Racial Crisis in American Higher Education.* Albany: State University of New York Press, 1991. A series of articles on issues of race and ethnicity relating to the academic community and curriculum. Topics include debates concerning affirmative action, admissions policies, and the difficulties of recruitment, retention, and campus life for African American, Latino, and Asian American students and faculty.

• Astin, Alexander. *What Matters in College?* San Francisco: Jossey-Bass, 1993. A comprehensive discussion of how undergraduates are affected by their college experiences. Topics include the impact of higher education on attitudes, behaviors, achievement, and other outcomes of college. Written in a style appropriate for both high school and college audiences. Several chapters can be read independently of others. Includes a bibliography and subject indexes.

• Bean, Frank D., and Marta Tienda. *The Hispanic Population of the United States.* New York: Russell Sage Foundation, 1987. One in a series of publications aimed at analyzing the 1980 census. The chapter on the educational standing of Hispanics is particularly informative. Contains footnotes, name and subject indexes, and a bibliography.

• Boswell, Thomas D., and James R. Curtis. *The Cuban-American Experience: Culture, Images, and Perspectives.* Totowa, N.J.: Rowman & Allanheld,

1984. An excellent account of the major social, economic, educational, and political topics relating to Cuban settlement and culture in the United States. Contains footnotes and a combined name and subject index.

• *College Blue Book: Degrees Offered by College and Subject*. 23d ed. New York: Macmillan, 1991. Comprehensive guide to undergraduate and graduate degree programs offered at colleges and universities throughout the United States and Canada. Updated annually.

• The Editors of the Chronicle of Higher Education. *The Almanac of Higher Education*. Chicago: University of Chicago Press, 1993. An annual publication offering an overview of the health and financing of U.S. higher education as well as state-by-state reports on demographics, political leadership, and key statistics about faculty and students. The almanac is filled with easy-to-use maps, tables, and charts.

• Olivas, Michael A., ed. *Latino College Students*. New York: Teachers College Press, 1986. A comprehensive collection of essays on Latinos in higher education. Discusses historical, political, economic, organizational, sociological, cultural, scientific, and policy-centered topics. Several chapters can be read independently of others. Includes a bibliography and subject indexes.

• Pascarella, Ernest T., and Patrick T. Terenzini. *How College Affects Students*. San Francisco: Jossey-Bass, 1991. A summary of findings and insights from twenty years of research on college students. Topics include the impact of higher education on attitudes, behaviors, achievement, and other outcomes of college. Contains name and subject indexes and a 150-page bibliography.

• Weis, Lois, ed. *Class, Race, and Gender in American Education*. Albany: State University of New York Press, 1988. A series of research articles in which the authors consider the particular situations of males and females of divergent racial/ethnic and class backgrounds, from childhood experiences through the adult university years.

Hijuelos, Oscar (b. Aug. 24, 1951, New York, N.Y.): Writer. Hijuelos, the son of a hotel worker and a homemaker, received his undergraduate education at the City College of the City University of New York and

Oscar Hijuelos, shown shortly after receiving the Pulitzer Prize in fiction. (AP/Wide World Photos)

completed his M.S. there in 1976. After working in advertising for several years, Hijuelos turned to writing full-time.

Hijuelos, a Cuban American, combines realism with certain Latin American attributes sometimes labeled "surreal" or "magical." His first novel, *Our House in the Last World* (1983), won for him the Rome Fellowship in Literature from the American Academy and Institute of Arts and Letters. He won the 1990 Pulitzer Prize in fiction for *The Mambo Kings Play Songs of Love* (1989). *The Fourteen Sisters of Emilio Montez O'Brien* (1993) was also well received.

Hinojosa, Rolando (Rolando Hinojosa-Smith, b. Jan. 21, 1929, Mercedes, Tex.): Novelist. Born to a Mexican American family of modest means, Hinojosa earned a bachelor's degree in education from the University of Texas at Austin, a master's degree from New Mexico Highlands University, and, in 1989, a doctorate from the University of Illinois.

After teaching high school in Brownsville, Texas, Hinojosa taught at Trinity University in San Antonio and Texas A&I University in Kingsville, where he became dean of the College of Arts and Sciences and vice president for academic affairs. During the 1970's, Hinojosa was a professor of Chicano studies at the University of Minnesota. He returned to Texas in 1981 and assumed the E.C. Garwood professorship at the University of Texas at Austin in 1985.

In 1973, Hinojosa published *Estampas del valle y otras obras/Sketches of the Valley and Other Works,* the first volume in his evolving "Klail City Death Trip" series. The series, which focuses on the inhabitants of a fictional Texas border town, has garnered substantial critical acclaim.

Hispanic: Refers to people of Latin American ancestry in the United States. The term dates to the 1960's, when it was created by bureaucrats of the United States Congress. The U.S. government used the term as a useful catch-all to include all Spanish-speaking people, enabling politicians to appeal to all Latinos at once. The term ignores the great diversity of cultural backgrounds in the Spanish-speaking population and falsely assumes that these groups have a common identity. The term also implies Spanish ancestry, as its literal meaning is "pertaining to ancient Spain," and does not account for the indigenous and/or African roots present in many Latino cultures. "Hispanic" is used more frequently than "Latino" by the politically conservative, marketers, and the general public than by the people it describes, some of whom find the term offensive. Among Latinos, it is used mostly by the middle and upper classes.

Hispanic Academy of Media Arts and Sciences (HAMAS): Nonprofit corporation. HAMAS was founded in 1984 to create a Hispanic network, with national and international influence, that would contribute to the development of positive media images of Hispanics. The national organization has offices in New York, New York; Los Angeles, California; Washington, D.C.; Miami, Florida; and elsewhere.

HAMAS advocates the fair and equal representation of Latinos in film and television, monitors how they are portrayed, and tries to find employment for Latinos at all levels of the television and film industries. HAMAS puts together a multiday educational, informational, and inspirational conference called the Annual U.S. Hispanic Media Conference at which HAMAS members and colleagues gather to exchange ideas concerning the challenges facing the media industries. Conference activities include workshops, film screenings, career counseling, social gatherings, and speeches. The group also sponsors an annual awards event that highlights the contributions of Hispanics to the media industries. HAMAS publishes a quarterly newsletter and the *Guide to Hispanic Media Professionals*, a comprehensive directory of Latinos in every industry pertaining to the media.

Hispanic American Festival (Washington, D.C.): Known under a variety of names, including El Festival Latino, the Hispanic American Festival, begun in 1970, takes place in the heart of a Latino district located in the Adams Morgan and Mount Pleasant section of WASHINGTON, D.C. It was instituted to celebrate the culture, customs, and traditions of Latinos living in the Washington area. Originally limited to folk dances and ethnic food, it has rapidly grown to include soccer matches; the festival queen's coronation; a gala ball; special events celebrating children, women, elders, and the undocumented; and the festival's centerpiece, a grand parade, on the last Sunday in July. Various organizations also sponsor contests and exhibitions, with an emphasis on music, dance, dramatic presentations, and food from more than thirty Latin American and other nations.

Hispanic Health and Nutrition Examination Survey (HHANES): Measured health and socioeconomic factors of the Latino population. This survey was conducted from 1981 to 1983. It was the first survey of its kind for Latinos and was designed to gather information on the health and the social and economic status of various groups of Latinos. It was carried out by the National Center for Health Statistics, an agency of the United States Health and Human Services Department.

Twelve thousand people of Puerto Rican, Cuban, and Mexican background were interviewed and medically tested. The results showed disparity in health care among the three subgroups. Health knowledge and needs varied substantially. This information allowed the targeting of these groups with health education. As a result of the survey, specific research began regarding particular health issues among the subgroups of Latinos surveyed. The Hispanic Health Research Consortium was established to keep track of research resulting from the study. Such projects included studies on dental care, drug and alcohol abuse, health risk factors, and medical care utilization.

Hispanic Heritage Awards (September): In conjunction with HISPANIC HERITAGE MONTH, the National Hispanic Heritage Awards are annually bestowed on Hispanic Americans for their contributions to U.S. national culture and the preservation of Hispanic heritage. The awards are made at the National Building Museum in Washington, D.C., at the end of the Hispanic Heritage Month celebrations.

Hispanic Heritage Festival (Miami, Fla.): The annual Hispanic Heritage Festival, although centered in Miami, is held throughout Dade County during the entire month of October. The part of the festival known as the Hispanic Folklore Festival features folk arts and crafts. Although most Latino participants are Cuban Americans, other groups, including Mexican Americans and Puerto Ricans, are represented. Other events in the Hispanic Heritage Festival include a gala ball, a discovery of America celebration (including a dramatic re-enactment of Christopher Columbus' preparations and voyage to the New World), a golf tournament, and the Festival of the Americas, featuring concerts by Hispanic musicians as well as children's attractions and arts and crafts booths. The festival attracts more than 300,000 visitors annually.

An event with the same name was begun in 1983 in Rock Springs, Wyoming, and held on the first Saturday after Easter. Like other community festivals, that in Rock Springs features folk music, dances, arts and crafts, traditional games, costumes, contests, and exhibits.

Hispanic Heritage Month: Proclaimed annually by the president of the United States, a Hispanic Heritage Week celebrates the contributions of Hispanic Americans to U.S. culture. Diverse events take place at the federal, state, and local levels, including seminars and lectures as well as cultural activities.

In Washington, D.C., the celebration is known as the Hispanic Heritage Month because its schedule extends to two or three weeks in September. It includes the annual Fashion Show Gala Benefit featuring fashions by Hispanic designers and the Hispanic Heritage Week Annual Dinner, sponsored by the Congressional Hispanic Caucus Institute. At the dinner, Medallion of Excellence Awards are given to Hispanics and non-Hispanics recognized for their contributions to the enhancement or promotion of Hispanic American culture and to citizens of Hispanic background who have made noteworthy professional or artistic achievements.

Hispanic Music Association: Musicians' group. The association formed in 1984 in EAST LOS ANGELES to promote Latino musicians in the area. Members are East Los Angeles Latino musicians, many of whom are Chicano. The founding officers were president and pianist Eddie Cano, vice president and saxophonist Tony Garcia, secretary and singer Jeri Gonzalez, and treasurer and saxophonist Adolfo Martinez. The group's goals are to arrange performances, increase the role of Latino musicians within the local musicians' union, and develop educational programs. In 1991, the association's salsa big band, the HMA Salsa/Jazz Orchestra, recorded the album *California Salsa*.

Hispanic National Bar Association (founded in 1972 as La Raza National Lawyers Association): Professional association. The Hispanic National Bar Association promotes the science of jurisprudence and reform in the law. The association was established with the goals of facilitating the administration of justice; advancing the standing of the legal profession; and promoting high standards of integrity, honor, and professional courtesy among Hispanic lawyers. It changed its name from La Raza National Lawyers Association to La Raza National Bar Association in 1978, then to the Hispanic National Bar Association in 1980.

The association facilitates mentorship through a counseling service provided to Hispanic students interested in careers in the law. As part of the mentorship process, the association offers placement services, bestows awards, and provides financial assistance. The association also compiles and disseminates statistical information pertinent to its goals.

As part of its community outreach, the association provides referral services for legal cases involving issues of relevance to the Hispanic community. Professional training seminars address race relations issues and other topics. The association offers computerized services through a database and produces a mailing list. Members participate in conferences (usually more than two per year) and an annual convention.

Membership in the Hispanic National Bar Association was more than thirty-eight hundred in the early 1990's. The organization included nineteen local and eight state bar associations. Publications included a semiannual *National Directory* and a quarterly *Noticias*. Its headquarters are in Washington, D.C.

Hispanic Policy Development Project: Community service organization. Founded in 1982, this agency seeks to correct what it calls "the long-standing neglect of the Hispanic population." It works by means of raising public interest in issues concerning Hispanics, by influencing lawmakers, by fostering grassroots participation of Hispanics in policy debates, and through workshops and other educational programs.

The project conducts research and sponsors competitions and seminars. One of the national activities it has sponsored is the National Commission on Secondary Schooling for Hispanics. One particular concern is fostering participation of young Hispanic policy analysts by creating forums and other avenues through which they can take part in policy debates.

The agency publishes *Hispanic Almanac* and the *Research Bulletin*, both periodicals. It also publishes reports, monographs, and books. The agency has an editorial office in Washington, D.C., and an operating office in New York, New York.

Hispanic Radio Network (founded 1982): Radio production company and syndicator. The Hispanic Radio Network is the first and, as of 1994, the largest producer and syndicator of daily Spanish-language radio programs.

The daily programs of the Hispanic Radio Network air on more than eighty full-time Spanish radio stations across the United States. Network affiliates are located in each of the top thirty U.S. Hispanic markets, covering 95 percent of the potential Hispanic audience. The network, with headquarters in Santa Fe, New Mexico, has most of its affiliates in California, Arizona, New Mexico, and Texas, but affiliates are spread across the United States.

Affiliated stations primarily air popular Spanish music. The Hispanic Radio Network takes pride in providing well-produced educational, cultural, and special interest programming to the Hispanic community.

Hispanic Walk of Fame (Miami, Fla.): Landmark. Also known as LITTLE HAVANA's Walk of Fame, the site features stars planted in the pavement between Twelfth and Seventeenth Streets in Miami to honor Hispanic screen and musical celebrities. It is modeled after the Walk of Fame in Hollywood, California.

The Hispanic Walk of Fame celebrates Hispanic stars such as Gloria ESTEFAN, Olga Gillot, and Jose Louis Rodriguez. It began when a star honoring "Hansel" was placed in the pavement without the permission of the City of Miami. A long battle followed between the city and Latin Stars, Inc., the organization managing the project. When permission was granted in 1988 to continue the project, Estefan's became the second star planted in the walk. The walk officially opened in 1989. In 1992, the city withdrew support after a long debate over the selection of stars and how star placements would be financed.

Hispanics in Public Radio (founded 1991): Nonprofit professional organization. Hispanics in Public Radio was founded to provide a forum for the expression of the needs and interests of Hispanic Americans involved with the radio broadcasting industry.

Hispanics in Public Radio represents the interests of Hispanic-controlled public radio stations and attempts to improve the financial resources of these stations. Its main activities are information sharing, joint fundraising, training, and program development. As of 1994, Hispanics in Public Radio controlled thirteen FM radio stations.

Hispaniola. *See* **Española, La**

Hispanos: One of several predominantly Spanish groups (including CALIFORNIOS and Tejanos) that settled the northern frontier of New Spain on the upper Rio Grande in northern New Mexico and southern Colorado. Hispanos are descended from the Spaniards who arrived in New Mexico in the seventeenth century and later established Santa Fe, Santa Cruz de la Cañada, and San Felipe Neri (Albuquerque). The majority were subsistence farmers and sheepherders who lived in small, isolated communities in or near the Rio Grande Valley.

By 1750, Hispano settlements had reached the present border of Colorado. By the 1790's, approximately

A Hispano family in a formal photograph taken in 1892 in Albuquerque, New Mexico. (Ruben G. Mendoza)

one-fourth of the Hispano population was MESTIZO (mixed Amerindian and Spanish). A distinct Mexican population settled southeastern New Mexico between 1820 and 1850.

After the MEXICAN AMERICAN WAR (1846-1848), Hispanos found themselves under the jurisdiction of the U.S. government and surrounded by English-speaking American culture. Unlike the Tejano and Californio cultures, however, Hispano society was never inundated by Anglos and was allowed to retain its relative isolation. Anglo settlers did not arrive in the region in significant numbers until the last quarter of the nineteenth century. Their arrival meant the loss of much Hispano grazing land, but this was offset by the increasing availability of jobs that paid wages. Many Hispanos welcomed the cession of territory to the United States, some serving as territorial administrators before New Mexico was granted statehood in 1912.

Between 1910 and 1930, large numbers of Mexicans migrated to NEW MEXICO. Some Hispanos identified with the new arrivals, espousing their values and traditions, but others revived the popular notion that Hispanos were essentially Caucasian, tending to assimilate Anglo culture. In 1930, Senator Dennis CHÁVEZ began a campaign to have all Hispanos learn English, arguing for future economic growth in an English-speaking world rather than retention of Spanish and the less economically productive traditions associated with it.

In the 1940's, Hispanos began a general exodus from rural communities to larger urban areas in New Mexico and other states. As they settled in larger numbers in cities, so did many Mexican immigrants. By late in the twentieth century, it was difficult to distinguish the descendants of Hispanos from those of Mexican Americans. Government statisticians make no such distinction. In 1990, the census recorded 579,224 Hispanics in New Mexico, or 38 percent of the state's population. Census analysts believe, however, that many Hispanos choose the labels "other Hispanic," "Spanish," or "Spanish American" when identifying themselves on government forms.

Hispanos have given a particular flavor to New Mexican culture with their dialect of Spanish, full of archaisms, and the use of distinctive given names and surnames. The extensive use of very hot chiles in New Mexican cooking is also a unique Hispano custom. In the arts, Hispano society has a long tradition of local theater and oral literature, particularly the use of the balladlike *DÉCIMA* form. Hispano families have long cultivated the art of making SANTOS, which are carved, gessoed, and painted figures of saints. Many are now collectors' items. The PENITENTE Brotherhood, an ascetic religious organization with strong Franciscan characteristics that dates from the late 1700's, still has its strongest support among Hispanos in the rural communities of upper New Mexico and Colorado.

Holidays and festivals, Cuban American: Cuban exiles and their American-born descendants maintain a lively calendar of celebrations. These events affirm their ties to faith, heritage, and community. Although some Cuban American holidays are celebrated behind closed doors in homes, churches, and social organizations, others spill out into the streets, asserting cultural pride and introducing Cuban customs to other Americans.

Religious Holidays. The vast majority of Cuban Americans are Catholics, and many of their celebrations center on religious observances. Perhaps the most important is the feast of the Epiphany, observed on January 6, the twelfth day after Christmas. It is the oldest festival on the church calendar, dating to the second century.

The Epiphany commemorates the arrival of the Magi at the manger in Bethlehem. It is an important date for Cuban Americans not only for its significance in the birth story of Jesus Christ but also because it is traditionally the day when Cubans exchange gifts and celebrate the Christmas season most joyfully. Although many Cuban Americans have adopted American ways and incorporate Santa Claus and gift exchanges on December 25 into their celebrations, many families still wait until Epiphany. In Miami, Cuban Americans celebrate with a parade that draws about a quarter of a million people. It includes floats, animals, and people dressed as the Magi. The culmination is a re-enactment of the Magi arriving and delivering their gifts to the newborn baby Jesus.

Another distinctive feature of Cuban American Christmas celebrations is that Christmas Eve (December 24) is traditionally the day for family gatherings and Christmas dinner. A pig is often roasted and wine is poured as relatives and friends congregate to share this important feast. On Christmas Day, the celebration continues with food, music, and more visits from family and friends.

Lent begins with Ash Wednesday, when the devout fast and attend Mass. Lenten promises of abstinence are made, and the season of Lent culminates in the celebration of Easter. Although the appearance of the Easter bunny and baskets of candy for children are

The Feast of Our Lady of Charity is celebrated on September 8; Our Lady of Charity is portrayed in this statue. (Martin Hutner)

now common in most Cuban American households, Easter has traditionally been celebrated in a more solemn manner marked by Masses and prayer.

September 8 is the Feast of Our Lady of Charity, a holy day of particular importance for Cuban Americans. In 1916, the Vatican proclaimed Our Lady of Charity the patron saint of Cuba. Devout Cubans have a deep reverence for Our Lady of Charity, who is associated with a miraculous story of deliverance by the Virgin Mary. According to the story, three fishermen were caught in a terrible storm at sea. Their boat was close to sinking when they noticed a wooden figurine floating in the water. The men grabbed the figurine, began praying to the Virgin Mary, and were saved from drowning. The men then brought the small statue to the seaport town of Santiago de Cuba and built a shrine to her.

In 1960, the Diocese of Miami held the first annual Mass for Our Lady of Charity, with eight hundred people in attendance. The next year, the Mass was celebrated at Miami Stadium before a crowd of twenty-five thousand. In 1966, on the fiftieth anniversary of the proclamation of Our Lady of Charity as the Patroness of Cuba, the bishop in Miami invited Cuban Americans to erect a shrine in her honor on Biscayne Bay. The shrine was erected on property donated by the church and was financed by money raised in the Cuban American community. Each year on September 8, thousands of Cuban Americans bring flowers to the shrine. In remembrance of the three fishermen, the statue is carried by boat to Miami Stadium, where twenty-five thousand people eagerly await its arrival before celebrating Mass.

National Holidays. Cuban Americans celebrate several important dates associated with Cuba's independence from Spain in 1898. The first on the calendar is January 28, the birthday of José MARTÍ, a poet and political activist who became the symbol of the Cuban struggle for independence. Martí organized and unified the movement for Cuban independence, then died on the battlefield in 1895, fighting for his homeland. Even today, throughout Latin America his name is synonymous with liberty.

May 20 is Cuban Independence Day, commemorating the official declaration of the Republic of Cuba in 1902. Cuban Americans mark this day with picnics

Cuban Independence Day is celebrated on May 20 with parades, picnics, and speeches. (Richard B. Levine)

and parades. In cities with large Cuban populations, such as Miami, city and state politicians join Cuban American leaders at banquets in honor of Cuban independence. Each year on May 20, the president of the United States delivers a message for Cuban Americans.

December 7 is a day of national mourning in Cuba and a holiday that is also observed by Cuban Americans. It is the day in 1897 that Antonio Maceo died. Maceo was a Cuban military leader and tactician who fought in both the Ten Years' War of 1868-1878 (an unsuccessful bid for independence) and the CUBAN WAR OF INDEPENDENCE (1895-1898). December 7 is to Cuban Americans what Veterans Day is to other Americans: a time to acknowledge those who gave their lives for their country. It is celebrated with speeches and special events.

Festivals. The largest Cuban American festival in the United States is Carnaval Miami, an annual nine-day festival in March celebrating Latin culture. It attracts more than a million people. The festival was conceived in the 1960's by Cuban Americans living in the LITTLE HAVANA section of Miami, as a way of sharing Latin American culture with their new Anglo and African American neighbors.

The festival begins with a giant *paseo* (parade) featuring floats, Cuban American and other Latin American celebrities, *comparsas* (large groups of conga musicians accompanied by paired male and female dancers performing choreographed routines), limbo dancers, SAMBA groups, and street bands from the Caribbean. Parties and special events are featured throughout the week, but the biggest bash is reserved for the last weekend of the Carnival. At this time, twenty blocks of CALLE OCHO (Eighth Street) in Little Havana are closed to vehicles, and the largest "Cuban street party," CALLE OCHO OPEN HOUSE—CARNAVAL MIAMI, gets under way. A panoply of color, dance, movement, and sound fills the street where thousands of people gather and some forty SALSA bands play throughout the day. At various intervals, dance troupes perform staged performances and musicians parade down the street. CONGA lines of more than fifty people snake through the crowds. Calle Ocho Open House is a celebration of Cuban music, food, and dance shared by Cuban Americans, other Latinos, and non-Hispanics alike. *—Suzanne Smith*

SUGGESTED READINGS: • Boswell, Thomas D., and James R. Curtis. *The Cuban-American Experience.* Totowa, N.J.: Rowman & Allanheld, 1983. • Brown, Ray B., ed. *Rituals and Ceremonies in Popular Cul-*ture. Bowling Green, Ohio: Bowling Green University Popular Press, 1980. • Kinser, Samuel. *Carnival, American Style.* Chicago: University of Chicago Press, 1990. • McNally, Michael J. *Catholicism in South Florida, 1868-1968.* Gainesville: University Press of Florida, 1982.

Holidays and festivals, Mexican American: Mexican Americans celebrate U.S. holidays, such as the Fourth of July and Labor Day, but historical and religious holidays that are celebrated in Mexico are also celebrated in the United States and Canada. Mexican Americans try to maintain their heritage by celebrating these holidays and passing their traditions to succeeding generations.

Historical Holidays. It is customary for Mexican Americans to make noise on New Year's Eve to celebrate *el año nuevo.* People celebrate on the streets or at parties with music and other noisemakers. Some celebrate with firecrackers to ward off evil spirits.

CINCO DE MAYO (May 5) commemorates the defeat of the invading French army by Texas-born General Ignacio Zaragoza and his Mexican forces at the Battle of Pueblo in 1862. His defense of the city prevented Napoleon III from establishing a permanent French colony and led toward eventual expulsion of the French from Mexico by Benito Juárez five years later.

Cinco de Mayo is symbolic of a bold stand against outside forces and oppression. It is celebrated in most schools and communities in the Southwest. Celebrations usually include MARIACHI music, food, and speeches. Cinco de Mayo is the most widely recognized Mexican American holiday and is celebrated by other cultures.

Many Mexican Americans celebrate Mother's Day on May 10, the official Mexican Mother's Day. Families usually celebrate Mexican Mother's Day for their parents, grandparents, and other relatives who come from Mexico; they additionally celebrate for themselves the traditional American Mother's Day on the second Sunday of May.

DIECISÉIS DE SEPTIEMBRE (September 16) commemorates the initiation of the Mexican independence movement by the GRITO DE DOLORES in 1810; the celebration is also known as Mexican Independence Day. Although festive, the holiday is celebrated less colorfully than is Cinco de Mayo by most Mexican Americans.

Religious Holidays. El Día de los TRES REYES MAGOS, or Three Kings Day, is observed on January 6 to celebrate the visit of the biblical wise men to the

Parades and other celebrations commemorate Cinco de Mayo and Dieciséis de Septiembre, two important days in the history of Mexican independence. (Ruben G. Mendoza)

El Día de los Muertos is celebrated by visiting graves as well as by more lighthearted costuming and festivities. (Diane C. Lyell)

infant Jesus. According to legend, the child was only twelve days old; thus, the holiday is celebrated on January 6, twelve days after Christmas.

It is customary for Mexican American children to leave their shoes on window ledges or doorsteps on the night of January 5. In the morning, their shoes are filled with candies, fruits, and little toys.

Lent, a forty-day commemoration of the events that led up to the death of Jesus, is observed by Roman Catholics. On Ash Wednesday, Mexican American believers go to church to have their foreheads smudged with ashes in the form of a cross. The final week of Lent is known as Holy Week, or la Semana Santa. During that week, some communities have sorrowful processions. Large, heavy platforms bearing statues of Jesus, Mary, and the saints are marched through the streets on the shoulders of the faithful. On Good Friday, most Mexican American Catholics attend church or observe silence and prayer at home. On the following Saturday (El Sábado de Gloria), the end of the Holy Week, many communities have noisy celebrations with music and food.

Many Mexican American communities have candlelight processions on the midnight before Easter Sunday. Easter morning is a time of joy, and the day is celebrated with a fiesta.

On November 1, Día de los Santos (All Saints Day), saints who do not have name days of their own are honored. November 2, DÍA DE LOS MUERTOS (Day of the Dead), is a time to pray for the souls of the dead who have not yet found a resting place. Deceased relatives are remembered and honored, and families visit cemeteries to pray for the dead. Family members dress in holiday clothing and bring special food dishes and flowers to the graves of their loved ones. Candles are lit, and incense may be burned.

Mexican Americans believe they have a responsibility to all their past relatives. Therefore, they pray for the dead each day during the month of November.

On December 12, many Mexican Americans attend church services to honor Our Lady of Guadalupe, the patron saint of Mexico (*see* GUADALUPE, VIRGIN OF). The VIRGIN MARY is believed by some to have appeared to Juan DIEGO on this date in 1531, leaving a picture of herself imprinted on his cloak. This feast is widely celebrated in the Southwest.

Christmas Observances. The festival of Christmas begins in mid-December. Starting on December 16, groups of children take part each evening in Las Posadas ("the inns" or "the resting places"). The children go from house to house, reenacting the wanderings of Mary and Joseph searching for a place for the Christ child to be born. For nine nights, the children set out on their procession. They carry lanterns and a small platform bearing figures of Mary and Joseph. They knock on the doors of friends and neighbors, sing or recite poems, and ask to enter. Everyone then enjoys a fiesta.

A *posada* fiesta can include a PIÑATA, which is a clay pot or a bamboo frame covered with crepe paper. The center is filled with candies, fruits, small toys, and sometimes coins. The piñata can be hung from a tree limb and raised or lowered by a rope. Children take turns being blindfolded and poking at the piñata with a long stick. When someone breaks it, the treats inside tumble to the ground for all to share. Piñatas are especially popular at birthday parties.

The last night of the *posada* is December 24, or Christmas Eve. By then, most Mexican American families have set up a *nacimiento*, or manger, in their homes. The NACIMIENTO is usually made of straw and is filled with figures of Mary and Joseph, shepherds, and farm animals. On Christmas morning, the tiny figure of the infant Jesus is laid in its cradle.

Some families have a big dinner on the afternoon of Christmas day, but most celebrate earlier with a meal on Christmas Eve, or Noche Buena. If the meal is eaten before midnight, it often does not contain meat. Food served may include TAMALES (bundles of corn meal wrapped in corn husks and filled with fruit, pork, chicken, or beef), BUÑUELOS (fried fritters sprinkled with cinnamon), and hot chocolate. On Noche Buena, many families go to church for midnight Mass, after which they return home to eat a festive meal. Many Mexican Americans spend Christmas Day visiting friends and relatives and exchanging gifts.

—*María L. Alonzo*

SUGGESTED READINGS: • Behrens, June. *Fiesta!: Cinco de Mayo.* Chicago: Children's Press, 1978. • Cohen, Hennig, and Tristram Potter Coffin, eds. *The*

Las Posadas observances include a procession, often followed by a party and religious services. (Robert Fried)

Folklore of American Holidays. 2d ed. Detroit: Gale Research, 1991. • Graham, Joe S., comp. *Hispanic-American Material Culture: An Annotated Directory of Collections, Sites, Archives, and Festivals in the United States*. New York: Greenwood Press, 1989. • Harper, Howard V. *Days and Customs of All Faiths*. New York: Fleet, 1957. • MacDonald, Margaret Read, ed. *The Folklore of World Holidays*. Detroit: Gale Research, 1992. • Perl, Lila. *Piñatas and Paper Flowers: Holidays of the Americas*. New York: Clarion Books, 1983.

Holidays and festivals, Puerto Rican: Festivals are an important medium for cultural groups to express their identity. Foodways, costume, music, and the arts frequently are parts of festivals. These expressions of cultural identity are also present in holidays and rituals. From an anthropological perspective, festivals are cultural texts that provide the participants with an opportunity to reflect upon and find meaning in their lives as well as to find and express support and unity.

For Puerto Ricans, religion is an important element in the context of many festivities, holidays, and rituals. Other cultural traits and traditions may decline in importance; it is through religion that most of the cultural traits of Puerto Ricans are maintained. The influence of religion in many festivities is typical of Latino cultures.

Festivals in the United States. The largest Latino festival in the United States is CALLE OCHO OPEN HOUSE—CARNAVAL MIAMI, held in Miami, Florida, during the second week of March. The event, begun in 1977, takes place on South West Eighth Street. By the early 1990's, an estimated 1.5 million people attended the annual festivities. About two-thirds of those in attendance were Latinos. Activities in this event include music, arts and crafts, folk dance, games, costumes, and a parade.

The Desfile Puertorriqueño (Puerto Rican Parade) held in New York City each year is surrounded by a festival atmosphere. The mayor of the city, a representative of the government of Puerto Rico, and other

A float in the third annual Puerto Rican Parade, held in 1960. (AP/Wide World Photos)

Three Kings Day celebrations often include a parade. (Frances M. Roberts)

political figures lead the parade. The parade begins at noon on Fifth Avenue and Forty-fourth Street and ends four hours later on Ninetieth Street. Latino businesses sponsor their floats with musicians, advertising, and women who dance to the music of the parade. The event is covered by the Spanish television networks of the area.

Other Puerto Rican festivals held in the United States include the Fiestas Patronales Puertorriqueñas (Puerto Rican Patron Saint Festivities) in Humboldt Park, Chicago, Illinois, during the second week of June; the Puerto Rican Festival in Phoenix Plaza in Pontiac, Michigan, during the last weekend of July; the Folklore Fiesta in Central Park, New York City, in late August; and the Harrisburg Hispanic Folk Festival held in April at the Rose Lehrman Arts Center in Harrisburg, Pennsylvania. The Harrisburg festival also includes Latino cinema. Festival del Barrio (Neighborhood Festival) is held in the 2700 block of North Fifth Street in Philadelphia, Pennsylvania, in late August. Philadelphia also hosts the Puerto Rican Week Festival, in late September. Puerto Rican Heritage Week is celebrated during the last week of September at Roger Williams Park in Providence, Rhode Island.

Religion and Puerto Rican Celebrations. During the Spanish colonization of Puerto Rico, elements present in public celebration or festivals included illumination, fireworks, military music, popular music, religious music, dance, and games. One Puerto Rican celebration that combines elements of a holiday with elements of a festival is the day of Saint John the Baptist. At Newport Beach Resort in Sunny Isles, Florida, the celebration includes music, foodways, folk arts, folk crafts, folk dance, and folk costumes. It is important that the celebration take place close to the sea, because at midnight on Saint John's Day people enter the water as a symbolic baptism. The belief is that through this ritual a person will be spiritually renewed.

Puerto Rico has numerous celebrations with significant influence from religion. The celebrations are associated with Catholic symbolism and patron saints. These celebrations include, among others, those honoring the Three Kings (January 6), the Sacred Family (January 9), Saint Anthony Abad (January 17), Saint Sebastian (January 20), the Virgin of Candelaria (February 2), Saint Patrick (March 17), Saint Joseph (March 19), Saint Peter (May 1), the Holy Cross (May 3), Saint Anthony of Padua (June 13), Saint Peter (June 30), Saint Lawrence (August 10), Our Lady of Monserratt (September 8), Saint Michael (September 29), Saint Francis (October 4), Our Lady of the Rosary (October 7), Saint Raphael (October 24), and Our Lady of Guadalupe (December 12).

The Christmas celebration is probably the most important among Puerto Ricans. In Puerto Rico, Christmas celebration ends on January 8 as a result of the influence of Roman Catholic views of this historical event. Noche Buena (Christmas Eve) is characterized by family gatherings and a traditional meal that includes rice, beans, pork, and a meat pie called PASTELES. Mass is held on Christmas Eve. Parents in Puerto Rico commonly give their children gifts on the day of Los TRES REYES MAGOS (Three Kings Day), January 6. Most Puerto Ricans in the United States, however, have adopted Christmas Day for the presentation of gifts.

Christmas carols called *parrandas navideñas* are also typical of the Puerto Rican culture. The PARRANDAS ritual usually involves people visiting friends' homes and singing Christmas carols. The group of singers and musicians continues visiting friends until the late hours of the night or even until the next day. Puerto Ricans in the United States have adapted this tradition by having a gathering at a house to sing carols, dance, and play instruments. The festivities are confined to a single location rather than traveling from home to home. Regardless of the adaptations, Christmas for Puerto Ricans in the United States remains an important occasion for expression of cultural identity.

—*Carlos I. Ramos*

SUGGESTED READINGS: • Babin, Maria Teresa. *La Cultura de Puerto Rico*. San Juan: Instituto de Cultura Puertorriquena, 1973. • Graham, Joe, comp. *Hispanic-American Material Culture: An Annotated Directory of Collections, Sites, Archives, and Festivals in the United States*. New York: Greenwood Press, 1989. • Ibrahim, Hilmi. *Leisure and Society: A Comparative Approach*. Dubuque, Iowa: W. C. Brown, 1991. • Lopez Cantos, Angel. *Fiestas y Juegos en Puerto Rico: Siglo 18*. San Juan: Centro de Estudios Avanzados de Puerto Rico y el Caribe, 1990. •Taylor, Dorceta. *Identity in Ethnic Leisure Pursuits*. San Francisco: Mellen Research University Press, 1992. •Turner, Victor. "Variations on a Theme of Liminality." In *Secular Ritual*, edited by Sally F. Moore and Barbara G. Myerhoff. Assen, The Netherlands: Van Gorcum, 1977.

Homar, Lorenzo (b. Sept. 10, 1913, Puerta de Tierra, Puerto Rico): Artist. Homar traveled to New York, New York, in 1928. He studied at the Pratt Graphics Center (1940-1942) and the Brooklyn Museum Art School (1946-1950). He received practical training at Cartier, where he designed jewelry from 1938 to 1950. Homar returned to Puerto Rico in 1950.

Homar is best known for the silkscreen posters produced at the height of his career, in the 1960's. He had given up painting around 1960 to concentrate on printmaking, though he continued to make caricatures of political personalities along with his political posters.

Homar also exhibited a strong interest in typography. Text was often an important component of his posters. He also designed such items as books, record jackets, and Christmas cards. During the 1960's, he became involved in stage design, working for the San Juan Ballet and other groups.

Homar was director of the Division of Community Education's print workshop from 1950 to 1956, when he was asked to organize the Graphic Arts Workshop of the Institute of Puerto Rican Culture, created in 1955. The institute was controversial because it espoused retention of Puerto Rican culture rather than assimilation into U.S. culture. Homar remained director of the Graphic Arts Workshop until 1972, when he became an instructor in the School of Plastic Arts run by the institute.

Homestead Act (1862): By this act, the U.S. government released public lands eight times the size of Kansas to those who agreed to improve them. Although the federal government did not offer free land to potential settlers until 1862, agitation for such land distribution had been afoot through the first half of the nineteenth century. Farmers argued that when they cultivated barren, sometimes arid land, they increased its value, so should reap the benefits of that increase.

With westward expansion, given the vast tracts of open land in the West and Southwest, a considerable amount of land was brought under cultivation. Much of it sold for about two dollars an acre, but by 1820, the price had declined from that high to about 40 percent less. By mid-century, unsold undeveloped land could sometimes be bought for ten to fifteen cents an acre.

The Republican Party favored offering free land to those who would develop it. New York's most powerful newspaper at mid-century, the *Tribune*, agitated for such distribution. A bill aimed at offering government lands passed the House of Representatives and the Senate in 1860, but President James Buchanan, pressured by Southerners who feared that the opening of new lands would disturb the balance between slave states and the free states in the northern part of the Mississippi Valley, vetoed the bill.

With the secession of the southern states in 1860 and the onset of the Civil War, the Confederacy and its individual states confiscated large amounts of federal land. This fact and the completion of the transcontinental railroad shortly thereafter relieved Congress and President Abraham Lincoln of the pressures that had influenced Buchanan. The Homestead Act, enacted by duly elected representatives of the free states, was passed in 1862. Lincoln signed it into law.

Under the Homestead Act of 1862, any citizen twenty-one years old or older or any person of like age anticipating citizenship was eligible to receive a quarter section—640 acres or 65 hectares—of land. Much of this land had been taken from Native Americans throughout the less developed regions of the United States, including Mexican Americans who lived in the areas ceded to the United States in the TREATY OF GUADALUPE HIDALGO (1848). No limit was placed on the amount of federal land the government could distribute. The only stipulation was that, beginning on January 1, 1863, the recipients had to improve and live on the land for five years, after which they received a clear title.

The Homestead Act of 1862 is largely responsible for the settlement of the rural West and Southwest. Many foreigners, including Latinos from Central and South America, applied for United States citizenship so that they could take advantage of the Homestead Act. By 1967, 2,992,058 people had staked claims, and more than half that number—1,623,691—had met all the stipulations required to receive titles. Nothing previous in the nation's history had created so many independent farms.

Honduran Americans: The second largest of the Central American countries (43,277 square miles), Honduras is located between Nicaragua to the south and Guatemala and El Salvador to the west. It had an estimated population of 4,949,000 in 1991, with most people living in the interior west and along part of the Caribbean coast. Predominantly MESTIZO, the population also includes several small indigenous groups.

Before 900 C.E., western Honduras formed part of the area of Classic-era MAYAN CIVILIZATION. Honduras was visited by Christopher Columbus in 1502 and by Hernán CORTÉS in the 1520's. Independence from Spain was declared on September 15, 1821. Honduras played a major role in the short-lived Federation of Central America. After 1850, Honduras gained control of both the Bay Islands, off the northern coast, and Mosquitia, the eastern quarter of the present country. During the Ronald Reagan and George Bush administrations, Honduras played a major role in supporting U.S. aid to the Nicaraguan Contras.

Hondurans have maintained ties with New Orleans since the late nineteenth century, but significant numbers of Hondurans did not immigrate to the United States until after 1950. The presence of foreign banana companies and their fleets of ships on the Caribbean coast facilitated this migration. In the late twentieth century, most Honduran emigrants continued to come from the coastal towns and cities of the country rather than the interior, but migration from the interior was increasing.

According to the 1990 census data, 131,066 people of Honduran descent lived in the United States. Estimates by Honduran Americans themselves suggest that their population approached 200,000 by early 1994. The largest concentration is in New Orleans, followed by New York City, Los Angeles, and Chicago. Honduran migration to Canada has been negligible.

Although a number of social organizations exist, Honduran Americans see themselves as less well organized than the Guatemalan and Salvadoran groups in the United States. An exception to this pattern are the GARIFUNA (also called Garinagu or Black Caribs), an ethnic minority descended from Arawak Indians and escaped slaves. In Chicago, Hondurans form part of the Central American Civic Society. Most communities have some religious activity associated with the

A participant in an Amnesty International project holds a Honduran refugee child. (Impact Visuals, Rick Reinhard)

STATISTICAL PROFILE OF HONDURAN AMERICANS, 1990

Total population based on sample: 131,066

Percentage foreign-born: 77%

Median age: 27.5 years

Percentage 25+ years old with at least a high school diploma or equivalent: 50%

Occupation (employed persons 16+ years old)

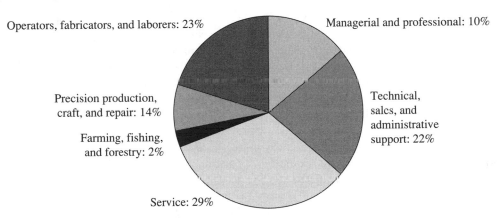

Operators, fabricators, and laborers: 23%

Managerial and professional: 10%

Precision production, craft, and repair: 14%

Farming, fishing, and forestry: 2%

Technical, sales, and administrative support: 22%

Service: 29%

Percentage unemployed: 12.2%

Median household income, 1989: $22,109

Percentage of families in poverty, 1989: 25.5%

Source: Data are from Bureau of the Census, *Census of 1990: Persons of Hispanic Origin in the United States* (Washington, D.C.: Bureau of the Census, 1993), Tables 1, 3, 4, and 5.

Virgin of Suyapa, the patron saint of Honduras. Honduran Americans return often to Honduras, particularly for Independence Day celebrations in September, as well as at Christmas and at Easter.

Horchata: Cool drink made from powdered rice, water, and flavorings. *Horchata* has its origins in Spain, where it was made from ground rice, ground almonds, and sugar, stirred into water. This kind of *horchata* still is popular, but other versions replace the rice with corn, add cinnamon, replace the almonds with melon seeds, or add fruit juices. *Horchata* is always milky and sweetened, and it is widely consumed in Mexico and parts of Central America. *Horchata* mixes can be purchased for convenient home preparation.

Hostos y Bonilla, Eugenio María de (Jan. 11, 1839, Rio Cañas, Mayagüez, Puerto Rico—Aug. 11, 1903,

Santo Domingo, Dominican Republic): Writer. Hostos received his education in Spain, earning a degree from the Central University of Madrid Law School about 1860. He was active in Spanish politics when, in 1869, he immigrated to the United States and supported Cuban activists in New York City. He traveled to South America to promote the cause; while there, he taught at the University of Santiago, Chile, before returning to New York.

During the 1880's, Hostos founded and served as dean of the Santo Domingo Normal School and was inspector general of public instruction. Later, he was headmaster of a Chilean secondary school and for about eight years taught constitutional law at the University of Chile. He wrote on various topics; many of his writings, however, remained untranslated until *Obras Completas* (1939; *The Complete Works of Eugenio María de Hostos*, 1979) was published. His criticism of William Shakespeare's *Hamlet, Prince of*

Denmark (pb. 1603) remains the leading Spanish-language study of that work.

Houston, Texas: Fourth largest city in the United States. Houston is the largest city in Texas, with a population of 1,630,553 according to the 1990 census. The consolidated metropolitan statistical area, a wider geographic area containing suburbs, was estimated to have a population of 3.7 million people, of which 21 percent were Latinos.

The original town was planned in 1836 as a real estate venture by two brothers, A. C. and J. K. Allen. The Allens purchased several thousand acres of land near Harrisburg, a town that burned during the Texas war for independence. The new town was to be called Houston in honor of Sam Houston, the first president of the Republic of Texas. In 1837, the town was chosen as the capital of the republic.

When the capital was moved to Austin in 1839, Houston was a budding commercial center. Completion of rail connections in the 1840's and 1850's led to considerable growth. In 1914, the Houston ship channel was opened, allowing Houston to become a seaport city.

Following discovery of oil in the area, Houston became an industrial city with emphasis on petroleum refining, production of petrochemicals, and production of steel pipe and oil field machinery. Several petroleum corporations located their headquarters in Houston. During the oil boom of the 1970's, 70 percent of the jobs in the Houston area were dependent, directly or indirectly, on the oil and gas industries.

Rice University was established in 1891, and the University of Houston was founded in 1927. The city became known for its medical care, with specialties in many areas including the diagnosis and treatment of cancer. In 1961, the Lyndon B. Johnson Space Center of the National Aeronautics and Space Administration was completed.

In the early 1880's, Hispanic people began to move into Houston, but the greatest population increase came after the beginning of the Mexican Revolution in 1910. In 1911, the Catholic church sent Oblate priests to establish a parish, Our Lady of Guadalupe, to minister to the spiritual needs of the Mexican American community. In the 1920's, more Mexican Americans moved into Houston, and the parish had to expand. Two more Catholic churches, Immaculate Heart of Mary and Our Lady of Dolores, were built. The city developed a distinct Mexican American area.

As the Mexican American community continued to grow, church organizations, social clubs, dance groups, and theater troupes fostered Mexican traditions and festivals. The social, economic, and political issues faced by Mexican Americans brought about the formation of civic organizations, business associations, and political groups.

The Hispanic community, composing about 28 percent of Houston's population in 1990, is divergent and well established. The people are distributed throughout the city, with little segregation. Mexican Americans account for about 80 percent of the Hispanic population.

Latinos have been elected to office at many levels of government. The city has both Hispanic and Mexican American chambers of commerce that assist small businesses. The Spanish-speaking community is served by a variety of radio stations, television channels, and newspapers.

LATINO POPULATION OF HOUSTON, TEXAS, 1990

Total number of Latinos = 772,295; 21% of population

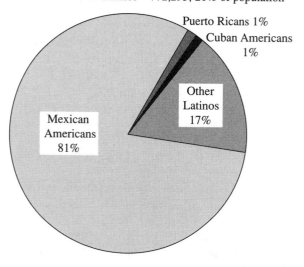

Source: Data are from Marlita A. Reddy, ed., *Statistical Record of Hispanic Americans* (Detroit: Gale Research, 1993), Table 110.

Note: Figures represent the population of the Houston-Galveston-Brazoria, Texas, Consolidated Metropolitan Statistical Area as delineated by the U.S. Bureau of the Census.

Huapango: Dance from Mexico. The *huapango* is called the dance of the platform because it is performed on rustic platforms. As is true for the JARABE TAPATÍO, the steps and accompaniment vary according to region. The *huapango* is sung exclusively by men, who alternate between normal voice and an artificial high pitch. Danced typically by six couples, using predominant foot movement and little facial expression, the dance can last twenty minutes. Male dancers take off their hats to initiate the dance. A man places his hat on another man's head when wishing to dance with that man's partner.

Huelga: Labor strike. *La huelga*, or the strike, represents one of the most common forms of protest for Latinos/Chicanos in the United States. Many Spanish-speaking people have used the strike not only to challenge unfair wages and dangerous working conditions but also to voice their discontent over issues of racial and ethnic discrimination. Latinos have contributed to a long and accomplished history of labor activism in the twentieth century (*see* LABOR UNIONISM). Significant leaders include Bert CORONA and Josefina Fierro de Bright of the Congress of Industrial Organizations, Luisa MORENO of the UNITED CANNERY, AGRICUL-

TURAL, PACKING AND ALLIED WORKERS OF AMERICA, and César CHÁVEZ of the UNITED FARM WORKERS.

Huerta, Dolores Fernández (b. 1930, Dawson, N.Mex.): Labor leader. Certainly the most prominent Mexican American woman in the struggle for farmworkers' rights, Huerta has been a vice president, lobbyist, and negotiator for the UNITED FARM WORKERS OF AMERICA (UFW). In the early 1950's she helped establish chapters of the COMMUNITY SERVICE ORGANIZATION. She met César CHÁVEZ in 1955 and began working with him and the union that became the UFW. Over the next four decades, she held several important and visible positions, gaining an international reputation as a powerful speaker and effective politician. In 1970, she helped the UFW negotiate contracts with grape and lettuce growers in California that resulted in substantial improvements in working conditions for migrant

Farmworkers' unions popularized the term huelga *during the 1960's.* (AP/Wide World Photos)

Dolores Huerta pictured at the end of the 1994 march by the United Farm Workers from Delano to Sacramento, California. (David Bacon)

workers. In 1988, she had six ribs broken and her spleen ruptured by police batons while protesting at a campaign rally in San Francisco. In 1993, she addressed the NATIONAL ASSOCIATION OF HISPANIC JOURNALISTS on unfair treatment of the UFW in the media.

Huerta, Jorge (b. Nov. 20, 1942, Los Angeles, Calif.): Director and writer. Huerta, a Mexican American, received his doctorate in dramatic literature and Chicano and U.S. Latino studies from the University of California, Santa Barbara, where he founded TEATRO DE LA

ESPERANZA during the early 1970's. He was the co-founder of Teatro Meta, the Hispanic theater and education wing at the Old Globe Theater in San Diego, and of Máscara Mágica, San Diego's first independent professional Latino theatrical company.

From 1989 to 1991, Huerta was director of the nation's first Hispanic American master of fine arts program, at the University of California, San Diego. The program's Teatro Ensemble de UCSD toured Chicano plays to Spain, France, and Germany during the summers and was the first Chicano troupe to perform in Barcelona and Madrid. Huerta has also directed at numerous regional theaters throughout California, the western United States, and New York.

Huerta is the author of *Chicano Theatre. Themes and Forms* (1982) and editor of *Necessary Theater: Six Plays About the Chicano Experience* (1990). In 1990, he was awarded a special citation by NOSOTROS for his contribution to Hispanic theater. In 1994, he was named first holder of the endowed Chancellor's Associate Chair III at the University of California, San Diego.

Huesero: Healer specializing in muscle problems and the setting of bones. Within the Mexican American community, *hueseros*, or bone setters, were healers specializing in setting bones and relieving muscle strains. Although few now exist, some of their practices were taken over by SOBADORES, or masseurs. *Sobadores* treat muscle soreness and strains by rubbing and manipulating the affected area. There are two kinds of treatments: *masajes*, or general body massages, and *sobaditas*, massages for the treatment of ankle sprains and leg cramps. *Sobadores* are a folk alternative to chiropractors.

Huevos rancheros: Mexican dish of fried eggs on tortillas, covered with a spicy tomato sauce. *Huevos rancheros*, or "ranch-style eggs," are a popular breakfast or luncheon dish, especially in northern Mexico and the adjacent United States. The dish consists of one or more fried eggs placed on an equal number of heated tortillas and covered with a spicy sauce, usually the local tomato-chile sauce. *Huevos rancheros* typically are accompanied by *FRIJOLES REFRITOS*.

Hypertension: Hypertension is a cardiovascular disease that, if left untreated, leads to stroke, kidney disease, diseases of the heart, and problems with coronary circulation.

Heart disease is the leading cause of death for all ethnic and racial groups in the United States. Heart disease manifests itself differently in different groups, and different groups exhibit different causes of death. Non-Hispanic whites are more likely to die of a heart attack than are Latinos and African Americans. Latinos and African Americans have higher incidences of mortality as a result of stroke, which is caused by hypertension.

Until recently, understanding of the role hypertension plays in the heart disease seen among Latinos was hampered by the paucity of research. Mortality statistics indicate that stroke is a leading cause of death among Latinos. There are only a few studies on Latinos and hypertension; most concern Mexican Americans. Only a few studies have focused on Puerto Ricans and Cuban Americans. These studies indicate that Latinos fall between non-Hispanic whites and African Americans in incidence of hypertension.

Several factors contribute to the incidence of hypertension among Latinos. The most common risk factors are obesity, DIABETES, and family history of myocardial infarction. Studies have demonstrated a high correlation between hypertension and socioeconomic factors. The rate of hypertension in Latinas was found in one study to decrease with an increase in socioeconomic status, but an increase in the socioeconomic status of Latino men did not reduce the rate of hypertension. Latinos have a higher incidence of obesity than does the U.S. population at large. Diet has also been associated with hypertension. The diet of Latinos tends to include more carbohydrates and fats than do the diets of other groups. Intake of carbohydrates and fats may also contribute to hypertension. Latinas diagnosed with hypertension were more likely to have it under control than were Latino males.

Latinos are at higher risk than the population as a whole for uncontrolled hypertension and stroke because they are often unaware that they have hypertension. Although Latinos lag behind non-Hispanic whites and blacks in the treatment and control of hypertension, studies indicate that Latinos can successfully control their blood pressure through compliance with a medication regimen. There is little information concerning how Latinos compare to others in responses to particular hypertension medication and other forms of treatment. Further study is needed to research all etiologic and environmental factors, psychosocial stresses, and cultural barriers that predispose people to the disease or affect the course it takes.

I

Iglesias, Julio (Julio José Iglesias de la Cueva; b. Sept. 23, 1943, Madrid, Spain): Singer and songwriter. Iglesias is the son of Julio Iglesias Puga, a gynecologist, and Maria del Rosario de la Cueva Perignat Iglesias. After he completed his secondary education, he began studying for a law degree. Iglesias also played soccer and was thought to be good enough to make it a career. A serious automobile accident in the summer of 1963 ended that possibility. During his convalescence, Iglesias occupied his time learning to play the guitar and listening to the radio. His decision to attempt a career in music surprised his parents.

Although he began to write songs in 1968, Iglesias continued his law studies out of respect for his father's wishes. His success with his songs convinced him to concentrate on his singing career. He became well known throughout Europe for his song "Guendoline" (1970). He traveled to Latin America to expand his popularity. By the early 1970's, Iglesias had become a top-selling recording artist in Europe, Latin America, Japan, and parts of the Middle East. His popular albums include *Como el Alamo al camino* (1972), *Soy* (1973), *El Amor* (1975), and *Emociónes* (1978). Iglesias specialized in singing elegant, romantic ballads. He received the first Diamond Disc Award in 1983 from the *Guinness Book of World Records* for being the world's best-selling recording artist, with more than one hundred million albums sold. In 1984, Iglesias released his first American-made, all English-language album, *1100 Bel Air Place*. He won a Grammy Award for Best Latin Popular Performance in 1987.

Illegal alien: Term used to refer to some noncitizens. The term is a misnomer for two reasons. First, a person, as an individual, cannot be deemed "illegal" under the U.S. Constitution. Second, under U.S. immigration law, only noncitizens who have failed to leave the United States after their cases have been fully adjudicated are legally considered to be in violation of the U.S. IMMIGRATION AND NATIONALITY ACT. Nevertheless, the term "illegal alien" has been accepted by the U.S. media and general public to identify undocumented immigrants, particularly those of Hispanic background.

Illegals, Los: Chicano new wave band. Los Illegals formed in the early 1980's. Members were lead singer, composer, and lyricist Willie Herron; Sandra Hahn, Bill Reyes, Manuel Valdez, and Jesus (Jesse) Velo. All are Chicano and grew up in East Los Angeles. Los Illegals brought a new style, new wave, to Chicano music, adding complex vocal rhythms and poetic, political lyrics. The band's songs were in English and Spanish. Themes included the struggles of undocumented workers, barrio slums, racism, and urban problems. The group recorded one album, *Internal Exile*, before disbanding in the mid-1980's.

Illegitimacy: Illegitimacy refers to a child born to an unwed mother. Some people have objected to calling any children "illegitimate," as that term questions the qualities of such children as people. A more accepted term is "children born out of wedlock."

Data compiled by the U.S. Bureau of the Census and other government statistics agencies reveal several trends. First, the percentages of births out of wedlock rose from 1985 to 1990 among black, white, and Hispanic mothers. The rates for out-of-wedlock births to Hispanic mothers were between those for black and white mothers. Among Latino groups, Cuban Americans had the lowest rate of out-of-wedlock births, nearly as low as for non-Hispanic whites.

The percentages of births that were out of wedlock were highest for younger mothers in all racial and ethnic categories. Data from 1985 for mothers under twenty years of age showed that of the births, 45.8 percent were out of wedlock for Mexican Americans. Corresponding figures were 73.9 percent for Puerto Ricans, 37.2 percent for Cuban Americans, and 59.1 percent for mothers of South American origin. In comparison, the rates were 90.2 percent for African Americans and 42.5 percent for whites. For mothers age twenty and older, percentages of births out of wedlock were approximately half those of younger mothers. The exception was for white mothers, for whom the proportion fell from 42.5 percent for young mothers to 8.9 percent for mothers age twenty and older.

Marriage behavior affects types of family groupings. Premarital childbearing has contributed to the rise in the number of one-parent families, as have rising rates of divorce and separation.

Level of education appears to play an important causal role in out-of-wedlock births. Education affects income, and women with higher incomes tend to delay

Julio Iglesias in a 1990 performance at New York's Radio City Music Hall. (AP/Wide World Photos)

childbearing. This delay makes it more likely that marriage will occur before a woman has her first child. Women who are committed to pursuing education are also more likely to take steps to prevent an out-of-wedlock birth from interfering with that education.

Illegitimacy also affects education. Teenage mothers have the highest rates of out-of-wedlock births. Young mothers, particularly from low-income families, find it difficult to re-enter school to complete their education. Unwed mothers also do not benefit from financial and childcare support from a spouse. (*See* PREGNANCY AND PRENATAL CARE.)

Illiteracy. *See* **Literacy and illiteracy**

Illness. *See* **Health and illness**

Immigration Act of 1917: This law imposed a literacy test on all would-be immigrants. The law also tightened restrictions on Asian immigration and refused admittance to certain political radicals.

The first two decades of the twentieth century saw a new social and political movement designed to limit immigration to the United States. The new science of genetics and the pseudoscience called eugenics encouraged many Americans to claim that the nation's genetic stock was being weakened by the introduction of "inferior" races and ethnic groups. U.S. labor unions joined the anti-immigrant crusade. Although many union members were first- or second-generation immigrants themselves, union leaders argued that unfair competition from immigrants lowered wages of American workers. Many social movements of this time were tied to restriction of immigration. Prohibitionists, for example, complained that urban immigrants in particular drank to excess, and the newly reborn Ku Klux Klan won millions of converts as it denounced immigrants, particularly Catholics and Jews.

One idea for limiting immigration was to require a literacy test of all would-be immigrants. Legislation imposing a literacy test met defeat several times, as members of Congress feared the wrath of their immigrant constituents. On three occasions the proposed literacy test passed Congress but met a presidential veto. Presidents William Howard Taft and Woodrow Wilson defended their vetoes by stressing the nation's need for labor, its willingness to educate immigrants, and the United States' traditional role as a haven for the world's oppressed. Southern and western members of Congress had few immigrant constituents and could push this legislation without fearing voter backlash.

Leadership from them resulted in passage of the Immigration Act of 1917, over President Wilson's veto.

The new law's most important provision was that each adult immigrant must be able to read in his or her native language. The law followed up earlier exclusion of Chinese immigrants by also excluding immigrants from most other Asian nations, with Japan as an exception. Finally, the law excluded political radicals who advocated revolution and stated that immigrants faced immediate deportation if they advocated revolution after arriving in the United States.

The Immigration Act of 1917 was of limited impact. The literacy test was abandoned in the 1920's. Two new laws, featuring immigration quota systems, won congressional approval in 1921 and 1924. These laws were much more effective in limiting immigration than was the act of 1917. As the first of three major restrictive laws, the Immigration Act of 1917 is important as a stepping-stone to more draconian legislation.

Immigration Act of 1924: One of several stringent pieces of immigration legislation from the post-World War I period, this law set an immigration quota for each nationality. Quotas were based on the number of persons living in the United States whose ancestors came from that nation. The effect of this statute was to favor immigrants from Northern and Western Europe over those from other areas.

This law was the last and most stringent in a series of restrictive laws Congress passed in the first half of the twentieth century. Earlier legislation had included the imposition of a literacy test on would-be immigrants through the IMMIGRATION ACT OF 1917 and the erection of a quota system based on national origins (1921). The Immigration Act of 1921 had called for a quota for each nationality equal to 3 percent of the persons of that nationality already in the United States, as reported in the 1910 census.

By 1924, nativist sentiment in the United States had reached an all-time high. Pressures for additional restrictions on immigration came from those who feared leftist political groups (which often had blocs of immigrant members), from prohibition groups (which believed that urban immigrants drank excessively), and from the Ku Klux Klan (a powerful organization that exhibited hatred for most immigrants, particularly Catholics and Jews). The goal of those who framed the Immigration Act of 1924 was to further limit the numbers of immigrants coming to the United States, particularly the so-called "new immigrants" coming from

Southern and Eastern European nations such as Italy, Greece, Poland, and Russia.

The 1924 act featured two quota systems, one of which was to go into effect immediately, the other by 1927. The first system set the quota for each nation at 2 percent of the total number of persons of that nationality living in the United States reported by the 1890 census. Members of Congress recognized that fewer immigrants from Southern and Eastern Europe were in the United States in 1890 compared with later years, so one effect of the Immigration Act of 1924 would be to favor the "old immigrant" groups over the "new immigrants." A second system, to be phased in more gradually, would allow a total of 150,000 immigrants annually, the quotas for each nation to be based on the "national origins" of all 1920 U.S. residents (stretching back many generations).

Under the new quota systems, the United States favored immigration from Northern and Western Europe while discouraging immigration from South-

ern and Eastern Europe. Under the national origins system, British immigrants would receive nearly half of all available immigration slots. For Mexican citizens interested in immigrating to the United States, the good news was that residents of the Western Hemisphere were exempt from the 1924 statute. The bad news was that a movement to set a quota upon Mexican immigrants began almost immediately.

Fearing a diplomatic incident with Mexico that would undoubtedly follow any such legislation, the State Department quietly began rejecting would-be immigrants from Mexico under existing laws that (for example) prohibited the immigration of persons likely to become "public charges." Later, the immigration of Mexicans to the United States fluctuated widely, depending upon the need for labor in the Southwest.

Immigration Act of 1990: Legislative reform that permitted the immigration of immediate relatives of U.S. citizens without any numerical limits. This act did es-

President George Bush hands a pen to Attorney General Dick Thornburgh after signing the Immigration Act of 1990. (AP/Wide World Photos)

tablish an annual cap on total worldwide immigration to the United States at 700,000 for the fiscal years 1992 through 1994 and at 675,000 for fiscal year 1995. Immigrant visas were to be allocated based on family relationships, employment qualifications, and a consideration of cultural diversity instead of the old seven-category system. The per country annual immigrant allowance was increased to 25,000.

Immigration and Nationality Act of 1952 (McCarran-Walter Act): The first major immigration legislation in three decades, this law retained the earlier quota system based on national origins. It did, however, give preferential treatment to certain would-be immigrants, including relatives of persons already in the United States and certain types of skilled workers. The law also provided for exclusion of certain groups, including political radicals, homosexuals, and those with a criminal past.

In the years immediately surrounding World War I, Congress passed a series of three major laws regulating immigration: the IMMIGRATION ACT OF 1917, the Immigration Act of 1921, and the IMMIGRATION ACT OF 1924. The effect of these laws was to reduce overall immigration and to favor immigrants from Northern and Western Europe over arrivals from other regions. In the 1930's and 1940's, however, public opinion began to retreat from support of this restrictive immigration policy.

Intellectual currents moved away from strict genetic determinism and eugenics, stressing instead the belief that environment was crucial in fostering human achievement. Adolf Hitler provided a telling example of the evils that could result from believing one race or ethnic group to be genetically superior to others. As the decades passed, early immigrants became increasingly assimilated, adopting much of the mainstream culture and often moving into the middle and upper-middle classes. As assimilation progressed, fear of various ethnic groups subsided and support for highly restrictive immigration legislation began to wane. Meanwhile, the second-generation immigrants themselves began to call for repeal of the most restrictive laws, and many other Americans supported their efforts.

The advent of the Cold War complicated the climate of public opinion. On one hand, many leaders called for a liberal immigration policy to handle refugees from communism, especially from the nations of Eastern Europe. At the same time, Cold War sentiment led to calls for caution in admitting immigrants so as not to admit persons sympathetic to socialism or communism. These dual concerns influenced Congress as it passed the Immigration and Nationality Act of 1952, commonly called the McCarran-Walter Act.

The 1952 law retained the quota system based on national origins that had been instituted by the Immigration Act of 1924. The new act, however, added several preferential categories of would-be immigrants, including relatives of persons who had already immigrated and certain categories of skilled laborers. The McCarran-Walter Act eliminated earlier blanket restrictions prohibiting immigration from China and other Asian nations. The law also provided a new list of reasons for exclusion of immigrants, including support of radical political beliefs, homosexuality, a criminal past, or narcotics addiction. Finally, the law incorporated several provisions of the Internal Security Act of 1950, making membership in the Communist Party or any totalitarian group cause for exclusion or deportation. All aliens were required to report their addresses to the federal government each year.

The McCarran-Walter Act, passed over the veto of President Harry S Truman, blunted efforts to liberalize the nation's immigration laws. The law's impact upon Latinos was somewhat muted because, like the IMMIGRATION ACT OF 1924, the new law kept the Western Hemisphere out of the quota system. New legislation, beginning in 1965, finally dismantled the system of giving each nation a quota, thus eliminating the appearance of favoring certain races and ethnic groups over others.

Immigration and Nationality Act of 1965: Legislation that abolished the discriminatory immigration quotas based on national origins that had been in effect up to that time. The new system was based on family preference, a system that gave priority to persons with family members in the United States. Total figures of new immigrants to be allowed entry to the United States were established for the Eastern and Western hemispheres, but individuals who had close relatives already living in the United States were exempt from being counted in these immigration targets. Refugees were also given preference in consideration for legal immigrant status.

The largest refugee group at the time of the act's passage came from Cuba and consisted primarily of middle-class families and well-educated individuals who had fled their country in the wake of Fidel Castro's rise to power. The largest immigrant group continued to come from Mexico, which sent more than

President Lyndon B. Johnson signed the Immigration and Nationality Act of 1965 into law at a ceremony on Liberty Island. (LBJ Library)

sixty thousand people per year during the 1970's. The elimination of the BRACERO PROGRAM in 1964 led to an unprecedented rise in unauthorized workers migrating to the United States for employment. Legal Mexican immigration totaled almost 38,000 persons in 1965 but increased to more than 92,000 in 1978.

Immigration and Naturalization Service (INS): Since its founding in 1891, the INS has enforced U.S. laws concerning immigration. On several occasions, it has engaged in anti-Latino practices and illegally expelled Latinos.

Congress created the INS to enforce laws concerning migration into the United States. In 1924, it created the Border Patrol as the INS's enforcement arm. Although the Immigration Act of that year placed a quota on European and Asian peoples, efforts to impose a quota on Latinos failed. Agricultural interests and railroads concerned with access to cheap labor successfully fought restrictions on immigration from south of the border. That immigration was affected most by a $10 visa fee, collected by the INS, for Latinos crossing into the United States. Until the 1930's, illegal entrance into the country resulted in only a minor fine and no expulsion.

During the Great Depression, when jobs became scarce, INS agents responded with more vigor to demands from state governors, particularly in Texas and California, to expel undocumented workers. Between 1931 and 1940, more than 250,000 Latinos were repatriated (*see* DEPORTATIONS, EXPATRIATIONS, AND REPATRIATIONS).

Border Patrol officers showed little respect for the constitutional rights of those they arrested. Frequently, deportations took place without any judicial proceedings or legal hearings for the deportees. In some cases, men, women, and children, were loaded onto trains and shipped south of the Rio Grande solely on the basis of their Mexican or Hispanic appearance. By 1941, perhaps half of the Latino population of midwestern states such as Michigan, Illinois, and Indiana had been returned to the Mexican border.

World War II changed INS policy again. Labor shortages developed, often in the same areas of the country from which Latinos recently had been removed. In 1943, Congress established a Bracero (hired hand) Program to bring workers back into the country. Under the Bracero Program, INS agents issued work

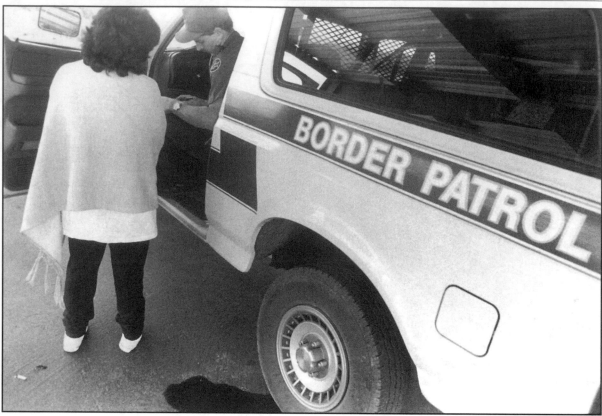

Border Patrol agents watch for people entering the United States without proper authorization. (Impact Visuals, Jeffrey D. Scott)

permits, good for one year, to Latinos available for labor in agriculture (primarily in the cotton and vegetable fields of the Southwest) and on railroads. The Mexican government pressed for and won Congressional support for minimum wages and improved working conditions for the braceros. The program lasted until 1964, with an average of 400,000 workers per year entering the United States under its provisions. Pressure from American growers kept the INS from stopping thousands of undocumented workers, not covered by minimum wage agreements, from entering the country at the same time.

Pressure from labor unions and fear of "radicals" led to the infamous OPERATION WETBACK in 1954. Border Patrol and INS agents arrested more than one million Latinos during this drive and violated the civil and human rights of thousands of arrested people. Many of those arrested had been in the United States for ten years or more but still were sent to the border without formal hearings. Only after loud protests by Mexican Americans and the beginning of court-ordered judicial proceedings did the INS end Operation Wetback.

In 1964, immigrants from the Western Hemisphere were included in an immigration ceiling. In the 1970's, Congress imposed a limit of twenty thousand per country on persons who could enter the United States as legal resident aliens.

INS efforts to control the southern border increased dramatically during the 1980's, under growing pressure from anti-immigrant voices in Congress and the nation. When the unemployment rate reached 10 percent in 1982, the INS announced Operation Jobs, which sought to "save jobs for Americans" by expelling undocumented workers. Roving bands of INS raiders arrested thousands of Latinos, but these sweeps had little impact on employment. Thousands more workers came in while the INS deported only hundreds. Still, the raids distressed the Latino community, because people were apprehended because of how they looked rather than who they were. The IMMIGRATION REFORM AND CONTROL ACT OF 1986 did little to reduce the influx of undocumented workers. The Border Patrol, in the early 1990's, reported apprehending more than 1,130,000 persons per year trying to enter the United States illegally.

Immigration legislation, U.S.: U.S. immigration laws have affected Latinos and their immigration throughout U.S. history. Although the U.S. Constitution empowered Congress in Article I, Section 7, "to establish an uniform Rule of Naturalization," it provided no other guidance, thereby resulting in more than two hundred years of experimentation.

Early Laws. The first Congress in 1790 passed a naturalization statute providing that free white persons who had been in the United States for two years could be naturalized in any American court. In 1798, the Alien Act required immigrants to reside in the United States for fourteen years before becoming eligible for citizenship. The Naturalization Act of 1801 changed the period of residency in the United States to five years.

During the Civil War, in response to the North's need for troops, an act was passed in 1864 to encourage immigration. A commissioner of immigration with a four-year term was appointed, subject to the direction of the secretary of state. This commissioner established regulations requiring immigrants to pledge their wages after admission for a period not to exceed twelve months, in order to repay the expenses of their emigration. It also provided that no immigrant would be compelled to enter military service during the war unless such person voluntarily renounced allegiance to the country of birth and indicated intent to become a U.S. citizen. A United States Immigrant Office was established under the direction of the commissioner of immigration. In 1868, the entire law of 1864 was repealed, leaving immigration regulation to the states.

Federal Control. On March 20, 1876, the United States Supreme Court decided in *Chy Lung v. Freeman* that the power to regulate immigration belongs to the national government and not to the states. Soon after that, the federal government passed laws requiring each immigrant to pay a duty of fifty cents and moving supervision of immigration from the secretary of state to the secretary of the Treasury. Foreign convicts, except those convicted of political offenses, were barred from entry. Contract laborers were barred as of 1885, and in 1888, the secretary of the Treasury was given authority to deport, within one year from arrival, any alien who had come to the United States in violation of this contract labor law. As of 1891, idiots, insane persons, paupers or persons likely to become public charges, persons suffering from a loathsome disease, polygamists, and persons encouraged to emigrate in promise of employment were all barred from entry. An Office of Superintendent of Immigration was established under the Treasury Department.

The immigration law of 1891, more comprehensive than any previous immigration law, required the inspection of immigrants and medical examinations by the Marine Hospital Service as well as prescribing rules for inspection of aliens along the borders of Mexico and Canada. Any alien who entered the United States in violation of the law or became a public charge within one year after arrival was to be deported. Any alien who was barred from entry had to be sent back at the expense of the person providing transportation to the U.S. border. In 1892, the federal government opened up Ellis Island in New York harbor as the

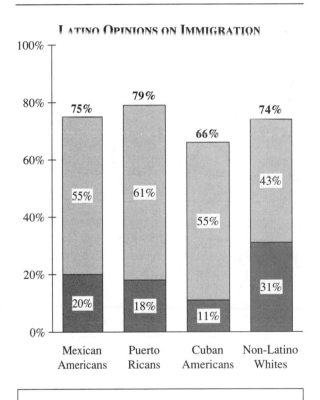

LATINO OPINIONS ON IMMIGRATION

"There are too many immigrants coming to this country."

■ Strongly Agree   ▨ Agree

Source: Data are from the Latino National Political Survey, which polled a representative sample of 1,546 Mexican Americans, 589 Puerto Ricans, and 682 Cuban Americans in forty metropolitan areas in 1989-1990. See Rodolfo O. de la Garza et al., *Latino Voices: Mexican, Puerto Rican, and Cuban Perspectives on American Politics* (Boulder, Colo.: Westview Press, 1992), Table 7.24.

Note: Respondents were asked their opinion on the statement "There are too many immigrants coming to this country." Response choices were Strongly Agree, Agree, Disagree, and Strongly Disagree.

The Statue of Liberty provided the backdrop for President Lyndon B. Johnson's signing of the Immigration and Nationality Act of 1965. (LBJ Library)

official debarkation point for immigrants into the United States. The Ellis Island reception center remained in use until 1932.

In 1897, Congress passed legislation requiring a literacy test, but President Grover Cleveland vetoed the law. Literacy tests introduced in 1913 and 1915 were vetoed by presidents William Howard Taft and Woodrow Wilson, respectively, but Wilson's veto was overridden.

Immigration Taxes. The law of 1903 was another comprehensive act, requiring the establishment of an Immigrant Fund to defray the expense of regulating immigration of aliens into the United States and levying a two dollar head tax. Upon arrival of a ship, the captain had to submit to the immigration officers at the port of arrival a list of all alien passengers that showed, for each, full name, age, sex, marital status, occupation, literacy, nationality, race, last residence, final destination, and whether the person was in possession of fifty dollars. The following year, that law was amended to exempt from the head tax all immigrants who arrived in the United States from Canada, Newfoundland, Cuba, and Mexico. The Bureau of Immi-

gration and Naturalization, established in 1906 under control of the secretary of commerce and labor, was put in charge of all matters concerning naturalization of aliens.

On February 20, 1907, another far-reaching law embodying the previous restrictions was passed. It provided for a tax of four dollars for each immigrant except those who entered from Canada, Newfoundland, Cuba, and Mexico.

In 1918, provisions relating to the literacy test, contract labor, and the head tax were suspended in order to admit unskilled laborers from Canada, Mexico, and the West Indies. That same year, a law was passed to exclude and expel aliens who were members of anarchist groups who either believed in or advocated the overthrow of the government of the United States by force or violence. The American Federation of Labor in 1919 sought to suspend immigration for four years, but the bill did not pass.

Quota Laws. On May 19, 1921, the first quota law was passed, the Immigration Act of 1921. It based quotas on data from the 1910 census identifying U.S. residents by country of descent. The law limited annual immigration of people from each country to 3 percent of the U.S. residents in 1910 identified as having roots in that country. The maximum quota was set at 357,000. Exceptions were made for immigrants from Canada, Newfoundland, Cuba, Mexico, and the countries of Central America and South America. Amended in May, 1922, the law provided that immigrants from Canada, Newfoundland, Cuba, Mexico, and Central and South America had to have resided in those areas for at least five years immediately preceding the time of their application for admission into the United States. The IMMIGRATION ACT OF 1924 set up quotas for certain areas of the world, but once again the quota system did not apply to Canada or Latin America.

Wartime Changes. On May 22, 1940, effective July 1, 1940, all immigration and naturalization matters were transferred from the Department of Labor to the Department of Justice, and all functions and powers of the secretary of labor relating to the administration of the Immigration and Naturalization Service were assumed by the attorney general. The Displaced Persons Act, passed on June 25, 1948, permitted entry of 205,000 persons over a period of two years; the number was later increased to 341,000. The Internal Security Act of 1950 temporarily slowed the process of immigration by requiring greater care in the screening of aliens.

The IMMIGRATION AND NATIONALITY ACT OF 1952 (McCarran-Walter Act) was passed by the House on June 9 and by the Senate on June 11. President Harry S Truman vetoed the bill as discriminatory, but it was passed over his veto with an effective date of December 24, 1952.

Quota Reform. John F. Kennedy spoke about immigration reform, but little was done in this area prior to the administration of Lyndon B. Johnson. The IMMIGRATION AND NATIONALITY ACT OF 1965 retained most restrictions that Congress had established since the late nineteenth century, including the public charge clause, requirements of physical and mental health, and various ideological tests, but it eliminated the variable quota system by country. The law placed annual caps of 170,000 on persons from the Old World and 120,000 on persons from the New World, with no country of the Old World having more than 20,000 visas. In 1978, the 20,000 figure applied everywhere, but a global annual ceiling of 290,000 was established. The Refugee Act of March 8, 1980, addressed problems of refugees from Cuba, Central America, and Haiti; the 20,000 limit was much lower than some refugee flows.

The IMMIGRATION REFORM AND CONTROL ACT OF 1986, otherwise known as the Simpson-Mazzoli Act, attempted to stem the flow of illegal immigrants into the United States from Latin America. The law provided limited AMNESTY for illegal immigrants, required verification by employers that their employees had the right to work in the United States, established harsh sanctions on employers who hired illegal aliens, and allowed farmers to import foreign agricultural workers. The agricultural workers provision primarily affected farmers in Texas and California.

As of 1994, immigrants could be naturalized as U.S. citizens in five major ways: through a family petition, through an employment-based petition, as a refugee, through a political ASYLUM petition, or through special programs such as amnesty. Eighteen classes of nonimmigrants could enter the country via VISAS for temporary residence.

Mexican Immigration. When Mexico won its freedom from Spain in 1821, it owned the area west of the Mississippi River south of the Louisiana Purchase. Texas won its independence from Mexico in 1836 and was annexed as a state to the United States in 1845; California, Arizona, New Mexico, and the remaining area north of the Rio Grande were taken from Mexico by the TREATY OF GUADALUPE HIDALGO in 1848; and the Gila River area was purchased from Mexico's dictator Antonio López de Santa Anna in 1853. These changes meant that approximately 100,000 Americans of Mexican extraction lived in the United States as of that date, perhaps 60,000 of them in New Mexico. Mexicans frequently crossed the border to the United States in search of jobs.

Immigration legislation passed in 1917 forbade the entry of contract laborers, but labor shortages resulting from World War I prompted use of a clause regarding "otherwise inadmissible aliens" to allow farmworkers to enter. The depression of the 1930's swept Mexicans in the United States out of jobs, and general labor surpluses prompted a massive repatriation program (*see* DEPRESSION, GREAT; DEPORTATIONS, EXPATRIATIONS, AND REPATRIATIONS).

Labor surpluses turned to shortages during World War II. In response, the U.S. government instituted the BRACERO PROGRAM in 1942. By the program's end in 1964, 4.8 million Mexicans had entered the United States under its provisions. Another 5 million who had entered illegally during that period were arrested by the IMMIGRATION AND NATURALIZATION SERVICE (INS). Braceros were under contracts stipulating eventual return to Mexico.

IMPORTANT EVENTS IN U.S. IMMIGRATION HISTORY

1790   Naturalization Statute establishes two-year residency for naturalization

1798   Alien Act establishes fourteen-year residency for naturalization

1801   Naturalization Act changes residency for naturalization to five years

1819   The United States, as a result of the Adams-Onís Treaty, acquires Spanish Florida

1836   Texas declares independence from Mexico, bringing many Mexicans into Texas citizenship

1845   Texas admitted as a state into the United States

1848   Treaty of Guadalupe Hidalgo signed, transferring about half of Mexico's territory to the United States

1864   Immigration Act encourages immigration to meet the North's need for troops in the Civil War

1885   Contract Labor Law bars contract laborers from entry into United States

1888   Secretary of Treasury given power to deport aliens who violate the Contract Labor Law

1891   Immigration legislation bars from entry idiots, insane persons, persons suffering from a loathsome disease, polygamists, and persons encouraged to emigrate in promise of employment

1892   Ellis Island becomes the official debarkation point for immigrants

1897   Literacy test vetoed by President Grover Cleveland

1898   The Treaty of Paris transfers control of Cuba and Puerto Rico to the United States from Spain

1900   Foraker Act establishes civil government in Puerto Rico

1902   Cuba declares its independence from the United States

1915   Literacy test passed by Congress over Woodrow Wilson's veto

1917   Jones Act extends United States citizenship to all Puerto Ricans

1917   Selective Service Act obligates noncitizen Mexicans in the United States to register for the military draft

1921   Quota law does not refer to persons from Western Hemisphere

1925   Border Patrol established by Congress

1933   English no longer required to be the official language of Puerto Rico

1934   Platt Amendment annulled

1940   Fascists barred from entry by Smith Act

1940   Immigration and naturalization matters transferred from the Department of Labor to the Department of Justice

1942   Bracero Program established for agricultural workers in the United States

1950   Internal Security Act passed, largely aimed at communists and subversive organizations

1952   McCarran-Walter Immigration and Nationality Act passed

1953   Refugee Relief Act passed

1953   Puerto Rico becomes a self-governing commonwealth

1964   Bracero Program ends

1965   Immigration Act scraps the national origins quota system in favor of a cap of 170,000 persons from Old World countries and 120,000 persons from the Western Hemisphere

1965   Border Industrialization Program initiated

1966   Airlift begins of more than 250,000 Cubans to the United States

1980   Mariel boat lift brings approximately 125,000 Cuban refugees to the United States

1980   Refugee Act eliminates the definition of a refugee as someone fleeing communism, permitting thousands of Latin Americans to enter the United States as refugees

1986   Immigration Reform and Control Act attempts to restrict illegal immigration

1990   Immigration Act attempts to streamline the citizenship process

This group of Mexican Americans returned to Mexico from Salem, Illinois, in 1946 when the labor shortage turned into a surplus. (AP/Wide World Photos)

During the Depression, the INS had arrested and repatriated approximately twelve thousand illegal entrants per year. This rose to seventy thousand by 1945 and one million by 1954. That year, the INS instituted the Special Mobile Force Operation to round up illegal immigrants. Although the INS was successful for a time, job availability in the United States proved too great an attraction. By 1960, the flood of illegal immigration was renewed. In 1956, for example, 455,000 legal braceros picked crops, but there were thousands more jobs open to Mexicans. In 1965, for example, 105,000 illegal immigrants were arrested.

Under the driving force of Senator Sam Ervin (D-North Carolina), President Johnson signed the IMMI-GRATION AND NATIONALITY ACT OF 1965, legislation establishing an annual ceiling of 120,000 legal immigrants from the Western Hemisphere. That did not prevent illegal entry. In 1968, 212,000 illegal immigrants were caught, and it became apparent that differ-

ent methods were required to stem illegal immigration.

Addressing Illegal Immigration. Under President Gerald Ford, the Domestic Council Committee on Illegal Aliens was appointed to study the situation. It came to several conclusions, including the following. There was a population explosion in Mexico, and economic conditions meant that the larger population could not be absorbed into the labor market. The United States needed to enforce its immigration laws more strictly because it presented such an attractive target destination for poor people leaving Latin America. The committee recommended several policy changes, including amnesty for the illegal residents of the United States under certain limited conditions, sanctions for employers hiring illegal immigrants, stronger penalties for people who aided illegal immigration, swifter deportation techniques, larger immigration quotas, and extension of family preferences to immigrants from Latin America. Despite recommendations, legislation passed in 1976 still permitted only twenty thousand immigrants from each Latin American country, regardless of its size or population.

Under President Jimmy Carter, another task force recommended employer sanctions of $1,000 for each illegal worker hired, a strengthened border patrol, amnesty, increased legal limits on annual immigration from Canada and Mexico of 50,000 immigrants each, and some form of identity card.

The problem of illegal immigration became more acute with the flood of refugees in the 1980's from Cuba, El Salvador, Nicaragua, Haiti, and Brazil. By 1981, an estimated three million to six million people resided illegally in the United States. Half of them were Mexicans, of whom about 15 percent worked in agriculture, 50 percent in service industries, and 30 percent in blue collar jobs.

The IMMIGRATION REFORM AND CONTROL ACT OF 1986 was signed into law by President Ronald Reagan on November 11, 1986, after a bitter five-year fight in Congress. Aimed at curtailing illegal immigration, it imposed civil penalties on employers of $250 to $10,000 for each illegal worker hired, in addition to criminal penalties of up to six months in jail and/or a $3,000 fine, with harsher penalties for repeat offenders. Prospective employers were required to make prospective employees produce documentary evidence that they were entitled to be in the United States. Illegal residents present in the United States since January 1, 1982, were eligible for amnesty.

The flow of illegal immigration to the United States, primarily from Mexico, nevertheless continued into the 1990's. Of all the applicants for AMNESTY between 1986 and 1988, 68.9 percent were from Mexico. The United States was willing to make exceptions for persons with a reasonable fear of persecution, or REFUGEES, but not for those who sought entry for economic reasons. As a result of large flows of Mexican immigration over long spans of time, by the 1990 census 21.9 million Americans reported Mexican ancestry.

Cuban Immigration. Although Thomas Jefferson thought perhaps that Cuba would one day become part of the United States, the Teller Amendment to the 1898 declaration of war against Spain made it clear that Cuba was to become a free country, albeit a protectorate. When Fidel Castro came to power in 1959, however, his devotion to communism eliminated Cuba as a protectorate. In January, 1961, President Dwight D. Eisenhower broke off U.S. relations with Cuba.

Largely as a result of dissatisfaction with Cuba's form of communism and the economic conditions under Castro, more Cubans fled to the United States in the thirty years following Castro's takeover than in all previous history (*see* CUBAN IMMIGRATION). The U.S. Census of 1960 counted 80,000 Cuban émigrés and 40,000 second-generation Cubans living in the United States, most of them in southern Florida, with Miami as the Cuban American center. An agreement between Castro's government and the Johnson Administration in 1965 established an airlift between Cuba and Miami that took 250,000 more Cubans to the United States before it ended in 1973. The chaotic MARIEL BOAT LIFT began on April 21, 1980, for the purpose of giving asylum to 3,500 Cubans who had taken refuge in the Peruvian Embassy in Havana by allowing them entry into the United States. The boat lift ultimately resulted in the immigration of 125,000 Cubans.

Originally it was expected that Cubans who fled the Castro regime would return to the island after Castro fell from power. As a second generation of Cubans grew up in the United States, passing through U.S. schools, speaking English, and absorbing U.S. culture, return to Cuba seemed less likely. According to the census of 1990, 1,053,197 persons of Cuban origin were living in the United States.

Puerto Rican Immigration. In 1898, the United States acquired Puerto Rico from Spain, and two years later, the FORAKER ACT declared Puerto Ricans nationals but not citizens. The JONES ACT of 1917 changed the status of Puerto Ricans to citizens unless they formally rejected citizenship.

After World War II, Congress allowed Puerto Ricans to select their own governor rather than having one appointed by the United States. Luis MUÑOZ MARÍN (1898-1980) was the first governor elected by the people of the island. In 1952, the Federal Relations Act allowed Puerto Ricans to draft a constitution of their own choosing, as long as it did not create independence or statehood, and in 1953, Puerto Rico became a self-governing commonwealth, remaining an American possession subject to U.S. federal laws. Although Puerto Ricans could not vote for the president of the United States or have senators and representatives in Congress, they were permitted a resident commissioner to sit in Congress but without a vote. The census of 1990 counted 2,651,815 Puerto Ricans residing in the United States (*see* PUERTO RICAN MIGRATION).

Central American Immigration. Many Nicaraguans who objected to the leftist Sandinista government that forced the brutal Somoza family dictatorship out of power in 1979 either sought entry into the United

The Freedom Airlift facilitated a huge wave of Cuban immigration. (AP/Wide World Photos)

Refugees from Central America and the Caribbean increasingly sought entry into the United States in the 1980's and 1990's. (Impact Visuals, Kathleen Foster)

States or joined the Contras, a rebel force at first legally and then illegally supported with financial and military aid by the United States. El Salvador and Guatemala were headed in the 1980's by anti-Marxist governments struggling against leftist rebels.

According to the 1990 Census, 565,081 Salvadorans, 268,779 Guatemalans, 202,658 Nicaraguans, 131,066 Hondurans, 57,223 Costa Ricans, and 92,013 Panamanians lived in the United States. A large percentage of the Central American immigrants took up residence in Southern California. Many received amnesty under the IMMIGRATION REFORM AND CONTROL ACT OF 1986.

Immigration from Hispaniola. The island of Hispaniola includes the two countries of Haiti and the Dominican Republic. Haiti, originally called St. Domingue when a French colony, occupies the western third of the island. During colonial times, it was perhaps the richest of France's colonies in the New World. In 1793, the black slaves rebelled and started the struggle for independence that ended with the victory of Jacques Dessalines in 1804. The United States started an occupation of Haiti in 1915 that lasted until 1934.

On the recommendation of the W. Cameron Forbes Commission to Haiti in 1930, President Herbert Hoover started the United States exodus.

François Duvalier became president in 1957. Upon his death in 1971, his son, Jean-Claude "Baby Doc" Duvalier, took over. He fled the country in 1986. Both Duvalier regimes were extremely oppressive, and Haitians fled the country. The Haitian people, who were perhaps 95 percent illiterate, in 1990 elected a former Catholic priest, Jean-Bertrand Aristide, as president with 67 percent of the vote. Aristide had strong leftist ideas for reform but seemed to exhibit almost the same brutish methods as used by the Duvaliers. After seven months of Aristide's rule, the military under Lieutenant General Raoul Cedras staged a coup that ousted Aristide and substituted another vicious rightist government. Aristide fled to the United States, requesting his return to office via United States military power.

In the meantime, thousands of Haitians resorted to small boats to cross the Caribbean and seek asylum in the United States. Under the Bill Clinton Administration, the Coast Guard turned back the HAITIAN BOAT PEOPLE, but in the late spring of 1994, the Clinton

Administration changed its view and gave orders that before any Haitians were returned to Haiti, a determination had to be made whether each was seeking entry into the United States for asylum or for economic reasons. Those genuinely seeking asylum were to be permitted to follow predetermined policies for United States entry. By the fall of 1994, the United States had invaded Haiti and demanded surrender of control by Cedras.

The Dominican Republic occupies the eastern two-thirds of Hispaniola. Between 1966 and 1976, more than a million people from the Dominican Republic were recorded as entering the United States on tourist visas. Many of them remained, some legally and many illegally. In 1986, fifteen thousand Dominicans applied for amnesty. The Census of 1990 listed 520,521 Dominicans in the United States. Dominicans primarily have come to the United States in search of a better economic life rather than out of fear of political persecution. —*Robert M. Spector*

SUGGESTED READINGS:

• Daniels, Roger. *Coming to America: A History of Immigration and Ethnicity in American Life.* New York: HarperCollins, 1990. A history of immigration by ethnic groups. Deals more with the social and cultural results of emigration than with details of immigration laws. Probably the best book for a general view of the effects of immigration laws on Latin Americans.

• Ehrlich, Paul R., et al. *The Golden Door: International Migration, Mexico, and the United States.* New York: Ballantine, 1979. Deals primarily with Mexican immigration to the United States, taking the position that Mexican immigration is a natural process. Anticipates the freeing of trade between the United States and Mexico.

• Kanellos, Nicolás, ed. *The Hispanic-American Almanac: A Reference Work on Hispanics in the United States.* Detroit: Gale Research, 1993. Excellent source with regard to Hispanic immigration. Covers virtually all aspects of Latino life. Provides a historical overview, historical landmarks, chronology, and significant documents.

• Kansas, Sidney. *Immigration and Nationality Act Annotated: With Rules and Regulations.* New York: Immigration Publications, 1953. The first chapter gives a reasonably good history of immigration legislation through 1952. Specifically covers the McCarran-Walter Act.

• Mitchell, Christopher, ed. *Western Hemisphere Immigration and United States Foreign Policy.* University Park: Pennsylvania State University Press, 1992. Deals mainly with U.S. immigration policy toward the Caribbean, Cuba, Central America, and Mexico, including Haiti's boat people and Dominican immigration.

• Spector, Robert. *W. Cameron Forbes and the Hoover Commissions to Haiti (1930).* Lanham, Md.: University Press of America, 1985. Gives a history of Haiti and relations with the United States through the Forbes and Moton Commissions, in addition to subsequent events.

• Teitelbaum, Michael S. *Latin Migration North: The Problem for United States Foreign Policy.* New York: Council on Foreign Relations, 1985. Presents a good overview of United States policy toward Latin American immigration to the United States but provides little coverage on the actual law regulating such immigration.

• United States. Bureau of the Census. *The Hispanic Population of the United States.* Current Population Reports, Population Characteristics, Series P-1-20, No. 455. Washington, D.C.: United States Department of Commerce, Economics and Statistics Administration, Bureau of the Census, 1991. Essential for determining the social and cultural results of Hispanic immigration into the United States.

• United States. Bureau of the Census. *1990 Census of Population: Social and Economic Characteristics, Metropolitan Areas.* Washington, D.C.: United States Department of Commerce, Economics and Statistics Administration, Bureau of the Census, 1993. Essential for determining the residential population of persons of Latin ancestry in the United States as of 1990 and their distribution throughout the country.

• United States. Bureau of the Census. *Statistical Abstract of the United States, 1993: The National Data Book.* Washington, D.C.: United States Department of Commerce, Economics and Statistics Administration, Bureau of the Census, 1993. Gives a digest of information contained in the 1990 census, providing immigration figures and residence by ancestry.

• Weyr, Thomas. *Hispanic U.S.A.: Breaking the Melting Pot.* New York: Harper & Row, 1988. Deals solely with Hispanic immigration into the United States and does not touch on immigration from Brazil, Haiti, or Quebec. Weak on presentation of immigration law.

Immigration Reform and Control Act of 1986 (IRCA): This act marked a major change in U.S. immigration policy with its provisions of amnesty for some illegal aliens and sanctions against employers who knowingly hired undocumented workers. A compromise among competing interest groups, IRCA (also known as the Simpson-Mazzoli Act for its key congressional sponsors) has been criticized on many counts.

The amnesty provision of IRCA extended legal status to illegal aliens who could prove they had entered the United States prior to January 1, 1982, and had lived in the country continuously since that time. They could apply for permanent residency after eighteen months and be eligible for citizenship in five years. The initial period for amnesty applications ended on May 4, 1988, but was later extended. The employer sanctions provision made it illegal to knowingly hire an illegal alien. Employers became subject to fines of up to $3,000 and six months imprisonment. The act created a new unit in the Justice Department to investigate possible employment discrimination against workers who might be perceived as foreign. The law also increased funding for Border Patrol surveillance and allowed for the temporary immigration of guest workers.

The act was the culmination of years of congressional debate on immigration. It combined provisions from bills in the Senate and House sponsored by Senator Alan Simpson (R-Wyoming) and Congressman Roman Mazzoli (D-Missouri). The 1986 law was a liberal-conservative compromise with elements intended to satisfy disparate interest groups such as Latinos, growers, civil rights groups, and local governments. In 1990, further legislation set aside fifty-five thousand visas per year for three years, for spouses and children of persons who had obtained amnesty under the 1986 act.

The amnesty provision of the act has been attacked for its ineffectiveness. Although more than three million persons took advantage of amnesty, many did not even apply. Some lacked the documentation to prove their cases or the skills needed to complete the complicated process. Others feared reprisals if they failed to prove residency, such as deportation of family members or friends. The amnesty provision was also faulted for causing increased trafficking in counterfeit papers.

Critics contend that employers' fear of sanctions led to employment discrimination against persons with valid work permits who looked foreign. An investigation by the General Accounting Office in 1990 uncovered this pattern. In addition, some employers used the threat of deportation to exploit and harass foreign workers. The sanction provision was also faulted for burdening employers with the duty of verifying the citizenship of prospective employees.

More broadly, the act has been criticized for failing to address such key issues as the appropriate number of immigrants to admit yearly, the plight of seasonal farmworkers, and the problems of UNAUTHORIZED WORKERS who do not seek permanent residence. Contrary to expectations that the law would discourage attempted illegal border crossings, the number of border apprehensions reported by the Border Patrol actually increased in some areas after 1986.

Imperialism: Process by which Europeans and the United States acquired markets, raw materials, and strategic interests throughout Latin America. Imperialism in the Americas began when Spain and Portugal constructed their empires during the sixteenth century. Both Spain and Portugal particularly emphasized silver and gold mining as a motive for imperial expansion. Spain immediately profited from rich MINING sites in northern Mexico, Peru, and Colombia. Later, at the end of the seventeenth century, Portugal found gold and diamonds in Brazil. These Iberian powers also sought to develop markets for their limited industrial sectors as well as to import luxury items for domestic use and for trade with other European countries. Spain and Portugal developed lucrative European agricultural markets for American cacao, tobacco, sugar, indigo, and henequen. Both nations insisted that their colonists trade only with Portuguese and Spanish merchants in selected ports. Convoys guarded the shipments of valuable commodities across the Atlantic, warding off attempts to seize coveted goods.

Colonial imperialism gave way to the modern period after many countries gained independence in the early 1820's. The early Spanish American republics as well as Brazil established free-trade policies from which Great Britain and the United States profited. As Spain and Portugal declined in power during the nineteenth century, Great Britain dominated trade and investments in Latin America. World War I enabled the United States to supplant Great Britain as the imperialist power with the greatest influence in Latin America.

Four basic factors motivated U.S. imperialism in Latin America. First, the U.S. domestic market was saturated: Industrialists produced more than U.S. consumers wished to purchase. Second, the country sought economic stability. Approximately half the years from 1873 to 1897 were characterized by economic depressions. Imperialists assumed that Latin American markets would stabilize production. Third, the United States was a debtor nation. Large amounts of European capital had to be brought in to develop

Basic commodities, such as sugar, and slave labor to produce them were primary motivations for imperial expansion. (Library of Congress)

mines, railroads, oil fields, and breweries. A trading surplus with Latin America was thought to be the best way to avoid increased indebtedness. Finally, many members of the elite feared that democracy had gone too far, as unusual criticism came from intellectuals as well as anarchists and socialists. The elite hoped that imperialism could unify the United States.

William Seward was among the first U.S. diplomats to envision a new empire formed by annexing Central America, so that the United States could control a canal between the Atlantic and Pacific oceans. To promote better relations with Mexico, Seward began to persuade the French to leave Mexico after Emperor Ferdinand Maximilian's empire began to collapse in the 1860's. A grateful Mexico allowed U.S. businesses to invest $1.5 billion in the Mexican economy by 1910. After becoming secretary of state in 1881, James Blaine promoted U.S. imperialism with the 1881 establishment

of the Pan American Union. Blaine also signed a reciprocity agreement with Brazil in 1891 that engaged Brazil in an alliance that lasted for many years.

U.S. imperialism later became more forceful. Eager to obtain markets in Cuba, the United States engaged in war with Spain. The 1898 victory in the SPANISH-AMERICAN WAR gave the United States control in Puerto Rico and the Philippines. Cuba was occupied for four years. The PLATT AMENDMENT (1901, formalized in 1903) made Cuba into a virtual colony until 1933.

The United States continued to expand its interests in Latin America, opening the Panama Canal in 1914 and intervening in Mexico's civil war. During Woodrow Wilson's presidency (1913-1921), the United States occupied Nicaragua, the Dominican Republic, and Haiti. Occupation ended under the promises of the GOOD NEIGHBOR POLICY promulgated in 1933.

Income and wage levels: Income and wages are defined as money income (wages, salaries, commissions, and tips) received, before deductions for personal income taxes, Social Security, union dues, and Medicare. Occupational distributions describe jobs held by different groups of workers (for example, Latinos, African Americans, men, and women) according to categories of job skill, education, and pay rate. Information derived from income and occupational distribution data is important to policymakers, employers, and labor unions in developing programs and policies that, among other goals, attempt to improve the income levels of minority groups. These types of data also enable evaluation of how Latinos have assimilated into the economy.

Data collection on income, wage levels, and occupational distributions was initiated by the federal Bureau of Labor Statistics and the Bureau of the Census. These agencies collect data on the jobs in which people are employed, how much income they and their families earn, and how these data differ from year to

year. The federal government collects this type of data to assist it in monitoring occupational distribution and earning patterns of all employed U.S. citizens. These patterns are then used to determine a general indicator of well-being and to monitor policy goals.

Earnings Distribution. Income levels are often grouped in distinct categories for comparative purposes. The distribution of family income in 1991 for all Latinos was heavily concentrated (29 percent) in the lowest category reported, an annual income of $14,999 or less. In other words, nearly one-third of Latino families were close to the poverty level defined by the federal government.

Only a small proportion of Latinos were at the highest income levels. Approximately 5.7 percent of all Latino families had incomes of $75,000 per year or higher. A comparison of figures for Latinos with those for African Americans and non-Hispanic whites shows large disparities.

African Americans had patterns similar to those of Latinos, but non-Hispanic whites diverged signifi-

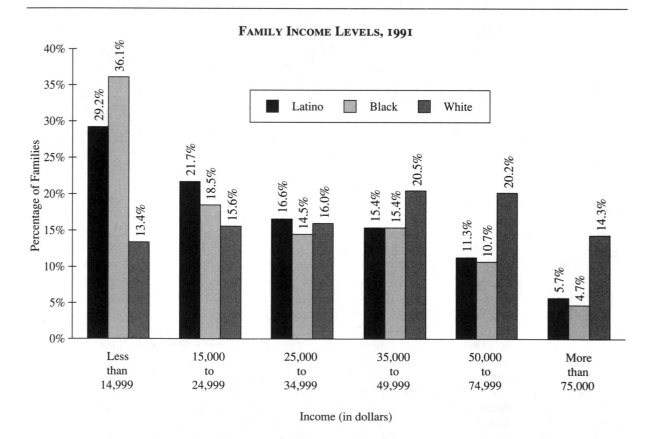

FAMILY INCOME LEVELS, 1991

Source: U.S. Bureau of the Census, *Statistical Abstract of the United States: 1990* (Washington, D.C.: Government Printing Office, 1991), p. 460, Table 717.

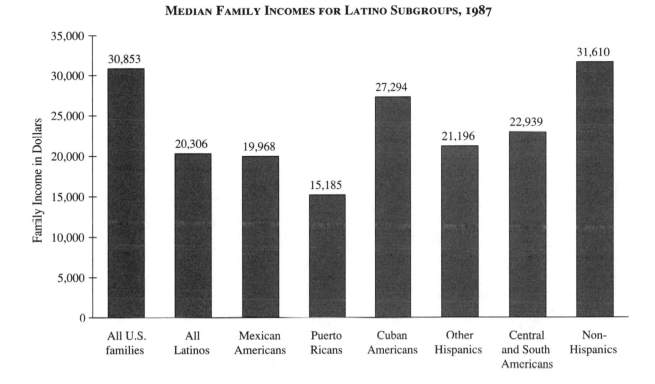

MEDIAN FAMILY INCOMES FOR LATINO SUBGROUPS, 1987

Source: Data are from *The Hispanic Population in the United States* (Washington, D.C.: U.S. Bureau of the Census, 1988), Current Population Reports, Series P-20, No. 438.

cantly. Only 13 percent of non-Hispanic white families had incomes of $14,999 or less, but almost 15 percent had incomes of $75,000 or more. Corresponding figures for African Americans show that 36.1 percent were in the lowest income category, a higher proportion than for Latinos, and 4.7 percent were in the highest category, a lower proportion than for Latinos. Thus, in terms of family income, Latinos appeared to be situated between African Americans and non-Hispanic whites.

Median Family Income. Income statistics often are presented as data points at different times to facilitate comparison between different years and to allow trends to be discerned. Median figures are often used. The median is the halfway mark; for family incomes, half of all families would have incomes below the median, and half would have incomes above it.

In addition, data presented over time often are adjusted for inflation, in terms of "constant dollars" of some year. If there has been inflation, for example, a dollar in 1990 would not buy as much as a dollar in 1980 would have. Adjusting for constant dollars would then make a 1980 dollar into more than one 1990 constant dollar.

The median family income for Latinos and African Americans fluctuated between $21,000 and $25,000 (expressed in constant 1991 dollars) between 1975 and 1991. During that time period, median family income for non-Hispanic whites fluctuated between $34,500 and $39,000. The differences among these groups remained relatively constant between 1975 and 1991 and may have been larger before 1975. Income patterns for all three groups showed a general upward trend.

Occupational Distribution. One way of explaining income differences among groups of workers is to examine differences in their occupations (*see* OCCUPATIONS AND OCCUPATIONAL TRENDS). The occupational distribution of Latino workers is one factor in their earning potential and economic assimilation. On average, weekly earnings for workers in managerial and professional occupations, for example, are significantly higher than those for persons working as operators, fabricators, and laborers. Distinguishing among Latino subgroups such as Mexican Americans, Puerto Ricans, and Cuban Americans can also help explain why one subgroup has an average income level higher than that of another subgroup.

MEDIAN FAMILY INCOME IN CONSTANT (1991) DOLLARS

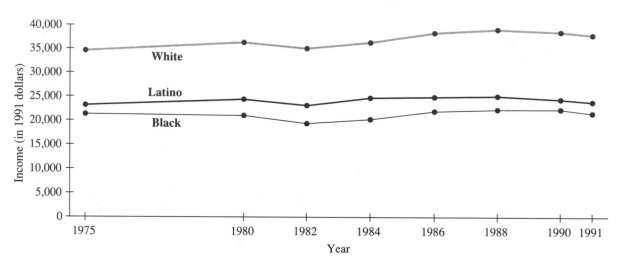

Source: U.S. Bureau of the Census, *Statistical Abstract of the United States: 1990* (Washington, D.C.: Government Printing Office, 1991), p. 457, Table 712.

Census data regarding occupational distribution for Latinos in 1992 showed that they were concentrated, as a group, primarily in three areas: technical, sales, and administrative support (24.8 percent); operators, fabricators, and laborers (22.2 percent); and service workers (20.3 percent). These concentrations differed somewhat for the subgroup of Cuban Americans, who had a higher percentage of workers (25.1 percent) in the higher-paying managerial and professional jobs than did Mexican Americans (10.8 percent) and Puerto Ricans (18.2 percent). Cuban Americans were more similar to non-Hispanic whites in their occupational distribution than they were to other Latino subgroups.

Occupational distribution thus helps to explain the disparity in incomes between Latinos and non-Hispanic whites. Latinos tended to be concentrated in the lower-paying occupations to a greater extent than were non-Hispanic whites. The reasons for the differences are beyond the scope of this article but include differences in skills, education, experience, and proficiency in use of the English language. Discrimination also has been argued to play a role. *—Abel Valenzuela, Jr.*

SUGGESTED READINGS: • Bean, Frank D., and Marta Tienda. *The Hispanic Population of the United States.* New York: Russell Sage Foundation, 1987. • Borjas, George J., and Marta Tienda, eds. *Hispanics in the U.S. Economy.* Orlando, Fla.: Academic Press, 1985. • DeFreitas, Gregory. *Inequality at Work: Hispanics in the U.S. Labor Force.* New York: Oxford

University Press, 1991. • Knouse, Stephen B., Paul Rosenfeld, and Amy L. Culbertson, eds. *Hispanics in the Workplace.* Newbury Park, Calif.: Sage Publications, 1992. • Melendez, Edwin, Clara Rodriguez, and Janis Barry Figueroa, eds. *Hispanics in the Labor Force: Issues and Policies.* New York: Plenum Press, 1991. • Moore, Joan, and Harry Pachon. *Hispanics in the United States.* Englewood Cliffs, N.J.: Prentice Hall, 1985. • Morales, Rebecca, and Frank Bonilla, eds. *Latinos in a Changing U.S. Economy: Comparative Perspectives on Growing Inequality.* Newbury Park, Calif.: Sage Publications, 1993. • Rodriguez, Clara. *Puerto Ricans: Born in the U.S.A.* Boulder, Colo.: Westview Press, 1989.

Indians. *See* **North American Indians**

Indígenas: Native inhabitants of America. *Indígenas* is the name given to the native inhabitants of the Americas by Europeans upon their arrival. By the time Europeans arrived in the Americas, three major indigenous civilizations had dominated what is now known as Latin America: the Aztecs, in central Mexico; the Maya, in the southern part of Mexico, the Yucatán Peninsula, and regions extending to Guatemala; and the Incas, in the Andean region and Peru. The term *indígenas* still designates indigenous groups that maintain a significant link to indigenous traditions and languages.

Industrial Areas Foundation: Community empowerment group. Founded in 1940, this organization supplies techniques and personnel to help people in poor, working, and middle-class communities, regardless of race or ethnicity, to organize for change. Its aim is to create democratic local organizations that work for change through political means.

The main focus of the Industrial Areas Foundation is to promote change by working against established authorities and created interests. In order to accomplish the shifting of political power to the local community, the group helps local residents to become organized and politically literate. This empowerment process helps the local community in taking power back from the hands of those with economic interests at stake and in cooping the effects of apathy of governmental officials.

The foundation works against slum dwellings, urban decay, racial discrimination, unresponsive politicians, and overcrowded schools. It maintains a training institute to develop citizens into politically literate, competent organizers and leaders. The foundation is actively involved in community development at the leadership training and organizing level.

Industrial Workers of the World (IWW): Labor union founded in 1905. The IWW promoted a radical approach to unionization—workers were organized on the basis of industry rather than craft (*see* LABOR UNIONISM). Previous attempts at unionization, most notably the American Federation of Labor (AFL), involved craft unions based on specific trades or skills. Some leaders in the union movement, including Eugene Debs of the Socialist Party and William ("Big Bill") Haywood of the Western Federation of Miners, opposed major policies of the AFL. The AFL worked within the capitalist structure and excluded unskilled labor from craft unions. During the national convention of the Socialist Party in 1904, the rift between the conservative and radical approaches deepened, resulting in a split in the party.

Acting on an invitation by Debs, radical socialists met in Chicago, Illinois, in June, 1905, to establish an industrial union that would include unskilled workers. Forty-three labor groups were represented at this first meeting, although Haywood's Western Federation of Miners was the only major established union present.

The IWW, or "Wobblies," included within its umbrella previously ignored laborers such as migrant workers from the West and Southwest and immigrant workers from the East. African Americans, Jews, Latin Americans, and Eastern European immigrants were all welcomed into the organization. Such was not true for other unions.

Unsuccessful at recruiting major unions, the IWW quickly evolved into a more radical organization. The Detroit faction, led by Daniel De Leon, argued in favor of political activity within the confines of law. The Chicago faction of Haywood and Vincent St. John opposed such political action, favoring instead sabotage or boycotts as a means of achieving their goals. By 1908, the latter faction prevailed.

Ultimately, the "Wobblies" hoped to end capitalism and establish a new government based on a classless, socialist society (*see* SOCIALISM). Government would be controlled through industrial unions. In this approach, the more radical branch of the organization embraced syndicalism, a movement popular at the time. The movement originated in nineteenth century France, and by the beginning of World War I it had made inroads in both Western Europe and Latin America. The premises of syndicalism included a concept of class warfare that would abolish capitalism. Later superseded by Communism, syndicalism was a major political movement during the peak years of the IWW.

Peak membership in the IWW was probably attained in 1906, when some 100,000 workers were members. By 1908, defections resulted in the union being predominantly associated with unskilled laborers, most of whom were immigrants. Although numbers of members remained in the thousands, by 1925 the IWW had ceased to exist as an effective tool of representation. The intervening years did see some successes. Among these were a strike by textile workers in the East (1912-1913) and the conflict among workers at the Pressed Steel Car Company in McKees Rock, Pennsylvania (1909). The IWW was most successful in the West and Southwest, among unskilled workers in agriculture, lumbering, and mining. It played a role in the Wheatland riot (1913) in California.

Few major objectives of the IWW were achieved, but the organization provided a voice for thousands of members, many of whom were unskilled and were ignored by other unions. The radical members of the IWW also provided a legacy for future unions, many of which incorporated tactics used by the IWW. Many Latino workers learned the value of unionization and developed leadership and organizing skills in the IWW. The Congress of Industrial Organizations, formed in 1935, organized workers by industry, as had the IWW.

Infant mortality: Death of an infant during the first year following birth. Neonatal mortality counts deaths

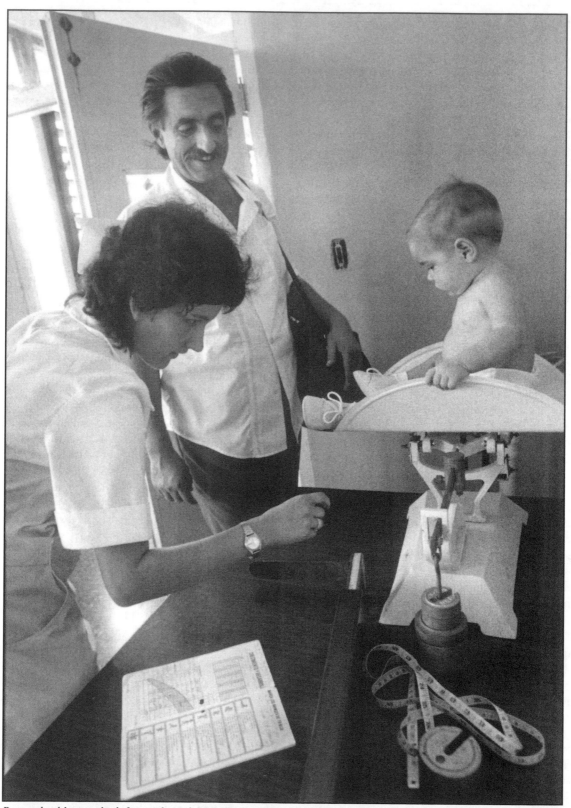

Proper health care, both for mothers during pregnancy and for babies, is vital in reducing infant mortality. (Hazel Hankin)

in the first twenty-eight days after birth; postnatal infant mortality counts deaths from twenty-nine days to one year. Many factors are associated with infant mortality. The most important are national place of origin, birth weight, and socioeconomic factors.

Data from U.S. census reports compiled during the 1980's showed that rates of infant mortality for Hispanics were similar to those for whites and were lower than those for African Americans. In 1984, for example, the rate of infant mortality for white children was 10.5 per 1,000 births. Corresponding rates were 19.8 for African Americans, 14.4 for Puerto Ricans, 7.6 for Mexican Americans, 11.0 for Cuban Americans, and 8.6 for people of South American origin.

A high mortality rate is believed to result from factors such as economic conditions, NUTRITION, education, sanitation, and medical care. Neonatal mortality rates are thought to be affected strongly by the health of mothers and the medical care received during pregnancy (*see* PREGNANCY AND PRENATAL CARE). The postnatal mortality rate is thought to be affected by living conditions and medical care for children as well as medical care for treatable conditions such as infections.

Low birth weight is an important problem affecting infant mortality. It is defined as a birth weight of less than 5.5 pounds and has been linked to 60 percent of all infant deaths. African Americans and Puerto Ricans have higher rates of low birth weight than do whites and other Hispanics, especially in large metropolitan areas. These higher rates of low birth weight are reflected in generally higher rates of infant mortality. These health outcomes likely result in part from the living and economic conditions of large cities, where most Puerto Ricans live.

It has been reported that the neonatal mortality rate for Mexican-born Hispanics is higher than for U.S.-born Hispanics. This difference results in part from cases in which more aggressive monitoring and intervention might have prevented death. U.S.-born babies were more likely to receive monitoring and intervention.

Maternal factors in low birth weight and high infant mortality rates can be significantly influenced by prenatal care. Examples are screening for DIABETES and HYPERTENSION, which are risk factors in Hispanic groups. Social health factors include smoking and alcohol consumption, which are associated with low birth weight and other significant health problems.

Institute for Puerto Rican Policy: Public interest group. The Institute for Puerto Rican Policy, Inc., is a

policy analysis group concerned with issues affecting the Puerto Rican community of the United States. As a nonprofit and nonpartisan organization, the institute does not accept government funding and operates through funds received from certain corporations and from individuals.

The institute sponsors the National Puerto Rican Policy Network, a fifteen-hundred-member information-sharing network extending through twenty-four states, Washington, D.C., and Puerto Rico. It encourages policymakers and the Puerto Rican community to reflect critically on problems affecting the community. Its research and analysis are community based and use action-oriented methods. Special reports, working papers, and other informational materials are researched through the institute's policy analysis and monitoring program. The institute publishes studies on Puerto Rican political participation, public sector employment, political campaign contributions, and related subjects.

Integration. *See* **Segregation, desegregation, and integration**

Intelligence testing: Measurement of human intellect. It is subject to variability in forms and in skills and abilities tested. Three main types have been used: tests of the ability to adapt to the environment, achievement tests, and measurements of abstract thinking skills.

Intelligence testing has been used since the early twentieth century to sort students into groups based on ability. This practice has been common at the elementary level in reading and math. In secondary schools, curriculum tracking puts students in vocational, business, or pre-college groups, with separation based on intelligence tests as well as previous achievements. Students have also been placed in special education classes based on IQ tests. Another type of placement is compensatory education, which is designed to remedy deficiencies resulting from economic or cultural deprivation.

There are several problems with the uses schools make of the results of intelligence tests. The most important purpose of an IQ test is to measure "native" ability, so that an individual student's progress can be compared to his or her potential. Tests consistently have been used, however, to determine funding needs of schools according to numbers of students in certain groups.

IQ tests contain many biases. Tests of verbal and other abilities, for example, often require reading. They actually test English vocabulary and therefore

Intelligence tests and other standardized tests can be biased against people from cultures different from the mainstream.
(James L. Shaffer)

are biased against Spanish-speaking students. Even nonlanguage tests exhibit this problem because directions have to be read and understood. Some tests are constructed to be "culture-free," but they sometimes retain certain biases. For example, questions regarding relationships with peers may be confusing because different ethnic groups value interpersonal relations differently, as in cases of cooperation versus competition.

Minority students have been placed disproportionately in slower academic tracks and have higher rates of grade retention. One significant court case, *Diana v.*

State Board of Education (1970), involved Chicano students and was filed in the U.S. Federal District Court of the Northern District of California. The plaintiffs made their case based on the evidence that when Chicano children who had been placed in remedial classes were retested in their own language, eight of nine scored above the IQ cutoff for those classes. The case resulted in a quota for Chicano representation in such classes.

Larry P. v. Riles (1979) was a case similar to *Diana* but concerned black students. It established additional procedural protection for students. The Association of

Black Psychologists reported that it defended parents who refused to allow their children to be tested by methods that disproportionately label minorities as inferior. This had much to do with the *Larry P.* suit, which resulted in various quota systems. These cases focused attention on the biases of intelligence testing and illustrated the need for culturally appropriate methods of evaluation.

Inter-Agency Committee on Mexican American Affairs: U.S. government commission. This commission was created in 1967, during the Lyndon B. Johnson Administration. Johnson was indebted to Mexican Americans for the "Viva Johnson" campaign that aided his election and thus was open to creation of the commission. The commission's goals were to find solutions to problems in the Mexican American community, reach Mexican Americans through federal programs, and create new programs when necessary. Its members were the cabinet secretaries of the departments of agriculture; health, education, and welfare; housing and urban development; and labor, along with the director of the Office of Economic Opportunity. Its first chairman was Vicente Treviño XIMENES. The committee was reconstituted in 1969 as the CABINET COMMITTEE ON OPPORTUNITIES FOR SPANISH SPEAKING PEOPLE.

Inter-American Music Festival (Washington, D.C.): The Inter-American Music Festival is sponsored by the Inter-American Music and Arts Festival Foundation, organized in 1958, in conjunction with the Organization of American States. The annual festival in May has presented an annual program of "Music of the Americas," both contemporary and traditional, at various locations in Washington, D.C., including the Library of Congress, the Pan American Union Building, and the John F. Kennedy Center Concert Hall. All kinds of music and dance are represented, including opera, chamber music, traditional choral pieces, experimental choral and instrumental works, *baile folklórico*, and classical and contemporary folk music. Performances are by professional ensembles.

Intermarriage: Marriage across ethnic, racial, or religious lines. The presence of such unions, and the reactions of society to them, can often reveal significant lines of stress within and among social groups, particularly when power is unequally shared among social groups. The phenomenon of intermarriage is of interest to political scientists as well as sociologists.

Early studies of intermarriage in the United States primarily concerned unions between African American and white partners. As Latino populations have increased in size and as intermarriage of Latinos has become more common, Latinos have received increased attention. Many of the theories of intermarriage apply to unions between members of any two different groups, but some are particular to Latinos.

Studies have shown that the intermarriage rate for Latinos with non-Latinos is rising, especially in areas with large Latino populations. For example, one study in three predominantly Mexican American communities found that in Texas, the rate rose from 5 percent in 1860 to 16 percent in 1973; in New Mexico, from 14 percent in 1916 to 39 percent in 1971; and in California, to 38 percent in the 1970's. This increase occurred despite the fact that measures of racial prejudice have consistently revealed that Mexican Americans are perceived by Americans of European background as near the bottom of the list for "acceptance levels" in wider American society. Intermarriage rates between Latinos

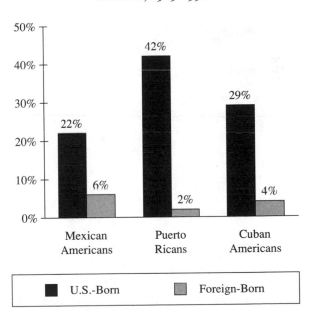

PERCENTAGE OF LATINOS MARRIED TO ANGLOS, 1989-1990

Source: Data are from the Latino National Political Survey, which polled a representative sample of 1,546 Mexican Americans, 589 Puerto Ricans, and 682 Cuban Americans in forty metropolitan areas in 1989-1990. See Rodolfo O. de la Garza et al., *Latino Voices: Mexican, Puerto Rican, and Cuban Perspectives on American Politics* (Boulder, Colo.: Westview Press, 1992), Table 2.6.

and non-Latinos are often cited as an indicator of the Latino community's level of acceptance by the surrounding community.

The Sociology of Intermarriage. It appears self-evident that intermarriage will be more common in mixed societies in which the availability of endogamous (same group) potential marriage partners is lower. Sociological analysis suggests, however, that the matter is more complex than relative numbers of available potential spouses. According to sociologist Robert Merton, endogamy (marrying within one's group) serves to maintain a group's social privileges. It helps prevent the diffusion of power, authority, and preferred status to persons who are not affiliated with a dominant group. It serves further to set the group off against other clearly observable social units and to maintain the social identity and culture of the group.

Merton's arguments are based on the "exchange theory" and the related "hypergamy" theories of intermarriage. In exchange theory, marriages are viewed as transactions between persons and groups who "exchange" things (such as socioeconomic status or racial

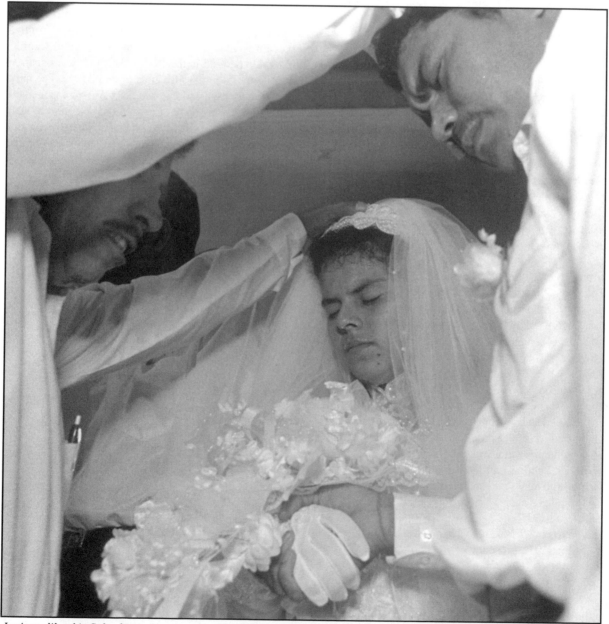

Latinos, like this Salvadoran American couple, tend to marry within their subgroups. (Impact Visuals, Donna DeCesare)

acceptability) through marriage. Although this is not conscious in most cases, it may explain some attraction between persons from different groups. The hypergamy theory states that persons involved in intermarriage will attempt to "marry up" toward the more socially acceptable social or ethnic group; persons attempting such social improvement must have something of value to offer to a potential partner in exchange for higher social status. According to this controversial theory, members of minority groups will attempt, whenever possible, to marry into the dominant social group.

Other social scientists emphasize group identity as the main factor in protecting "boundaries" between groups. Some argue that intermarriage, as a "violation" of ethnic boundaries, is mainly romantically motivated, while others believe that such unions result from deviance or alienation from the strictures of a specific ethnic or cultural group. If mixed marriages of Mexican Americans are viewed from the perspective of hypergamy theory, marriages to Americans of European background generally would involve an increase in status. One study, conducted in 1963, found that about one-fourth of the marriages studied, all involving Mexican Americans, were cases of intermarriage. Very few of the partners who were not Mexican American were members of other Latino groups.

Social Identity. Many sociologists have noted that immigrant men are often more willing to marry local women of the host culture when the local immigrant community is small and not well established. Once the immigrant group establishes itself as a viable community and the pressure of being a member of a disadvantaged group decreases, intermarriage rates tend to fall and endogamous marriages become more common.

Some sociologists see prohibitions against intermarriage as an indicator of worries by a group about its own identity and cultural survival. When a human group finds itself uprooted and isolated, facing strong pressure to conform to alien standards, the group will depend on the primary ties of the kinship network both to reaffirm its individuality in the face of threats of extinction and to maintain some form of normal existence amid unforeseeable and stressful contingencies.

Mexican Americans. Mexican Americans compose the largest subgroup of Latinos in the United States, and as such, their behavior is of particular interest. One study of the history of Mexican American intermarriage found the nature of these marriages to change over time. When Anglo settlers began to arrive in the Southwest in areas of high Mexican concentration in

the nineteenth century, mixed marriages were common. Anglo settlers typically attempted to marry into local aristocratic Mexican American families that controlled land. Thus, the historic attempt to marry into upper-class Mexican American and CALIFORNIO families supported the hypergamy theory, with Anglos being the lower class.

After the western conquests by the United States and the coming of the railroad, Mexican Americans were relegated to a lower status, and European Americans controlled more aspects of economic life. Intermarriage rates dropped significantly, except in Southern California and Los Angeles in particular, where acceptance of mixed marriages was historically higher.

With increased immigration and the growth of the Mexican American middle class in the late twentieth century, marriages between Mexican Americans and Anglos again increased. Rarely did Mexican Americans marry people from other Latino subgroups.

Factors Discouraging Intermarriage. Studies stress a combination of factors that tend to prevent intermarriage between Latinos and others. These include ethnicity, race, class, and religion. Ethnicity refers to cultural differences between the countries of Latin America and the United States, especially outside the Southwest. Race factors stress the continuing problems of racial intolerance, especially for people of dark SKIN COLOR. Class factors emphasize the large socioeconomic gaps between most non-Latinos and the Latino community as a whole. Finally, religion plays a role because many Latinos are Catholic, but that religion is less dominant among non-Latinos. Intermarriage thus often involves unions across religions as well as across racial and ethnic groups, causing further social disapproval.

There are also geographic factors that may be important in the Mexican American case. With a constant flow of people between Mexico and the southwestern United States, the number of potential Mexican marriage partners is always high, and the constant "cultural reminders" of this recently immigrated population increase the socialization pressures to marry within the group. Sociologists expect that the incidence of intermarriage in Mexican American and other Latino communities will increase as their socioeconomic levels improve and as Latinos gain increasing acceptance within mainstream U.S. society.

—*Daniel Smith-Christopher*

SUGGESTED READINGS: • Aldridge, Delores P. "Interracial Marriages." *Journal of Black Studies* 8 (March, 1978): 365-368. • Lazar, Robert J. "Toward a

Theory of Intermarriage." *International Journal of Sociology of the Family* 1 (1971): 1-9. • Murguia, Edward, and Ralph Cazares. "Intermarriage of Mexican-Americans." In *Intermarriage in the United States*, edited by Gary Crester and Joseph Leon. New York: Haworth Press, 1982. • Porterfield, Ernest. "Perspectives on Black-White Intermixture." In *Black and White Mixed Marriages*. Chicago: Nelson-Hall, 1978. • Stephan, Cookie W., and Walter G. Stephan. "Ethnic Identity Among Persons of Mixed Heritage." *Journal of Marriage and the Family* 51 (May 1, 1989): 507-519.

Internal colonialism: Theories of internal colonialism attempt to explain the POVERTY and powerlessness of the Latino community in terms of its exploitation by members of the majority group. These theories view BARRIOS as "internal colonies" of the dominant non-Latino society.

Internal colonialism is an adaptation of models of classic colonialism to the situation of American minority groups. Both models involve one group of people exploiting another in an unequal relationship. Under classic colonialism, one nation or society dominates another within the dominated group's own territory. Under internal colonialism, the colonized minority population has the same formal political and legal status as the dominant group. Some political sociologists combined the internal colonialism model with Marxist analysis to stress the importance of social class in patterns of domination.

The internal colonial interpretation suggests that Latinos entered U.S. society involuntarily. The initial contact between Anglo society and Latinos was the conquest of former Spanish lands by the United States. A significant Mexican population was absorbed into the United States as a result of the MEXICAN AMERICAN WAR (1846-1848). The Mexican community was treated like a conquered population by the U.S. government. This legacy of conquest in the Southwest has created a crucial difference between Latinos and other immigrant groups.

The internal colonial model claims that the disadvantaged position of Latino groups is in large part the result of past oppression. The United States adopted policies that denigrated Latino values and culture, including the Spanish language. Racist policies were established at both the individual and institutional levels (*see* RACISM). Political and economic control continued to rest with persons and institutions outside the Latino community, with few Latinos in positions of real power.

The legacy of oppression has persisted, according to proponents of the internal colonialism model, although that oppression is no longer overt or directly supported by formal government policies. This legacy is manifested in the relatively disadvantaged socioeconomic position of Latinos.

International Ladies' Garment Workers' Union (ILGWU): Labor union. The ILGWU was founded in 1900. It focuses on improving wages and working conditions of female workers in the textile and clothing industries. In the western part of the United States, Latinas have been excluded from union leadership positions even though they make up the majority of the textile laborers. Latinas are, however, given minor leadership positions within the union. By the early 1990's, the union claimed more than 170,000 members.

Islas, Arturo, Jr. (May 24, 1938, El Paso, Tex.—Feb. 15, 1991): Novelist. Islas, the eldest of three children, was the son of one of the first Hispanic police officers in El Paso, Texas. His mother worked as a secretary. Upon graduation from El Paso High School, he was awarded a scholarship to Stanford University, from which he was graduated with distinction. He completed his doctorate in English there in 1971.

After completing his academic work, Islas was appointed to a tenure-track position at Stanford in 1970. During this period, he became increasingly interested in Chicano-related issues and turned to more autobiographical writing. *The Rain God: A Desert Tale* (1984), which brought literary success and awards, reached its twelfth printing in 1990. His second novel, *Migrant Souls* (1990), was published eight years after its completion. During the 1970's, Islas received a diagnosis of cancer, and his career was cut short by his death in 1991.

Iturbi, José (Nov. 28, 1895, Valencia, Spain—June 28, 1980, Hollywood, Calif.): Classical pianist and conductor. Iturbi, the son of a piano builder, got his first piano lesson at the age of five. As a young man, he earned his living playing in street cafés before moving to Paris, where he studied with Victor Staub at the conservatory. He was graduated in 1913 with the highest honors.

Iturbi had a memorable concert career and also served as head of the piano department at the Geneva Conservatory in Switzerland from 1919 to 1923. His American debut took place in 1929. During his second American tour, in 1930, he gave sixty-seven concerts.

José Iturbi at home, with his piano. (AP/Wide World Photos)

He also toured throughout Europe and the Americas playing in a piano duo with his sister Amparo.

Iturbi was also a much-sought orchestra conductor in Mexico, Europe, and the United States. He led the Rochester Philharmonic Orchestra from 1936 to 1944.

Iturbi appeared in several Hollywood films, and his hands substituted for those of actor Cornel Wilde in *A Song to Remember* (1945), a film about the romantic composer Frederic Chopin.

In 1950, he became the first classical musician to sell more than a million copies of a single recording. Iturbi became the most famous Spanish American pianist of his day, especially acclaimed for his interpretations of the music of his native country.

J

Jaar, Alfredo (b. Feb. 5, 1956, Santiago, Chile): Sculptor. Jaar's works attempt to force viewers to consider the relationship of the industrialized world to less developed countries and the people who live there. His work can be found at the High Museum of Art in Atlanta, Georgia; in the La Jolla Museum of Contemporary Art in California; and at L'Arche de la Fraternité, La Défense, in Paris, France. He participated in several major exhibitions in the late 1980's and early 1990's. Jaar was the recipient of a John Simon Guggenheim Foundation Grant in 1985.

Jackson Heights (New York, N.Y.): Neighborhood. Located in the Queens borough, Jackson Heights is an area of South American settlement. Jackson Heights and the adjacent neighborhoods of Corona and Elm-

hurst experienced a trickle of Colombian immigration in the 1930's and 1940's. The vast majority of these arrivals were professional people who had attended U.S. colleges and universities.

A second and much larger wave of South and Central American immigration began in the 1970's. In the 1980's and 1990's, the area received an increasing influx of undocumented people. Jackson Heights in particular became an important base of operations for Colombian drug dealers.

Jai alai: Sport of Basque origin. Jai alai originated in the Basque region of Spain, then spread throughout Spain and to France. The form called *cestapunta* gained popularity in Mexico, Cuba, Argentina, Uruguay, and the United States. The game is played in a

A couple from the Grupo de Danzas Folklóricas performs the jarabe tapatío. (Impact Visuals, Marvin Collins)

court called a *frontón*, consisting of three playing surfaces: a frontal wall, or *frontis*, a left lateral wall, and a wall parallel to the *frontis*. Players use a wicker basket attached to a leather glove that can be tied to the arm with leather straps. The ball, made of rubber, wool, and leather, is scooped and thrown against the wall at high speeds. A player or team loses a point by failing to scoop the ball before it bounces twice.

Jalapeño: Moderately hot chile, used extensively in Mexican cooking. Although not as fiery as their reputation suggests, jalapeños are quite spicy and should be used guardedly by the uninitiated. They can be used green and underripe (the usual way) or red and fully ripe, in which case they have a fruitier taste. Jalapeños are most often used fresh as seasonings to dishes, but they also can be pickled. Many Mexicans call the fresh green chile *cuaresmeño* and only the pickled form jalapeño. Fresh jalapeños are eaten raw, sometimes as a show of MACHISMO, as at TEX-MEX chile-eating contests. Because jalapeños do not air-dry well, they normally are not available in the dried or powdered state. *Chipotle* is a special smoke-dried, fully ripe jalapeño used to impart a distinctive taste to certain Mexican dishes; it is called *chile huachinango* in Oaxaca.

Jarabe tapatío: Mexican courtship dance. The *jarabe tapatío* is the dance of the CHARROS (horsemen) of Jalisco, known as the "hat dance" in the United States. This ten-minute dance is performed by a persistent man and a flirtatious girl, both of whom dance around the man's hat, becoming more boisterous as the man wins the girl. The meaning, music, and *zapateado* steps, which quicken as the dance progresses, vary according to region and are often adapted to the dancers' skills. It was banned by Mexican officials between 1802 and 1862. It is commonly danced on Independence Day in cabarets, at fiestas, and at RODEOS.

Jaramillo, Cleofas Martinez (1878, Arroyo Hondo, N.Mex.—1956): Folklorist and writer. Jaramillo was one of seven children in a family descended from original pioneer families of Arroyo Hondo. Following her elementary education in Arroyo Hondo, she attended the Loretto Sisters' academies at Taos and Santa Fe. In 1898, she was married to her politically prominent cousin, Venceslao Jaramillo. All three of their children died, however, and her husband succumbed to cancer in 1920.

When Jaramillo was left a widow, she became a businesswoman as the family fortunes declined. Jara-

millo began her literary career by writing a cookbook; later, she translated twenty-five of her mother's stories and published them. These endeavors also led to Jaramillo's founding of La Sociedad Folklórica to keep Hispanic folklore alive. Her *Shadows of the Past* (1941) is probably her best-known folklore work. In 1955, her autobiographical *Romance of a Little Village Girl*, written in English, shared her perspective of almost seventy years. Her works provide a record of traditions, customs, and social conventions from the standpoint of an upper-class Hispanic female trying to preserve a rapidly vanishing culture.

Jaramillo, Mari-Luci (b. June 19, 1928, Las Vegas, N.Mex.). Educator and diplomat. Jaramillo, a Mexican American, was born into a poor family that placed a high value on education and academic achievement. She completed her undergraduate studies in 1955 and a master's program four years later. Jaramillo earned her Ph.D. in 1970. All of her studies were completed at New Mexico Highlands University.

Jaramillo taught elementary school and concentrated her efforts on increasing educational levels of Latino children. She eventually went on to become a professor in the Department of Elementary Education at the University of New Mexico, then chair of that department.

Jaramillo traveled extensively in Latin America, conducting workshops on education and school development. In 1977, President Jimmy Carter appointed her to serve as ambassador to Honduras. During Jaramillo's tenure, Honduras experienced its first free election in years. After a brief stay at the State Department, Jaramillo returned to teaching.

Jaramillo, Pedro (c. 1850, near Guadalajara, Mexico—July 3, 1907, Paisano, Tex.): Spiritualist and healer. Jaramillo is perhaps the best-known Mexican American folk healer. He claimed that God had bestowed on him the power to heal the sick. Jaramillo moved to southeastern Texas in the 1880's and settled at the Los Olmos Ranch, where he continued to practice folk medicine as he had in Mexico.

In an area with few doctors, Jaramillo's fame spread quickly among the poor Mexican and Mexican American population. At first, Jaramillo visited individual ranches, but increasingly people came to his home at Los Olmos for treatment and remedies. His renown was enhanced by the fact that he did not charge for the medicines he prescribed.

After nearly thirty years of unselfish service, Jara-

Jesuit missionary Eusebio Francisco Kino was an important explorer. (Arizona Historical Society)

millo died and was buried in a cemetery near present-day Falfurrias, Texas. Jaramillo's grave became a shrine visited by people whose parents or relatives had been helped by his remedies.

Jarocho: Designates the population of Veracruz. Jarocho was used as a derogative term by the colonial Spaniards to designate the mulattoes of Veracruz, particularly of the region of Sotavento. The etymology points at two sources: *jaro* (wild boar) or *jara* (thicket), added to the derogative suffix *cho*. The second source seems more substantial, for even today *jarales* abound in Veracruz. After the seventeenth century, the term lost its derogative connotation and became associated with robust horsemen. The term is often used in conjunction with other words to indicate a relationship to Veracruz: *puerto jarocho* (Veracruz port) and *pueblo jarocho* (people from Veracruz).

Jesuit missionaries: Priests who played an important part in spreading the Catholic faith in Latin America and in extending the northern frontier of NEW SPAIN. The Compañía de Jesús, better known as the Jesuits, has a twofold purpose: spiritual growth of members and salvation of all people. Jesuit missionaries played a crucial role in taking Catholicism to Asia, Africa, and Latin America. In spreading their faith, Jesuit missionaries made daring experiments in adapting Christianity to other faiths, thus becoming the most important new missionary agency of modern times.

The Jesuit constitution provided for more centralized authority than did earlier religious orders. This policy was evident in Jesuit missionary work. In Paraguay, at the beginning of the seventeenth century, the order established the *reducciones*, which were political and social organizations among the Indians. Eventually they organized approximately thirty *reducciones* composed of approximately 300,000 Guaraní Indians and 75 Jesuits. The prosperity and judicial exemptions of the *reducciones* caused envy in other communities of the region. This, coupled with attacks from Portuguese adventurers, treaties between the Spanish and Portuguese governments, and the suppression of the Jesuits in 1767 put an end to this socioreligious experiment. The Indians from the *reducciones* dispersed, returning to the jungle or becoming absorbed into the ethnic and cultural MESTIZAJE (intermixing) of the times.

Jesuits were also actively present in North America. In 1570, Jesuit missionaries attempted to found a colony near what would later be Jamestown, Virginia.

They started a school for Indian boys, but disaster struck the following year, when all the Jesuits there were put to death by the Indians. Among the most notable Jesuit missionaries in North America were Saint Jean de Brébeuf, Jacques Marquette, and Eusebio Francisco KINO, a pioneer in Arizona and California.

Born of Italian parents and educated in Austria, Kino pioneered the introduction of Christianity into the northwestern frontier of New Spain after several years of labor in Baja California. Kino arrived in PIMERÍA ALTA in 1687. He founded the mission of Nuestra Señora de los Dolores and then extended the mission frontier into Arizona to the Gila and Colorado Rivers. After the expulsion of Jesuits in 1767, the missionary phase of the movement was placed in the trust of Franciscan friar Junípero SERRA.

Jesuit missionaries were also present in other parts of North America. As early as 1593, a Jesuit had been sent to Durango to maintain permanent residence. In 1566, Jesuits arrived in Florida, but they were ordered to withdraw to concentrate forces in New Spain. They established settlements in various other areas.

Jews: Persons can be members of the religion of Judaism either through descent from the ancient Israelite tribe of Judah or through conversion. The first European Jews to arrive in the Americas were crypto-Jews, considered New Christians as a result of forced conversions, and sometimes pejoratively referred to as Marranos. These included Luis de Torres, an interpreter for Christopher Columbus during his fifteenth century voyages, and members of the retinue of Hernán CORTÉS in the early sixteenth century. As a result of the Spanish Inquisition, large numbers of Sephardic Jews from the Iberian Peninsula began arriving in Latin America during the latter part of the sixteenth century. By 1550, there were more Jews in Mexico than there were Spanish Catholics, although it was still illegal to openly practice Judaism.

During this period, most Jewish immigration was centered in Central America and the northern portion of South America. A large proportion of the trade and commerce that developed during this period was carried out by these Jewish immigrants, including much of the nascent sugar and tobacco business. When Brazil fell briefly under Dutch rule (1620), crypto-Jews were finally allowed to openly practice their religion, and large numbers of Dutch Jews began to arrive.

Modern Jewish settlement in Latin America dates from the early nineteenth century. In the 1820's, German Jews established colonies in Mexico, heralding a larger influx during later decades of the century. Jews, mainly Sephardic in origin, were prohibited from practicing Judaism in Portuguese-owned Brazil, but following Brazil's independence in 1822, Jews from Spain and Portugal began additional settlements in that country.

The number of Jews remained relatively small until the period following World War I. With the borders of the United States essentially closed to European Jews after the war, Eastern European Jews turned to South America as a haven, settling mainly in established communities of Mexico and Brazil as well as in the growing community of Argentina.

Although Jewish communities are found throughout Latin America, most are centered in the large cities of Mexico, Brazil, and Argentina. The largest community as of the early 1990's was that of Argentina, with 80 percent of the approximately 200,000 Jews in the country living in the capital of Buenos Aires. The lack of separation of church and state in that predominantly Catholic country has fostered extensive bigotry, resulting in the highest rate of *aliyah* (migration to Israel) in Latin America.

A more tolerant atmosphere is found in Mexico. Of the approximately 50,000 Mexican Jews, about 40,000 lived in Mexico City. The large number of Jewish day schools and low rate of assimilation have contributed to a thriving community in that country. A tolerant government and society in Brazil, with approximately 150,000 Jews, has likewise contributed to a thriving Jewish community.

Both Sephardic and Ashkenazi (Eastern European) congregations are found throughout Latin America. The Ladino and Yiddish languages unique to the early immigrants have largely been replaced by modern Spanish and Portuguese. Many of the immigrants from earlier centuries intermarried with the indigenous population, resulting in extensive assimilation. Ironically, it is not uncommon for Catholic families in northern Mexico, and even in the southwestern United States, to maintain Jewish customs such as candle-lighting for the Sabbath, reflecting the Jewish origins of their ancestors.

Jíbaro: Peasant mountain worker of Puerto Rico. *Jíbaros* were poor peasant farmers who resided in the hills of Puerto Rico. Many were illiterate, and unemployment was frequent among them. Luis MUÑOZ MARÍN, the governor of Puerto Rico from 1948 to 1964, took a special interest in their plight and at-

tempted to bring them into the developing economy. In the process of industrialization, the *jíbaros'* rural lifestyle was lost. Muñoz Marín later tried to slow the country's industrialization and bring back some of the serenity found in the *jíbaro* lifestyle, but without success. The image of the *jíbaro* remains as a symbol of the rural past, a folk icon with specific language, cultural, and lifestyle traits. This image serves as a form of ethnic identification, though the *jíbaro* of yesteryear no longer exists. The image of the *jíbaro* is not representative of the true ethnic background of Puerto Ricans, since *jíbaros* were white and a large population of Puerto Rico is of mixed ancestry.

Jiménez, Leonardo "Flaco" (b. Mar. 11, 1939, San Antonio, Tex.): Accordionist and songwriter. Jiménez's father, Santiago Jiménez, Sr., was a well-known accordion player. Jiménez's younger brother, Santiago Jiménez, Jr., also became an important accordionist.

With his father, Flaco Jiménez played bajo sexto, recording for the first time on "Los Tecolotes" in the early 1950's. Most of his early recordings were singles released in the San Antonio area. He had his first hit single, "Hasta La Vista," in the mid-1950's. Jiménez had many other Spanish-language hits in the years to follow. In 1973, he worked with Doug Sahm on *Doug Sahm and Band*. Besides Jiménez, Bob Dylan and Dr. John appeared on the album.

Jiménez's reputation grew, and he received more invitations to work with mainstream recording artists. He has worked with Ry Cooder on various projects, including Cooder's *Chicken Skin Music* (1976), *Showtime* (1977), *The Border* (1982), and *Get Rhythm* (1987). In 1986, Jiménez's album *Ay Te Dejo en San Antonio* won a Grammy Award. Jiménez joined Doug Sahm, Augie Meyers, and Freddy FENDER in 1989 to create the TEXAS TORNADOS. The group released its first album, *Texas Tornados*, in 1990, and won a Grammy Award for Best Mexican-American Performance in 1991. When not involved with projects for the Texas Tornados, Jiménez continued to record and tour on his own.

Jiménez, Luis Alfonso, Jr. (b. July 30, 1940, El Paso, Tex.): Artist. Jiménez, a Mexican American, grew up and received his early education in El Paso. He also began to learn art by learning his father's trade of sign painting.

Jiménez began studying architecture, first at the University of Texas at El Paso and then at the University of Texas at Austin. He switched his concentration to art and earned a bachelor's degree in fine arts in 1964. While a student, he created a mural on the engineering building of the university. In 1964, he received a scholarship from the Universidad Nacional Autónoma de México that allowed him to study and travel for several months in Mexico.

Jiménez's work of the late 1960's and early 1970's incorporated pre-Columbian concepts. He became concerned with the relevance of his art to society and interested in machines as part of American culture. His brightly colored fiberglass and epoxy sculptures blend the human form and machinery, offering a commentary on American society.

In 1966, Jiménez moved to New York, New York, without his wife and daughter. He soon had several one-man shows, but the move resulted in a divorce. His sculptures have also been included in important group shows. One of his best-known works is *Man on Fire* (1969-1970), inspired by the work of muralist José Clemente OROZCO. Jiménez moved back to El Paso in the early 1970's, then to Roswell, New Mexico. After working in several cities and again living briefly in El Paso, he settled in Hondo, New Mexico.

Sculptures are not Jiménez's only works of art. *Illegals* (1985) is a lithograph showing five Mexican family members trying to cross a busy road. It is dedicated to Jiménez's father, who crossed the border between the United States and Mexico in 1922. The creation of his lithograph *The Rose Tattoo* (1983) was the subject of a Public Broadcasting Service documentary.

Jobim, Antonio Carlos (Jan. 25, 1927, Rio de Janeiro, Brazil—Dec. 8, 1994, New York, N.Y.): Composer, pianist, guitarist, and singer. As a child, Jobim learned to play the piano. He studied architecture in school but was drawn to Brazilian music and decided to make it the center of his life. Over the years, he gained a reputation in his native country.

In 1959, Jobim and Luiz Bonfa wrote the film score for *Orfeo Negro* (*Black Orpheus*). With this score, Jobim earned an international reputation. In the early 1960's, his songs such as "A felicidade" and "Desafinado" helped to spark fresh variations on the BOSSA NOVA style. His newfound popularity led Jobim to tour the United States.

During the 1960's, he wrote a number of haunting and sophisticated songs, including "Chega de saudade" ("No More Blues"), "Agua de beber" ("Drinking Water"), "Garota de Ipanema" ("The Girl from Ipanema"), and "Por causa de você" ("Don't Ever Go Away"). Jobim wrote the soundtrack for the film *Copacabana*

Palace (1963). He continued to compose romantic and urbane music, becoming one of the most respected composers of popular music in the twentieth century. He was inducted into the Songwriters Hall of Fame in 1991.

Jones Act (1917): From the time of its acquisition in 1898, at the end of the SPANISH-AMERICAN WAR, until 1917, Puerto Rico and its people were ruled as subjects of a colonial government. The Jones Act granted Puerto Ricans citizenship in the United States.

When Puerto Rico became a ward of the United States at the end of the Spanish-American War, the island was designated by the United States Supreme Court as "unorganized," in contrast to the Hawaiian Islands and Alaska, which were considered potential new states. Accordingly, the Senate passed the FORAKER ACT in 1900 to establish colonial government in Puerto Rico, modeled on the British "crown colony" system. An upper and a lower legislative body were formed. The former was selected by popular election, and the latter, an eleven-member council, was appointed by the president of the United States, as was the governor. The U.S. Senate retained full veto and recall power.

At the time, U.S. senators were appointed by state legislatures rather than being elected directly. Most relied heavily on the financial assistance of business and commodity interests, some of which were tied closely to the enormous and largely untapped agricultural potential in the new possessions. Colonial policy in the United States thus served partially or largely to benefit U.S. lawmakers.

This situation resulted in the government of Puerto Rico sitting at the indulgence of the enormously lucrative sugar market and the few large landholders who produced the crop. Their influence on the Senate through the appointment system ended, at least temporarily, in May, 1913, when the Seventeenth Amendment to the U.S. Constitution was ratified, providing for popular election of the Senate.

Although President Woodrow Wilson described the United States as more concerned with "human rights, national integrity, and opportunity" than with "material conquests," the "crown colony" rule established by the Foraker Act extended in Puerto Rico until 1917. At that time, the United States had just released another acquisition from the Spanish-American War by giving the Philippines independence and a limited self-rule. It also had supplied Cuba with a constitution under which it could "learn" to govern itself.

In the spirit of Wilson's new liberalism, the citizens

The Puerto Rican constitution created in 1952 extended the self-governance of Puerto Ricans while maintaining their U.S. citizenship, granted under the Jones Act. (AP/Wide World Photos)

of Puerto Rico, although not allowed autonomy, were made citizens of the United States by the Jones Act. It was not until 1946, however, that Puerto Ricans were given the right to elect their governor. The Jones Act also retained the exemption from federal taxes established by the Foraker Act.

Removal of the influence that financial interests had on the island's government made exploitation of the people by local landowners more difficult. No longer could landowners buy influence through their financial support of U.S. senators. The Puerto Rican economy, unlocked from rule by monied interests and the burden of taxation to support the growing U.S. bureaucracy, was able to take advantage of free market forces.

U.S. citizenship allowed free movement from Puerto Rico to the mainland for employment. Many Puerto Ricans either repatriated their earnings from mainland jobs or returned home, relatively wealthy, after having worked on the mainland. Without the bur-

den of federal taxes, Puerto Rico is attractive to investors. As a result of these and other factors, this once poor agricultural land burgeoned into a diverse economy of intensive farming and technical industry.

Jones-Costigan Act: Trade legislation. This law was passed by the U.S. Congress and signed by President Franklin D. Roosevelt on May 9, 1934. The legislation established a system whereby sugar sold in the United States would be allocated between domestic and foreign producers according to a quota system. The act derives its name from its congressional sponsors, John Marvin Jones, a congressman from Texas and chairman of the House Agriculture Committee, and Edward P. Costigan, a senator from Colorado.

The Jones-Costigan Act, also known as the Sugar Act of 1934, was part of the New Deal efforts to stabilize the price of agricultural commodities during the Depression of the 1930's. The goal was to establish a quota system that would provide a protected market for cane and beet sugar produced in the continental United States and that would at the same time keep down the cost of sugar.

The bill authorized the secretary of agriculture to determine the annual sugar needs of the U.S. market. Domestic and foreign producers were then allotted a percentage of the market based on their respective market percentages during the 1931-1933 period. A tax was assessed on all sugar consumption, with the revenues used to subsidize domestic producers of both sugar beet and sugarcane as well as sugarcane producers in Puerto Rico.

In addition to its domestic goals, the Jones-Costigan Act provided a means of improving economic conditions in Cuba. The declining price of sugar in the late 1920's and early 1930's had put the Cuban economy in a downward spiral. Furthermore, the adoption by the United States in 1930 of the protectionist Smoot-Hawley tariff resulted in a decline in Cuba's share of the U.S. sugar market. Disastrous economic conditions in Cuba resulted in massive unemployment, social unrest, and increased political opposition to the dictatorial government of President Gerardo Machado. Following the overthrow of Machado, the U.S. ambassadors to Cuba in 1933 and 1934, Sumner Wells and Jefferson Caffery, both urged reduction of the tariff on sugar and the establishment of an import quota for Cuban sugar as a way of improving the economic and political situation on the island.

Because the Jones-Costigan Act used the 1931-1933 period as the base for determining the quota for various producers, Cuba's share was less than it would have been if an earlier period had been chosen. Nevertheless, the market stability provided by the act did help to restore the Cuban sugar industry. The quota system introduced by the 1934 act, although revised in 1937, 1948, 1951, and 1956, remained the basis for the sale of Cuban sugar in the United States until deteriorating relations between Fidel Castro and Washington led to the breaking of diplomatic ties in 1961. Furthermore, by ensuring a market for Cuban sugar, the Jones-Costigan Act alleviated problems associated with the Cuban economy's dependence on sugar exports.

Jordan, Steve (Estaban Jordan): Accordionist and songwriter. In the 1960's, Jordan, a Mexican American, began recording music that was rooted in the *MÚSICA NORTEÑA* tradition, but he added a rock flavor to his accordion playing. He recorded for a number of regional record labels, including Falcón, Fama, Fred-

die, and Aguila. When Jordan was recording for Falcón, he worked with his brothers Bonnie and Silver. His showmanship and aggressive approach to playing earned him the title of the "Jimi Hendrix of the accordion" from those who respected his work. He also became known for wearing an eyepatch.

In his repertoire, Jordan mixed polkas, *CORRIDOS*, and *rancheras* with rock music through the use of synthesizers, phase shifters, and other technological devices. Although Jordan began recording in the 1960's, he came to prominence with his appearance in David Byrne's 1986 film *True Stories*. Also in 1986, he was featured on the *Born in East L.A.* soundtrack, and his album *Turn Me Loose* was nominated for a Grammy Award. He continued to expand his idiosyncratic musical style into the 1990's.

Jornaleros: Day laborers working throughout the American Southwest. The term refers to a large segment of the Mexican American and Mexican immigrant occupational pool during the first third of the twentieth century. Regarded as members of the working class, *jornaleros* frequently organized with skilled and semi-skilled Mexican American workers to form *MUTUALISTAS*, which helped to protect and assist Mexican families living and working in the American Southwest.

Joropo: Venezuela's national dance. The *joropo* can be accompanied by the *pasaje* or the *golpe*, two entertainment music forms mixing syncopation with Venezuelan melodies and rhythms. African influence is shown in versions played exclusively on drums, while Spanish influence is evident in musical ensembles using harp melodies to contrast with the harmony and rhythm provided by the *bandola* (flat-backed lute), *CUATRO*, and MARACAS. A courtship dance, the *joropo* is danced by couples. It begins with the *valseo* (waltz step), followed by a variety of steps during which the man dances around the girl, getting progressively closer, while the girl rejects him. It is unique among Venezuela's folk dances.

Journalism: Activity in Spanish and bilingual (English-Spanish) publications and broadcasting exploded late in the twentieth century in the United States and Canada. Many Latinos started Spanish or bilingual newspapers in urban areas, often operating as small businesses on shoestring budgets. Latino publications were tied together by the Hispanic Link News Service, which provided news, columns, cartoons, and commentary from Washington, D.C. Meanwhile, other

Latino participation in both print and visual journalism has been restricted largely to Latino-oriented news outlets. (Robert Fried)

Latinos found work in the mainstream media, although in 1994 the percentage of Latino journalists employed was still far below Latinos' proportion of the general population.

Latino Publishers. By the 1990's, most major cities in the United States hosted at least one newspaper that published in Spanish, or in English and Spanish. Some cities even had competing papers, ranging from those that were principally advertising vehicles to others with political and social motivations. Publishing and broadcasting became more viable career options for ambitious Latinos who wanted to fill a need in their communities.

In 1990, Benito Salazar was an attorney in his early forties in Omaha, Nebraska. He saw the need for a Spanish news source not only for Omaha's Latino community but for the rest of the state's forty thousand Latinos. They lived widely scattered in rural areas, with relatively large concentrations in several western Nebraska farming communities. Salazar likened his audience to a small town that happened to be four hundred miles wide. He abandoned his law career to launch *Nuestro Mundo* in 1990.

The paper has maintained a strong activist stance from its premier issue. For example, it questioned the circumstances under which Miguel Angel Valdez, a Mexican immigrant, was shot to death by police near Gothenburg, Nebraska. It tackled English-only laws (*see* ENGLISH-ONLY CONTROVERSY) and joined a broad community effort in 1992 to pressure the IMMIGRATION AND NATURALIZATION SERVICE (INS) to return two deported Mexican teenagers to their legal parents in the United States. The paper also pushed general community news, from profiles on local Latinos serv-

Mainstream journalism tends to ignore Latino issues; only the largest events and those involving celebrities such as César Chávez have tended to receive coverage. (AP/Wide World Photos)

ing in the armed forces to marriages, deaths, and school honor rolls.

Latinos in Mainstream Journalism. While the number of Latino-owned independent media has grown, more Latinos have been taking jobs with mainstream daily and weekly newspapers. This increase is part of a general rise in minority employment in the news industry, a trend encouraged and monitored by the American Society of Newspaper Editors (ASNE).

Minority employment in print journalism was practically zero in 1955, when an *Ebony* magazine survey counted thirty-one African American journalists in the entire United States. By 1978, it had grown to 4 percent, and by 1991 to 8.72 percent. In 1993, 10.5 percent of newspaper professionals were non-white, including about 3 to 4 percent who were Latino. Although these percentages remained lower than the combined proportion of minorities in the U.S. population (about 25 percent), they represented a dramatic increase from earlier years. The ASNE has pledged to achieve parity in minority employment (equal to the minority proportion of the population) by the year 2000, when minorities are projected to comprise one-third of all Americans.

According to a 1991 survey by the NATIONAL ASSOCIATION OF HISPANIC JOURNALISTS (NAHJ), roughly 2 percent of newsroom managers, 3 percent of copy editors, 4 percent of reporters, and 5.5 percent of photographers and artists were Latino. NAHJ president Don Flores, publisher of the Iowa City *Press-Citizen*, said that the organization's main purpose is to create a bridge between the industry and the pool of Latino journalists through networking, while providing its two thousand members with successful role models.

Newsroom managers are hiring more Latinos and other minority journalists not only for the sake of equal employment opportunity but also because their audiences have become more diverse. The rapid growth of the Latino population, especially in the Southwest, represents a new potential readership. The *Los Angeles Times*, for example, added a Spanish-language edition and boosted its number of Latino editorial writers, columnists, and reporters in its main English-language edition.

Multicultural Issues and Perspectives. Aside from the media's economic self-interest, many people believe that the number of nonwhite journalists must rise to present American society with an accurate mirror of itself. In the 1950's, virtually all-white newspaper staffs ignored the social and economic changes that brought millions of African Americans from the rural South to the urban North, until a nationwide wave of riots made

problems evident in the 1960's. The *Los Angeles Times* hired its first black reporter to cover the 1964 Watts riots, largely because white reporters lacked access to the story. During the 1960's, newspaper executives were similarly slow to realize that although substantial Latino communities were growing in their circulation areas, Latino concerns were receiving scant coverage.

Thirty years later, news and views from the African American community were still far more common in the mainstream media that were stories by and about Latinos. This became evident during the 1992 LOS ANGELES RIOTS, in which the media focused on black-white and black-Korean American conflicts rather than on the thousands of Latino immigrants who participated in and were affected by the disturbances. The deep-rooted frustration that Latino rioters were expressing came as a surprise to many non-Latinos, perhaps because this long-simmering story had been ignored by the mainstream media.

Some Latino activists have charged that their community is virtually invisible in the news, except when there is bad news. The Latino beat tends to get stereotyped in news that is limited to immigration problems, drugs and gangs, migrant labor, and illiteracy, notes NAHJ head Flores. The same handful of Latino celebrities, such as Gloria ESTEFAN, Lee TREVINO, and Chi Chi RODRIGUEZ, grab the other Latino-related headlines. Meanwhile, the daily issues faced by a wide spectrum of Latinos go unreported. Latino professionals such as Flores hope that as more Latino youth enter journalism school and pursue careers in journalism, the media will become more relevant to Latino readers and more reflective of multicultural American society.

—*Bruce E. Johansen*

SUGGESTED READINGS: • Johansen, Bruce E. "Race, Ethnicity, and the Media." In *Mass Media and Society*, edited by Alan Wells. 4th ed. Lexington, Mass.: Lexington Books, 1987. • Marzolf, Marion, and Melba Tolliver. *Kerner Plus 10: Minorities and the Media—A Conference Report.* Ann Arbor: University of Michigan School of Journalism, 1977. • Salwen, Michael B., and Bruce Garrison. *Latin American Journalism.* Hillsdale, N.J.: Lawrence Erlbaum, 1991. • Wilson, Clint C., II, and Felix Gutierrez. *Minorities and Media: Diversity and the End of Mass Communication.* Beverly Hills, Calif.: Sage Publications, 1985.

Jueyes: Land crabs. *Jueyes*, the Puerto Rican Spanish word for land crabs, are closely related to their marine cousins and can be cooked and eaten in the same ways. Although they are eaten around the world, they hold a

Raúl Julia and Diane Salinger in a scene from The Morning After. *(AP/Wide World Photos)*

special place in Puerto Rican cuisine, where they formerly were very common in cane fields. In Puerto Rico, *jueyes* often are made into *asopao de jueyes*, a thick soup with rice, SOFRITO, and peas. They also are eaten boiled, deviled, and as a filling for EMPANADAS.

Julia, Raúl (Mar. 9, 1940, San Juan, Puerto Rico— Oct. 24, 1994, New York, N.Y.): Actor. Julia was educated at the University of Puerto Rico and made his stage debut in 1964 in Pedro Calderón de la Barca's classic *La vida es sueño* (*Life Is a Dream*). His first of many appearances with the New York Shakespeare Festival was in a 1966 production of *Macbeth*; he debuted on Broadway in *The Cuban Thing*. He was nominated for Tony Awards on four occasions.

Julia's film debut came in the 1969 film *Stiletto*, which he followed with *The Organization* and *Panic in Needle Park* in 1971. His other films include *Gumball Rally* (1976); *The Eyes of Laura Mars* (1978); *Isabel*

negra (1979), a film from Puerto Rico; *One from the Heart* (1982); *Compromising Positions* (1985); *Kiss of the Spider Woman* (1985), by Brazilian director Hector Babenco; *The Morning After* (1986), with Jane Fonda; *La gran fiesta* (1986), another Puerto Rican film; *Florida Straits* (1986); *Trading Hearts* (1987); *Moon over Parador* (1988); *Tequila Sunrise* (1988); *Romero* (1989), in which he portrayed slain Salvadoran archbishop Oscar Romero; *The Rookie* (1990); *Presumed Innocent* (1990); and *The Addams Family* (1991) and its sequel *Addams Family Values* (1993). Julia also played the title role in the television film *Onassis* and had a recurring role on the children's program *Sesame Street*.

Jurado, Katy (María Cristina Jurado García; b. Jan. 16, 1927, Guadalajara, Mexico): Actress. Jurado, a onetime film columnist for Mexican publications, made her Hollywood debut in the 1951 feature *The*

Actress Katy Jurado. (AP/Wide World Photos)

Bullfighter and the Lady. Her Hollywood career gained momentum in 1952, when she played Gary Cooper's jilted lover in *High Noon*. Many critics and fans believed that she should have been nominated for an Academy Award for that performance; nine years later, she was nominated for her supporting work in *Barabbas* (1962).

Jurado's list of film credits includes *Arrowhead* (1953), *Broken Lance* (1954), *The Racers* (1955), *Trial* (1955), *Trapeze* (1956), *The Man from Del Rio* (1956), *The Badlanders* (1958), *One-Eyed Jacks* (1961), *Smoky* (1966), *Covenant with Death* (1967), *Stay Away Joe* (1968), *Pat Garrett and Billy the Kid* (1973), *The Children of Sanchez* (1978), and *Under the Volcano* (1984). She has also appeared in a number of Spanish-language films made in Mexico and Spain, including *Un hombre solo* (1964), *El elegido* (1977), *Los albaniles* (1977), and *El recurso del método* (1978). Her television credits include the film *Evita Peron* and a recurring role in the short-lived 1984 series *AKA Pablo*. Jurado was married to actor Ernest Borgnine during the early 1960's.

Justice for Janitors: Labor organization. Justice for Janitors is made up of Latino members of Local 399 of the Service Employees International Union of Los Angeles, California. The Latinos are primarily Central American and Mexican, and the majority live in the inner city. The subgroup was formed to address the needs of Latinos within the union. Various demonstrations have been organized to demand fair wages and safer working conditions for union members.

Kachinas: Powerful spirits of the dead. From the Hopi, the word *kachina* is a general term used by outsiders to identify powerful spirits of the dead among Pueblo peoples. *Kachinas* are said to promote fertility and growth, beneficial rains, and healing; they also enforce communal laws. Pueblo peoples believe that these spirits take the shape of plants, animals, birds, and people. Ceremonial depictions of *kachinas* include masks and dolls. Many Pueblo *kachinas* paral-

lel main deities of ancient Mesoamerica. QUETZAL-CÓATL, for example, is represented by a plumed serpent and associated with water and fertility. He is a deity equivalent to Kolowisi, for the Zuni, and Palulukong, for the Hopi.

Kahlo, Frida (Magdalena Carmen Frida Kahlo y Calderón; July 6, 1907, Coyoacán, Mexico—July 13, 1954, Coyoacán, Mexico): Artist. Although she was

Frida Kahlo and Diego Rivera, shortly before their remarriage in 1940. (AP/Wide World Photos)

born in 1907, Kahlo reported her birth year as 1910, to correspond with the beginning of the Mexican Revolution. She was political throughout her adult life and joined the Mexican Communist Party in 1928; she had a brief relationship with Communist leader Leon Trotsky in 1937. She also supported the Spanish Republicans in the Spanish Civil War (1936-1939).

Kahlo met muralist Diego RIVERA in 1923 and was married to him on August 21, 1929. Kahlo had suffered a serious accident in 1925, when a bus in which she was riding collided with a trolley car. During her convalescence, she devoted herself to painting. Rivera encouraged her after viewing her work. Kahlo endured Rivera's extramarital affairs, becoming friends with some of the women with whom he had relationships. Kahlo and Rivera were divorced in 1939 but remarried in 1940.

Kahlo and Rivera traveled together through the 1930's, with a tour of Europe at the end of the decade. Kahlo received her first major recognition in 1938, with a show at the Julien Levy Gallery in New York, New York. In 1941, Kahlo was selected as one of the founding members of the Seminaria de Cultura Mexicana by the Mexican Ministry of Education. In 1943, she was appointed a professor of painting at La Esmeralda, the ministry's school of painting and sculpture in Mexico City. In 1946, she won the National Prize of Arts and Sciences awarded by the Ministry of Education.

Many of Kahlo's works are self-portraits that reflect her relationships to Rivera and to Mexico and the United States. She began to paint in earnest in the early 1930's, as a way of coping with physical and psychological problems including a miscarriage in 1932 and recurring difficulties related to a spinal injury she suffered in the 1925 accident. Rivera encouraged her to paint in a style more similar to folk art. Through *RETABLOS*, paintings that showed miracles performed by saints, Kahlo expressed her physical and psychological pain. Much of her work adapts traditional Mexican forms, and much of it is in a surrealist style.

Kanellos, Nicolás (b. Jan. 31, 1945, New York, N.Y.): Scholar and editor. Kanellos, of Puerto Rican descent, launched the *Revista Chicano-Riqueña* in Gary, Indiana, in 1973. The magazine led to the establishment of ARTE PÚBLICO Press in Houston in 1979. In 1987, the *Revista Chicano-Riqueña* became *The Americas Review*.

A longtime professor of Hispanic and classical languages at the University of Houston, Kanellos in 1990 published *The History of Hispanic Theater in the United States: Origins to 1940*. He is also the coauthor of *Nuevos Pasos: Chicano and Puerto Rican Drama* (1989), written with Jorge Huerta. Kanellos served as editor of and a writer for *The Hispanic-American Almanac* (1993) and also edited the *Biographical Dictionary of Hispanic Literature in the United States: The Literature of Puerto Ricans, Cubans and Other Hispanic Writers* (1990) and the anthology *Short Fiction by Hispanic Writers of the United States* (1993). In 1988, Kanellos received a White House Hispanic Heritage Award for Literature; in 1990, he won an American Book Award.

Kansas: Latinos represent a small, generally young segment of the population of Kansas and are centralized in the five largest cities and the rural southwest of the state. Since the 1800's, Latinos have worked as migrant agricultural laborers in Kansas. Since the 1950's, many Latinos have also worked as unskilled laborers in food-processing industries.

According to the 1990 census, Kansas ranked twenty-second among states in Latino population, with 93,670 Latinos, or 4 percent of the state's population. Most of the Latinos in Kansas belong to the three largest subgroups of Latinos—Mexican Americans, Puerto Ricans, and Cuban Americans.

Francisco Vázquez de CORONADO reached Kansas in the 1540's in his search for a powerful Indian kingdom. That mission did not succeed, but other similar efforts by other explorers followed. Part of what is now Kansas was ceded by Mexico to the United States in the TREATY OF GUADALUPE HIDALGO.

Latinos first came to Kansas in large numbers in the early nineteenth century, to work in the sugar beet fields and on the railroads. By the 1950's, center-pivot irrigation made cultivation possible even on marginal lands. Productive agriculture meant the availability of abundant feed grain, which was instrumental in building the cattle industry. In 1985, Kansas was the leading beef-packing state. By the 1990's, more than eighty feed yards were located in the nineteen counties of southwest Kansas. Meatpacking companies lowered costs by relocating in rural nonunion areas and hiring immigrant labor.

About half of the Latino population of Kansas resides in the state's ten largest cities. The largest number of Latinos live in the eastern part of Kansas; however, their presence is more strongly felt in the southwestern part of the state, where they represent more than 10 percent of the population.

LATINO POPULATION OF KANSAS, 1990

Total number of Latinos = 93,670; 4% of population

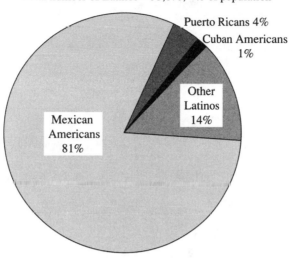

Puerto Ricans 4%
Cuban Americans 1%
Other Latinos 14%
Mexican Americans 81%

Source: Data are from Marlita A. Reddy, ed., *Statistical Record of Hispanic Americans* (Detroit: Gale Research, 1993), Table 106.

Latinos tend to be underrepresented in Kansas state universities. In 1993, Latinos represented approximately 4 percent of the population of Kansas but received only 2 percent of the bachelor's degrees awarded by these institutions. Among adults in Kansas who have less than a ninth grade education, Latinos make up 8.2 percent. Per capita, Latinos earn less than any other minority group in the state. Almost 20 percent of all Kansas Latinos were below the poverty level in 1990, while only 9.9 percent of the white population fell into this category.

Food processors, truck farms, feed lots, fish farms, orchards, and vegetable and fruit farms are the primary sources of employment for Kansas Latinos. Many work as migrant agricultural laborers, and children often work alongside parents in the fields. More than five thousand migrant workers, for example, move in and out of Garden City in a given year. Both the meatpacking and the agricultural industries have been attractive for new immigrants because little or no English is required of employees.

Approximately 8 percent of Latinos in Kansas work in precision production and repair services. Another 5 percent work as machine operators, assemblers, or inspectors. About 3 percent are employed in executive, administrative, and managerial positions, and 3 percent are represented in professional or specialty occupations.

Kapp, Joseph Robert (b. Mar. 19, 1938, Santa Fe, N.Mex.): Football player and coach. Kapp, the son of a German American father and a Mexican American mother, was reared in farmworking communities near Salinas, California. After an outstanding high-school career in both basketball and football, he received an athletic scholarship to the University of California at Berkeley, and he soon won the starting quarterback position on the school's football team. In his senior season, Kapp and halfback Jack Hart combined to lead the once-struggling team to the Pacific Coast Conference championship and a Rose Bowl appearance.

Drafted thirteenth overall by the Washington Redskins of the National Football League (NFL) in 1959, Kapp instead signed with the Calgary Stampeders of the Canadian Football League (CFL). Traded to the Vancouver Lions in 1961, he went on to lead the team to the 1964 Grey Cup. Remarkably, Kapp did not miss a game during his eight years in the CFL.

In 1967, Kapp moved to the NFL as a twenty-nine-year-old rookie with the Minnesota Vikings. In 1968, he led the Vikings to a division title. In the second game of the 1969 season, he threw seven touchdown passes against the Baltimore Colts, tying an NFL record. Kapp then led the Vikings to an NFL championship and into the 1969 Super Bowl against Kansas City. An injury took him out of the game, however, and

Joe Kapp tied an NFL record by completing seven touchdown passes in a 1969 victory by the Minnesota Vikings over the Baltimore Colts. (AP/Wide World Photos)

the favored Vikings lost to the American Football League champion Kansas City Chiefs.

In 1970, Kapp, whose agreement with the Vikings had expired, became the subject of a heated contract dispute. After refusing to sign with Minnesota, he accepted an offer from the floundering New England Patriots, with whom he finished the 1970 season. Before the 1971 season, however, Kapp refused to sign a standard players' contract and left training camp, never to return. He filed suit against the NFL, alleging that the league's policies violated antitrust laws, and in 1974 he won a landmark decision in U.S. District Court. Kapp's actions caused his early retirement, but he set an important precedent for future dealings between players and team owners. Kapp later became a successful coach at the University of California at Berkeley.

Katz, Leandro (b. June 6, 1938, Buenos Aires, Argentina): Artist and filmmaker. After earning a bachelor's degree at the Universidad Nacional de Buenos Aires, Katz lived in Peru, Ecuador, and Mexico before settling in the United States in the mid-1960's. He studied at the Pratt Graphic Arts Center in New York, New York, from 1965 to 1967. Katz began exhibiting in the United States in 1964 and has had his work shown at the Whitney Museum of American Art, the New Museum of Contemporary Art, and the Museum of Contemporary Crafts at the Smithsonian Institution, among other major museums.

Katz has worked in photography and film. In addition, he created radio pieces broadcast between 1966 and 1970 on station WRVR in New York City and worked as an editor with TVRT Press beginning in 1970. He began teaching pre-Columbian art at the School of Visual Arts in New York City in 1970. In 1981, he became an instructor in semiotics and cinema at Brown University, and in 1986, he moved to the New School of Social Research in New York City as a faculty member in the film department. Katz was awarded a John Simon Guggenheim Memorial Fellowship in 1979 and has received other prestigious honors.

Kerr, Louise Año Nuevo (b. Dec. 24, 1938, Denver, Colo.): Educator and administrator. Kerr was encouraged by a high-school typing instructor to apply for a four-year *salsipuedes* ("get out if you can") scholarship, which she received. Few other instructors had offered encouragement. Kerr went on to earn a bachelor's degree in sociology (1960) and a master's degree in history (1966) at the University of California, Los Angeles, and a Ph.D. in history from the University of Illinois, Chicago (1976).

Kerr, the daughter of a Mexican American mother and a native Filipino father, grew up in California, where her family worked on farms. She married Howard Kerr in 1963 and moved to Illinois with him when he was offered a teaching position at the University of Chicago. She learned about the large Latino community in Chicago and took a course to learn more about it. She took an assistant teaching position at the University of Illinois and later finished her Ph.D. there. She taught at Loyola University in Chicago from 1973 to 1980, when she was made an assistant dean. She rose to the position of associate dean, then in 1988 was named associate vice chancellor for academic affairs at the University of Illinois, Chicago. Along with her academic activities, Kerr served on the Committee on Decent and Unbiased Campaign Tactics, becoming its chair in 1989. She has published scholarly articles and worked on several academic publications, including serving on the editorial board of *Aztlan: International Journal of Chicano Studies* from 1981 to 1985. In 1979, she was given the Congressional Hispanic Caucus Humanities Award.

Kid Frost (Arturo Molina, Jr.): Mexican American rapper. Kid Frost emerged on the rap scene with his hit single *La Raza*, released in 1990 on the *Hispanic Causing Panic* album. Reared in East Los Angeles, Kid Frost was a gang member and LOW RIDER. He brings these experiences to his bilingual raps, which focus on political and social issues. He views rap as a unifying art for Latinos and in 1991 formed Latin Alliance, a like-minded group of rappers of Central American, Cuban, Mexican, and Puerto Rican descent.

King Ranch: HACIENDA in South Texas. This expansive hacienda, which covered fifty thousand acres during Richard King's lifetime, exemplified the typical Anglo-owned, self-sufficient ranch. It contained a commissary and store, stables, corrals, carriage and wagon sheds, blacksmith's shop, and houses for five hundred workers and their families. Richard King and his family effectively emulated and extended the feudal world of the Spanish and Mexican HACENDADOS. Anglo pioneer ranchers such as King acquired the traits of earlier Spanish/Mexican hacendados—a paternalistic bond with the VAQUEROS (ranch hands) and peons, an identification with the ranch, and an obsession to expand one's landholdings.

A statue of Eusebio Francisco Kino stands in the U.S. Capitol. (Library of Congress)

Kino, Eusebio Francisco (Eusebio Francesco Chino; August 10, 1645, Segno, Tirol [now Italy]—Mar. 15, 1711, Magdalena de Kino, Sonora, Mexico): Missionary and explorer. Kino received his education in Germany. In 1665, he joined the Jesuit order. In 1681, the order sent Kino to Mexico, where he went first to Mexico City and then to Veracruz. From Veracruz, he ranged widely through the region that today includes the Mexican state of Sonora and the American state of Arizona. There, Kino found numerous Jesuit missions among the Indians. The first of these was a Sonoran mission, Nuestra Señora de los Dolores, begun in 1687.

From 1691 on, Kino, often called "the padre on horseback," undertook more than forty expeditions ranging throughout what is now Arizona. During these expeditions, he explored the Rio Grande and the Gila and Colorado rivers.

In the course of establishing his missions, Kino helped Arizona's Pima Indians to expand and to diversify their agriculture, introducing fruits, grain, and vegetables until then unknown to this tribe. He also gave instruction in raising cattle, sheep, and horses. Kino reportedly fought the enslavement of Indians in the silver mines of Mexico. His other accomplishments include preparing a map of lower California and Pimería Alta that was used for more than a century after his death and writing *Las Misiones de Sonora y Arizona*.

Kit Carson National Forest takeover (Oct. 22, 1966): Protest concerning Spanish land grants. National Forest Service lands in New Mexico had been carved from Spanish land grants dating back to the 1560's. Large numbers of poor Mexican Americans had lived in these areas since long before New Mexico had become a state in 1912. In 1966, the Forest Service began charging higher fees for grazing privileges on these lands. Most of the farmers had small herds of sheep and cattle and could not afford the increased fees.

In response, Reies López TIJERINA, a former evangelist, organized the Alianza Federal de Mercedes (the federal alliance of land grantees). This group took over a parking lot in Kit Carson National Forest, put up a tent city in the campground, and announced plans to stay until the farmers' grazing fees were reduced. Violence broke out on October 22, when two forest rangers were stoned by a mob. Tijerina and his brother were arrested, convicted of assault, and sentenced to two years in prison. Over the next few months, fires were set in the forest and white ranchers had their fences cut. The tent city was finally abandoned, and the protest ended.

L

Labarthe, Pedro Juan (b. 1906, Puerto Rico): Writer. Labarthe received attention in the United States for his *The Son of Two Nations: The Private Life of a Columbia Student* (1931). This autobiographical work tells of Labarthe's experiences at Columbia University and his efforts to improve his socioeconomic status.

The work has been referred to as "proto-NUYORICAN" because of its emphasis on assimilation as a means to success. Labarthe's experiences are those of a person from the middle and upper classes, explaining the assimilationist viewpoints expressed in his work.

Labat, Tony (b. Nov. 14, 1951, Havana, Cuba): Artist. Labat moved to the United States in 1965, but his father stayed behind. Labat visited Cuba in 1983, but his father had died earlier and Labat reported feeling as much a foreigner in Cuba as he had in the United States. The visit transformed his work, from showing a bicultural experience to becoming more personal as well as more universal. Much of his work is in the video medium.

Labat moved to San Francisco, California, from his original place of settlement in Miami, Florida. He earned B.F.A. (1978) and M.F.A. (1980) degrees from the San Francisco Art Institute. His work is in the Centre Pompidou in Paris, France; the Museum of Modern Art in New York, New York; the Oppenheim Collection in Bonn, Germany; and other major collections throughout the world. Labat won National Endowment for the Arts fellowships in 1983 and 1988 and has received numerous awards for his work.

Labor force, Latinas in the: In 1992, there were slightly more than four million Latinas in the U.S. labor force, that is, either working or actively seeking work. This compares with 6.1 million Latino men in the labor force. Although it became increasingly common for Latinas to work outside the home in the late twentieth century, their labor force participation remained constrained by both socioeconomic and cultural factors such as the value placed on women's domestic role in traditional Latino culture.

Latina Labor Force Participation. The labor force participation rate of Latinas, that is, the proportion of all Latinas over the age of sixteen who are in the labor force, has increased significantly in the late twentieth century. The overall labor force participation rate for Latinas in 1990 was 56 percent, substantially higher than the 1980 rate of 49.4 percent. By contrast, the Latina participation rate was 27.2 percent in 1950, 32.7 percent in 1960, and 36.8 percent in 1970.

The pattern of rising labor force participation applies to all Latina subgroups, to one extent or another. Among Central and South American women in the United States, labor force participation increased the most, from about 50 percent in 1980 to about 63 percent in 1990. The proportion of mainland Puerto Rican women in the work force rose from 40 to 51 percent, and that of Mexican Americans from 49 percent to 55 percent during the same time period. Labor force participation changed the least among Cuban American women, rising from 55.3 percent in 1980 to 56 percent in 1990. These numbers illustrate the diversity in the labor force experiences of the various Latina groups.

The rising labor force participation rate of Latinas is partly associated with changes in the national economy and society. The overall female labor force participation rate in the United States increased from 49.8 percent in 1980 to 57.4 percent in 1990. There are, however, specific factors influencing Latina labor force participation.

Determinants of Labor Force Participation. A broad set of demographic and socioeconomic factors influences labor force participation. For the Latino population, the presence of a significant foreign-born labor force exerts an important effect. The labor force participation of immigrants is generally different from that of U.S.-born women. These gaps are related to differences in the economies and societies involved (such as the role of agriculture versus industry and the role of women in work for pay) as well as the nature of the particular immigrant group (urban versus rural migrants, for example, and different socioeconomic classes). Latina immigrants tend to have a lower rate of labor force participation than do women born in the United States. For example, in 1990, the participation rate among foreign-born Latinas was 53 percent, compared to 59.5 percent among U.S.-born Latinas.

Education is another critical factor. As educational attainment rises, the income that can be earned in the labor market increases, making work outside the home more likely. Career aspirations are also stimulated by higher education, leading to a greater attractiveness of work for pay. For the Latino population, greater educational attainment is closely related to the increased labor force participation observed in the 1980's and earlier. For example, among U.S.-born women, the proportion of Latinas twenty-five years of age or older with less than a high school diploma or equivalent declined from 48.6 percent in 1980 to 37.2 percent in 1990. The proportion of Latinas with a college degree rose from 6.4 percent in 1980 to 9.5 percent in 1990.

The situation of the local labor market is important in influencing labor force participation. Among women, employment in clerical, office, and other white-collar occupations has traditionally absorbed a large portion of the labor force. The relative strength of the service sector in the 1970's and 1980's served to increase the number of job opportunities available to women. In New York City, for example, employment in services expanded by 311,780 jobs from 1970 to 1990, compared to a drop of more than 275,000 jobs in manufacturing during the period.

Other variables influencing labor force participation rates of women include age, marital status, presence of children, disability status, labor market skills, and proficiency in the English language. The influence of each of these variables on Latina labor force participation depends on the group being considered.

Earnings of Latinas. The earnings received by women in the American labor market traditionally have been substantially below those of men, although the gap began to shrink as the twentieth century came to a close. For example, Latinas earned 58.7 cents per dollar earned by men in 1979, but the ratio had increased to 69.2 cents per dollar by 1989. The gender gap in wages narrowed considerably in the 1980's, with women's salaries catching up significantly with those of men. This pattern occurred both for the overall

CHANGES IN LATINA LABOR FORCE PARTICIPATION, 1980-1990
(persons 16 years of age or older)

Ethnic Group	Labor Force Participation Rates (percentages)	
	1980	1990
Latino population, overall	49.4	56.0
Central Americans	50.6	62.7
Cuban Americans	55.3	56.0
Dominican Americans	46.1	52.8
Mexican Americans	49.2	55.3
Puerto Ricans (mainland)	40.3	50.8
South Americans	50.0	63.2

Source: Data are from U.S. Department of Commerce, *1990 United States Census of Population and Housing Public Use Microdata Samples.*

labor force and for the Latino population (*see* INCOME AND WAGE LEVELS).

There are various reasons for this gender gap. One is that part-time employment traditionally has been more prevalent among women. This reduces women's earnings relative to men because the wages of part-time workers lie below those of full-time laborers. Among the Latino population, 51.2 percent of men aged twenty-five to sixty-four were working full-time, year-round in 1989, compared to 27.8 percent of Latinas.

Even among those persons employed full-time, there is substantial inequality in the income received by men and women. Among Latinos, the annual earnings of full-time, year-round male workers between the ages of twenty-five and sixty-four was $24,087 in 1989. Comparable Latinas earned $17,950. This means that, in 1989, full-time, year-round Latina workers made 74.5 cents per dollar earned by men. The earnings of full-time, year-round Latina workers were much closer to those of Latino men in 1989 than they had been in 1979, when full-time Latina workers made, on average, 63.9 cents per dollar earned by men.

Occupational Distribution. Labor market inequities are reflected in the diverse occupational distributions of men and women (*see* OCCUPATIONS AND OCCUPATIONAL TRENDS). Women are heavily concentrated in administrative support, clerical, and private household occupations, which tend to be lower paying. For example, in 1990, 41 percent of all the Latino workers employed in the executive, administrative, and managerial occupations were women. By contrast, 95 percent of all Latino workers employed in private household occupations were female. Latino women are concen-

LABOR FORCE PARTICIPATION OF LATINAS IN THE UNITED STATES
(persons 16 years of age or older)

Year	Labor Force Participation Rates (percentages)
1950	27.2
1960	32.7
1970	36.8
1980	49.4
1990	56.0

Source: Data are from U.S. Department of Commerce, *1980 and 1990 United States Census of Population and Housing Public Use Microdata Samples.* The data for 1950, 1960, and 1970 are from Gregory DeFreitas, *Inequality at Work: Hispanics in the U.S. Labor Force* (New York: Oxford University Press, 1991), p. 80.

trated in white-collar occupations, and within those occupations, they are clustered in the lower-paying categories. Only in the professional occupations—which include a large share of high-paying jobs—are women overrepresented. That phenomenon, however, is relatively recent.

The growing presence of Latinas in traditionally male occupations reflects a nationwide pattern associated with the growth of professional training for women and the breakdown in hiring barriers for women, through policies such as AFFIRMATIVE ACTION. The 1980's saw significant gains in educational attainment for women, as seen in the increase in degrees granted by professional schools. Among the Latino population receiving law degrees, the proportion of women grew from 30.9 percent in the 1980-1981 academic year to 44.1 percent in 1990-1991. Among Latino business and management college graduates, women constituted 35 percent in 1980-1981 but 48.1 percent ten years later. Even engineering, a traditionally male field, had a larger proportion of female graduates in 1990-1991 (16.7 percent) compared to 1980-1981 (9.2 percent).

Despite significant educational progress, Latinas' occupational status in the United States remained significantly below that of Latino men. Furthermore, within the female population, the occupations that Latinas hold are lower-paying and have lower status than those held by non-Hispanic white women. Differences in education, age, part-time employment, immigrant status, and other variables influence the relative occupational position of Latinas. There is evidence, however, that after taking into account these factors, Latino women still have lower wages than non-Hispanic

WOMEN AS A PROPORTION OF THE LATINO LABOR FORCE, BY OCCUPATION, 1990	
Occupational Group	*Latinas as a Percentage of All Latino Workers in the Occupational Group, 1990*
Executive, administrative, and managerial	41.0
Professional	57.5
Technical	42.0
Sales	58.2
Administrative support	70.9
Private household occupations	95.0
Protective services	17.1
Other services	51.6
Farming, forestry, and fishing	25.3
Precision production, craft, and repair occupations	14.3
Machine operators, assemblers, and inspectors	46.9
Transportation workers	6.0
Handlers, equipment cleaners, helpers, and laborers	21.1

Source: Data are from U.S. Department of Commerce, *1990 United States Census of Population and Housing Public Use Microdata Samples.*

white females. Such is the conclusion of a sociological study done in 1985, which showed that if Latino women had the same demographic characteristics, such as age and education, as their white counterparts, only between 27 and 57 percent of the gap in occupational status would be closed. The remaining portion can be attributed to employment DISCRIMINATION based on ethnicity or other unidentified factors.

—Francisco L. Rivera-Batiz

SUGGESTED READINGS:

• Barry Figueroa, Janis. "A Comparison of Labor Supply Behavior Among Single and Married Puerto Rican Mothers." In *Hispanics in the Labor Force: Issues and Policies*, edited by Edwin Melendez, Clara Rodriguez, and Janis Barry Figueroa. New York: Plenum Press, 1991. Study of the determinants of labor force participation among Puerto Rican women in New York City.

• Blau, Francine D., and Marianne Ferber. *The Economics of Women, Men, and Work.* 2d ed. Englewood Cliffs, N.J.: Prentice-Hall, 1992. Review of the determinants of female labor force participation in the United States, including Latinas.

• DeFreitas, Gregory. *Inequality at Work: Hispanics in the U.S. Labor Force.* New York: Oxford University Press, 1991. Presents and analyzes trends in Latina labor force participation, earnings, and other labor market variables since 1950.

THE GENDER GAP, 1979-1989		
(employed persons 16 years of age or older)		
	Annual Earnings of Women as a Percentage of Men's Earnings	
Ethnic Group	*1979*	*1989*
United States, overall	51.2	58.1
Latino population, overall	58.7	69.2
Central Americans	67.0	71.2
Cuban Americans	60.3	66.1
Dominican Americans	73.8	78.1
Mexican Americans	56.8	70.1
Puerto Ricans (mainland)	66.7	72.4
South Americans	71.9	60.0

Source: Data are from U.S. Department of Commerce, *1990 United States Census of Population and Housing Public Use Microdata Samples.*

- Goldin, Claudia. *Understanding the Gender Gap: An Economic History of American Women*. New York: Oxford University Press, 1990. Provides a survey of the factors determining women's participation in the U.S. labor force.
- Ong, Paul M. "Immigrant Wives' Labor Force Participation." *Industrial Relations* 26 (Fall, 1987): 296-303. Examines the labor supply decisions of immigrant women.
- Ortiz, Vilma, and Rosemary Santana Cooney. "Sex-Role Attitudes and Labor Force Participation Among Young Hispanic Females and Non-Hispanic White Females." In *The Mexican American Experience: An Interdisciplinary Anthology*, edited by Rodolfo O. de la Garza et al. Austin: University of Texas Press, 1985. Determines the impact of sex-role attitudes on the labor force participation of several generations of Hispanic women in the United States.
- Reimers, Cordelia. "A Comparative Analysis of the Wages of Hispanics, Blacks, and Non-Hispanic Whites." In *Hispanics in the U.S. Economy*, edited by George J. Borjas and Marta Tienda. Orlando, Fla.: Academic Press, 1985. Provides estimates of the role played by labor market discrimination in determining the wages of Latinas and other women in the United States.
- Tienda, Marta, and J. Glass. "Household Structure and Labor Force Participation of Black, Hispanic, and White Mothers." *Demography* 22 (August, 1985): 381-394. Examines the determinants of labor force participation among Hispanic and other women in the United States.
- Tienda, Marta, and Patricia Guhleman. "The Occupational Position of Employed Hispanic Women." In *Hispanics in the U.S. Economy*, edited by George J. Borjas and Marta Tienda. Orlando, Fla.: Academic Press, 1985. Studies the determinants of occupational status and the extent of labor market discrimination against Latinas in the United States, relative to non-Hispanic white women.

Labor force, Latinos in the: The U.S. Latino labor force in 1991 consisted of 9.8 million persons, including 6.0 million Mexican Americans, 930,000 mainland Puerto Ricans, 543,000 Cuban Americans, and 2.3 million members of Central, South American, and other Latino groups.

Official labor market statistics consider persons in the labor force to be those individuals sixteen years of age or older who are either employed or actively seeking employment (unemployed). The remaining

LATINO LABOR FORCE PARTICIPATION RATES, 1990
(persons 16 years of age or older)

Ethnic Group	Labor Force Participation Rates (percentages)	
	Male	Female
United States, overall	75.9	57.4
Latino population, overall	80.6	56.0
Central Americans	86.7	62.7
Cuban Americans	76.3	56.0
Dominican Americans	77.1	52.8
Mexican Americans	81.8	55.3
Puerto Ricans (mainland)	74.0	50.8
South Americans	86.3	63.2

Source: Data are from U.S. Department of Commerce, *1990 United States Census of Population and Housing Public Use Microdata Samples.*

group—persons not in the labor force—includes individuals who have stopped looking for work (discouraged workers), full-time students, retirees, persons performing unpaid family work, and those unable to work.

Latino Labor Force Participation. The proportion of Latinos in the labor force—their labor force participation rate—varies significantly, depending on gender and on the particular subgroup considered. The overall labor force participation rate for Latino males in 1990 was 80.6 percent. This rate exceeds the average for the U.S. general male population, which was 75.9 percent in 1990. There is, however, considerable diversity in labor market participation within the Latino population. Among men of Central and South American origin, for example, labor force participation in 1990 was substantially above the average (more than 86 percent), and among Puerto Ricans it was lower (74 percent). For Cuban American men, the 1990 labor force participation rate was 76.3 percent; for men from the Dominican Republic it was 77.1 percent; and for Mexican American men it was 81.8 percent.

Among Latino women in the United States, the overall labor force participation rate in 1990 was 56 percent, slightly below the rate for the general American female population (57.4 percent). There is also diversity in the labor market participation of Latinas. As was true for men, the labor force participation rate of women of South and Central American origin was higher than the average in 1990 (approximately 63 percent), and that of Puerto Ricans was below the average (50.8 percent). Labor force participation was 56 percent for Cuban American women, 52.8 percent for Dominican American women, and 55.3 percent for Mexican American women.

Most of the Latino labor force was employed. In 1992, for example, the fraction of the Latino labor force that was gainfully employed was, on average, 88.6 percent. This employment rate was much lower than that of other groups in the population. The average employment rate for the overall U.S. labor force in 1992 was 92.6 percent. Among non-Hispanic white Americans, it was 93.5 percent. Furthermore, there is considerable diversity of employment experience within the Latino labor force. In 1992, the average employment rate for Mexican Americans was 88.3 percent, among Puerto Ricans it was 85.9 percent, and among Cuban Americans it was 92.1 percent.

Determinants of Latino Labor Force Participation. Differences in the participation rates of various Latino groups in the labor force result from a wide array of demographic and socioeconomic factors. There are, for example, significant differences between the foreign-born and the native born populations. Among men, the labor force participation rate of Latino immigrants generally exceeds that of Latinos born in the United States. In 1990, the labor force participation of U.S.-born Latinos was 76.9 percent, while it was 83.3 percent for foreign-born Latinos. Among Latinas on the other hand, the labor force participation rate of immigrants is significantly lower than that of persons born in the United States: In 1990, the participation rate among foreign-born Latinas was 53 percent, compared to 59.5 percent among U.S.-born Latinas.

Other variables influencing labor force participation rates include potential workers' age, marital status, presence of children, disability status, human capital endowments (such as schooling, on-the-job experience, and proficiency in use of the English language), and local labor market conditions facing the worker, including the unemployment rate and prevailing wage rates. The influence of each of these variables on Latino labor force participation depends on the group being considered.

Puerto Ricans. One of the key factors associated with the lower labor force participation rates of Puerto Rican men and women relative to other Latino groups is the deteriorating labor market faced by Puerto Ricans in the northeastern United States. The northeastern area has undergone massive economic restructuring that has shifted employment from manufacturing to services. In New York City alone, employment in manufacturing declined by 117,580 jobs in the 1970's

Lack of skills or undocumented status force some Latinos to take jobs in the underground economy. (Impact Visuals, Donna DeCesare)

and by 158,200 jobs in the 1980's. Service jobs expanded by 56,880 in the 1970's and by 254,900 in the 1980's. Most studies of employees displaced in the 1970's and 1980's have found that workers leaving manufacturing jobs often face extended periods of unemployment (*see* UNEMPLOYMENT AND UNDEREMPLOYMENT). When job offers are forthcoming, the wages offered are substantially below those earned by workers in their previous positions. These factors push some workers to withdraw from the labor force. Manufacturing has been one of the largest sectors of employment among Puerto Ricans, accounting for close to one-third of the Puerto Rican labor force in 1980, so the deteriorating market for these laborers has affected Puerto Ricans substantially.

Disability and handicapped status are also related to the lower labor force participation rates of Puerto Ricans in the United States. Significant improvements have been made since the 1970's regarding job access for persons with disabilities. Nevertheless, disabled people traditionally have suffered from limited employment opportunities and have comparatively low labor force participation rates. This is critical for the Puerto Rican population on the U.S. mainland, which has handicapped and disability rates exceeding those of other groups in the population. Among Puerto Ricans in New York City in 1990, for example, 43.9 percent of the men not in the labor force had a handicap or disability, compared to 38.3 percent of all Latino men, 34.1 percent of non-Latino white men, and 35.8 percent of non-Latino black men.

Among women, the corresponding figures were 29.8 percent for Latinas overall and 34.5 percent for Puerto Rican women. Supporting these data are several

SCHOOLING AND THE EARNINGS OF LATINO WORKERS, 1989
(employed persons 16 years of age or older)

Educational Attainment	Annual Earnings (dollars)	
	Male	Female
Less than high school diploma	14,869	9,100
High school diploma or equivalent	19,683	13,128
Some college education	22,843	15,834
College degree	30,746	20,205
More than a college degree	39,543	25,196

Source: Data are from U.S. Department of Commerce, *1990 United States Census of Population and Housing Public Use Microdata Samples.*

studies documenting the greater incidence of health problems among Puerto Ricans. According to a 1991 report in the *Journal of the American Medical Association*, on almost every health indicator, Puerto Ricans fared worse than did Mexican Americans or Cuban Americans.

Earnings of Latino Workers. In 1989, male Latino workers earned, on average, $17,154. This was substantially lower than the earnings for the overall U.S. male work force, which received an average of $24,632 (*see* INCOME AND WAGE LEVELS).

There is considerable diversity in the labor market rewards received by various Latino subgroups. Cuban American men, for example, earned an average of $23,256 in 1989, an amount substantially higher than the average for Latinos, while Central American workers made an average of $14,961 a year. Dominican American workers had an average annual income of $15,619 in 1989, Mexican American workers received $15,631, Puerto Ricans $19,021, and South Americans $21,457.

Among women, Latinas earned an average of $14,160 in 1989. This is less than the $14,306 earned by the average U.S. female worker. Within the Latina labor force, Cuban American women earned the most, with average annual wages of $15,385, followed by Puerto Rican women with $13,790, South Americans with $12,885, Dominican Americans with $12,193, Mexican Americans with $10,970, and Central Americans with $10,661.

One of the most disturbing trends in Latino labor force statistics in recent years has been the declining average earnings of the Latino male work force. The earnings of Latino male workers in the United States declined by 4.8 percent in the 1980's, measured in constant 1989 dollars. This is in contrast to marked

EARNINGS OF LATINO WORKERS, 1989
(employed persons 16 years of age or older)

Ethnic Group	Annual Earnings (dollars)	
	Male	Female
United States, overall	24,632	14,306
Latino population, overall	17,154	11,879
Central Americans	14,961	10,661
Cuban Americans	23,256	15,385
Dominican Americans	15,619	12,193
Mexican Americans	15,631	10,970
Puerto Ricans (mainland)	19,021	13,790
South Americans	21,457	12,885

Source: Data are from U.S. Department of Commerce, *1990 United States Census of Population and Housing Public Use Microdata Samples.*

A billboard in Atlanta, Georgia, reminds workers and employers of immigrants' rights. (Envision, Jean Higgins)

increases in the inflation-adjusted earnings of non-Latino white, black, and Asian men.

The earnings of men in all the major Latino subgroups increased on average in the 1980's, except those of the most numerous group, Mexican American workers, whose pay declined on average by 9 percent. To understand this reduction in earnings, especially in comparison to wage changes for members of other Latino subgroups, one must examine the factors that determine wages and earnings in the labor market.

The Determinants of Earnings. Variations in the earnings received by workers largely reflect differences in the skills that persons bring to the labor market. All other things being equal, the greater the skills that a person is endowed with, the higher his or her productivity on the job and, therefore, the higher his or her earnings. A significant portion of a person's skills are obtained through formal education in school, although many workers also acquire skills through on-the-job training and vocational education.

The average male Latino worker between the ages of twenty-five and sixty-four with less than a high school diploma or equivalent earned $14,869 in 1989. For Latinos with a high school diploma, earnings went up to $19,683. Some college education increased earnings to $22,843, and a college degree raised earnings to $30,746. Latino men with education beyond an undergraduate degree earned an average of $39,543 in 1989.

The same pattern can be observed among Latinas. For Latinas with less than a high school diploma or equivalent, annual earnings were $9,100 in 1990. Those with a high school diploma earned an average of $13,128. Latinas with some college received $15,834 in earnings, and those with a college degree earned $20,205. Latinas with education beyond an undergraduate degree earned $25,196.

Educational differences explain much of the variation in the earnings of workers from different Latino subgroups. The higher earnings of Cuban and South American workers as compared to Mexican and Dominican American workers can be linked to the greater average educational attainment of Latinos of Cuban and South American descent. In 1990, the proportions of the population twenty-five years of age or older who had not completed high school were 42.2 percent and 28.6 percent for Cuban and South American Latinos, respectively. By contrast, the corresponding proportions for Mexican and Dominican Latinos were 56.2 percent and 58.1 percent.

Variation in educational attainment is embodied in the occupations that persons hold. The more formal education an individual has, the more likely it is that he or she will be in a white-collar occupation (managerial, professional, technical, sales, or administrative support) instead of a blue-collar occupation (production, craft, or repair work or equipment operation). Among Cuban Americans, the proportion of workers with white-collar jobs was 57.3 percent in 1990. By contrast, only 35.2 percent of employed Mexican Americans were in these occupations in 1990.

The Deteriorating Labor Market for Unskilled Workers. Educational attainment gaps also help explain changes in Latino earnings. The labor market for workers with comparatively low educational attainment collapsed in the United States during the 1980's. This means that higher education earned a larger return and persons with lower levels of education suffered in relation. As these changes occurred, unskilled workers suffered a deterioration in employment opportunities and earnings. The Mexican American population, with a relatively low average level of education, suffered from this effect.

The collapsing labor market for unskilled labor has had a tremendously negative impact on unskilled Latino immigrants. The annual earnings of Mexican immigrants spiraled downward in the 1980's, when adjusted for inflation. For men in this group, annual earnings in 1979 (expressed in 1989 dollars) were, on average, $15,467. By 1989, male Mexican immigrants' earnings had fallen to $13,515, a drop of 12.6 percent from 1979. Among Mexican immigrant women, annual earnings changed little in the 1980's, from $9,087 in 1979 to $9,120 in 1989.

The key reason why Mexican immigrants fell back in economic status during the 1980's is related to the deteriorating labor market position of unskilled workers in the United States. The proportion of Mexican immigrants lacking a high school diploma is relatively high, and these people fell into the category of unskilled workers. In 1990, 74.8 percent of the Mexican immigrant population in the United States aged twenty-five years or older had not completed high school or the equivalent. The average educational attainment of the Mexican immigrant population did not improve much during the 1980's. By contrast, most other groups in the U.S. population exhibited substantial improvement in educational attainment.

Labor market research suggests that, apart from economic restructuring, most of the decline in the wages of unskilled workers relative to educated workers in the United States during the 1980's was related to technological change in the workplace. Technological changes, such as increased use of computers, reduced

The market for unskilled factory workers declined in the 1980's, with disproportionate effects on Latinos.
(David Bacon)

the demand for unskilled workers while increasing the demand for highly educated labor. The result was an increase in the wage premium paid for education in the labor market.

It is often argued in the press and in some policy circles that the growth of immigration is linked to the deteriorating condition of less-educated workers in the labor market. The argument made is that immigrants displace unskilled workers in U.S. labor markets, reducing their wages. There is, however, no substantive evidence indicating that inflows of unskilled immigrants have depressed economic conditions. On the contrary, research results on the issue suggest that, both for the United States overall and for specific labor markets (such as Miami after the MARIEL BOAT LIFT from Cuba), the impact of immigration on wages in the 1980's and 1990's has been small. These studies find that the lower wages received by unskilled workers over the 1980's were not associated with immigration but rather with economic restructuring and technological changes in the workplace.

Discrimination. Educational attainment and other productive characteristics are critical in determining labor market success. Skill differences, however, do not explain all the shortfall in the employment rates of Latinos relative to the non-Hispanic white population or Latinos' comparatively lower earnings. Research evidence suggests that labor market discrimination against Latinos explains a substantial part of the differences in UNEMPLOYMENT rates and wage rates.

In a pathbreaking 1989 study, the Urban Institute undertook an analysis for the U.S. government of the extent of employment discrimination against Hispanic U.S. citizens in Chicago and San Diego. To measure discrimination, the study used a so-called "hiring audit" methodology similar to that used in studies of housing discrimination. Pairs of individuals, Latino and Anglo, were carefully matched in all personal characteristics— other than ethnicity—that could influence hiring decisions. These persons were then sent to apply for low-skilled, entry-level jobs, and their experience in the hiring process was measured and compared. The study found evidence of widespread discrimination against Latino applicants. Latinos received unfavorable treatment from three out of every ten employers, with Anglos receiving 33 percent more interviews and 52 percent more job offers than Latinos.

Evidence on DISCRIMINATION against Latinos in the United States is available from other sources. In an influential 1985 study using the Survey of Income and Education, Cordelia Reimers estimated that 86 percent

of the shortfall in the wages of Central and South American men relative to non-Hispanic white men could be attributed to discrimination. The comparable figure for Puerto Ricans was 50 percent, and for Mexican Americans it was 20 percent.

Explicit information concerning UNAUTHORIZED WORKERS (sometimes referred to as "illegal" or "undocumented") is scarce and based on relatively small surveys. Most of the figures cited above are based on census or census-type surveys, which tend to undercount unauthorized workers. Experts are concerned that the census of 1990 seriously undercounted unauthorized workers, as well as persons from minority groups in general, particularly those in urban areas. These questions were taken up by the U.S. court system in the early 1990's in response to challenges made to the census population count by certain state and city governments (*see* CENSUS, TREATMENT AND COUNTING OF LATINOS IN THE).

Evidence suggests that unauthorized workers, in comparison with legal workers, keep longer work hours and receive lower wages. In a study carried out by sociologist Douglas Massey, legal Mexican immigrants in the United States were found to have earned an average hourly wage of $9.54 during 1983 and 1984. By comparison, undocumented Mexican workers earned an average of $5.98 an hour. These sharply lower wages are partly related to the lower average age of the undocumented workers and their more limited educational attainment. Exploitation and wage discrimination, however, probably explain a significant part of the wage shortfall of unauthorized workers.

—*Francisco L. Rivera-Batiz*

SUGGESTED READINGS:

• Bean, Frank D., and Marta Tienda, *The Hispanic Population of the United States.* New York: Russell Sage Foundation, 1987. Provides a general survey of the Hispanic population in the United States, using 1980 census data. Chapter 9, "Hispanics in the U.S. Labor Force," is a summary of the labor force status of Latinos.

• Borjas, George J., and Marta Tienda. "Introduction." In *Hispanics in the U.S. Economy,* edited by George J. Borjas and Marta Tienda. Orlando, Fla.: Academic Press, 1985. Examines Latino labor market trends and their consequences up to the early 1980's.

• Cross, Harry, et al. *Employer Hiring Practices: Differential Treatment of Hispanic and Anglo Job Seekers.* Washington, D.C.: The Urban Institute Press, 1990. Surveys the literature and estimates the extent of discrimination against Latino job seekers.

• DeFreitas, Gregory. *Inequality at Work: Hispanics in the U.S. Labor Force*. New York: Oxford University Press, 1991. Analysis of trends and determinants of shifts in labor force participation among Latinos in the United States from 1949 to the late 1980's.

• Melendez, Edwin, Clara Rodriguez, and Janis Barry Figueroa. "Hispanics in the Labor Force: An Introduction to Issues and Approaches." In *Hispanics in the Labor Force: Issues and Policies*, edited by Edwin Melendez, Clara Rodriguez, and Janis Barry Figueroa. New York: Plenum Press, 1991. Survey of labor force trends among Latinos in the United States. Considers policy issues related to improving the labor force status of Latinos.

• Morales, Rebecca, and Frank Bonilla. "Restructuring and the New Inequality." In *Latinos in a Changing U.S. Economy: Comparative Perspectives on Growing Inequality*, edited by Rebecca Morales and Frank Bonilla. Newbury Park, Calif.: Sage Publications, 1993. Examines the impact of economic restructuring in the United States on labor force indicators among Latinos.

• Reimers, Cordelia. "A Comparative Analysis of the Wages of Hispanics, Blacks, and Non-Hispanic Whites." In *Hispanics in the U.S. Economy*, edited by George J. Borjas and Marta Tienda. Orlando, Fla.: Academic Press, 1985. Provides estimates of the role played by labor market discrimination in determining the wages of Latinos and members of other ethnic and racial groups in the United States.

• Rivera-Batiz, Francisco L. "The Effects of Literacy on the Earnings of Hispanics in the United States." In *Hispanics in the Labor Force: Issues and Policies*, edited by Edwin Melendez, Clara Rodriguez, and Janis Barry-Figueroa. New York: Plenum Press, 1991. Examines the role played by education, language skills, and literacy in determining the employment success of Latinos and members of other ethnic and racial groups in the U.S. economy.

• Rivera-Batiz, Francisco L., and Selig L. Sechzer. "Substitution and Complementarity Between Immigrant and Native Labor in the United States." In *U.S. Immigration Policy Reform in the 1980s: A Preliminary Assessment*, edited by Francisco L. Rivera-Batiz, Selig Sechzer, and Ira Gang. New York: Praeger, 1991. Provides a survey of the literature examining the impact of Latino immigrants on the U.S. labor market.

Labor-Management Relations Act (Taft-Hartley Act): Labor legislation. This act was passed in 1947, following a wave of labor strikes in 1946. Policymakers believed that the balance of power had shifted in favor of workers and against management and that it was time to curb the power of organized labor.

The Labor-Management Relations Act amended the NATIONAL LABOR RELATIONS ACT of 1935, also known as the Wagner Act. The new legislation prohibited unions from engaging in unfair labor practices and outlawed the closed shop, which required that anyone hired be a member of the union before beginning employment. It also gave states the option of prohibiting union shops—in which all workers had to belong to the union before being hired or join soon after being hired—through "right to work" laws. The act also gave the president of the United States the right to issue an injunction against a strike.

The Wagner Act had protected workers from discrimination or harassment by employers in response to union activities. The Taft-Hartley Act protected workers' right not to join a union. Unions were prohibited from discriminating against workers who were not members. In addition, the act gave workers the right to decertify a union, or to stop being represented by it.

Historically, unions have benefited workers by bargaining for pay rates higher than those of nonunion workers (*see* LABOR UNIONISM). Latinas in particular have benefited from unionization. Prior to unionization, many employers of Latinas paid extremely low wage rates and offered poor working conditions. Unions aided Latinas in enforcing their legal rights and in organizing to bargain for pay and working conditions better than the minimum required by law. The provisions of the Taft-Hartley Act thus indirectly harmed Latinos by making it more difficult to organize unions and keep them in place. As of the early 1990's, Texas, Arizona, and Florida—all states with large Latino populations—all had right to work laws that diminished the power of unions.

Labor unionism: The deplorable economic conditions of Latinos in the United States during the nineteenth and early twentieth centuries resulted in the emergence of numerous labor unions. Latino laborers demonstrated a remarkable degree of self-organization. The goals of these unions usually included increased wages and improved working and living conditions.

One of the myths concerning Latino laborers is that they were docile and not prone to unionization; in truth, many Latino unions were extremely militant, and strikes were common. Most of these strikes were vigorously opposed by companies, farmers, and local authorities. Coercive tactics were routinely used against strikers and pickets, including lockouts, deportations, arrests and incarcerations, excessive bail, and beatings by vigilante groups and local police officers.

Latino unions often failed to receive support from the larger U.S. labor movement. In some cases, incipient Latino unions were strongly opposed by traditional U.S. labor organizations. Discrimination against Latinos by established unions, including the American Federation of Labor (AFL), was widespread.

Early Organizational Efforts. In the southwestern United States, the organization of Mexican workers dates from at least the 1880's. One of the earliest records of labor organizing activity occurred in the Texas Panhandle in 1883, when several hundred cowboys went on strike against several large cattle companies. Strike leaders included several Mexican *vaqueros.*

One labor movement that attracted Mexican workers in the Southwest was the Knights of Labor (*see* CABALLEROS DE LABOR). The Knights of Labor was started in Philadelphia in 1869 with the organization of garment workers. The union grew slowly until the 1880's, when membership increased to 700,000, mak-

ing it the largest labor union in the United States. The union effectively organized miners, including many Mexican Americans and Mexicans in the West in the mid-1880's. In New Mexico, the Knights of Labor supported local Hispanos against illegal land-grabbing schemes on the part of non-Latinos.

Agricultural Workers. Although labor unionism in the southwestern United States can be traced to the late nineteenth century, union activity increased sharply in the early twentieth century. This increased union activity paralleled the development of large-scale commercial agriculture throughout the Southwest. Militant Mexican workers were at the forefront of strikes in California in the 1920's and 1930's. These work stoppages included the famous Imperial Valley cantaloupe strike (1928), the Imperial Valley lettuce strike (1930), the EL MONTE BERRY STRIKE (1933), the California cotton strikes (1933), and the agricultural strikes of 1936.

During the first three decades of the twentieth century, hundreds of efforts were made to organize Mexican farmworkers throughout the Southwest. Union leaders found it difficult to organize farmworkers. This difficulty can be attributed to the strong opposition of landowners and farm organizations; the instability of the migrant labor force, composed largely of minorities; the seasonal and migratory nature of much of the work; and a large surplus of workers.

During the early twentieth century, however, several Mexican farm labor organizations came into existence, particularly in California. One of the most important of these was the CONFEDERACIÓN DE UNIONES OBRERAS MEXICANAS (CUOM). CUOM was modeled after the major Mexican labor union, the Confederación Regional Obrera Mexicana, with the purpose of organizing all Mexican workers in the United States. At the first CUOM meeting in April, 1928, twenty-two local unions with a combined membership of about three thousand workers were represented. CUOM was important as the first large-scale effort to organize Mexican workers in the United States in order to improve their economic welfare.

One of the most active local farmworker unions in Southern California during this era was La Unión de Trabajadores del Valle Imperial (the Imperial Valley Workers' Union), organized in the spring of 1928. It soon claimed nearly twenty-eight hundred members. In May, 1928, the union requested a wage increase of one-half cent per crate for cantaloupe picking, free picking sacks and ice for drinking water, materials for sheds and outhouses, and several other improvements

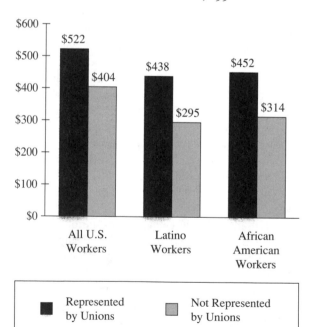

LABOR UNION REPRESENTATION AND WEEKLY WAGES, 1991

Source: Data are from U.S. Bureau of the Census, *Statistical Abstract of the United States 1992* (Washington, D.C.: Bureau of the Census, 1992), Table 672.

The United Farm Workers union has sponsored many strikes and boycotts. (Impact Visuals, Rick Gerharter)

in working conditions. Growers in the Imperial Valley ignored the request, and a spontaneous strike ensued. Efforts were promptly initiated to break the strike. The local sheriff, Charles Gillett, deputized more than forty farm foremen (employees of the growers) and began arresting strikers by the dozens for vagrancy, disturbing the peace, and other alleged crimes. Bail was set between $250 and $1,000 for many of those arrested, too high for them to obtain their release. Gillett closed the union office and some Mexican businesses, and strikers were threatened with mass deportation. The strike was soon broken by the concerted efforts of the growers, the sheriff, and other local authorities.

As economic conditions deteriorated during the Great Depression, wage rates for farm laborers declined sharply. By 1933, wage rates as low as ten cents per hour were common in California. Workers simply could not exist on such low wages. In El Monte, California, the Confederación de Uniones de Campesinos y Obreros Mexicanos (CUCOM) struck Japanese strawberry growers for higher wages. The union, which represented more than five thousand Mexican workers, eventually prevailed, and wages were increased to twenty cents an hour.

A prominent agricultural labor organization, the UNITED FARM WORKERS ASSOCIATION (UFWA), gained prominence in the 1960's under the leadership of César CHÁVEZ. In September, 1965, the UFWA struck major table grape growers near Delano, California, for higher wages. Five thousand workers walked off the job. The strike was not particularly effective in the fields but captured the attention of the nation. Eventually a national consumer boycott of table grapes developed. Declining grape sales and the pressure of the ongoing strike forced the growers to settle the strike in July, 1970, when Chávez signed a contract with twenty-six growers who produced more than half of the California table grapes.

Industrial Workers. By the 1930's, relatively large numbers of Latinos were members of industrial unions that frequently engaged in work stoppages in order to improve their economic welfare. Latino workers engaged in labor activities in industrial plants throughout the Midwest and East. In Texas, Mexican pecan shellers, garment workers, and cigar rollers, many of whom were women, engaged in numerous strikes during the 1930's. Immigrant cigar workers from Cuba also formed strong unions during the early twentieth

Various agricultural and factory operations have been targets of strikes and boycotts. (David Bacon)

century and demanded higher wages and improved working conditions.

Magdaleno Rodriguez was one of the first important organizers of the Mexican pecan shellers. By 1934, Rodriguez's Pecan Shelling Workers' Union in San Antonio claimed ten thousand members. The organization was ineffective, however, and membership rapidly declined. Remnants of this union reappeared as the Texas Pecan Shelling Workers' Union (TPSWU) in 1937. In January, 1938, the Southern Pecan Shelling Company, the major employer of pecan shellers in San Antonio, announced a significant pay reduction for workers, prompting a spontaneous walkout. The TPSWU failed to immediately support the strike, which lost momentum. The TPSWU was replaced by the UNITED CANNERY, AGRICULTURAL, PACKING AND ALLIED WORKERS OF AMERICA (UCAPAWA), a union affiliated with the Congress of Industrial Organizations (CIO) that had begun organizing workers shortly before the strike. In a few weeks, UCAPAWA had recruited about half of the twelve thousand pecan shellers in the city.

From the outset, the PECAN SHELLERS' STRIKE met with strong opposition from community leaders and authorities in San Antonio. UCAPAWA's leadership was branded as communist by opponents of the strike, although there was no evidence to support this accusation. Even traditional supporters of Mexicans, including the LEAGUE OF UNITED LATIN AMERICAN CITIZENS and the Mexican Chamber of Commerce, refused to support the strike unless the workers renounced the UCAPAWA's leadership. Strikers were continually harassed. More than one thousand picketers were arrested and charged with disturbing the peace, blocking sidewalks, and unlawful assembly. Picketers were also the frequent targets of tear gas attacks by police. Following intervention in the strike by Governor James V. Allred, it was settled by arbitration in May, 1938.

Another industrial union important to the history of the Latino labor movement was the INTERNATIONAL LADIES' GARMENT WORKERS' UNION (ILGWU). By the 1930's, this union had hundreds of members in various locations across the United States. Invariably, Mexicans were among the most militant workers. In 1933, a local ILGWU affiliate in Los Angeles went on strike for higher wages. In less than a month, the strike was settled, with many of the workers' demands met.

Fully half of the members of this local were Mexican women.

Similarly, in 1937, the ILGWU in San Antonio struck the largest garment manufacturer in the city, the Shirlee Frocks Company. Virtually all the members of this local were Mexican women. Following a three-month work stoppage, most of the labor issues were resolved in favor of the workers, and the strike ended. Other garment manufacturers in the city signed similar labor agreements.

Cigar Workers. Another industry long associated with Latino unionism in the United States is CIGAR MANUFACTURING. By the late nineteenth century, Tampa, Florida, was the focus of the U.S. cigar industry, which was dependent on immigrant Cuban cigar workers. Cuban workers initiated major strikes in 1899, 1901, 1910, 1920, and 1931. The 1901 strike was begun by La Sociedad de Torcederes de Tabaco de Tampa. This union, with about five thousand members, challenged the combined wealth and power of the cigar manufacturers, the newly formed tobacco trust, the International Cigarmakers Union, and Tampa officials. During the early 1900's, members of the union were kidnapped and forcibly deported, arrested and jailed for vagrancy, and victimized by vigilante groups.

Following the 1901 strike, the power of this incipient union was broken.

Smaller unions of cigar rollers existed elsewhere in the United States. For example, 350 Mexican cigar workers, the majority of whom were women, formed a union in San Antonio, Texas, in 1933. Following a short strike that year, wages were increased and working conditions improved. Another strike by the San Antonio cigar workers failed completely in 1935. The union soon ceased to exist.

Mine Workers. Latino union activity in the United States was not limited to agricultural and industrial workers. By 1900, thousands of Mexican miners had joined the United Mine Workers of America. In Texas, for example, the coal mines at Lyra, Strawn, Rock Creek, Alba, and Bridgeport were unionized by the United Mine Workers of America by 1900. Mexicans usually composed the largest immigrant group in these mines, although a number of other ethnic groups were represented. In many cases, Mexican workers were among the most militant union members and strongly supported the union.

Mexican mineworkers throughout the West were relatively well-organized. The Western Federation of Miners (WFM) was perhaps the most important min-

In the West, mine workers formed an early stronghold in the Latino union movement. (University Libraries, Arizona State University, Tempe)

ing union in this region. In 1903, Mexican workers in the Clifton-Morenci copper mining district struck when mine owners lowered wages by 10 percent. The strike failed, and union leaders were subsequently arrested, tried, convicted, and sentenced to the territorial prison in Yuma.

The WFM continued to gain strength, however, and in 1915 it demanded that Mexican miners receive the same pay as non-Hispanic white miners. Mine owners ignored the demand, and the Mexican miners struck. Following a five-month strike, the mine owners agreed to establish uniform wages for all workers. The CLIFTON-MORENCI STRIKES were not all as successful as the 1915 effort. When mine workers initiated labor stoppages in 1917 and 1918, vigilante groups supported by the mine owners rounded up and deported militant Mexican workers. These strikes were quickly broken.

As the foregoing examples illustrate, Latino workers have participated in a variety of unionization efforts. Many of their unions were mainstream, but many others reacted to the unique needs of Latino workers, particularly those engaged in farm labor.

—*Robert R. McKay*

SUGGESTED READINGS:
• Kern, Robert, ed. *Labor in New Mexico: Unions, Strikes, and Social History Since 1881.* Albuquerque: University of New Mexico Press, 1983. This excellent history covers all facets of unionism in New Mexico, much of it focusing on Hispano labor activity.
• Landolt, Robert Garland. *The Mexican-American Workers of San Antonio, Texas.* New York: Arno Press, 1976. This reprint of Landolt's 1965 doctoral dissertation at the University of Texas examines labor movements in San Antonio, Texas. Includes a number of case studies of Mexican labor union activity.
• Long, Durward. "'La Resistencia': Tampa's Immigrant Labor Union." *Labor History* 6 (Fall, 1965): 193-213. Examines labor union activity among Cuban cigar workers in Tampa, Florida, during the nineteenth and early twentieth centuries. Focuses on the rise and fall of a single union, representative of many Latino unions.
• Menefee, Selden C., and Orin C. Cassmore. *The Pecan Shellers of San Antonio.* Washington, D.C.: Government Printing Office, 1940. Examines the Mexican pecan shellers of San Antonio, Texas, documenting the important role of unions and the impact of pecan sheller strikes on Mexican residents of San Antonio during the Great Depression.
• Zamora, Emilio. *The World of the Mexican Worker in Texas.* College Station: Texas A&M University

Press, 1993. This excellent study provides detailed information on union activities in various locations across Texas.

Ladino: Group identification. "Ladino" can refer to Spanish Jews, Spanish-speaking black people, and Central Americans with European backgrounds. The term refers to descendants of Spanish Jews who were exiled from Spain in the fifteenth century, as well as to the language spoken by these people. The language combines archaic Spanish and some Hebrew elements. It still is spoken by Sephardic Jews in the diaspora, though its use is limited. "Ladino" took a second meaning as a name for African slaves who spoke Spanish; eventually the term came to mean any Spanish-speaking black person born in the New World. A third meaning of "Ladino," used in Central America, is a person of predominantly Spanish, as opposed to indigenous, origin. A more general meaning of the term is any Spanish-speaking Latin American who has become Westernized.

Laguerre, Enrique A. (b. May 3, 1906, Moca, Puerto Rico): Novelist. Laguerre was born to Juan N. Laguerre and Atanasia Velez Vargas. After he received bachelor's and master's degrees from the University of Puerto Rico, he did doctoral work at Columbia University.

In the 1920's, Laguerre worked as a teacher in rural Puerto Rico. Later, he worked for the Puerto Rico Department of Education, taught at the University of Puerto Rico at Rio Piedras, and was a consultant for the Department of Public Instruction. In the United States, he was a visiting professor at the City University of New York and a research adviser to the Higher Council on Education. His ten novels include *La llamarada* (1935), now considered a modern classic. The novels focus on problems of Puerto Rican groups both on the island and in the United States.

Lamas family: Actors. Fernando Lamas and his son Lorenzo have captivated film audiences portraying "Latin lover" types for more than forty years. Fernando, the son of electrical engineer Emilio Lamas, was born on October 8, 1915, in Buenos Aires, Argentina. At an early age, he began acting in school plays. He later studied law in college and drama in various schools in Argentina, Spain, and France, including the Teatro Experimental in Buenos Aires.

Fernando was an avid sportsman, becoming an expert swimmer, boxer, and fencer. He won the Intercol-

Fernando Lamas. (AP/Wide World Photos)

legiate Boxing championship in Argentina and the South American freestyle swimming championship in 1937.

In 1934, he made his stage debut with a Buenos Aires repertory theater company. Three years later, when he won the swimming title, he was offered a dramatic role in an Argentine radio program. In 1939, he made his first film, but he became a star in South America with his fifth film, *Lady Windermere's Fan* (1942). He went to Hollywood in 1949 to dub the Spanish version of an American film and was soon spotted by talent scouts from Metro-Goldwyn-Mayer (MGM).

After more than a dozen Spanish-language films to his credit, he decided to move to the United States. MGM cast him in "Latin lover" roles, and he had to follow in the footsteps of superstars Rudolph Valentino and John Gilbert. Fernando appeared in the films *The Law and the Lady* (1951), *The Merry Widow* (1952), *The Girl Who Had Everything* and *Sangaree* (1953), *Jivaro* (1954), and *The Girl Rush* (1955).

By the end of the 1950's, he had decided to expand his artistry, and he began to pursue a career as a director, producer, and writer for both television and motion pictures. He directed episodes for the popular television series *Run for Your Life*, *Mannix*, *Starsky and Hutch*, *Maverick*, and later the successful *Falcon Crest* (on which his son Lorenzo appeared in 1981) and *Flamingo Road*.

In 1982, Fernando Lamas returned to acting for the series *Gavilan*, but after a few episodes he was hospitalized. He died of cancer on October 8 in Los Angeles, California.

Lorenzo Lamas was born on January 20, 1958, to Fernando Lamas and actress Arlene Dahl in Santa Monica, California. Lorenzo was brought up in the United States but traveled to South America with his father. Like his father, he was drawn to both sports and the theater. He attended the Jim Russell School of Motor Racing and won the Pro/Celebrity competition of the 1985 Toyota Grand Prix in Long Beach, California. He also practices surfing, skiing, golf, and karate.

Lorenzo received his professional training at Tony Barr's Film Actors Workshop. He began to appear in television episodes of *The Love Boat*, *Sword of Justice*, *California Fever*, *Switch*, and *Secrets of Midland Heights*. He appeared in the musical film *Grease* (1978), followed by *Tilt* (1978), *Take Down* (1978), and *Body Rock* (1984). For this last film, Lorenzo worked with choreographer Susan Scanlan and other professional ballet dancers in a sequence that included break dancing.

Lorenzo Lamas. (AP/Wide World Photos)

Lorenzo caught the attention of millions of television viewers when he starred as the villain Lance Cumson in the successful series *Falcon Crest* in 1981. Soon he was called one of Hollywood's heartthrobs. He later hosted a syndicated show called *Dancin' to the Hits*.

Lambada: Dance of Brazilian origin. Lambada dancing is a mixture of SALSA, MERENGUE, and TANGO, performed by couples in close embrace. With their hips in contact, the man's right leg between the woman's legs, the dancers perform hip-rocking motions, moving in circles on the floor and adding occasional deep back bends. The lambada originated in Brazil in the 1980's. Mixed with other dance forms, it was revived in France in 1989 and from there spread to the United States, where it gained extreme popularity, particularly in cities with large Latino communities.

Land Act of 1851: Law covering review of land grants. Through this legislation, Congress created a three-man Board of Commissioners to review the land claims of all California grant holders between January of 1852 and March of 1856. All land that remained unclaimed or had no legal title established was declared to be public domain and would be open for settlement. This situation was particularly hard on CALIFORNIOS, or native Spanish-speaking ranchero owners. Unscrupulous individuals managed to wrest nearly two-fifths of all land that originally belonged to the Californios. As a result, many Californios lost their wealth and economic position in California society.

Land tenure issues: Centuries of Spanish and Mexican laws and customs in the southwestern United States have influenced judicial decisions on land tenure and water rights. Questions of legal rights to the use of land and water resources have persisted over many years in the Southwest. Spanish and Mexican custom and law have served as precedents for American courts' decisions regarding land and water allocation and use in the Southwest.

Origins. These issues of land tenure have their origin in the right of eminent domain over all lands by Spain's kings. The Spanish Crown gave town governments authority over Crown lands under their jurisdiction, establishing municipal control. These Castilian practices were transferred to the southwestern United States.

Both the Spanish Crown and Mexico awarded land grants for the purpose of colonization. One of the most important institutions left in the Southwest by Spain and Mexico was the land grant. From the 1820's through the 1840's, several thousand colonists received land grants on the Mexican frontier, where they lived in relative isolation.

The Treaty of Guadalupe Hidalgo. The U.S. government, inspired by the doctrine of MANIFEST DESTINY and wanting to take over Mexican territory for western expansion, went to war with Mexico in 1846. The MEXICAN AMERICAN WAR ended through the TREATY OF GUADALUPE HIDALGO (1848), by which the United States acquired Mexico's northern frontier territories. The treaty stipulated that Mexicans in the territories would become citizens of the United States and would retain their property; if they chose not to become citizens, they could move from their property while retaining ownership of it. The right of absentee ownership was not respected and led to disputes concerning land ownership.

Land grants provided a land-based subsistence for Hispanics in the Southwest, especially in what later became New Mexico and California. In 1897, in *United States v. Sandoval*, the United States Supreme Court upset traditional and fundamental Hispanic land policy when it decided that common lands of Spanish and Mexican community grants belonged to the United States public domain. Millions of acres of common lands that had been part of community land grants in northern New Mexico became government land administered by the U.S. Forest Service.

Water Rights. Water rights were also an issue in the former Mexican territories. In *State of New Mexico ex rel. Reynolds v. R. Lee Aamodt, et al.*, a U.S. district court case filed in 1966, the court adjudicated the water rights of more than twenty-two hundred non-Indian persons and twenty-eight community ditches.

New Mexico water law had been based on the principle that surface and ground water belonged to the public and was subject to appropriation of the right to divert it for beneficial use. Although water rights accompanied specific lands, they could be sold, exchanged, and severed from those lands. New Mexico did not distinguish among the beneficial uses of water; agricultural, industrial, and recreational uses were all considered to be equal.

Water rights adjudication usually was based on a hydrographic survey to ascertain the status of water use in a particular stream system. Traditional subsistence-based communities had developed irrigation systems as one of the first acts in creating settlements in New Mexico. Dates were determined for establishment of

Many conflicting claims to land and water rights date back to the Spanish colonial period and land grants made at that time. (Security Pacific Bank Collection, Los Angeles Public Library)

community ditch systems, and their pattern of individual use was determined. This information formed the basis for determining priorities for appropriation of water. Each water user was then sent an offer defining the amount, purpose, ownership, place of use, source of water, and priority date of a water right.

In the twentieth century, much of the litigation emanating from the Treaty of Guadalupe Hidalgo focused on water rights. Many judicial decisions on southwestern water rights used expert testimony concerning the history of Hispanic water law. The Treaty of Guadalupe Hidalgo was determined to be the applicable law in many cases, with judges in every state

bound to respect it. Thus Spanish colonial and Mexican land and water law was to be considered American law.   —*Santos C. Vega*

SUGGESTED READINGS: • Blawis, Patricia Bell. *Tijerina and the Land Grants: Mexican Americans in Struggle for Their Heritage.* New York: International Publishers, 1971. • Briggs, Charles L., and John R. Van Ness, eds. *Land, Water, and Culture: New Perspectives on Hispanic Land Grants.* Albuquerque: University of New Mexico Press, 1987. • Clark, Ira G. *Water in New Mexico: A History of Its Management and Use.* Albuquerque: University of New Mexico Press, 1987. • Ebright, Malcolm. *Land Grants and*

Lawsuits in Northern New Mexico. Albuquerque: University of New Mexico Press, 1994. • Ebright, Malcolm, ed. *Spanish and Mexican Land Grants and the Law*. Manhattan, Kans.: Sunflower University Press, 1989. • Meyer, Michael. *Water in the Hispanic Southwest: A Social and Legal History, 1550-1850*. Tucson: University of Arizona Press, 1984.

Language bias, history of: Language bias refers to unequal treatment received by members of a society who do not speak the language of the dominant group. Language bias has a long history in the United States; English has been the language of the dominant group since the country's inception, despite the fact that the area was populated by non-English speakers long before the arrival of English-speaking explorers.

Background. English has always been the language of those in power in the United States. For this reason, those who speak languages other than English have suffered from various forms of bias. From de facto segregation in public schools in which instruction is based on knowledge of English to the widespread use of English-only signs and documents, the "supremacy" of English disfranchises speakers of other languages.

Those who speak various languages derived from Spanish make up the largest segment of non-English speakers in the U.S. population. As a group that has experienced language bias, this segment of the population is the largest and has probably experienced the most biased treatment. In *Borderlands: The New Mestiza/La Frontera* (1987), Gloria Anzaldúa makes

During the 1920's, when this school photograph was taken in Arizona, many schools prohibited the use of Spanish. (University Libraries, Arizona State University, Tempe)

Basic informational signs increasingly use both English and Spanish, particularly in areas with large Latino populations. (James Shaffer)

the issue of language bias clear. According to Anzaldúa, "Ethnic identity is twin skin to linguistic identity—I am my language. Until I can accept as legitimate Chicano, Texas Spanish, Tex-Mex and all the other languages I speak, I cannot accept the legitimacy of myself."

Language Bias in Schools. Until 1974, English was considered the sole essential language of instruction in schools. In 1974, however, the Supreme Court, in the case of *LAU V. NICHOLS*, interpreted Title VI of the Civil Rights Act of 1964 to mean that children have a right to understand the language of their instruction. The Court's ruling meant that schools were required either to teach a student English before forcing the student to take other courses taught in English or to teach other subjects in the student's native language until the student's English was sufficiently developed to allow instruction in other subjects. BILINGUAL EDUCATION is proposed by many as the solution to the issue that

Lau v. Nichols raised; however, bilingual education requires financial support and teacher training, and it often flounders from inadequate attention and support in school districts where it is most needed.

Many standardized tests used for everything from grade-level placement to college entrance criteria have been widely alleged to have language (and cultural) bias. Many IQ tests have also been alleged to be biased against non-English speakers.

Bias in Other Areas. In other arenas of life, there is also a long history of language bias. Before being outlawed, literacy tests were used as a prerequisite for registering to vote, thus disfranchising the non-English speaker. Even though literacy tests eventually disappeared, it was not until the VOTING RIGHTS ACT OF 1975 that bilingual ballots come into use in U.S. elections. Signs—from road signs to labels on rest rooms—are usually English-only in most parts of the country, making many everyday choices difficult for the non-English speaker. For many years, completing job applications, driver's license applications, and applications for public assistance required knowledge of English. Moreover, because language and culture are inextricably woven together, the imposition of an "English-only" atmosphere in the United States also denies non-English speakers a vital connection to their native cultures (*see* ENGLISH-ONLY CONTROVERSY).

Latinos, depending on their origins, tend to differ in their assessment of the importance of speaking Spanish. Puerto Ricans are generally the most interested in having their children become literate in Spanish. Many Puerto Rican parents hope to return to their native land, where fluency in Spanish and knowledge of the culture is important. Cuban Americans have adopted English as their primary language somewhat more quickly, as a group, than Mexican Americans or Puerto Ricans.

Controversies. The most common view of schools (and other institutions that socialize citizens) is that they are relatively neutral and that the language used is immaterial or irrelevant. Radical educators do not accept that notion. Such theorists point out the social and political constraints on language and argue that the primacy of English helps to perpetuate Anglo culture. For example, the radical theorist Henry Giroux has argued that the language of schooling is "implicated in forms of racism that attempt to silence the voices of subordinated groups whose primary language is not English." The same point can perhaps be made with respect to the arenas of politics, work, and community life.

Impact. Obviously, the impact of language bias on Spanish-speaking individuals in the United States is and has been far-reaching. Partly as a result of such bias, Latinos have had to take inferior jobs, have been denied access to political power, have had their culture and language denigrated in the schools, and have been forced into ghettos or other enclaves where they can preserve their culture. As a large group, numerically, they have been denied the right to translate their numbers into power or political action, in part because of the effects of language bias.   —*M. C. Ware*

SUGGESTED READINGS: • Anzaldúa, Gloria. *Borderlands: The New Mestiza/La Frontera*. San Francisco: Spinsters/Aunt Lute Press, 1987. • Giroux, Henry. *Border Crossings*. New York: Routledge, 1992. • Meier, Kenneth, and Joseph Stewart, Jr. *The Politics of Hispanic Education*. Albany: State University of New York Press, 1991. • Ramirez, Manuel, and Alfredo Castaneda. "Culturally Democratic Educational

Environments: Language, Heritage, and Values." In *Cultural Democracy, Bicognitive Development, and Education*. New York: Academic Press, 1974. • Valencia, Richard R., ed. *Chicano School Failure and Success*. New York: Falmer Press, 1991.

L'Archeveque, Sostenes: Folk hero. L'Archeveque was a nineteenth century contemporary of New Mexican folk hero Elfego Baca. Born in Santa Fe, New Mexico, to parents of Mexican and French background, L'Archeveque went on a killing rampage when several Americans murdered his father. Within a short time, he had killed more than twenty Americans. Nuevo mexicanos ambushed and killed him because they feared retaliation by Americans.

Laredo, Texas: Laredo is the seat of Webb County and the city in Texas with the largest proportion of Latinos—94 percent of the total population of 133,000 counted in the 1990 census.

San Agustín de Laredo was founded in 1755 by Tomás Sánchez de la Barrera y Gallardo as a small Spanish settlement on the Rio Grande's north bank. In the 1800's, the first adobe and stone buildings were

---

LATINO POPULATION OF LAREDO, TEXAS, 1990

Total number of Latinos = 125,069; 94% of population

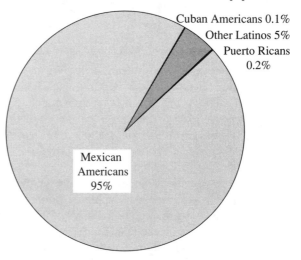

Source: Data are from Marlita A. Reddy, ed., *Statistical Record of Hispanic Americans* (Detroit: Gale Research, 1993), Table 111.

Note: Figures represent the population of the Metropolitan Statistical Area as delineated by the U.S. Bureau of the Census. Percentages are rounded to the nearest whole number except for Cuban Americans and Puerto Ricans, for whom rounding is to the nearest 0.1%.

constructed. Laredo played a major historical role as the headquarters for Mexico's war with Spain that resulted in independence in 1821. Laredo was also the capital of the independent Republic of the Rio Grande during the early 1840's.

In 1846, Laredo was occupied by U.S. troops led by Zachary Taylor, who declared Laredo to be part of the United States. The TREATY OF GUADALUPE HIDALGO (1848), which ended the MEXICAN AMERICAN WAR, placed the new U.S.-Mexico border at the Rio Grande. Many of the Mexican residents of Laredo moved across the river into territory that remained in Mexico, establishing Nuevo Laredo. Local politics in Laredo has been dominated by Latinos.

The two Laredos (commonly known as Los Dos Laredos) form one of the most important crossing points for U.S. commerce with Mexico. Residents of the two towns have extensive cross-border family ties, and the communities and economies are integrated (*see* BORDER REGION AND CULTURE). The cities are situated on the highway connecting San Antonio, Texas, and Monterrey, Mexico, and are about 150 miles from each of these cities. The most important issues for this border community relate to trade, bridges, and water quality of the Rio Grande.

Laredo is the site of Texas A&M International University, which in 1994 had plans to begin offering four-year degrees. In 1994, this was the only university in Texas authorized to offer joint degree programs with universities in Mexico.

The economy of Laredo is centered on border trade, retail sales, and tourism. Los Dos Laredos are supply centers for the ranching and farming industries. The oil and gas industry was important for most of the twentieth century but declined drastically in importance in the 1990's. Drug traffic to the United States and illegal sales of firearms to Mexico posed major problems.

Maquiladora factory activity in Nuevo Laredo in the early 1990's was small in comparison to that of other border cities. The anticipated increase in trade resulting from the NORTH AMERICAN FREE TRADE AGREEMENT that went into effect in 1994 appeared likely to affect trade between Los Dos Laredos. Three bridges across the river were in operation by 1991 to deal with the ever-increasing traffic of trucks through Los Dos Laredos.

Water pollution and environmental health hazards were major issues for Los Dos Laredos in the early 1990's. Untreated sewage was discharged on the Mexican side of the Rio Grande. A U.S.-Mexico agreement signed in 1989 provided for development of sewage treatment plants in Nuevo Laredo that would meet U.S. standards.

Larraz, Julio F. (b. Mar. 12, 1944, Havana, Cuba): Artist. Larraz began drawing and painting as a youngster. He recalls that art was his only basic interest as a child. He attended a military school where his artistry was not encouraged; he hoped in the United States to find the freedom to be a painter. He arrived in Miami, Florida, in 1961.

Larraz's art training in the United States was primarily informal. By 1973, he had begun exhibiting his work. In 1976, he traveled to Spain and elsewhere in Europe, observing nature. Larraz works primarily in oils and watercolors, painting mostly from memory. He became a U.S. citizen but retained the hope of returning to Cuba, seeing himself as a political exile.

During the 1980's, Larraz participated in numerous group and solo shows throughout the United States and Latin America. His work is held in the Museo de Arte Moderno in Bogotá, Colombia; the Museo de Monterrey in Mexico; and the collection of the Cintas Foundation. He was awarded a Cintas Foundation Fellowship in 1975.

Lasuén, Fermin Francisco de (1720, Vitoria, Spain—June 26, 1803, Mission San Carlos, Calif.): Missionary. Father Lasuén, born in Basque Spain, entered the Franciscan order at an undocumented time and migrated to Mexico. At first a missionary in Sierra Gorda, Lasuén in 1767 took over Francisco de Borjia, an isolated and deprived California mission. During five years there, he introduced farming and cattle to the Indians and made the mission much more prosperous. In 1773, Lasuén was ordered to Alta California and assigned to Mission San Gabriel. He arrived when a severe famine was in progress and trouble with the Indian population was mounting as a result of improper conduct of the local Spanish garrison. Lasuén quickly made the mission prosperous and defused the trouble.

In 1775, during the San Diego Indian revolt, he moved to San Diego. Remaining there until 1785, Lasuén conciliated the Indians and improved their living conditions. At that time, Lasuén became the president of California's Franciscan missions. During the eighteen years of his presidency, nine missions were founded. Under Lasuén, the inhabitants of the Franciscan missions enjoyed a lifestyle unequaled elsewhere in New Spain. Lasuén so impressed English and French explorers that modern Point Fermin and Point Lasuén in the bay near Los Angeles were named for him.

Latifundios: Vast extensions of large, landed estates during the Spanish colonial period. The early Spanish MERCEDES (land grants) had granted use of vast tracts of land to Spaniards and the Catholic church in New Spain but had retained ownership by the Crown. The early conquistadores needed Indian labor to work the large estates they were granted. The REPARTIMIENTO SYSTEM and the ENCOMIENDA SYSTEM developed as a result. In these systems, the landowner became master of large groups of *indios* (Indians) but was subject to certain moral and legal obligations to his workers.

The disappearance of the *repartimientos* and *encomiendas* left vacant land in the fertile valley of central New Spain that could be sold or granted to a new class of landholders, the HACENDADOS. Their haciendas became LATIFUNDIOS as they increased in size, at times encompassing several haciendas. Severe depopulation of the area, economic depression, and the large fortunes invested by CRIOLLO (Spaniards born in New Spain) mine operators all hastened the rapid growth of the *latifundio*.

By the end of the eighteenth century, most of the land of the Central Valley not owned by the church belonged to a few landowners. The *hacendados* enlarged the boundaries of their estates, claiming that the lands they occupied belonged to the Crown, and because Indian villages had never obtained royal grants, they could not assert ownership of land. Deliberate marriage alliances also merged large estates.

Ownership of such estates was the pinnacle of prestige in the Spanish colonial world. Although these vast agricultural plantations were inefficient and produced little surplus to be sold for profit, the owners lived in luxury. Life was generally miserable and hopeless for the workers.

Latifundios appeared on the frontier of New Spain as new markets and techniques induced expansion in the north and south. Hacienda grants were given for both agriculture and livestock. In the east, far north, and south, *latifundios* were organized and managed with considerable efficiency; nevertheless, most of the produce went abroad. The profits that did return went to the city banking system. On the frontier, the size and economic power of the *latifundios* gave their owners great political influence.

Latifundios dominated Coahuila. The *latifundio* of the heirs of José Miguel Sánchez Navarro encompassed seventeen haciendas and more than sixteen million acres. The Escandón holdings in the northeast were so vast that a train could not cross them in a day. *Latifundios* were scarce in New Mexico, and in Texas, RANCHOS or stock farms predominated.

As haciendas grew richer and more powerful, they engulfed and dominated entire regions and states. By the end of the nineteenth century, at least half of the territory of the Mexican Republic belonged to a few thousand families and foreign investors. More than half of the cropland was divided among fewer than ten thousand families. Agricultural reforms in the first half of the twentieth century sought to end *latifundios*. Many continued, but their political power was broken.

Latin Breed: Tejano band. Latin Breed was a ten-member orchestra from San Antonio, Texas. Fronted by lead singer Adalberto Gallegos, originally from Sonora, Mexico, the group played tejano music, with pieces ranging in style from polka to rock.

Latin jazz: Jazz, Latin jazz, and fusion are interrelated genres of music, with many artists crossing the boundaries of the forms. Jazz developed in the United States within African American communities in such areas as New Orleans, Chicago, New York, Kansas City, Philadelphia, and Los Angeles. In many of these same areas, Latinos performed their own styles of music, drawing on Latin American traditions and cultures.

Music based on Caribbean rhythms, especially AFRO-CUBAN, were popular within these communities. The musical forms include MÚSICA TROPICAL, Afro-Cuban music that became known as SALSA in the 1950's. Prior to this transformation, cities across the United States experienced a "RUMBA craze" in the 1930's. This movement influenced African American jazz performers who were popular during the same period.

As a result of segregation in housing and entertainment, many Latinos and African Americans lived and worked in close proximity and shared musical experiences. Clubs hosting major Latino, Mexican, and African American acts drew combined black and Latino audiences. Joint appearances facilitated cultural borrowing.

Latin American and Latino bandleaders, such as Tito PUENTE (New York), Mongo SANTAMARÍA (Cuba), and Lionel "Chico" Sesma (East Los Angeles), popularized "Latin" music between 1930 and 1960. Such bandleaders played a significant role in influencing future Latin jazz artists. Inspired by these early percussionists, Ildefonso "Poncho" SANCHEZ became one of

Bandleader Tito Puente helped popularize Latin music in the United States. (AP/Wide World Photos)

the most successful Latin jazz musicians. Throughout the late 1970's and early 1980's, Sanchez performed in Cal Tjader's Latin jazz group, perfecting the blend of Afro-Cuban music, jazz, and other contemporary musical components. Sanchez and other percussionists contributed a distinguishable sound to Latin jazz.

Latin rock: Rock music performed by American musicians of Latino ancestry. Although Latin rock can be straightforward rock and roll, it often incorporates Latin musical genres and Spanish lyrics.

Since the inception of rock and roll music in the mid-1950's, Latino musicians have contributed a con-

sistent stream of major hit songs. Examples of Latino artists and their popular songs (not all of them rock and roll) include Santo and Johnny ("Sleep Walk"), Rosie & the Originals ("Angel Baby"), Chris Montes ("Let's Dance"), Tony ORLANDO and Dawn ("Tie a Yellow Ribbon Round the Ole Oak Tree"), Freddy FENDER ("Wasted Days and Wasted Nights"), Linda Ronstadt ("You're No Good"), and Irene Cara ("Flashdance . . . What a Feeling"). Latin rock becomes more innovative, however, when it blends rock and Latin music.

Early Major Players. Ritchie VALENS' classic "La Bamba" (1958) was a prototype of Latin rock with its mixture of Mexican folk rhythms, rhythm and blues, and all-Spanish lyrics. "La Bamba" pushed rock and roll forward by introducing a sound used in subsequent rock classics such as the Isley Brothers' "Twist and Shout" (popularized by the Beatles) and the Rascals' "Good Lovin'."

The East Los Angeles urban rock scene of the 1960's produced numerous musicians of local fame whose exciting yet marginalized sounds rarely garnered mainstream attention. Thee MIDNITERS (1964-1970) were the quintessential Chicano rock band of this era, specializing in romantic ballads such as "Sad Girl" and foot-stomping dance numbers such as their *grito*-punctuated instrumental "Whittier Blvd." Ironically, the fame that eluded Thee Midniters was bestowed upon Cannibal and the Headhunters, who scored a Top 40 hit with Thee Midniters' staple "Land of 1000 Dances," which they performed in Pasadena while opening for the Beatles in 1965.

Meanwhile, in Texas, SUNNY AND THE SUNLINERS scored a Top 10 hit with "Talk to Me" in the early 1960's. The outrageous Sam the Sham and the Pharaohs followed with the Tex-Mex rock classic "Wooly Bully," which hit number two on the charts in 1966 with the most famous countdown in rock ("Uno, dos, one, two, tres, cuatro!"). The Sir Douglas Quintet similarly scored a Tex-Mex rock hit in 1965 with "She's About a Mover," as did ? (question mark) and the Mysterians, five young Mexicans living in Michigan whose classic "96 Tears" reached the top chart position in 1966.

On the East Coast, the Latin *bugalú* (boogaloo) sound dominated the late 1960's by blending brassy mambo, early rhythm and blues, and mostly English lyrics. This brash and exhilarating music was performed by mostly younger, American-born Latinos who were as interested in 1960's black music as in their rich inheritance of traditional Cuban and Puerto Rican music. Early important singles include Pete Rodriguez's "I Like It Like That," Johnny Colon's "Boogaloo Blues," and Joe CUBA's million-seller "Bang Bang" from 1966. A variation on the Latin *bugalú* known as "Latin soul" was best exemplified by Joe Bataan from El Barrio, a largely Latino area of New York City. Bataan recorded more than a dozen albums, which included heartfelt, Latinized versions of soul classics such as the Impressions' "Gypsy Woman" as well as his own "My Cloud" and "Ordinary Guy."

Rock and the Chicano Movement. As the CHICANO MOVEMENT of the 1960's peaked in the early 1970's, its consciousness became reflected in East Los Angeles groups such as El Chicano and Tierra, whose names connoted prideful self-affirmation and whose music more consciously blended rock and Latin sounds. In 1970, El Chicano's first single, "Viva Tirado," an organ-driven instrumental cover of Gerald Wilson's jazz composition, topped Los Angeles radio station charts for more than three months. Tierra's silky version of the Intruders' "Together" sold more than a million copies and won the band national exposure on televised rock shows such as *American Bandstand* and *Soul Train*.

Carlos SANTANA is an international superstar and guitar virtuoso on the level of Jimi Hendrix and Eric Clapton. The son of a mariachi musician, Santana was born in Autlan, Mexico, in 1947. He played the nightclubs of Tijuana in the 1960's. In 1967, he relocated to San Francisco's Latino Mission District, where he formed the six-piece Santana band. The band's ticket to stardom was its show-stopping performance of "Soul Sacrifice" at the legendary Woodstock music festival of 1969. The electric guitar-driven, Afro-Caribbean polyrhythms of Santana have spanned more than a dozen gold albums, including exemplars of Latin rock such as *Santana* and *Abraxis*. Younger brother Jorge Santana formed the eight-piece Malo band, which adopted Santana's musical direction with the addition of heavy brass. In 1972, Malo released its superb namesake debut album, which spent several weeks in the Top 15 and contained the romantic single "Suavecito."

Latin Rock Since the 1980's. Los LOBOS became the ultimate Chicano rock band, with its impressive ability to play seemingly all genres of popular music with equal grace, beauty, and power. The band delivered accordion-based Mexican RANCHERA MUSIC, Tex-Mex, and rockabilly as well as searing blues-based rock, folk, and alternative experimental music. In 1984, *Rolling Stone* magazine selected the band's anthemic *How Will the Wolf Survive?* as album of the year and the band itself as one of two bands of the year. Los Lobos is best known for its number one single "La Bamba" from the 1987 motion picture soundtrack. The band's nine-album body of work from 1978 to 1994 is noteworthy for its wide range, from all-Spanish, traditional acoustic work to all-English, eclectic rock and roll.

Cuban-born Gloria ESTEFAN and her Miami Sound Machine perfected a formula for mainstream success by blending mild salsa and rock to create Latin-influenced pop. Estefan and her band have enjoyed numerous platinum albums and number one hit sin-

Gloria Estefan has had a major influence on pop music. (AP/Wide World Photos)

Rock bands in the Southwest have adapted rock and roll to add Chicano and Latin influences. (Mary LaSalle)

gles, some of which, including "Coming Out of the Dark," were written by their one-time backup singer, Jon SECADA. Cuban-born Secada sold six million copies of his namesake debut album of Latinized pop and later released a second album more flavored by rhythm and blues. —*Kurt C. Organista*

SUGGESTED READINGS: • DeCurtis, Anthony, and James Henke, with Holly George-Warren, eds. *The Rolling Stone Album Guide: Completely New Reviews.* New York: Random House, 1992. • Gillett, Charlie. *The Sound of the City: The Rise of Rock and Roll.* New York: Outerbridge & Dienstfrey, 1970. • Loza, Steven. *Barrio Rhythm: Mexican American Music in Los Angeles.* Urbana: University of Illinois Press, 1993. • Mendheim, Beverly. *Ritchie Valens: The First Latino Rocker.* Tempe, Ariz.: Bilingual Press/Editorial Bilingüe, 1987. • Roberts, John Storm. *The Latin Tinge: The Impact of Latin American Music on the United States.* New York: Oxford University Press, 1979.

Latina writers: Latina writers of the Southwest have described the experience of living between two cultures, the Mexican and the American. Their literary production illustrates the problematic merging of the two worlds to create a third one—a borderland culture. Their works are written in Spanish, English, or both.

Sociohistorical Context. The Spanish-speaking Southwest was integrated into the United States after the MEXICAN AMERICAN WAR (1846-1848). Women's personal narratives responded in the 1870's to the dilemma of assimilation versus ethnic preservation in a new border culture, initiating the Mexican American or Chicana tradition of autobiographical expression. María Amparo RUIZ DE BURTON published in English the historical romance *The Squatter and the Don* (1885). This text, the first used to reconstruct the literary history of Hispanics in the United States, reflects the conflicts between two cultures.

In the early 1900's, feminist issues were discussed in Spanish-language periodicals by Leonor Villegas de Magnón and others. She also challenged stereotyped misconceptions of Mexican Americans in her autobiography *The Rebel*, written in the 1920's and published in 1994 as part of the Recovering the U.S. Hispanic Literary Heritage Series.

An ambivalent cultural attitude permeated writings from the 1920's to the 1950's. María Cristina Mena, who was born in Mexico, expressed dual consciousness in the satirical story "The Education of Popo" (1915), criticizing both the Mexican and the American value systems. Jovita González reflected resistance and assimilation in her collection of sketches *Among My People*, published in the 1930's. María Otero Warren (*Old Spain in Our Southwest*, 1936), Josephina NIGGLI (*Mexican Village*, 1945), Fabiola CABEZA DE BACA Gilbert (*We Fed Them Cactus*, 1954), and Cleofas Martinez JARAMILLO (*Romance of a Little Village Girl*, 1955) conformed to conventional views of their Hispanic culture, concentrated on the landscape, and searched for an ideal distant past.

The Chicano Movement. The CHICANO MOVEMENT of the 1960's led to a Latino search for political, social, and cultural self-affirmation. The feminist movement inspired some CHICANAS to view writing and publishing as empowerment. In the 1970's, they re-examined their history and re-evaluated their gender and cultural identity. Poetry and fiction became politicized, interlingual texts, blending Spanish and English. In the 1980's, Chicana literature matured in all genres, exploring creatively the self, sexuality, and sexual relationships, as well as issues of gender, class, race, and ethnicity. Many highly educated authors became teachers or writers in residence at American institutions, and many won national and international awards.

Estela PORTILLO TRAMBLEY was the first woman to win the Premio Quinto Sol (1972) for Chicana literature. Known for her play about restrained sexuality, *The Day of the Swallows* (1972), she received the award for *Rain of Scorpions and Other Writings* (1975), a book containing a novella and short stories. In 1977, she edited the first issue of *El Grito*, a major journal devoted to Chicana creative expression. In *Sor Juana and Other Plays* (1983), she focused on the intellectual quest of the seventeenth century Mexican nun Sor Juana Inés de la CRUZ, who might serve as a model for Chicanas. In her novel *Trini* (1986), she again presented women's strong resistance to predetermined sex roles.

The poet Bernice Zamora created a feminist manifesto in *Restless Serpents* (1976), responding to Chicano male oppression. Angela de Hoyos, socially conscious in *Arise Chicano and Other Poems* (1976) and *Chicano Poems: For the Barrio* (1975), focused on the erotic tension between the sexes in *Woman, Woman* (1985). Alma Villanueva celebrated a universal female identity, as well as the connections between a woman's body and spirit, in *Bloodroot* (1977) and *Mother, May I?* (1978). In *Life Span* (1985), she affirmed female desire. Lorna Dee CERVANTES held firm to her ethnic roots, expressed the struggles between cultures, and gave a human feminist vision in *Emplumada* (1981).

Crossing Boundaries. Genre boundaries disappeared in *This Bridge Called My Back: Writings by Radical Women of Color* (1981), a collection of essays, poems, tales, and testimonies edited by Cherríe MORAGA and Gloria ANZALDÚA. Moraga battled myths of defined sex roles and proclaimed solidarity with Third World people in *Loving in the War Years* (1983). Anzaldúa introduced the new mestiza, a woman who straddles several borders and exists in a space where cultures converge, in *Borderlands: The New Mestiza/ La Frontera* (1987). Both writers, examining the dynamics of race, class, gender, and sexual orientation, have helped to shape Chicana feminism.

Helena María VIRAMONTES portrayed life at the borders of society and powerlessness in *The Moths and Other Stories* (1985). Margarita Cota-Cárdenas also exposed the power of the dominant culture in her experimental novel *Puppet* (1985). Many fictional narratives followed the pattern of "growing up" stories, reviewing the childhood years through memories and noting the influential sociocultural forces. *The House on Mango Street* (1983) by Sandra CISNEROS and *The Last of the Menu Girls* (1986) by Denise CHÁVEZ emanated from barrio experiences, had a home as a central metaphor, and depicted protagonists coming to terms with their womanhood and emerging as writers. *The Mixquiahuala Letters* (1986) by Ana CASTILLO is an epistolary novel reflecting the limitations in both U.S. and Mexican cultures, expressing the same concerns that others have since 1848. The same interest was evident in Roberta Fernández's *Intaglio: A Novel in Six Stories* (1990), about six women at the turn of the century on the United States-Mexico border.

Laura Esquivel's Like Water for Chocolate *was a best-seller and the basis for a popular film.* (AP/Wide World Photos)

Impact. Chicana writers added a new vision and dimension to American literature, making it richer and more representative of the culturally and linguistically diverse society in the United States.

—*Ludmila Kapschutschenko-Schmitt*

SUGGESTED READINGS: • Calderón, Héctor, and José David Saldívar, eds. *Criticism in the Borderlands: Studies in Chicano Literature, Culture, and Ideology.* Durham, N.C.: Duke University Press, 1991. • Herrera-Sobek, María, ed. *Beyond Stereotypes: The Critical Analysis of Chicana Literature.* Binghamton, N.Y.: Bilingual Press, 1985. • Herrera-Sobek, María, and Helena María Viramontes, eds. *Chicana Creativity and Criticism: Charting New Frontiers in American Literature.* Houston, Tex.: Arte Público Press, 1988. • Horno-Delgado, Asunción, et al., eds. *Breaking Boundaries: Latina Writing and Critical Readings.* Amherst: University of Massachusetts Press, 1989. • Sánchez, Marta Ester. *Contemporary Chicana Poetry: A Critical Approach to an Emerging Literature.* Berkeley: University of California Press, 1985.

Latinas, history and issues of: The term "Latinas" refers to women of Spanish or Latin American descent, primarily those living in the United States. The stereotypical role of the Latina is one of powerlessness and submission in a predominantly patriarchal society in which MACHISMO (a feeling of male superiority) is prevalent. Men are seen as the heads of their households; women manage households and assume responsibility for children. The Catholic church, a major religious influence in Latino cultures, has contributed to hierarchical gender roles and expectations.

By the end of the twentieth century, many women in Latin American countries as well as in the United States were in the labor force. This entrance into the larger culture served to break down stereotypes of roles and to show Latinas what was possible for them (*see* STEREOTYPES OF LATINAS; STEREOTYPES OF LATINOS). Feminist movements began among Latinas, and many women became politically active.

Male and female societal roles and expectations appear to have been less strictly defined in the United

As Latinas entered the labor force, their attitudes toward societal roles changed. (Martin Hutner)

States than in Latin America. Many Latinas believe that they reached a higher degree of independence as emigrants to the United States, but others often feel caught between the demands of two cultures. They struggle against the ethnic prejudice and DISCRIMINATION of the larger culture as well as the sexism and sex discrimination that exist in both the U.S. mainstream culture and the Latino subculture. The extent of acculturation has varied, depending on how many generations a family has been in the United States.

Historical Perspective. From the time of Spanish arrival in the Americas, Latinas have been influential in shaping values and defining female roles in society. The historical roots of Latinas can be traced to Africa, Asia, Europe, and the Americas. Spanish and Portuguese cultures, themselves influenced by Middle Eastern and North African traditions as well as European culture, have played an important role in the lives of Latinas. Latinas also have been influenced by pre-Columbian indigenous cultures and the roles of women in those ancient civilizations. In the fifteenth century, Spanish and Portuguese conquest and colonization in the Americas led to intermarriage between Europeans and Native Americans and a mixing of cultures.

The influence of Latin America is evident in many areas of U.S. culture. Music, dancing, language, art, literature, and food reflect Latin American heritage. Women have played important roles in the development of Latino culture in America.

Latinas and the Family. The family has been the central unifying force of Latino culture (*see* FAMILY LIFE). The concept of family goes beyond the typical U.S. view of the nuclear family of mother, father, and children. For Latinos, the extended family is extremely important. Members of the extended family— grandparents, aunts, uncles, cousins, and others—form a close circle of mutual respect and nurturing. Children are taught to respect older family members and to accept their advice.

Historically, the extended patriarchal family was most prevalent among the elite. Industrialization affected the structure of families; poor women were most affected. The women who entered factories received low wages as unskilled laborers, but sometimes factory jobs were the only ones available. Most Latinas, particularly in Latin America but also in the United States, remained engaged in primitive agriculture and handicrafts that contributed to family income. As industrial work for women became established, women were instrumental in the struggles for collec-

tive bargaining rights as union members. Latina feminist reformers fought for the rights of poor, underclass women. Within the middle and upper classes, it became relatively common to have female servants who performed some of the duties previously the responsibility of the female head of household.

Latinas' socioeconomic and political lives have been intricately tied to their role within the family structure. Latinas, especially CHICANAS, are perceived as guardians of traditional social customs and morality. Living in, and by the rules of, two cultures—Latino and Anglo—often leaves these women marginalized, confused, and angry.

Cubanas and Puertorriqueñas have shared similar feelings of cultural displacement, but there are contrasts. Many Cuban women who came to the United States were educated, professional, political exiles, unlike Chicanas and Puertorriqueñas, many of whom were from lower classes. Despite differences in social class, all three groups of women shared the goal of maintaining their Latino traditions, which include respect for motherhood and protection of women.

Religion, particularly Catholicism, has played an important role in the lives and societal role of Latinas. Women traditionally were entrusted with the social and religious upbringing of children. The Virgin of GUADALUPE became the symbol of purity for Chicanas. Latinas have been reared to believe that suffering, forgiveness, and purity provide salvation and moral authority over their male counterparts.

The double standard for marital fidelity among Latinos existed through the twentieth century. Promiscuity by males was accepted and even encouraged but was considered deplorable for women and was punishable by society. The Concordata, an agreement between the Catholic church and many Latin American countries, did not recognize divorce or remarriage. Such agreements, however, were almost nonexistent by the end of the twentieth century. Some researchers argue that the institution of marriage in Latin American cultures has perpetuated inequity for Latinas. Another religious issue that affects Latinas is reproductive rights, especially the issue of BIRTH CONTROL.

Latinas and Feminism. As more Latinas became educated and empowered, they became involved in the socioeconomic betterment of other Latinas. Although Latinas were largely voiceless during the American feminist movement and the Chicano movement of the 1960's and 1970's, their voices and concerns began to be heard in mainstream society in the 1980's and 1990's. Through collective organization and common

Traditionally, women as homemakers formed the core of intergenerational relationships in extended families. (James Shaffer)

goals, Latinas expressed their views and took action against oppression and discrimination. Despite objections by some of their male counterparts, Latinas began fighting for equity without necessarily giving up their feminine side and their family responsibilities.

The National Network of Hispanic Women was formed by professional women to focus on specific concerns of Latinas in the labor force. Organizations within the barrios have worked to improve education, housing, and social services for the Latino community. THE NATIONAL ASSOCIATION OF LATINO ELECTED AND APPOINTED OFFICIALS, with many female members, has provided opportunities for young Latinos to pursue higher education and worked to reduce dropout rates in secondary and higher education.

Contributions. Latinas have made numerous contributions to American culture. Antonia NOVELLO, a Puertorriqueña, served as U.S. surgeon general under President George Bush. Sandra CISNEROS, a Chicana writer and former teacher, has written about the emotional struggles of Mexican American women. Other Latina writers include Ana CASTILLO and Mary Helen PONCE. Cuban American entertainer Gloria ESTEFAN delights audiences with her Latin American songs and music. Vicki CARR and Linda RONSTADT are singers of Mexican American heritage. Many of Ronstadt's works of the 1980's and 1990's focused on her Chicano experiences. Latino actresses Rita MORENO and Rosie Perez, both Puertorriqueñas from New York, have become popular in film, television, and theater. Mexican American Nancy LOPEZ is well known as a professional golfer.

Latinas have also distinguished themselves in the political arena. Linda CHÁVEZ, author of *Out of the Barrio: Toward a New Politics of Hispanic Assimilation*, served in the Ronald Reagan Administration and was Maryland's Republican nominee for the U.S. Senate in 1986. Gloria MOLINA, from California, served

As a public figure and author, Linda Chávez has raised issues important to Latinas. (AP/Wide World Photos)

for two years in the White House during the Jimmy Carter Administration. With other Latinas, she helped bring feminism to Latino politics. Many other Latinas have provided effective role models and flourished in the arts, the sciences, education, business, entertainment, and politics. —*Maria A. Pacino*

SUGGESTED READINGS:

• Abalos, David T. *Latinos in the United States: The Sacred and the Political*. Notre Dame, Ind.: University of Notre Dame Press, 1986. Provides an understanding of the threats and opportunities facing Latinos in American society. The chapter titled "The Politics of Liberation Versus the Politics of Assimilation" deals with issues of marginalization, ethnic identity, and empowerment as a result of living in both the U.S. and the Latino culture.

• Alvarado, Elvia. *Don't Be Afraid Gringo: A Honduran Woman Speaks from the Heart: The Story of Elvia Alvarado*. Edited and translated by Benjamin Medea. New York: Harper and Row, 1989. Oral history of a Honduran peasant activist. As a *campesino* (peasant) organizer, Alvarado organized women's groups to fight malnutrition and enforce land reform laws. Includes black and white maps and photographs, a fact sheet, a list of organizations, and statistics.

• Cisneros, Sandra. *Woman Hollering Creek and Other Stories*. New York: Vintage Books, 1992. An emotional taste of Latino culture in the powerful voice of a Chicana feminist. Vivid fictional portrayals of Mexican American women as submissive wives and mothers living among macho attitudes.

• Flores, Bettina R. *Chiquita's Cocoon: The Latina Woman's Guide to Greater Power, Love, Money, Status, and Happiness*. New York: Villard Books, 1990. Flores tackles Latina issues including female submissiveness, relationships with men, the Catholic church, physical abuse, and birth control. Latinas are encouraged to maintain valued cultural traditions while giving up traditions that demean women and leave them powerless. Includes a list of suggested readings.

• McKenna, Teresa, and Flora Ida Ortiz, eds. *The Broken Web: The Educational Experience of Hispanic American Women*. Claremont, Calif.: Tomas Rivera Center, 1988. Documents the educational inequities faced by Latinas, identifying core issues that require dramatic changes in public policy. Includes statistics and bibliography.

• Mirande, Alfredo, and Evangelina Enriquez. *La Chicana: The Mexican American Woman*. Chicago: University of Chicago Press, 1979. Comprehensive study of Mexican American women, including cultural heritage from Mexico and the American Southwest. Identifies the role of the Chicana within the family structure, education, work, media images, and the Chicana feminist movement. Includes black-and-white photographs, bibliography, and a glossary of Spanish terminology.

• Seller, Maxine Schwartz, ed. *Immigrant Women*. Philadelphia, Pa.: Temple University Press, 1981. While revealing issues of discrimination and other socioeconomic problems, the work emphasizes the strengths and resourcefulness of immigrant women, including Latinas, in coping with cultural change. Includes a bibliographic essay.

• Shorris, Earl. *Latinos. Biography of the People*. New York: W. W. Norton, 1992. Perceptive, analytical, and reflective account of America's fastest-growing minority. Migrant workers, educators, business leaders, social workers, gangsters, and others express their struggles against oppression and discrimination. Includes historical perspective, oral histories, bibliography, and glossary.

• Stoner, K. Lynn. *Latinas of the Americas: A Source Book*. New York: Garland, 1989. Perspectives on history, education, household and family views, and feminist studies, including an extensive bibliography. A biographical section gives an intimate portrayal of Latinas.

Latino National Political Survey: This survey collected data on the political attitudes and values of the three largest Hispanic subgroups in the United States. The U.S. Bureau of the Census reported that the Latino population in the United States grew seven times faster than the rest of the nation between 1980 and 1990. Increased immigration from Central and South America during this period contributed greatly to the changing nature of the Hispanic population. Historically, Latinos had not been included in research such as public opinion polls to ascertain their views on social and political issues. As a result, misconceptions about Latinos dominated their interactions with the rest of American society. Between July, 1989, and March, 1990, Latino researchers conducted the Latino National Political Survey (LNPS) to gather detailed data on this increasingly important segment of the American population.

The LNPS research team consisted of Rodolfo O. de la Garza, Angelo Falcón, F. Chris Garcia, and John A. Garcia. Their objective was to gather data on issues such as the fundamental political values of Lati-

Latinos attempt to unify for various reasons, but subgroups have distinct characteristics and opinions. (Robert Fried)

nos in the United States and the factors that influenced these values. The LNPS also looked at gender, immigration history, and such factors as citizenship and socioeconomic status. The survey's subjects comprised Mexican Americans (1,546), Puerto Ricans (589), and Cuban Americans (682) because these were the largest and most politically significant Latino subgroups in the United States. The forty Standard Metropolitan Statistical Areas selected for the LNPS yielded a sample that was representative of 91 percent of the three targeted Hispanic populations in the United States. The research sample included both foreign- and native-born respondents, not all of whom were U.S. citizens.

The LNPS findings indicated that members of the three subgroups, particularly those who were U.S. citizens, had much in common. Large percentages of each subgroup, for example, preferred to identify themselves in terms of national origin rather than with such pan-ethnic terms as "Latino" or "Hispanic." The survey also revealed that the three subgroups shared views on domestic policy issues, generally looking to government for solutions to social problems. The

LNPS indicated that these three subgroups agreed that increased government spending was appropriate in addressing issues such as health, crime and drug control, bilingual education, services for children, and the environment.

Significant differences were also revealed. Survey results indicated that government spending on welfare and programs intended to assist minorities was favored by Puerto Ricans but not by Cuban Americans. The LNPS illustrated the difficulty of attaching such political labels as "liberal" or "conservative" to the three subgroups: A subgroup may hold a liberal view on one particular social issue and a conservative view on another. This indicates the futility of simple categorization when discussing the diverse Latino population in the United States. The LNPS also illustrated the need for researchers to include Latinos in their work, providing them with a model that clearly distinguishes the variances among the United States' three largest Hispanic groups in the 1990's.

Latino World Festival (Detroit, Mich.): Sponsored by the Latin American Cultural Institute, the Latino

World Festival is a three-day music festival that was inaugurated in 1971. It takes place in Hart Plaza, in downtown Detroit, and features both traditional and contemporary music from throughout Latin America and other Spanish-language countries. Its headliners are major local, national, and international artists. Although its focus is on music, the family oriented festival includes ethnic food, folk arts and crafts, children's games, and dancing. It also includes a Sunday Mass. The July event has drawn more than a quarter million people in some years.

Latinos: People of Latin American ancestry in the United States. This term, literally "Latins" in Spanish, encompasses many groups yet recognizes the cultural differences among them. The term has grown in popularity since its inception in the mid- to late 1980's and has been more popular than "Hispanic" in areas where many varied groups of Latin Americans live together. Politically, the term is favored by liberals and moderates.

Latins Anonymous: Comedy troupe. Latins Anonymous comprised four Latino members: Luisa Leschin, Armando Molina, Rick Najera, and Diane Rodriguez. Disgruntled with the lack of good Hollywood roles for Latinos, the four actors created a show to express their views. Their sketches expressed the diversity of Latino culture, poking fun at the cultural clichés that often surround Latinos.

Lau v. Nichols (U.S. Supreme Court number 72-6520): Litigation involving education. The case was brought before the U.S. Supreme Court by students of Chinese ancestry who did not speak English. The petitioners argued that the non-English-speaking students of Chinese ancestry were not provided equal educational opportunities because they did not receive courses in the English language.

The U.S. Supreme Court held that the public education programs in the California school system programs were in violation of Title VI of the CIVIL RIGHTS ACT OF 1964, in that the California school system failed to provide English-language instruction to students who did not speak English, thus denying them a meaningful opportunity to participate in public education. The Court held in its 1974 decision that under the provisions of the Civil Rights Act of 1964, children who could not understand the language in which they were being taught were not offered equal education.

The impact of *Lau v. Nichols* for Spanish speakers who do not speak English well or at all is that the Court ruled that a school's failure to provide an educational program for non-English-speaking students violated the 1964 Civil Rights Act's proscription of discrimination on the basis of national origin. The Court held that school districts receiving federal funds cannot discriminate against schoolchildren who come to the classroom with limited speaking ability in English by denying them the necessary language training needed to participate meaningfully in the education process.

In a related case, SERNA V. PORTALES (1972), lawyers from the Mexican American Legal Defense and Education Fund argued that the inadequacy or absence of educational bilingual or bicultural programs in New Mexico schools that may have had many Mexican American students violated the FOURTEENTH AMENDMENT's equal protection clause. Both *Lau v. Nichols* and *Serna v. Portales* illustrate the efficacy of using the courts to legally establish programs for non-English-speaking students.

Laviera, Jesús Abraham "Tato" (b. Sept. 5, 1950, Santurce, Puerto Rico): Poet and community worker. Laviera accompanied his family to New York in 1960. He lived in a Lower East Side ghetto, but his work as an altar boy at church enabled him to maintain pride and stability during a difficult period of adjustment. He received his high school diploma in 1968.

Laviera has used his talents both professionally and as a community volunteer. For fifteen years, he was involved in directing the Association of Community Services. He served on the boards of Madison Neighbors in Action and Mobilization for Youth and was involved with the Jamaica Arts Center, the Puerto Rico Family Institute, and United Bronx Parents. He was a producer for the sixteenth Annual Puerto Rico Parade of Chicago, the First Latino Book Fair and Writers Festival in Chicago, and the second such event in Houston. He was commissioned playwright for the Henry Street Settlement New Federal Theater. At President Jimmy Carter's invitation, Laviera read his poetry at the White House in 1980. His poetry, including *La Carreta Made a U-Turn* (1979) and *Enclave* (1981), provides a record of the exile who learns to be at home in a sometimes hostile environment.

Law enforcement and the Latino community: Latino interactions with law enforcement agencies are often complicated by misunderstanding and fraught with prejudice. Historically, U.S. police have often

Top Ten Cities for Latino Representation Among Police Officers, 1988

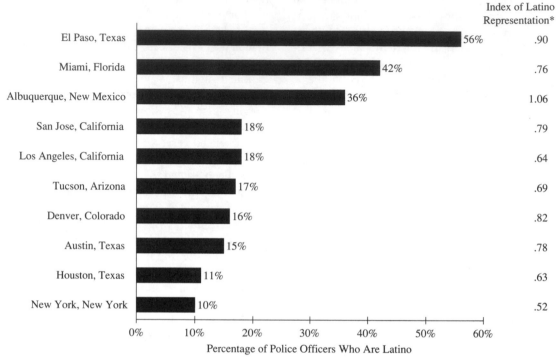

Index of Latino
Representation*

City	Percentage	Index
El Paso, Texas	56%	.90
Miami, Florida	42%	.76
Albuquerque, New Mexico	36%	1.06
San Jose, California	18%	.79
Los Angeles, California	18%	.64
Tucson, Arizona	17%	.69
Denver, Colorado	16%	.82
Austin, Texas	15%	.78
Houston, Texas	11%	.63
New York, New York	10%	.52

Percentage of Police Officers Who Are Latino

Source: Data are from Marlita A. Reddy, ed., *Statistical Record of Hispanic Americans* (Detroit: Gale Research, 1993), Table 901.
*The index of Latino representation is the percentage of Latino law enforcement officers divided by the percentage of Latinos in the population as a whole.

assisted in the maltreatment of Latinos and ignored their need for protection. The combined experience of Puerto Ricans in the Northeast and Mexican Americans in the Southwest offers a profile of the situation.

The relationship between law enforcement and Latinos also concerns many issues other than those directly related to the police. Particularly relevant to the Latino community are such topics as SEGREGATION and DISCRIMINATION with respect to residence, education, and employment; health coverage; political representation; immigration; and labor-organizing efforts. Nevertheless, the significance of the police-Latino relationship necessitates attention. Latino critics of law enforcement typically make three broad claims: that police help groups to discriminate against or abuse Latinos; police officers themselves often do the same; and police often fail to protect Latinos.

Mexican Americans. In 1967, a U.S. Commission on Civil Rights investigation uncovered evidence of police abuse of Mexican Americans in the Southwest. Victims testified about incidents in which police offi-

cers used excessive force and had also expressed their alleged authority to do so because the victims were Mexican. Sometimes, especially in cases regarding resistance to arrest and attempts to escape, police actions had resulted in Chicano deaths. Witnesses maintained that police officers would not likely have used deadly force against non-Hispanic whites under similar circumstances.

Witnesses also alleged that police engaged in unequal treatment of Anglo versus Chicano youth. Anglo juveniles detained by police were customarily released and left to the custody of their parents, critics said, but Chicano juveniles in similar circumstances were charged and jailed or sent to reformatories. For the same faults in conduct, police records were thus established for the Mexican American youths and not for Anglo ones.

Mexican Americans who testified in the hearings also made various claims about how their right to vote had been undermined by police action. They cited increased police presence and ticketing for minor of-

Police departments have tried to increase the number of Latino officers and their presence in Latino areas. (James Shaffer)

fenses on election day as attempts to discourage Latino voting participation.

Witnesses also complained about a perceived lack of respect from police, a lack reflected in verbal abuse, rudeness, insults, and threats. They perceived themselves as being more frequently stopped for minor violations and argued that Latinos were often stopped for minor offenses in order to anger them and provide an excuse for arresting them.

A number of Mexican Americans also declared that police had interfered with their organizational efforts. For example, in the TIERRA AMARILLA incident in the summer of 1967, police arrested the officers of the Alianza Federal de Mercedes—an organization dedicated to improving the status of Chicanos—on the eve of a planning rally.

Chicano citizens and communities also complained that they were victims of inadequate police protection. Many times, critics said, officers were simply not around in rural Latino-populated areas; in urban areas, it was alleged, officers seemed annoyed to be working in Latino communities. According to one witness, police officers in Latino communities saw their jobs as an effort to protect the communities from residents. Outside the BARRIOS, though, police officers remembered their protective duty toward people.

Complaints did not end with that investigation. Similar allegations of abuse by police officers, disregard for civil rights, and discriminatory treatment of the Mexican American community as a whole persisted.

Puerto Ricans. Puerto Ricans in the Northeast have echoed the claims of Mexican Americans in the Southwest. In 1993, the NATIONAL CONGRESS OF PUERTO RICAN RIGHTS (NCPRR), which had been working on issues of police brutality and racially motivated violence for eight years, announced that it had identified a pattern of discrimination in the ways in which the police handled cases involving Latino victims.

According to the NCPRR, the following scenario was typical: After a person of color was attacked and race or ethnicity could have been the motive, police arrived and asked the victim why he or she was there at that time. The blame thus began to be shifted toward the victim. Instead of starting to address the problem of violence motivated by prejudice, the inquiry started from the assumption that such violence was inevitable.

Latinos have protested what they believe to be biases against Latinos on the part of police departments and officers. (Impact Visuals, Andrew Lichtenstein)

The discussion assumed that the victim should have known this "fact" and thus should have expected the violence. Therefore, police tended to assume, the victim probably provoked violence by, many times literally, walking into the situation.

Moreover, the NCPRR alleged, there existed an "institutional reluctance" on the part of law enforcement agencies to classify incidents as racially motivated because of the paperwork involved and the "negative image" associated with precincts that had high numbers of racially motivated cases. Thus, many racially motivated incidents involving Latinos were never classified correctly and, therefore, never investigated properly.

The list of specific incidents of abuse and discrimination adduced by both the NCPRR and the Commission on Civil Rights was long. The commission's 1970 statement transmits the attitude that investigators, though not necessarily witnesses, can have: "Although the Commission cannot establish the validity of each of the complaints [it heard] . . . their prevalence suggests a serious problem."

Some scholars have proposed the theory that an unfair burden may be brought upon people who live in BARRIOS and other minority neighborhoods. In this view, the dominant U.S. culture does not know how to deal with the truths of poverty or with other ills of urban life. The police, as representatives of the dominant culture, are thus inevitably drawn into conflicts with and misunderstandings of those who live in the barrios.　　　　　　　　　　　　*—Yara I. Alma Bonilla*

SUGGESTED READINGS: • Cooper, J. L. *The Police and the Ghetto.* Port Washington, N.Y.: Kennikat Press, 1980. • U.S. Commission on Civil Rights. *Mexican Americans and the Administration of Justice in the Southwest.* Washington, D.C.: Government Printing Office, 1970. • U.S. Commission on Civil Rights. Texas Advisory Committee. *The Civil Rights Status of Spanish-Speaking Americans in Kleberg, Nueces, and San Patricio Counties, Texas.* Washington, D.C.: Government Printing Office, 1967.

Lazaro, Ladislas (June 5, 1872, near Ville Platte, La.—Mar. 30, 1927, Washington, D.C.): Politician. Lazaro, a Mexican American, received a well-rounded education, attending both public and private schools, then Holy Cross College in New Orleans, Louisiana. He was graduated from a medical school in Louisville, Kentucky, in 1894. Lazaro then returned to Louisiana and practiced medicine in the town of Washington until 1913. At that time, he became interested in agriculture.

Lazaro was also intrigued by politics. He served in the Louisiana state senate between 1908 and 1912 and was elected to Congress as a Democrat in 1913. Lazaro served in Congress until his death.

League of United Latin American Citizens (LULAC): Founded in 1929 in San Antonio, Texas, LULAC is the oldest existing Latino nonprofit civic, social, and political organization in the United States. It emerged from negotiations between leaders of the Order of Sons of America, the League of Latin American Citizens, the SONS OF AMERICA, and the Knights of America with the goal of successfully integrating Latinos into mainstream U.S. culture.

From its founding until World War II, LULAC experienced rapid growth, especially in South Texas. It advocated equal rights and opportunities for Mexican Americans, also urging their assimilation into and loyalty to the United States. LULAC fought the classification of Mexican Americans by race and engaged in voter registration drives, petition campaigns, and legal pressure against employers and local governments that discriminated against Mexican Americans. Believing that access to education would hasten Mexican American assimilation into and acceptance by the American middle class, LULAC organized back-to-school campaigns for children and adults, the renovation of Mexican American elementary schools, and citizenship training.

The focus on EDUCATION continued after the war with citizenship and English classes provided by volunteers. Under the presidency of Felix Tijerina (1956-1960), LULAC established the Little School of the Four Hundred, a preschool program that taught non-English-speaking children four hundred basic English words. LULAC raised funds for charities and held campaigns to integrate civic groups such as the Boy Scouts, Red Cross, and 4H. The organization also continued its crusade for educational reform by participating in the important legal cases of *MÉNDEZ V. WESTMINSTER SCHOOL DISTRICT* (1947) and *DELGADO V. BASTROP INDEPENDENT SCHOOL DISTRICT* (1948) in addition to other civil rights suits. Integration and economic mobility continued to be a primary concern, but in 1953 LULAC fought for recognition of Mexican Americans as a discrete sector of the population that suffered from DISCRIMINATION (*see* SEGREGATION, DESEGREGATION, AND INTEGRATION).

The 1960's was a period of instability for LULAC. As economic opportunities for Latinos expanded, members from the postwar period saw less need for the organization. LULAC criticized the confrontational tactics of the newer Chicano organizations, which in turn challenged LULAC'S goals of integration and service. Internal conflict over ideology, tactics, and the organization's role created inertia and financial strain. Ironically, the availability of federal funds for social service programs was a boon for LULAC. For example, in 1964, LULAC and the AMERICAN G.I. FORUM established Project SER (Service, Employment, and Retention), which provided employment banks in the Southwest. By 1994, there were forty-two affiliates in seventeen states. LULAC also sponsored six federally funded housing projects worth more than $17 million and centers offering counseling and technical assistance to Latinos enrolled in higher education. In 1974, the LULAC Foundation was established to seek out and disperse corporate grants.

Membership peaked at sixty-three hundred in 1981, during the presidency of Rubén Bonilla. Financial difficulties plagued the organization, forcing it to close its headquarters in Washington, D.C. The misappropriation of funds by the LULAC Foundation in 1989 caused additional internal tension and discord.

League of United Latin American Citizens v. Pasadena Independent School District (June 10, 1987): Litigation involving employment practices. This case from the United States District Court for the Southern District of Texas bears the number Civ. A. No. H-87-935. The plaintiffs were illegal aliens who were suing the Pasadena, Texas, school district after being terminated from their jobs as custodians for using false Social Security numbers on their job applications. Interpretation of the IMMIGRATION REFORM AND CONTROL ACT OF 1986 was central to the case. The court ordered the school district to reinstate the plaintiffs, who claimed that they had been fired in violation of the act's antidiscrimination provisions.

In this case, the League of United Latin American Citizens represented fired custodians Maria Olympia Hernandez, Reina Raquel Gullen, Bianca Lopez, and Maria Garza, and all persons similarly situated against the Pasadena Independent School District. The school district fired the named plaintiffs when their use of false Social Security numbers on job applications became known.

District Judge McDonald ordered the school district to rehire the plaintiffs. He held that firing these custodians for no reason other than their use of false Social Security numbers amounted to an unfair immigration-related employment practice under the Immigration

Reform and Control Act of 1986. All the named plaintiffs were eligible for legalization under the act, and their continued employment by the school district was permissible under its grandfather clause.

Under the Immigration Reform and Control Act of 1986, undocumented aliens who could prove that they had been in the United States on January 1, 1982, became eligible for legalization and permanent lawful residence. Another provision of the act made it illegal to hire undocumented aliens after November 6, 1986, and provided penalties for unlawful hiring. The act also contained provisions against discrimination based on national origin or citizenship status. These provisions were intended to avoid injuring minority groups such as Hispanics.

The school district supported its termination of the workers by pointing to a longstanding policy that required the firing of workers who had lied on their applications. The court, however, noticed that the district had failed to carry out its existing policy of verifying the information on employee applications within thirty days. In addition, the Immigration and Naturalization Service testified that their loss of employment drastically reduced the named plaintiffs' chances of legalization. This decision provided crucial aid to illegal Hispanic immigrants seeking legalization under the Immigration Reform and Control Act of 1986.

Leal, Luis (b. Sept. 17, 1907, Linares, Mexico): Writer and educator. Leal has written extensively in both Spanish and English on Mexican folklore, literature, and culture, and has edited several anthologies. Among his works is *A Decade of Chicano Literature, 1970-1979: Critical Essays and Bibliography* (1982).

Leal holds degrees in Spanish from Northwestern University (B.A., 1940) and the University of Chicago (A.M., 1941; Ph.D., 1950). He worked as an instructor at the University of Chicago from 1942 to 1943 and 1946 to 1948, then was promoted to assistant professor of Spanish. In 1952, he left the University of Chicago to take a position as associate professor of modern languages at the University of Mississippi, where he taught until 1956. He was an associate professor of Spanish at Emory University from 1955 to 1959, then joined the faculty of the University of Illinois at Urbana-Champaign. He was promoted to the rank of professor in 1962 and became professor emeritus in 1976. In 1980, he was named acting director of the Center for Chicano Studies at the University of California, Santa Barbara.

Lolita Lebrón Soto claims during a press conference that the attack on the House of Representatives was her idea. (AP/Wide World Photos)

Lebrón Soto, Lolita (b. 1919, Lares, Puerto Rico): Puerto Rican nationalist. Lebrón Soto was born in Lares, the rural village in which Ramón Emeterio BE-TANCES proclaimed a free and independent Puerto Rico in EL GRITO DE LARES (1868).

Lebrón joined the Nationalist Party, which had consistently sought a free Puerto Rico. She moved to New York in 1940 and became deeply involved in nationalist politics. Lebrón led three other nationalists—Andrés FIGUEROA CORDERO, Rafael CANCEL MI-RANDA, and Irving Flores—in an armed assault on the U.S. House of Representatives on March 1, 1954. Five congressmen were wounded. For her role in this attack, Lebrón was sentenced to serve between sixteen

and fifty years in prison at Alderson, Virginia. Before her pardon by President Jimmy Carter in 1979, Lebrón was allowed to return to Puerto Rico for the funeral of her daughter.

Lechón: Suckling pig. Roast suckling pig, *lechón asado*, is traditional fare for Christmas in the Spanish-speaking Caribbean. Stuffed with a mixture of beans, rice, and guava paste, it takes on a distinctive fruity flavor. At other seasons, it may be cooked on a spit over an open fire on a bed of stones, usually accompanied by roasted green plantains. In Puerto Rico, *lechón asado* is usually served with a sour garlic sauce (*aji-li-mójili*). In the Dominican Republic, *lechón asado* is a traditional dish for a wedding feast. Most other *lechón* dishes in the Caribbean are based not on suckling pig but on beef eye of round, also called *lechón* because of its purported resemblance to the silhouette of a pig.

Lecuona, Ernesto (1895 or 1896, Guanabacoa, Cuba—Nov. 29, 1963, Santa Cruz de Tenerife, Canary Islands): Bandleader, composer, and pianist. Lecuona began composing dance music when he was eleven years old. When he was seventeen, he gave his first recital in New York City. Lecuona's Palau Brothers Cuban Orchestra was featured in the 1931 film musical *Cuban Love Song*. The film starred Jimmy Durante, Lawrence Tibbett, and Lupe VELEZ. During the 1930's, his group, the Lecuona Cuban Boys, toured Europe and recorded for Columbia.

Lecuona composed music for a variety of different venues, including musical shows and cantatas. He is probably best known for various songs that have been rerecorded by other artists. His song "Siboney" was a hit for Alfredo Brito in 1931. It was recorded again in 1953 by a quartet that included Dizzy Gillespie and Stan Getz. "Para Vigo Me Voy" ("Say 'Si Si'") was recorded by Xavier CUGAT in 1933. The song later became a hit for Glenn Miller, with English lyrics by Al Stillman. The Andrews Sisters, the Mills Brothers, and others would also record the song.

Other songs by Lecuona that had numerous cover versions include "Canto Karabali" ("Jungle Drums"), "La Comparsa," "Malagueña," and "Andaluzia" (which Stillman turned into "The Breeze and I"). Lecuona is one of the most successful Cuban-born composers. In addition, his daughter Ernestina sang in Lecuona's band, and his niece Margarita made a name as a mezzo-soprano and a songwriter.

Legal system, Spanish/Mexican colonial: The legal system of the Spanish New World, especially in New Spain or Mexico, was a sophisticated law-enforcement machine that reflected the complexity and special features of colonial Latin America.

History. Spain governed its American possessions through the Council of the Indies, founded in 1511. This body, presided over by the king, acted as a sort of court of last appeal for the colonies. Below the council, there were ten *audiencias*, modeled after the Royal Chancellery of Valladolid in Castile and founded in the sixteenth century. The *audiencias* served as local law courts. Not all these institutions possessed equal status, however; the two major *audiencias*—in Mexico City, New Spain (founded in 1533), and in Lima, Peru (founded in 1544)—acted as supreme courts for the New World.

The bureaucracy of the Spanish empire was staffed by *letrados*, university-trained legal officials. *Letrados* could be found in each *audiencia* acting as *oidores*, or judges, and as *fiscales*, or public prosecutors. In addition, the *audiencias* relied on the services of *escribanos de camara*, *relatores*, and several other categories of legal clerks who handled the abundant paperwork. Spaniards were preferred for these appointments in the belief that they would more keenly enforce royal legislation and would not be exposed to the influence of local interest groups. Not surprisingly, this policy of discrimination brought forth bitter protest by "American" *letrados* and became a permanent source of discontent among the white elite in the colonies.

In New Spain there was, in addition to the *audiencia* of Mexico City, a second *audiencia* in Guadalajara with jurisdiction over northern Mexico as well as over what would become California, Arizona, and New Mexico. There was also a special court designed specifically for Indians and Indian affairs: the Juzgado General de Indios, or General Indian Court, established in 1592. This tribunal dealt with the distribution and supervision of Indian tribute labor as well as with lawsuits involving Indians. The court provided its services free of charge and tried in earnest to ameliorate the lot of the natives and to prevent their abuse by Spanish settlers. Although many instances of illegal exploitation of Indians never reached this tribunal, its proceedings were relatively quick for the period and quite accessible to complainants. The absence of similar institutions elsewhere in the Hispanic world hurt the interests of native populations, who were forced to use the slower, more aloof, and more complex *audiencias*.

The question of which legal system should apply in the Indies was a major intellectual and political problem for Spanish jurists in the sixteenth century. Originally, the Crown intended to maintain the Indian population under its own system of law. Thus in 1530 King Charles V ordered that native Indian laws and customs should be respected as long as they did not violate Christian religion and morals. In 1543, the New Laws of the Indies became the first comprehensive European code of law meant exclusively for America. Despite these precedents, in the late sixteenth century, Philip II called for a uniform legal system for Spain and its colonies. Philip's opinion prevailed, and pre-Columbian laws—except at the level of Indian villages, and as long as there were no appeals—were disregarded in favor of the traditional principles of Spanish legislation. Thus, in effect, Indians were placed under an alien legal system that they largely did not understand, a situation that naturally lent itself to abuse.

Although the legal principles behind law in the New World stemmed from European models, local circumstances eventually forced the Madrid government to abandon its efforts to apply a single code of law on both sides of the Atlantic. In 1614, Philip III gave the Council of the Indies the authority to pass legislation for America. In 1680, the special rules applied to the colonies were published as the *Recopilación de las Leyes de los Reynos de las Indias*, which became the basic law code for Spain's American possessions.

Impact. It is difficult to generalize about the effect of the colonial legal system on the majority Indian and mestizo population of the Indies. On one hand, the Indian and mestizo population, like the mulattoes and blacks, lived under severe legal restrictions and were barred from most offices and prestigious ranks, on the political, religious, and professional levels. On the other hand, the Crown took very seriously its self-imposed role as benefactor and protector of the native population against the excesses of the settlers, and royal legislation clearly shows this concern. The 1543 New Laws put an end to the enslavement of the native population and reaffirmed both the humanity and the personal liberty and civil rights of the Indians.

In the 1570's, the king exempted the Indians from the jurisdiction of perhaps the most feared tribunal of all, the Inquisition. Although Indians, like religious minorities in Spain itself, were often prone to backsliding, the king placed them outside the scope of the Holy Office, in marked contrast to the plight of the Jews and Muslims in the metropolis. Furthermore, the *audiencias*, especially in New Spain, meted out considerably milder punishments to Indian lawbreakers than to white criminals. The most common penalty even for violent crimes was a term of forced labor, instead of the more common European measures of torture, mutilation, and execution. In its relative mildness, the colonial legal system appears to have been ahead of its time, foreshadowing the widespread use of incarceration that became a major feature of modern penal systems.   —*Fernando González de León*

SUGGESTED READINGS: • Arregui-Zamorano, Pilar. *La Audiencia de México Según Los Visitadores: Siglos XVI y XVII.* 2d ed. Mexico City: Universidad Nacional Autonoma de Mexico, 1985. • Borah, Woodrow. *Justice by Insurance: The General Indian Court of Colonial Mexico and the Legal Aides of the Half-Real.* Berkeley: University of California Press, 1983. • Burkholder, Mark, and D. S. Chandler. *From Impotence to Authority: The Spanish Crown and the American Audiencias, 1687-1808.* Columbia: University of Missouri Press, 1977. • Parry, John Horace. *The Audiencia of New Galicia in the Sixteenth Century.* Cambridge, England: Cambridge University Press, 1948. • Soberanes Fernandez, Jose Luis, ed. *Los Tribunales de la Nueva España.* Mexico City: Universidad Nacional Autonoma de Mexico, 1980.

León, Alonso de (1637, Spain—1691, near San Antonio, Tex.): Soldier and explorer. León, a Spanish officer, was governor of Coahuila (Nueva Estremadura), Mexico, in 1688. Later known as "the conqueror of Texas," León first entered that area in early 1688 in search of an East Texas French settlement founded by René-Robert Cavalier, Sieur de la Salle, in 1685. León had been given orders to find and destroy the settlement, the existence of which threatened Spanish claims to the area. Those claims were founded on sixteenth century explorations of Hernando DE SOTO, and Francisco Vázquez de CORONADO as well as on the foundation, in 1682, of Franciscan missions near the site of modern El Paso.

This León expedition, the first of five that he undertook, enabled León to ascertain that La Salle's settlement, Fort St. Louis, had been destroyed by local Indians and that the French had abandoned the ruins. In 1690, León and several Franciscan friars, including Damian Massanet, laid a firm foundation for future Spanish settlements in East Texas. During León's expeditions, he crossed and named many of the rivers of Texas. Among the other accomplishments of León and the priests and soldiers who made up his expeditions were the foundings of two missions, San Francisco de los Texas and Santa Maria.

Lezama Lima, José (José María Andres Fernando Lezama Lima; Dec. 19, 1910, Campamento Militar de Columbia, Cuba—Aug. 9, 1976, Havana, Cuba): Poet and novelist. Until the publication of *Paradiso* (1966, rev. ed., 1988; *Paradise*, 1974), Lezama Lima was virtually unknown outside Cuba. *Paradise*, which is his first novel, has been influential and has become established as a classic of Cuban literature.

Primarily a poet, Lezama Lima can be considered a member of the generation of writers of the Latin American "Boom." His rich and ornate style has influenced a generation of poets. He founded *Orígenes*, an influential pre-revolutionary journal. Alienated from power, at least in part because of his highly metaphorical, Byzantine writing, which was described by some as counterrevolutionary, he spent his later years in poverty and isolation that he might have been able to alleviate had his requests to leave the island been granted.

Liberation theology: Radical Catholic movement that began in Latin America in the 1960's and had some influence on Latinos in the United States. It attempts to reinterpret Christianity using sociopolitical criteria, urging the church to side with the poor and the oppressed in social struggles.

The Beginnings of the Movement. Liberation theology appears to have exploded on the Latin American scene in the late 1960's and early 1970's, much like Martin Luther's Protestant Reformation suddenly appeared in Wittenburg, Germany, in 1517. Like the Reformation of the sixteenth century, liberation theology

Liberation theology stresses efforts to bring religion to the common people and address everyday concerns. (Robert Fried)

in the twentieth century was the culmination of development over time. Liberation theology drew out the social and political implications of the Christian faith and applied them to the problems of modern Latin American society, asserting that God is on the side of the poor.

The spirit of this theology can be traced back four hundred years to Bartolomé DE LAS CASAS, who defended the rights of the Indians in Valladolid, Spain, in a dispute with a scholastic theologian in the 1550's. More recent roots can be found in the Catholic youth movements such as Juventud Obrero Católico (Catholic Worker Youth) and Juventud Estudiantil Católico (Catholic Student Youth), which began in the 1930's to unite faith with political commitment. The worker priest movement beginning in the 1950's also tied faith to social issues. Political changes brought momentum to these movements. The CUBAN REVOLUTION of 1959 became a model of revolution, showing that countries could break free of domination by the United States.

The Second Vatican Council II (1962-1965) signaled a tremendous change in Catholic theology that helped prepare the foundations for liberation theology. Pope John XXIII convened the council for the purpose of opening the CATHOLIC CHURCH to the modern world in a process known as *aggiornamiento*. The key documents produced at Vatican II redefined the church as the people of God including masses of believers. They called on theologians to become conversant with the social sciences to make theology more relevant to society. Paul IV extended the reforms of VATICAN II in his encyclical *Popularum Progressio*, which set forth a theology of development and defended the right of the oppressed to overthrow tyrannical regimes. The theology of development claimed that social, economic, and political reforms to promote development would bring about justice.

A theology of revolution emerged in reaction to the reformist attitudes of the theology of development. This theology was articulated in 1966 at the Church and Society meeting of the World Council of Christian Churches in Geneva, Switzerland. It challenged the socioeconomic theories of development underlying the World Bank, the International Monetary Fund, and President John F. Kennedy's Alliance for Progress by suggesting that the theory of dependence was an appropriate model.

In this view, the poverty of Third World countries was explained not as a result of underdevelopment but as a product of capitalism. Third World countries were being kept in a state of economic and political dependence on the advanced industrial nations of the Northern Hemisphere. These poor countries needed a sociology of liberation to free them from this dependency.

The Formulation of Liberation Theology. As Latin American theologians reflected on these socioeconomic insights into the plight of their countries, the theology of liberation was born. The way had been paved in Petropolis, Brazil, as early as 1964, when theologians met to discuss the meaning of faith in contemporary Latin America. Gustavo Gutierrez, a Peruvian priest, taught a course in Montreal, Canada, in 1967 on the church and poverty. His notes were later published in the epoch-making book *A Theology of Liberation* (1973). Gutierrez continued to set forth the basic outlines of the theology of liberation at meetings in Peru and Colombia from 1968 to 1970.

At the Second Latin American Episcopal Conference in Medellín, Colombia, in 1968, Latin American bishops met to apply the ideas of Vatican II to Latin America. Gutierrez was there as a theological consultant, and he probably wrote the Medellín documents on peace, justice, and poverty. These documents spoke of institutionalized violence, structural sin, and integral liberation—key ideas in the theology of liberation.

Latin American theologians and sociologists began to further develop liberation theology ideas at conferences such as the Faith and Development meetings of the Mexican Theological Society in 1969; Iglesia y Sociedad en América Latina in Buenos Aires in 1970; and Seminario de la Theologia de Liberación in Juárez, Mexico, in 1970. A meeting in Escorial, Spain, in 1972 signaled the formulation of the principal ideas of liberation theology. The Christians for Socialism Conference in Santiago, Chile, in 1973 discussed the socialist implications of the theology.

Political movements continued to provoke debate among Latin American liberation theologians, who were divided between populist and Marxist approaches. They monitored developments such as the CUBAN REVOLUTION, Salvador Allende's Popular Unity government in Chile (1970-1973), and the return of Juan Perón in Argentina in 1973. They also evaluated activities of Priests for the Third World and the progress of Christian-based communities outside the church hierarchy in Brazil, Chile, Nicaragua, and El Salvador. The controversial Rockefeller Report (1969) also stimulated thinking about liberation movements. It stated that the security of the Western Hemisphere required support for military governments in Latin America because those governments were de-

A Central American refugee at a shelter in Brownsville, Texas, works on religious handicrafts. (Impact Visuals, Philip True)

fenders of order and of the values of Western Christian civilization.

The full range of political and theological debate was evident in a crop of new journals espousing liberation theology that began to appear throughout Latin America. These included *Vispera* (Montevideo, Uruguay), *Service of Documentation* (Lima, Peru), *Christus* (Mexico City), *Revista Ecclesiastica Brasileira* (Petropolis, Brazil), *Dialogo* (Panama), *Amanecer* (Managua, Nicaragua), *Paginas* (Lima, Peru), *Stromata* (San Miguel, Argentina), *Cristianismo y Sociedad* (Mexico City), and *Servir* (Mexico City). Such journals helped to bring liberation theology to the center of academic debate as well as to the attention of the general public.

The journals popularized the biblical theme of liberation that is the movement's inspiration. The key model of the concept is the Exodus—the liberation of the Hebrew slaves from bondage in Egypt. Liberation theologians see in Exodus a case for interpreting God as the God of the oppressed and salvation as liberation. Another important model is the Marxist idea of the liberation of the working classes. Herbert Marcuse, the German émigré philosopher in the United States, focused on the theme of liberation in philosophy and popularized the concept for the 1960's generation. Paulo Friere, the Brazilian educator, wrote about liberating education. Argentine philosophers drew on the ideas of Emmanuel Levinas, the French Jewish philosopher, to construct an authentic Latin American philosophy of liberation that took the fact of oppression as its point of departure.

Growth and Opposition. Developments in the 1970's changed the tenor of liberation theology as its influence spread. First, it began to inspire similar movements in the United States and other countries. Advocacy groups in the United States met with Latin American theologians to discuss the possibilities of applying liberation theology to the United States at meetings such as Theology in the Americas in Detroit in 1975. Feminist theologies, Chicano theologies, and Afro-American theologies took root. Some American churches set up community action organizations to help their poor Latino parishioners.

At the Third Latin American Episcopal Conference in Puebla, Mexico, in 1979, the conservative church leadership tried to oppose liberation theology; ironically, many insights of the movement were integrated with more traditional teachings. Pope John Paul II's encyclical *Laborem Exercens* (1979) equally condemned capitalism and socialism and advocated a

third way that became convincing to some liberation theologians. The Nicaraguan Revolution of 1979 installed Catholic priests with sympathies toward liberation theology in official positions with the Sandinista government, such as Ernesto Cardenal as the minister of culture and Fernando Cardenal as minister of education. The Sandinista government also produced a sympathetic document on the role of religion in society.

In the 1980's, liberation theology encountered some significant opposition. In 1980, the Ronald Reagan Administration's Santa Fe Document declared that U.S. foreign policy must begin to counter liberation theology because it threatened American business interests in the region. In 1984, after the publication of a provocative book by Brazilian theologian Leonardo Boff, the Vatican condemned liberation theology. A Vatican document called *Instruction on Certain Aspects of the Theology of Liberation* called attention to what were called "deviations" in liberation theology that were harmful to Christian living and drew heavily from Marxism. This negative treatment was followed, however, by the more positive *Instruction on Christian Freedom and Liberation*. Although this document did not affirm liberation theology, it was produced as a result of the movement.

Chicano Theology. Mexican Americans began to use liberation theology to reflect on their situation in the United States as an oppressed minority. Virgil Elizondo was one of the pioneer thinkers in this field. He articulated two of the key concepts of Chicano theology—*mestizaje* and Our Lady of Guadalupe. Mestizaje refers to the fact that Mexican Americans have always been bicultural as people of mixed race, and that experience must be taken into account in their talking about God. Our Lady of Guadalupe functions as a major religious and ethnic symbol for the Mexican American community, showing that divinity can take the form of a brown woman (*see* GUADALUPE, VIRGIN OF).

In 1981, Elizondo brought together Mexican American doctoral students in theology at the Mexican American Cultural Center in San Antonio, Texas, to discuss major problems facing the church and Mexican Americans. They were concerned about religion and mental health, cultural disintegration, assimilation, identity problems, growing secularism, and the price of capitalism. They agreed that Christians must work together on social problems such as the rights of farmworkers and the plight of the undocumented. They also decided to begin constructing a systematic theology for Mexican Americans that would be based on ancestral identities and popular expressions of faith.

Our Lady of Guadalupe is an important figure in Latino religious identity. (James Shaffer)

Through Chicano theology they hoped to find the language of ultimate resistance to the gods of the threatening Anglo empire and strengthen their people's connection to their heritage. —*Michael Candelaria*

SUGGESTED READINGS:

• Candelaria, Michael. *Popular Religion and Liberation: The Dilemma of Liberation Theology*. Albany: State University of New York Press, 1990. Discusses liberation theology's appraisal of the liberating and alienating qualities of popular religion.

• Deck, Allan Figueroa, ed. *Frontiers of Hispanic Theology in the United States*. Maryknoll, N.Y.: Orbis Books, 1992. An anthology of Hispanic American studies on religion and theology.

• Gibellini, Rosino, ed. *Frontiers of Theology in Latin America*. Translated by John Drury. Maryknoll, N.Y.: Orbis Books, 1979. A classic anthology of writings by some of the foremost exponents of liberation theology.

• Gutierrez, Gustavo. *A Theology of Liberation*. Translated and edited by Sister Caridad Inda and John Eagleson. Maryknoll, N.Y.: Orbis Books, 1973. Principal early work of liberation theology that lays out its main ideas.

• Hennelly, Alfred T., ed. and trans. *Liberation Theology: A Documentary History*. Maryknoll, N.Y.: Orbis Books, 1990. A thorough collection of primarily ecclesiastical documents on liberation theology.

Libraries and archives: Libraries are repositories of knowledge or information gathered by individuals or groups, most often in written form. Because the term "Latino" includes several cultural and historical groups, a discussion of libraries and archives in the context of Latinos necessitates consideration of the emergence of writing, books, and libraries within these specific groups.

Mesoamerican Writing. The first known writing in Mesoamerica was produced by Zapotecs. Although writing was present in Mayan culture, it flourished during the Classic Period (about 300 to 800 C.E.). Most writing of this period has been found inscribed on stone public monuments such as stelae and pyramids. Public Mayan writing and inscriptions documented the Mayan life cycle, wars, ruling dynasties, mythology, astronomy, and rituals and offerings.

Most written documents of Mesoamerica were destroyed during the Spanish colonial period. For example, in 1562, Bishop Diego de Landa burned many Mayan books. Those that survived include the Dresden Codex, Madrid Codex, Paris Codex, and Grolier Codex. The best-known pieces of Mayan literature are the Books of CHILAM BALAM and the epic POPOL VUH.

Nahuas, often referred to as Aztecs, had a rich language called Nahuatl. Their scribes, called *tlacuilo* or *tlamatini*, were honored functionaries in charge of composing and preserving written records. Scribes attended *calmecac* (schools for the nobles), where they learned to write. *Amatl* (books) were preserved in *amoxcalli* (libraries). Like Mayan writing, Nahuatl was a logographic as opposed to alphabetic system. Writing was used to preserve tribal lists, records of individual landholdings, historical annals, king lists and royal genealogies, works on gods and ritual, divinatory manuals, and other types of works. Thousands of books were burned by the Spanish conquerors, thus destroying the Aztec libraries.

The Mixtec, another major Mesoamerican group, also practiced writing. Their scribes were called *huisi tacu*. They used paper, hide, and cloth to write their books. Their texts are primarily genealogical and dynastic but include mythology and astronomy.

Writing in New Spain During the Colonial Period. Post-Conquest Nahua writing can be divided into three general stages. During the first stage, early in the sixteenth century, Nahua writing remained largely intact in indigenous form, with few words borrowed from Spanish. Spanish ecclesiastics began to experiment with Nahua writing and to teach the Nahua the Latin alphabet. The second stage, beginning around 1540, was marked by increased borrowing of words, with Nahua grammar remaining intact. The third period, beginning around 1640, was marked by changes in grammar, lexicon, and pronunciation. By this final stage, many Nahuas were bilingual.

Spaniards had a strong tradition of record keeping, associated with reports of the Conquest to the king. The first documentation sent to Charles V were the letters of Hernán CORTÉS (later published as *Cartas del relación*), the military leader of the Conquest. Later, Bernal Díaz del Castillo documented his recollections of the Conquest in *Historia verdadera de la conquista de la Nueva España*. In 1529, Father Bernardino de Sahagún arrived in Mexico. His interest in preserving Nahua culture motivated him to learn Nahuatl. Together with Nahua scribes, he wrote *Historia general de las cosas de Nueva España* (the Florentine Codex). This work contains Nahua logograms as well as symbols from the Latin alphabet. Other post-Conquest writings include annals; testaments; municipal documents including council minutes, internal tax records, and land documentation; petitions; and correspondence. The *Relaciones geográficas*, surveys of localities compiled by Spanish administrators, are a rich source of information.

Early Printing and Libraries. More than half a century before the Pilgrims landed at Plymouth Rock, New Spain had established its first post-Conquest library and printing press. In 1528, Bishop Juan de Zumárraga had brought his private library of almost two hundred volumes with him to New Spain. In 1533, he met with Viceroy Don Antonio de Mendoza and requested establishment of a library and a printing press in the New World. On January 6, 1536, a library was established at the Colegio Imperial de Santa Clara, containing some of the books from the Zumárraga library. Later, the collection would be sent to the Franciscan Friary Santiago de Tlatelolco. In 1834, it was transferred to the Library of the Convent of San Francisco.

In 1551, the Royal and Pontifical University was founded. It was later renamed the National Autonomous University of Mexico. A National Library was established around the same time and was associated with this university. During the sixteenth century, libraries in the Americas were most often housed in monasteries.

In 1534, when Zumárraga returned to Mexico, he was accompanied by Esteban Martin, a printer who brought a small press. Although items published on Martin's press have been reported, none are extant.

Other early printers in Mexico included Juan Carlos and Antonio Espinosa. By 1543, printing had spread throughout Mexico. Early printing was primarily focused on the production of religious and teaching texts. Although Zumárraga can be hailed as promoting printing and libraries in the New World, he also encouraged the destruction of Nahua manuscripts and artifacts.

Sources for the study of New Spain are scattered across the Americas and Europe. The most important European collections about New Spain are the Archive of the Indies in Seville, the National History Archive and the Royal Academy of History in Madrid, the Vatican Library and National Library in Rome, the British Museum in London, the Bodleian Library in Oxford, and the Nacionale Library in Paris. In Mexico, the major libraries that cover the era of New Spain are the Mexican National Archives, the National Library administered by the National University of Mexico, the National Museum of History and Anthropology, and the privately owned Center for the Study of the History of Mexico. In the United States, important collections for this period are the Huntington Library in San Marino, California; the Newberry Library in Chicago; the Bancroft Library at the University of California, Berkeley; the Latin American Collection at Tulane University, New Orleans, Louisiana; the John Carter Brown Library at Brown University, Providence, Rhode Island; and the Benson Latin American Collection at the University of Texas at Austin.

Early Private Collections. Joaquin García Icazbalceta, a nineteenth century bibliophile and scholar, created the most extensive collection of sixteenth century Mexican imprints of his time. A significant portion of the sixteenth century Mexican documents were part of Zumárraga's collection. He reprinted many of these works in a series titled *Nueva Colección de documentos para la historia de México*. His unique collection is now housed at the Benson Latin American Collection at the University of Texas at Austin.

Documents relating to the sixteenth through eighteenth centuries are represented in the Genaro García collection. García was a noted Mexican bibliophile. Represented in his collection are twenty-five thousand printed items including bibliographies, newspapers, documentary sources, rare editions, and manuscripts. His collection was bought by the University of Texas in 1921 and formed the base for the present-day Benson Latin American Collection.

Juan E. Hernández y Davalos was a historian and bibliophile who collected material on Mexico's struggle to gain independence from Spain. The majority of the documents in his collection represent the period from 1797 until 1826. He eventually republished six volumes in the series *Colección de documentos para la historia de la Guerra de Independencia de Mexico de 1808 a 1821*. In 1943, the Latin American Collection at the University of Texas acquired this unique collection.

Writing, Printing, and Libraries in Northern New Spain. The Spaniards provided a rich source of documentation on northern New Spain. Explorers and priests wrote a host of exploration narratives. These authors include Álvar Núñez CABEZA DE VACA, Fray Marcos de NIZA, Francisco Vázquez de CORONADO, and Antonio de Espejo.

Printing in northern New Spain began in the early part of the nineteenth century. The first Spanish-language newspaper in the Americas, *El Misissippi*, was published in 1808 in Louisiana. In 1834, Ramon Abreu established the first printing press in New Mexico. In California, Augustin Zamorano operated a press in 1834.

Several major collections exist that are devoted to keeping the history of early publications. Herbert Howe Bancroft was a historian, collector, and book dealer and publisher. He not only collected materials but also had a team of biographers who compiled a series of oral histories on early Californios. His collection, which included manuscripts, rare books, maps, and oral histories, became part of the University of California, Berkeley, in 1905. It forms the nucleus of the Bancroft Library.

The Benson Latin American Collection also houses unique materials on northern New Spain. The Eugene C. Barker Texas History Center is the most comprehensive collection on Texana. The Huntington Library in San Marino, California, contains a collection of early editions of works in Americana. Also important is the Newberry Library in Chicago, an independent research center that specializes in the humanities, with important collections on Western Americana. The Zimmerman Library at the University of New Mexico has a rich collection of the cultural history of northern New Spain. The New Mexico State Archives and Record Center is a major resource for New Mexican history that covers the period between 1621 and 1821 but is especially strong in eighteenth and nineteenth century material. In Los Angeles, the Southwest Museum has emphasized cultural history.

Contemporary Latino Collections. All Latin American countries have national libraries that contain important information for the study of Latinos. Important Caribbean collections are the Puerto Rican Collection at the University of Puerto Rico, the José Martí National Library, the Cuban Archives, and the University of South Florida Archives.

Chicano, Puerto Rican, and Cuban collections in the United States emerged during the late 1960's and throughout the 1970's as general responses to the curricular and scholarly needs of relatively small but growing populations of Latinos on college campuses. As part of the development of Chicano and Puerto Rican studies departments, centers, and projects, Chicano and Puerto Rican collections began to emerge. These collections can be considered to be archives because the material they collected was usually of a dated nature, such as personal papers and periodicals.

Major collections that focus on Latinos in the United States are the EVELINA LÓPEZ ANTONETTY PUERTO RICAN RESEARCH COLLECTION housed at Hunter College, City University of New York; the Cuban American Archives at Florida International University; the CHICANO STUDIES LIBRARY at the University of California, Berkeley; the CHICANO STUDIES RESEARCH LIBRARY at the University of California, Los Angeles; the Mexican American Library Program housed in the Benson Latin American Collection at the University of Texas at Austin; the CHICANO RESEARCH COLLECTION at Arizona State University in Tempe; the Southwest Resource Center located within the Zimmerman Library at the University of New Mexico at Albuquerque; the Mexican American archival program at Stanford University; and the COLECCIÓN TLOQUE NAHUAQUE at the University of California, Santa Barbara. Although all have established core Latino collections, the libraries in Berkeley and Los Angeles have emphasized strong bibliographic programs while the others have focused on the development of archival collections. — *Richard Chabrán*

SUGGESTED READINGS: • Beers, Henry Putney. *Spanish and Mexican Records of the American Southwest*. Tucson: University of Arizona Press, 1979. • Chabrán, Richard. *Guide to Hispanic Bibliographic Services in the United States*. Ann Arbor: Survey Research Center, University of Michigan, 1980. • Coe, Michael D. *Breaking the Maya Code*. New York: Thames and Hudson, 1992. • Griswold del Castillo, Richard, and Julio A. Martinez. "A Selective Survey of Chicano Manuscript Collections in U.S. Libraries." In *Biblio-Política: Chicano Perspectives on Library Service in the United States*, edited by Francisco Garcia-Ayvens and Richard Chabran. Berkeley: Chicano

Studies Library Publications Unit, University of California, 1984. • Guerena, Salvador, ed. *Latino Librarianship: A Handbook for Professionals*. Jefferson, N.C.: McFarland, 1990. • Marcus, Joyce. *Mesoamerican Writing Systems: Propaganda, Myth, and History in Four Ancient Civilizations*. Princeton, N.J.: Princeton University Press, 1992. • Schele, Linda, and Mary Ellen Miller. "The Mayan Hieroglyphic Writing System." In *The Blood of Kings: Dynasty and Ritual in Maya Art*. New York: George Braziller, 1986.

Life cycle customs: For Latinos, each stage of life is marked by a celebration that has evolved from community traditions, family obligations, and religious rites. Events such as the beginning of life (birth, baptism), entry into adulthood (confirmation, QUINCEAÑERA), entry into married life (betrothal, wedding), and the end of life (funeral, El DÍA DE LOS MUERTOS), are accompanied by ritual celebration. The customs described are traditional; constant evolution means that customs may take many different forms.

Links to Religion. The celebration of milestones in human life are, among Latinos, closely linked to the traditions and sacraments of the Roman CATHOLIC CHURCH. Brought to the New World by Jesuit and Franciscan missionaries, Catholicism remains a vital force among Spanish-speaking peoples of the United States, even as it has evolved and absorbed variations of indigenous customs. In some communities, the parish church is the focal point of various sacraments connected to life patterns, including baptism, confirmation, marriage, the last rites, and Requiem Mass. Other nonsacramental celebrations that receive religious blessing include the *quinceañera* and betrothal. Although the majority of U.S. Latinos and Latin Americans are Catholic, some are evangelical Protestants, Mormons, or members of other denominations, and their life cycle celebrations follow the traditions of their churches.

Birth Customs. Until recently, women in Latin American regions most often gave birth in the home, attended by the local doctor or a midwife (*partera*). Increasingly, however, giving birth in a hospital or clinic has become common. Expectant mothers traditionally stayed in their homes, curtailing travel, and received gifts and good wishes from visiting family and friends. Beginning around the 1970's, baby showers as celebrated by non-Latinos became increasingly popular among Latinos.

For Latino Catholics, the sacrament of baptism is given for infants. Both boys and girls wear a white,

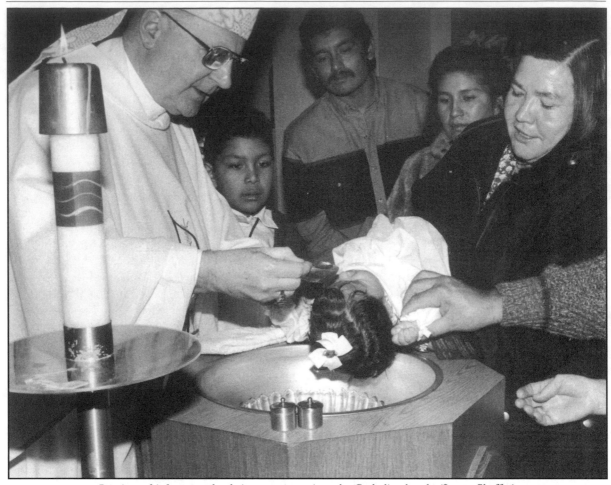

Baptism of infants marks their acceptance into the Catholic church. (James Shaffer)

full-length baptismal gown, and the baptized infant receives, in addition to the sprinkling of Holy Water, a baptismal name. This carefully chosen name may be from the Bible or may be a saint's name, sometimes chosen for the Saint's Day on which the baby's birthday falls. Occasionally a familial or legal name not from biblical or Catholic tradition is chosen, in which case two names are given, a familial name and what is called a Christian name. Godparents, or *PADRINOS*, play a significant role in the baptismal celebration. Chosen by the parents, the godparents most often are a married couple. They agree to assist in the child's religious and moral education, provide advice and comfort, and assume the duties of rearing the child should the baby's parents die.

Young Adulthood. The first participation in the Eucharist, also called Communion by Catholics and the Lord's Supper by Protestants, is called First Communion. For Latino Catholics, this usually takes place between the ages of seven and ten, after preparatory instruction has been completed. Girls traditionally wear a long white dress, while boys wear suit and tie. A girl may choose a female family member or friend as her godmother (*madrina*); the boy likewise chooses his own male godfather (*padrino*). These may be different from baptismal godparents. The chosen godparent teaches the communicant special prayers and provides advice.

Confirmation denotes entry into the church as a full participating member and usually occurs between the ages of twelve and fourteen, after the child has completed catechism, which consists of classes in Catholic doctrine and practice taught by the parish priest or a trained lay teacher.

Quinceañera marks a major milestone in a Latina girl's life. If she chooses to have a quinceañera celebration and if her family can afford one, it takes place in a hall where a dinner and dance can be held following a church blessing. On her fifteenth birthday, the *quinceañera* celebrant and her attending girlfriends dress in formal wear and participate in both a church service and later festivities that mark symbolic entry into womanhood, with its attendant privileges such as dating and dancing.

Betrothal and Marriage. After a period of courtship, men and women may follow the traditional betrothal pattern. First, the man and his father or other adult family member visit the bride's father. The husband-to-be asks the woman's father for her hand, and the betrothal is announced. The groom traditionally pays wedding expenses, including the cost of the wedding dress. The groom's family and friends contribute to the cost of the wedding arrangements, which traditionally include a MARIACHI band, a full meal, and a dance. The bride and groom each select godparents for the wed-ding. These can be the same couple or two couples and are not necessarily the baptismal or communion god-parents of either spouse. Before the bride leaves her family home for church on her wedding day, she receives her parents' blessing to make a new home with her husband. After the sacrament of marriage is performed in church, a meal is served, then dancing begins. Customarily, men may dance with the bride and women with the groom, but only after placing dollar bills in the couple's clothing, to help them start their new household. After the wedding waltz, men must ask the husband's permission to dance with his wife. Weddings, like other social customs, evolve over time, and less traditional ceremonies are practiced as well.

These girls are jointly celebrating their quinceañeras. (James Shaffer)

Funeral proceedings may have uniquely Latino aspects. (James Shaffer)

Death. When a Catholic Latino dies, a funeral Mass is held in the parish church. It may be followed by an all-night prayer vigil at the home of the deceased. This Hispanic Catholic version of a wake may include a meal and may occur after the graveside burial ceremony.

Annual remembrances for those who have passed away occur on November 2, EL DÍA DE LOS MUERTOS (the day of the dead). November 1, All Saint's Day, is celebrated in Latino communities as El Día de los Niños, a day honoring babies and children who have died. These two holidays include the decorating of graves, prayers at graveside, and the placement of gifts and tokens of remembrance on the graves of deceased loved ones.   —*Keith Atwater*

SUGGESTED READINGS: • Espinosa, Aurelio. *The Folklore of Spain in the American Southwest*. Norman: University of Oklahoma Press, 1985. • Reyna, Jose R. *Readings in Southwestern Folklore*. Tucson: Mexican American Studies and Research Center, University of Arizona, 1988. • West, John O. *Mexican-American Folklore*. Little Rock, Ark.: August House, 1988.

Liga Femenil: Women's organization. The Liga Femenil was established in Laredo, Texas, during El Primer Congreso Mexicanista on September 11, 1911. Its president was Jovita Idar. The Idar family was intensely involved in the Congreso and other organizational activities. Many of the women who joined the Liga Femenil were teachers, and education was an important issue at the Congreso. The Liga Femenil organized free tutoring for poor Mexican American children unable to attend school. The group lasted less than a year but had an important role in the history of Chicano organizing.

Liga Obrera de Habla Español: Labor union. Jesús Pallares and other miners founded this union in New Mexico in 1934. Mexican Americans and undocumented Mexicans composed its eight thousand members. The union attempted to protect the health and improve the wages of miners. One of its successful projects was a march to Washington, D.C., to protest the Criminal Syndicalism Bill, which would have suppressed unionization drives. The union's leadership included workers who were not U.S. citizens. In 1935, the union was terminated as a result of the deportation of its undocumented leaders and members.

Liga Protectora Latina: Social service agency. The Liga Protectora Latina was founded in Arizona in 1914. Among its first activities was lobbying against passage of the Clayton-McKinney bill, which would have excluded Mexicans from Arizona MINING. The organization provided social and educational assis-

tance, gave financial aid to unemployed and sick members, and paid funeral expenses. One of its most notable achievements was uniting Mexican American and Mexican miners. The group ensured proper care and treatment of the miners.

The organization had expanded to California, New Mexico, Pennsylvania, and Texas by 1920. Increases in dues led to the decline of the organization, which dissolved during the Great Depression.

Limón, José Arcadio (Jan. 12, 1908, Culiacán, Mexico—Dec. 2, 1972, Flemington, N.J.): Choreographer. The son of a musician father and a devoutly Catholic mother, Limón moved to Arizona with his family in 1915. He studied painting at the University of Califor

José Limón (background) dances with two students. (AP/Wide World Photos)

nia, Los Angeles, before going to New York in 1927 to study dance with Doris Humphrey, Charles Weidman, and Martha Graham. In 1930, he choreographed his first piece, *Bacchanale*. His notable early works include *Danzas Mexicanas* (1939) and the solo *Chaconne* (1942).

In 1945, Limón established his own company in New York. He earned considerable praise for his choreography of the 1949 production *The Moor's Pavane*. In 1964, Limón was chosen to direct the American Dance Theater in residence at Lincoln Center in New York City. That same year, he was selected by the State Department to tour South America as part of a cultural exchange program. Limón taught at the Juilliard School in New York, Bennington College in Vermont, and the Instituto Nacional de Bellas Artes in Mexico City. His extensive honors include the 1957 *Dance Magazine* Award and the 1964 Capezio Award. The Limón Dance Company continued his work after his death.

Lincoln County War (1876-1878): Dispute between farmers and cattle ranchers. Small farmers, primarily of Mexican ancestry, and cattle ranchers fought for political and economic control within Lincoln County, in New Mexico Territory.

Although events of the Lincoln County War occurred most notably between 1876 and 1878, the roots of the conflict were in the years following the Civil War. During the early postwar years, persons of Mexican ancestry settled in regions of southeastern New Mexico, primarily as small ranchers or farmers. At the same time, Texans established large cattle ranches. The result was that the eastern portion of the county was predominantly American, while the western portion remained native New Mexican.

Disputes began over economic control of the region and the political control that inevitably would follow. Juan Patrón became the recognized leader of the native New Mexican community, while Lawrence Murphy, a probate judge and political boss, represented the leadership of the American community. Murphy would later be succeeded by James Dolan. For personal reasons, John Chisum, owner of the largest cattle herd in the territory, refused to do business with Murphy and sided with the small ranchers. His decision was the spark that ignited the conflict.

The arrival of two individuals established the sides of the conflict. In 1875, Alexander McSween arrived in Lincoln. McSween, a Canadian-born lawyer, soon established a thriving practice known for aggressive

tactics and for strong moral scruples. John Henry Tunstall, a twenty-three-year-old British subject who had ideas of investing in the growing economy of the territory, came to Lincoln County in 1876. Tunstall opened a bank and store, placing him in direct conflict with the Murphy-Dolan interests. McSween and Tunstall formed a partnership, with the aim of providing competition for Dolan and a better deal for the farmers. Among Tunstall's employees was a young gunslinger, Henry McCarty, also known as Billy the Kid.

The McSween-Tunstall faction retained the support of the small ranchers and farmers, many of whom resented Dolan's tactics. The cattle ranchers, opposing the power of Chisum and the preemption of land by the farmers, aligned themselves with Dolan. By 1876, armed conflict between the sides had become common. On February 18, 1878, Tunstall was murdered in an ambush by members of the Dolan faction.

McSween, a peaceful man, found himself the nominal head of his faction. He recognized that a major fight had become inevitable. On July 15, 1878, McSween returned to Lincoln County with a group of forty-one men, following a meeting with Chisum. Opposing him was an equal force of Dolan's supporters. McSween deployed his forces throughout the town and returned to his ranch with ten men. For the next several days, the two factions fought a continuing gun battle. Among the wounded was a soldier from nearby Fort Stanton. This wounding provided an excuse for arrival of an army contingent that threw its support to the Dolan side. McSween and several others attempted to surrender when the house they occupied caught fire. All were shot by members of Dolan's forces. Billy the Kid escaped unharmed.

The ongoing conflict finally forced the hand of Lew Wallace, a Civil War general who was the new territorial governor. Wallace established federal control over the area and eventually pardoned the participants in exchange for peace. Billy the Kid continued to extract his own revenge until his death in 1881 at the hand of Sheriff Pat Garrett.

Lisa, Manuel (Sept. 8, 1772, New Orleans, La.— Aug. 12, 1820, St. Louis, Mo.): Explorer and trader. Lisa, a Louisianan of Spanish descent, entered the FUR TRADE in his late teens. By 1802, he and Pierre Chouteau had opened the Missouri Fur Company, which operated many trading posts along the Missouri River. The company at first traded with many tribes, especially the Osages. After the LOUISIANA PURCHASE of 1803, Lisa lost his favored position with that tribe.

Over the next five years, he led several exploration trips that resulted in the opening of other trading posts and forts. These included Fort Raymond, at the mouth of the Bighorn River in territory that became Montana. There, he traded with the Crow tribe.

In 1812, Lisa opened Fort Lisa, near the later site of Omaha, Nebraska. This fort was the most important trading post on the Missouri River for the next ten years, controlling trade with many Indian tribes including the Omaha and Pawnee. In 1814, Lisa became subagent for all the Missouri River Indian tribes located above the mouth of the Kansas River. Lisa's influence was largely responsible for keeping the Indians of the Western Plains from helping the British in the War of 1812. He is credited with opening up the Missouri River to Americans.

Literacy and illiteracy: Literacy involves the ability to process information and is more than decoding words. American society is becoming increasingly complex, technical, and interdisciplinary. Reading a typical newspaper requires at least an eighth grade education; understanding editorials and complex political ideas and events requires even higher reading skills. Literate people have facility in reading, writing, speaking, and listening. These skills are often acquired as much through daily activities outside school as through formal education, although most Americans acquire written literacy in Standard English in school rather than at home. Functional illiteracy is the inability to cope with everyday practical communication needs at an adult level.

According to data from the U.S. Bureau of the Census and independent studies such as the Audit Performance Study conducted by the Office of Education, more than one out of five Americans aged twenty-five and older lacked the literacy skills and knowledge to cope successfully with day-to-day living. Corrobora-

The New York literacy program offers basic courses and instruction in English as a Second Language to high school dropouts and adults. (Impact Visuals, H. L. Delgado)

tive evidence showed that in 1988, 23.8 percent of all Americans aged twenty-five and older had not completed high school (*see* DROPOUTS AND DROPOUT RATES).

In the 25-to-34-year-old group, the highest rate of high school dropouts was for Mexican Americans, at 45.7 percent. The Hispanic group with the lowest rate of dropouts was Cuban Americans, who had a dropout rate of only 16.1 percent in the 25-to-34-year-old group. Since the 1950's, the percentage of dropouts in each age group has fallen steadily, with the largest decreases being for African Americans. The dropout rate was 77.6 percent for Hispanics aged sixty-five and older; it fell to 38.3 percent for the 25-to-34-year-old group.

Illiteracy can have substantial economic consequences for an individual or a group. For example, 35 percent of Mexican Americans held white-collar jobs in 1989, compared to 57 percent of the total population. In addition, 41 percent of Mexican Americans were blue-collar workers, compared to 27 percent of the total population. These employment patterns result in part from illiteracy, or at least low academic achievement. They mean that Mexican American families earn less than the average family. Children may have to work to help support their families and may be forced to neglect their studies as a result, perpetuating the cycle. Many Hispanics drop out, and many Hispanic children have parents who did not complete high school. If Hispanics are to lower their illiteracy rate, which has been estimated to be almost double the national average of 20 percent, they will need to continue to raise their high school completion rates.

Literary history and criticism: Spanish American literature, from its beginning, clearly reflects the political, social, economic, and religious realities occurring within the particular environment in which works were written. It is important for Latinos to be aware of their indigenous and contemporary literature; this awareness helps them in their search for their own identity and promotes pride in their culture.

Early Writings. Spanish American literature began in the pre-Columbian era. Prose and poetry are found in the native literatures of these three major tribes; the Maya, who lived in Honduras, Guatemala, northern Belize, and northern Yucatán; the Quechuas (known commonly by the name of their rulers, the Incas), who inhabited Peru, Bolivia, and Ecuador; and the Aztecs, who lived in central and southern Mexico. These three

important Indian tribes left advanced examples of art, literature, and architecture, such as the pyramids of Mexico and the hieroglyphics found therein.

Because most of pre-Columbian literature was in oral form, much has been lost. What remains is really indirect transcriptions from the Latin and Spanish. Probably between 1554 and 1558, an Indian educated by the Spaniards wrote, in a mixture of the *quiche* and Spanish languages, the POPOL VUH, an account of the various legends, history, and fables of his people. His aim was to counteract the disappearance of the *Book of Counsels*, lost during the SPANISH CONQUEST. Popol Vuh translates as the "book of counsels." Although the original manuscript has been lost, there exists a copy translated into Spanish by Francisco Ximénez, a Spanish priest. The Books of CHILAM BALAM were also written after the Conquest, adapting the Maya phonology to the Latin and Spanish. These books, although written after or during the Conquest, provide representative samples of pre-Columbian literature and thought.

The Spanish Conquest. With the beginning of the Spanish Conquest in 1492, an entirely new way of life, including cultural, economic, religious, and social realms, was imposed on the Indian population. Through different forms of censorship and the prohibitive fear engendered by the Catholic Inquisition, the Indian culture was in large part destroyed.

The Spanish government ruled the New World through the Council of the Indies, which in turn imposed a series of vertical bureaucracies such as the *audiencias*, which relegated the role of the Indian to that of a servant to the conquerors, in an imposed system of slavery called ENCOMIENDA or REPARTIMIENTO. Indian protests against Spanish domination came in the form of covert guerrilla attacks and a literature of protest. The evolution of politics in Latin American literature can be perceived as a form of protest against an established and nondemocratic system of government.

Political reaction in literature against the Spanish regime was, surprisingly, initiated by a member of the Spanish clergy, Bartolomé DE LAS CASAS (1474-1566), who resided in Santo Domingo but visited most of the Spanish colonies, particularly Guatemala. In his *History of the Indies* and his *Short Account of the Destruction of the New World*, he angrily denounced the atrocities committed against the Indians by his fellow Spaniards. His texts were important because they constituted a verifiable account of the destruction of the Indians and because they initiated the artistic era in

Latin American writing, through which political and social problems could be expressed, criticized, and articulated.

Literature During Independence. In the nineteenth and early twentieth centuries, the colonies of the New World gained their independence from Spain. One of the results of independence was the beginning of dictatorial regimes in Spanish America. These regimes sometimes saw continued conditions of serfdom of the native Indian population. Dictators such as Porfirio Díaz of Mexico were primarily interested in preserving their wealth and power, even at the expense of the general population. This led to popular protests. These protests were heightened by the introduction of foreign corporations, such as the United Fruit Company, into Latin American cultures and societies. Motivated primarily by profits, these corporations were instrumental in furthering the exploitation of the Indians through their payment of low wages. Unable to resist by force of arms, the native population, which represented the majority, expressed opposition through literature, including newspaper articles, songs, poetry, short stories, and novels. Mexico, for example, is credited with producing the first Latin American novel.

In 1816, the Mexican José Joaquín Fernández de Lizardi (1776-1827) published a novel, *El periquillo sarniento* (*The Itching Parrot*), in which Pedro Sarmiento, the protagonist, describes his apprenticeships with various Mexican masters. Through the novel and its protagonist, Lizardi describes and criticizes the political, social, economic, and religious problems that plagued Mexico before the 1910 revolution. Spanish American writers continued this criticism of contemporary society through their writings. Among the earliest are José Mármol (1817-1871), Estéban Echevarría (1805-1851) and Domingo Sarmiento (1811-1888), all from Argentina.

Latin American writers came to the forefront of international literature during the literary boom in the region that occurred in the 1950's and 1960's. The main focus of writing, whether prose or poetry, was to expose the general environmental problems plaguing Latin Americans, whether they lived in Spanish American countries or elsewhere. It is important for Latinos in North America and elsewhere to be aware of these writings, as it makes them understand and have pride in their culture.   —*Víctor Manuel Durán*

SUGGESTED READINGS: • Fuentes, Carlos. *The Death of Artemio Cruz*. Translated by Sam Hileman. New York: Farrar, Straus and Giroux, 1964. • Menton, Seymour. *Latin America's New Historical Novel.* Austin: University of Texas Press, 1993. • Moyano Martin, Dolores, ed. *Handbook of Latin American Studies*. Austin: University of Texas Press, 1979. • Pike, Fredrick B. *The United States and Latin America*. Austin: University of Texas Press, 1992. • Puig, Manuel. *Heartbreak Tango*. Translated by Suzanne Jill Levine. New York: Dutton, 1973. • Torres-Rivas, Edelberto. *History and Society in Central America*. Translated by Douglas Sullivan-González. Austin: University of Texas Press, 1993.

Literatura chicanesca: Literature about Chicanos written by non-Chicanos. *Literatura chicanesca* is a category coined by Francisco A. Lomelí and Donaldo W. Urioste in *Chicano Perspectives in Literature: A Critical and Annotated Bibliography* (1976). Leading authors include Paul Horgan (*The Common Heart*, 1942); Frank Waters (*People of the Valley*, 1941); Eugene Nelson (*The Bracero*, 1972); and John Nichols (*The Milagro Beanfield War*, 1974; *The Magic Journey*, 1978; and *The Nirvana Blues*, 1981). Chester Seltzer, a journalist, published short stories depicting Mexican and Chicano characters under the pseudonym of Amado Muro, and Daniel James, a playwright, assumed the identity Danny Santiago when publishing his *Famous All Over Town* (1983).

Literature, American, Latinos in: The portrayal of Latinos in American literature by non-Latinos has generally reflected the views and prejudices of the broader society of the time. Early images of Latinos in American literature can be found in the journals of adventure, exploration, and trade from the early nineteenth century, when United States settlers entered Mexican territory. These works began a long tradition of negative stereotypes of Mexicans based on ignorance and distrust.

Toward the end of the nineteenth century, American writers began to emphasize the vitality of Mexican American culture and to find inspiration there for their own lives. After the mid-1900's, the Latino community became more diverse with the arrival of Puerto Ricans, Cubans, and eventually Central and South Americans. As more Latinos wrote memoirs, poetry, and fiction, more non-Latinos became aware of Latino culture, and Latino characters were presented with more realism and sympathy in literature.

Early Stereotypes. The European pioneers had an individualistic, Protestant ethic of hard work, technological progress, cleanliness, and strict faith that clashed with their image of the Mexican people. In the settlers' eyes, the Mexicans appeared to neglect work, technological advancement, and hygiene while advocating priestly power, social stratification, sensuality, violence, and the veneration of death (*see* STEREOTYPES OF LATINOS). By the 1830's, pioneers had stereotyped Mexicans as lazy, dirty, showy, cowardly, brutal, and sensual people who tended to be liars, thieves, and murderers. For example, J. Ross Browne, in *A Tour Through Arizona, 1864: Or, Adventures in the Apache Country* (1950), portrayed idle people of mixed race playing cards and smoking in filthy little huts. His characters chose not to work, stating that work would make them ill. This image of laziness and filthiness was accentuated by the term "GREASER," attached to Mexicans by early American settlers and reinforced by descriptions of greasy houses and dogs in *Bernard Lile: An Historical Romance* (1856) by Jeremiah Clemens.

The pioneers were particularly alienated by the Mexicans' elaborate form of religion with its unfamiliar ceremonies around colorful altar, chanted litany, and idolatrous depiction of and communication with Mary and the saints. The early American settlers also attributed the Mexicans' proud style of manners and dress to their lack of moral character. Their courtesy was perceived by the Americans as insincerity.

Elliott Arnold, in *The Time of the Gringo* (1953), clarified the concept of excessive Mexican style. According to Arnold, Mexicans treated style as a significant element of their strict code of honor that the Anglos failed to understand.

The labels of coward, liar, and murderer applied by the settlers to the Mexican people were linked to supposed character flaws. The self-confident settlers in the borderlands thought the Mexicans were weak; they were apparently unaware of the struggles of the *CRIOLLO* class in the Mexican independence movement. The early settlers were so distrustful of the Mexicans as liars that they were even reluctant to ask them for directions. The Anglos also feared the Mexicans as excessively violent. In *The Personal Narrative of James O. Pattie of Kentucky* (1930), Pattie, an American pioneer acquainted with the Southwest, described as typical the murders of ten people.

Modern Developments. In the twentieth century, negative stereotypes gave way to more positive portrayals of Latino culture as writers probed the origins of Latino behavior and modified their attitudes toward sex, death, and other themes. Literary historian Cecil Robinson traces some of these changes in attitude to a recognition of the influence of Mexicans' ancestors,

the Aztecs, on Mexican notions regarding courage, religious representations, and death (*see* AZTEC CIVILIZATION).

Advances in social sciences offered new perspectives to Anglo writers. They began to see, for example, how a stereotype of thievery among Mexican people might be rooted in poverty and neglect of the poor by the Mexican government. *In the American Grain* (1925) by poet William Carlos Williams signaled the gradual change of attitude toward Mexicans by twentieth century American writers. Whereas early settlers had been shocked at the sensual atmosphere and blood-stained images of Mexican American chapels, modern Anglo writers began to appreciate the colorful Mexican religious rites as part of a rich heritage and a link with primal instincts and spontaneous emotion.

Changing images of Latinos in literature also reflected changing perceptions of Latinos within mainstream American society. Before the twentieth century, Mexican Americans composed most of the Latino population, and their history was that of a conquered, impoverished people. As immigration from Mexico and Latin America increased, Latinos became assimilated into American society, with two consequences important to their portrayal in literature.

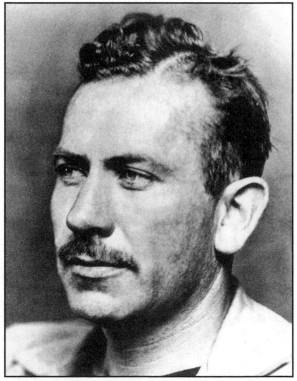

John Steinbeck's writing contains realistic depictions of Mexican Americans. (AP/Wide World Photos)

First, exposure to Latino cultures sensitized Anglo writers, so that their portrayals of Latino characters became less stereotyped and more appreciative of cultural differences. Latinos became less foreign to Anglo writers and thus less likely to be stereotyped. Second, Latino authors began to emerge within the American literary mainstream. These authors explained their heritage and cultural background in their works and incorporated their belief systems into their plots and characterization. Latino writers presented Latinos as primary characters rather than as background characters or antagonists, and these writers filled out their Latino characters' personalities realistically rather than relying on stereotypes. Latino characters in American literature thus began to resemble a cross section of the Latino population. —*Linda Prewett Davis*

SUGGESTED READINGS: • Arnold, Elliott. *The Time of the Gringo*. New York: Alfred A. Knopf, 1953. • Browne, J. Ross. *A Tour Through Arizona, 1864: Or, Adventures in the Apache Country*. Tucson: Arizona Silhouettes, 1950. • Clemens, Jeremiah. *Bernard Lile: An Historical Romance*. Philadelphia: J. B. Lippincott, 1856. • Pattie, James O. *The Personal Narrative of James O. Pattie of Kentucky*. Edited by Timothy Flint. Chicago: R. R. Donnelly & Sons, 1930. • Robinson, Cecil. *With the Ears of Strangers: The Mexican in American Literature*. Tucson: University of Arizona Press, 1963. • Williams, William Carlos. *In the American Grain*. Norfolk, Conn.: New Directions, 1925.

Literature, Cuban American: Cuban American literature developed early in the nineteenth century, as Cuban authors traveled to the United States to avoid censorship or imprisonment by Cuba's Spanish colonial government. Many prominent writers such as José María Heredia and Cirilo Villaverde fled from Cuba. Perhaps the most significant of these nineteenth century exiles was the poet and revolutionary José MARTÍ, who lived in the United States from 1881 to 1895. Martí helped to popularize the cause of Cuban independence and became one of its chief martyrs when he died in battle in 1895.

Nineteenth and Early Twentieth Century Literature. During the nineteenth century, poems, essays, dramas, and short stories by Cuban Americans proliferated in Spanish-language U.S. newspapers. Cuban American novelists of the period included Cirilo Villaverde and Anselmo Suárez y Romero. Villaverde was a practitioner of *costumbrismo*, the literature of manners. Both authors produced works calling for the end of slavery, which was not abolished in Cuba until 1886. By the

Poet José Martí promoted Cuban independence while in exile. (Library of Congress)

mid-nineteenth century, Cuban plays were being produced in the United States. The Cuban genres of serious drama, comedy, *teatro frívolo* (frivolous theater), and *teatro bufo* (low farce) were brought to the United States, where a lively theater scene sprang up in New York City and Tampa, Florida.

After Cuba won independence from Spain in 1898, many Cuban writers chose to remain in their homeland and publish their work there rather than in the United States. Much of the Cuban American literature produced in the United States in the early twentieth century has not been properly archived. Theatrical history, however, has been somewhat better preserved. Tampa and New York continued their shared dominance of Cuban American theater, in New York through theatrical clubs and in Tampa through mutual aid societies (*MUTUALISTAS*) made up of the families of tobacco workers. Important Cuban playwrights working in the United States during this period include Alberto O'FARRILL, Arquímides POUS, and Juan C. Rivera.

The Literature of Exile. The production of literature by exiled Cubans boomed after the CUBAN REVOLUTION of 1959, when Fidel CASTRO took power. During the 1960's, large numbers of upper- and middle-class Cubans immigrated to the United States. The works produced during this time are often called "the literature of exile." This literature is predominantly written

Oscar Hijuelos has become well known in the United States. (AP/Wide World Photos)

in Spanish and is characterized by nostalgia for a lost, idealized Cuba, strong anticommunist sentiment, and isolation from the dominant U.S. culture. Writers of the literature of exile include Luis Ricardo Alonso, René Ariza, Pura del Prado, Raoul A. Fowler y Cabrera, Celedonio González, Carlos Alberto Montaner, Hilda Perara, Tomás Travieso, and Ana Alomá Velilla. Other writers used some of the themes of the literature of exile but combined them with a greater awareness of the issues facing immigrants to the United States. Examples of this second group include Octavio Armand, María Irene Fornes, Matías Montes Huidobros, Maya Islas, Eduardo Machado, Lino Calvo Novás, Isel Rivero, Mireya Robles, and José Sánchez Boudy.

Other varieties of exile literature have been created by the *grupo Areíto* and *marielito* writers. The *grupo Areíto* (Areíto group) was composed of a mixture of intellectuals and artists, including the writers Lourdes Casal and Eliana Rivero. The group was formed during the 1960's by young Cuban exiles who rejected the vehemently anti-Castro, pro-U.S. politics of their parents. They longed for a dialogue and eventual reconciliation with postrevolution Cuba. The *marielito* writers, on the other hand, immigrated to the United States later, during the MARIEL BOAT LIFT of 1980. They repeated the pattern of other immigrants in their isolation from the dominant culture but faced the additional problem of discrimination against them by earlier Cuban exiles. The writers of this group include Reinaldo ARENAS, Heberto PADILLA, and Virgil SUÁREZ.

Many literary critics who believe that a true Cuban American literature did not begin to emerge until the 1980's prefer the terms "exile literature" or "U.S. Cuban literature" to describe earlier works. Such critics believe that Cuban American literature is centrally concerned with the search for dual Cuban and American identities and the accompanying tension, humor, and frustration. This search has historic resonance: *La cubinidad* (the Cuban national identity) has been obscured by Cuba's long period of Spanish rule and by the island's proximity to the United States. Writers often described as "Cuban American" include Iván Acosta, Cristina GARCÍA, Oscar HIJUELOS, Manuel Martín, E. Miguel Muñoz, and Dolores PRIDA. The roster of Cuban American writers also includes the group known as *Los Atrevidos* (the daring ones), such as Roberto G. FERNÁNDEZ, Lourdes Gil, Iraida Iturralde, Pablo Medina, Ricardo Pau-Llosa, and Gustavo Pérez-Firmat. These writers are somewhat controversial and have been criticized for their use of English or

bilingual forms, which has led some critics to accuse them of being too assimilated.   *—Kelly Fuller*

SUGGESTED READINGS: • Angebraum, Harold, and Ilan Stavans, eds. *Growing Up Latino: Memoirs and Stories.* New York: Houghton Mifflin, 1993. • Boswell, Thomas D., and James R. Curtis. *The Cuban-American Experience: Culture, Images, and Perspectives.* Totowa, N.J.: Rowman & Allanheld, 1984. • Cortina, Rodolfo J. *Cuban American Theater.* Houston: Arte Público Press, 1991. • Cortina, Rodolfo J. "Cuban Literature of the United States: 1824-1959." In *Recovering the U.S. Hispanic Literary Heritage,* edited by Ramón Gutiérrez and Genaro Padilla. Houston: Arte Público Press, 1993. • Hospital, Carolina, ed. *Cuban American Writers: Los Atrevidos.* Princeton, N.J.: Ediciones Ellas/Linden Lane Press, 1988. • Ortega, Eliana, and Nancy Saporta Sternbach. "At the Threshold of the Unnamed: Latina Literary Discourse in the Eighties." In *Breaking Boundaries: Latina Writing and Critical Readings,* edited by Asunción Horno-Delgado, et al. Amherst: University of Massachusetts Press, 1989. • Rivero, Eliana S. "From Immigrants to Ethnics: Cuban Woman Writers in the U.S." In *Breaking Boundaries: Latina Writing and Critical Readings,* edited by Asunción Horno-Delgado, et al. Amherst: University of Massachusetts Press, 1989. • Rivero, Eliana S. "(Re)Writing Sugarcane Memories: Cuban Americans and Literature." In *Paradise Lost or Gained? The Literature of Hispanic Exile,* edited by Fernando Alegría and Jorge Ruffinelli. Houston: Arte Público Press, 1990.

Literature, Mexican American: A common heritage inspired Mexican American and Chicano writers to express their life experiences through writings. This body of literature is often divided into four periods, corresponding to general historical periods: Spanish colonial (1492 to 1810), Mexican colonial (1821 to 1848), Mexican American (1848 to 1959), and Chicano (beginning in 1959). Chicano literature in the 1960's and 1970's was highly political and closely identified with the Chicano movement.

Common Literary Heritage. The meeting of European and American cultures provided Mexican American writers with a collective historical experience as a source of material for their writings. This encounter brought together different languages, religions, and cultures. The conflicts and events that resulted from this encounter inspired writers' themes and characters.

The anonymously written epic poem "Mio Cid" (1140-1157), which narrates the exploits of Don Rodrigo Díaz de Vivar, is considered to be the first great Spanish-language literary achievement. Literature developed rapidly in Spain after "Mio Cid" and reached its pinnacle in Spain's Golden Age in the sixteenth century. The Basques, Visigoths, Galicians, and Catalans who came across the ocean from Spain with the Castilians in 1492 brought this literature with them to the New World. Works by Miguel de Cervantes, exemplified by the novel *El ingenioso hidalgo don Quijote de la Mancha* (part 1, 1605; part 2, 1615; *Don Quixote de la Mancha*, 1612-1620, 2 vols.) and works by Félix Lope de Vega y Carpio (Spanish poet and playwright) in time were joined by the works of writers in New Spain, including Juan Ruiz Alarcón, Sor Juana Inés de la CRUZ, and Carlos de Siguenza y Gongora.

American indigenous peoples differed in culture, language, religion, and mode of life from the Spanish explorers and colonists. In Mexico, the ancient Toltecs, Maya, and Aztecs produced impressive works in religion, philosophy, astrology, mathematics, and astronomy. Aztec codices and other types of oral and graphic expressions, such as the Mayan Books of CHILAM BALAM and the sacred POPOL VUH (Eng. tr. 1950), provided literary inspiration and insight for Mexican American and Chicano writers in the twentieth century. The Aztecs used color as an element of writing-painting and focused on harmony with the forces of creation. Spanish comprehension of Aztec writing-painting was extremely limited when Don Antonio Mendoza, the first viceroy of New Spain, gave the conquered Aztec nobles an opportunity to tell their stories. Their work, the "Codex Mendoza" (Eng. tr., 1938, 3 vols.), was intended as a gift to Carlos V, King of Spain and emperor of the Holy Roman Empire.

This early literary heritage from Spain and indigenous Mexico helped form the Mexican American collective subconscious, from which evolved myths, legends, and story. Spanish poetic and folklore forms gave rise to the development of early Spanish colonial and later Mexican folk expressions. For example, the roots of the popular ballad known as the *CORRIDO* can be found in the Spanish *romanza*. The legend of La Llorona (The Weeping Woman), originating in the sixteenth century, is a true synthesis of Spanish and Indian traditions. La LLORONA became a cultural symbol used to frighten Mexican American children as well as the prototype of numerous female figures who were later incorporated into Mexican and Chicano literature.

Spanish Colonial Literature. The main literary forms in New Spain during the Spanish colonial period were historical, epic, oral folk, and religious. Among the earliest writings were travel narratives by explorers such as Alvar Núñez CABEZA DE VACA (*Relaciones*, 1542) and Fray Marcos de Niza (*Relación del descubrimiento de las siete ciudades*, 1539; *The Journey of Fray Marcos de Niza*, 1949). These accounts helped motivate Francisco Vázquez de Coronado's explorations of Mexico's northern territories that eventually became the Provincias Internas (Internal Provinces), later called AZTLÁN by Chicano writers.

In 1598, Juan de OÑATE led a contingent of more than five hundred colonists from Mexico into what is now New Mexico. Captain Marcos Farfán composed a play describing the Spanish feat. One of Oñate's officers, Gaspar Pérez de VILLAGRÁ, published an epic poem, *Historia de la Nueva México* (1610); *History of New Mexico, Alaca, 1610*, 1933), during the colonization of New Mexico. It was a rhymed history of the conquest of New Mexico in thirty-four cantos.

Religious themes inspired the early tradition of folk drama in the 1500's. Short religious plays called *autos de fe* were used to teach and convert the natives during the seasons of Christmas and Lent in Mexico. This form of conversion was promoted by Archbishop Fray Juan de Zumárraga (1468-1548).

The art of writing religious plays moved into Mexico's northern territories with Spanish explorers and later with Mexican colonizers. Juan de la Peña created a religious play titled *Las cuatro apariciones de la Virgen de Guadalupe* (the four apparitions of the Virgin Mary of Guadalupe, 1600) that gained popularity in New Mexico. This play documented the experience of Juan DIEGO, an Aztec Christian convert, who in 1531 saw a vision of a young brown-skinned woman who identified herself as being the Virgin Mary of GUADALUPE, mother of God.

The colonists performed another type of play in New Mexico, *Los Moros y los cristianos* (1598; the Moors and the Christians), by Capitán Farfán. This tradition of using drama to teach or to celebrate had later influence on the use of *CARPAS* (tents) for informal outdoor performances that traveled to Mexican towns and rural areas. In forming El TEATRO CAMPESINO in the 1960's, playwright Luis VALDEZ looked back to the tradition of the *autos de fe* and *carpas*.

Folk drama flourished in New Mexico and throughout the Internal Provinces (now the Southwest of the United States) until the late nineteenth century. Particularly popular were religious *pastoreles*, which originated in medieval Spain and were presented between Christmas and March.

The whole area of Spain's Mexican northern territories was governed from 1776 to 1789 from Arizpe, Sonora, Mexico, a mission town founded in 1641. The seat of government was then changed to Chihuahua, Mexico. Mexican settlers, miners, prospectors, and sheep and cattle ranchers moved into this vast area and helped found the cities of Santa Fe, New Mexico (c. 1609), Tucson, Arizona (1774), San Francisco, California (1776), and many others. Numerous explorers, military commanders, government administrators, soldiers, and colonizers kept diaries, descriptive narratives, and verse. An example is the *diario* or journal of the founder of San Francisco, Juan Bautista de Anza, written in 1775-1776.

Francisco Palou, a Franciscan priest, wrote a four-volume work about California, *Noticias de la Nueva California* (1874). A *pastorela* was also written in California in 1820 by Francisco Ibáñez of Soledad Mission.

Spanish-language newspapers in the colonies often published anonymous verse similar to folk verse. This generally followed traditional Spanish forms, such as the CANCIÓN and the DÉCIMA, a type of folk song. These rhymes became very popular in the settled localities.

The Mexican Colonial Period. The Spanish-speaking people in the Southwest first bound themselves in language, culture, and literary sources to Spain, and then to Mexico. By 1848, they already had a firmly established set of oral and written literary traditions. Besides the CORRIDO ballads, there were *cantos* (folk songs), CUENTOS (folktales), DICHOS (proverbs), and *leyendas* (legends) in the oral tradition. Poetic forms included the *décima*, *redondillos*, and the sonnet. In prose, there were autobiographical accounts, satire, legends, and the picaresque novel. With the proliferation of printing presses in the nineteenth century, romantic prose and poetry in Spanish were widely distributed. Liturgical and religious literature appeared in all genres.

Social and political life in Mexico influenced literary creativity by Mexican Americans before and after incorporation into the United States in 1848. By 1807, Southwestern Mexicans felt the growing migration of Anglos into their homelands, as well as the pressure of U.S. land acquisition. By 1821 there were Anglo settlements in Texas, and the Santa Fe Trail opened trade from Santa Fe to Independence, Missouri. Conflicts between Anglos and Spanish-speaking peoples, such as the Texas revolution (1836) and the MEXICAN AMERICAN WAR (1846-1848), found expression in literature. The Texan expedition to Santa Fe from Austin, made in an effort to extend territory, ended in misery with the Texans lost, hungry, dispirited, and captured. The episode was transformed into a play.

The Early American Period. Mexican American literature after 1848 changed in theme, style, tone, and language. The signing of the TREATY OF GUADALUPE HIDALGO (February 2, 1848), more than any other event, compelled Mexicans in the Southwest to reassess their relationship to Mexico and to the United States. According to the treaty, Mexico ceded its Provincias Internas north of the Rio Grande to the United States. Mexicans in the area who chose not to leave for Mexico became U.S. citizens. They were allowed to keep their language, culture, and traditions. English, however, was fast becoming the second language of the younger generation.

The new minority of Mexican Americans was created with all that such status implied and forbode. Their poets wrote about the intrusion of Anglo technology and expressed their concern about the erosion of their heritage and way of life. Mexican Americans not only endured the changes brought about by the imposition of a new government, a new language, and new social, cultural, and legal systems after 1848, but they also successfully responded to and acted upon these changes.

The literature of the Mexican Americans at this time was influenced by war and the concerns of a conquered people. *Corridos* described border conflict and the consequences of being a territorial minority. One famous *corrido* tells of a Mexican-born VAQUERO who protests his innocence of the accused crime of horse stealing to an Anglo sheriff. The *vaquero*, Gregorio CORTEZ, shoots the sheriff in self-defense. *Corridos* such as that of Gregorio Cortez indicated the psychology of border Mexicans, telling about their deep resentment of Anglos and denouncing Anglo views of Mexican character. In "The Ballad of Gregorio Cortez," which was made into a motion picture of the same name, in 1982, Mexicans reclaimed what was valued in *vaquero* culture.

Corridos and other types of folk song retained Mexican forms and language, but their themes, emotion, and cultural awareness departed from Mexican models. Many of these changes were evident by the 1920's. The Spanish language of Mexican Americans was infested with *pochismos* (Americanisms); some Mexican Americans preferred English. During the last half of the nineteenth century, more poems by Mexican Americans began to be written in English, and by 1900 it was common for poets to write entirely or predominantly in English.

The Mexican American War inspired many works of literature. (Institute of Texan Cultures)

From 1912 to 1959. The wave of Mexican immigration to the United States prompted by the MEXICAN REVOLUTION (1910-1921) marked a period of transition in Mexican American community life and Mexican American literature. As the population increased dramatically, so did awareness of anti-Mexican prejudice and discrimination. Major Latino organizations formed to protect Mexican American rights to further social and economic advancement. Spanish newspapers were also established in major Mexican American cities, such as *La Prensa* in San Antonio and *La Opinion* in Los Angeles. The popular press became an important vehicle for the Mexican American literary output of the day (*see* NEWSPAPERS AND MAGAZINES). By the 1940's, most Mexican American writers were writing in English.

Among the Mexicans who came to the United States at this time were writers such as Benjamín PADILLA, who wrote satirical sketches about the Mexican American community, and Adolfo Carillo, who published a series of *Cuentos Californios* in the 1920's. Two well-known female authors of the period were Maria Christina Mena Chambers and Josephina NIGGLI. Their writings, such as Niggli's novel *Mexican Village* (1945), were set in Mexico and attempted to bring a more realistic portrayal of Mexican life and characters to English-speaking readers. The prolific Fray Angélico Chávez wrote poems, stories, novels, and essays centered on the history and legends of his native New Mexico. The stories of Mario SUÁREZ in the 1940's were the first widely circulated fiction to depict barrio life, building on the urban themes of Mexican American playwrights in the 1920's and 1930's.

The postwar years signaled a transformation in Mexican American life. The BRACERO PROGRAM, begun in 1942, brought new waves of immigrants as temporary workers. Many settled in the United States. Mexican Americans who served in World War II took advantage of veterans' benefits to attend college or become homeowners. The population shifted from primarily rural to primarily urban, and a thriving business sector developed. New organizations sprang up to meet new needs.

In 1959, José Antonio VILLARREAL published *Pocho*, a novel that told the story of a family's migration from Mexico during the revolution and the eventual rebellion of the American-born *POCHO* generation against its immigrant parents. Although this book presaged themes that would preoccupy Chicano writers, it remained obscure until its rediscovery in the early 1970's.

The Chicano Renaissance. It was not until the 1960's that the leaders of the CHICANO MOVEMENT succeeded in popularizing the concept and term "Chicano" to describe the unique culture, identity, and concerns of Mexican Americans born in the United States. The movement was modeled in large part on the African American Civil Rights movement but took on its own character through key issues such as farmworkers' rights and its emphasis on cultural expression.

As the Chicano movement grew politically during the 1960's, there was an outpouring of literary, musical, theatrical, and artistic activity that became known as the Chicano Renaissance. Artists and writers were determined to dispel the negative stereotypes about their people, protest social injustice, and reclaim a proud past. The poet ALURISTA, for example, introduced the concept of the legendary homeland of AZTLÁN in 1968. The peak years of the renaissance in the late 1960's and the early 1970's saw the founding of literary journals such as *El Grito*, the staging of literary and theatrical conferences, the rise of Chicano publishing houses, the distribution of the Quinto Sol National Literary Awards, and the founding of the first CHICANO STUDIES PROGRAMS at universities. The writing of the period tended to be highly critical of the status quo and the dominant Anglo culture.

Chicano Poetry. Chicano literature was at first mainly in the form of poetry. Chicanos turned to the literary genre of poetry because it was easier to publish and circulate than novels and drama. They were also continuing a strong oral and written tradition, which had always valued quick verse. Chicano movement newspapers such as *La voz de la Justicia*, *El Gallo*, *El Grito del Norte*, *Regeneración*, and many others gave space to poetry. Later, short stories and novels began to appear with increased frequency as the number of authors grew.

Chicano poetry served as both a social and an artistic expression. It was divided into two categories: poetry of the Chicano movement and postmovement poetry. A rallying point for movement poetry was the year 1967, when Rodolfo "Corky" GONZÁLES, founder of the Denver-based CRUSADE FOR JUSTICE, circulated a lengthy epic poem entitled *Yo Soy Joaquin/I am Joaquin* (1967). The poem enjoyed wide circulation and was later made into a film by El TEATRO CAMPESINO. It is credited with succinctly capturing the nationalist ideology of the movement. It reclaimed the Mexican Indian/mestizo heritage of the Chicano while attacking Anglo oppression. The poem refers to many symbols of Mexican culture, such as Cuauhtémoc (last

Luis Valdez wrote Zoot Suit *and many other plays about Chicanos, particularly farmworkers.* (AP/Wide World Photos)

ruler of the Aztecs), Benito Juárez, and the Virgin of Guadalupe (Mexico's patron saint), as reminders of a proud heritage.

Chicano movement poets declared their unique heritage, cultural pride, and linguistic richness. Movement poetry was often moral and political, and poets sought to incite the reader to political action or to greater self-awareness. The Chicano movement motivated a renewed use of Spanish and pride in Chicano culture.

Other Chicano Writers. Chicano and Chicana writers were inspired by political movements such as the Chicano/Chicana movement, the antiwar movement of the 1960's and 1970's, and the feminist movement, as well as protests against U.S. policy in Central America and elsewhere. They were also influenced by Latin American literary creativity such as the "new novel," which provided literary models, and the works of their fellow Chicano/Chicana writers.

The first major Chicano novel of the period was Raymond BARRIO's *The Plum Plum Pickers* (1969), which attempted to do for Mexican American migrant workers what John Steinbeck's *The Grapes of Wrath* had done for Okie migrants in the 1930's. Richard VÁSQUEZ's *Chicano* (1970) was the first novel that was explicitly Chicano in its orientation and theme of the search for identity and struggle with assimilation. Tomás RIVERA won the first Quinto Sol award for his novel *...y no se lo trago la tierra/And the Earth Did Not Part* (1971), another tale of an alienated young protagonist, which pioneered a unique literary language. *Bless Me, Ultima* (1972) by Rudolfo A. ANAYA moved Chicano literature into new realms of expression influenced by myth and Latin American literary style. Other important novelists of the early 1970's were Ernesto GALARZA, Miguel MÉNDEZ, Rolando HINOJOSA, and Estela PORTILLO TRAMBLEY.

Luis VALDEZ continued in the vein of movement poetry and Chicano novels with his play *Zoot Suit*, which combined the history of the SLEEPY LAGOON CASE with magical/mythical elements. It was highly successful both on stage in 1978-1979 and as a motion picture in 1981.

By this time, however, the Chicano movement had lost much of its drive and popularity, and Chicano writers had diversified in their style and concerns. Prominent poets included Gary SOTO and Bernice Zamora. Novelists such as Alejandro MORALES used stark social realism. Richard RODRIGUEZ published his controversial autobiography *Hunger of Memory: The Education of Richard Rodriguez* (1982), which in effect rejected his Mexican heritage.

Chicana writers became so numerous that by the 1980's they appeared to dominate the Chicano literary scene. They took on the dual challenges of gender and ethnic issues in probing autobiographical and other works, while experimenting with language and form. Among the best-known Chicana writers are Cherríe MORAGA in theater, Sandra CISNEROS in the novel, Helena María VIRAMONTES in short stories, and Pat MORA in poetry. Their rise in popularity corresponded with the advent of the publishing of Chicano/Chicana writers by mainstream presses in the late 1980's, including a number of important anthologies and works of literary criticism (*see* LITERARY HISTORY AND CRITICISM).

Distinctive Language. Contemporary Chicano literature has been characterized by experimentation with language. In a fluid, complex, and expressive manner, Chicano authors wrote in various combinations of English and Spanish. This process involved the forging of new vocabularies and new images of reality. A single piece of writing might contain several variations of these linguistic modes. The interspersing of Chicano words with English or Spanish gave the literature much of its originality, energy, and effectiveness.

Chicano writers never adopted an official tongue. Rather than any single Chicano spoken language, there were several: exclusively Spanish; exclusively English; bilingualism using standard English and standard Spanish; and CALÓ, *POCHO*, or PACHUCO slang, which combined English and Spanish grammar, structure, and vocabulary with new words to form a hybrid language.

Most Chicano fiction and poetry was written in English. The use of common Spanish words, especially those referring to food or culture in the Southwest, gave a distinctive touch to the style of Chicanos writing in English, such as Anaya, since the words did not have to be translated. When Villarreal used slang terms in *Pocho* in 1959, he translated them for his readers. In some parts of the Southwest, writers were influenced by the distinctive speech of young pachucos. Tomás Rivera excelled at using simple and natural expression of Texas-Chicano speech in a voice like the remembered speech of family, friends, and neighbors along the Mexican border.

Many novels and short stories were published in Spanish, some with a considerable amount of Caló. New immigrants able to read only in Spanish, Chicanos who retained Spanish, and students of the language enjoyed literary works in Spanish such as Méndez's *Peregrinos de Aztlan* (1974). Frequently, poets used English, Spanish, and Caló within the same poem or even the same line, reflecting a phenomenon in Mexican American speech called CODE SWITCHING.

Chicano literature is unique, then, not only because of its rich blend of indigenous American and Spanish American heritage. Mexican American writers used language creatively to explore their complex history, religion, traditions, and cultural values, as well as their personal struggles for identity. These characteristics made Mexican American and Chicano literature markedly different from other types of literature of the United States. —*Santos C. Vega*

SUGGESTED READINGS:

• Baker, Houston A., Jr. *Three American Literatures: Essays in Chicano, Native American, and Asian-American Literature for Teachers of American Literature.* New York: Modern Language Association of America, 1982. This literature sourcebook provides information not only in broad overviews of different literary forms but also in detailed analyses of the contents of these literary genres.

• Calderon, Héctor, and José David Saldivar, eds. *Criticism in the Borderlands: Studies in Chicano Literature, Culture, and Ideology.* Durham, N.C.: Duke University Press, 1991. Provides a re-evaluation of American literary history and representations of Chicanos, including race, class, and gender. Bibliography.

• Jiménez, Francisco, ed. *The Identification and Analysis of Chicano Literature.* New York: Bilingual Press/Editorial Bilingüe, 1979. Studies in the language and literature of United States Hispanics. Covers the role of women in Chicano literature.

• Lomelí, Francisco A., and Donaldo W. Urioste. *Chicano Perspectives in Literature: A Critical and Annotated Bibliography.* Albuquerque, N.Mex.: Pajarito, 1976. A comprehensive book covering poetry, novels, short fiction, theater, and anthologies, with literary criticism. Contents include Chicana literature and the oral tradition in print.

• Martínez, Julio A., and Francisco A. Lomelí, eds. *Chicano Literature: A Reference Guide.* Westport, Conn.: Greenwood Press, 1985. Treats Chicano literature as part of the Chicano movement of the mid-1960's. Defines Chicano literary works since 1848, including backgrounds and traditions since the sixteenth century.

• Saldivar, Ramón. *Chicano Narrative: The Dialectics of Difference.* Madison: University of Wisconsin Press, 1990. A comprehensive text on the history and theory of Mexican American authors, with an analysis

of their literary products. Examines various aspects of Mexican American narrative forms.

• Shirley, Carl R., and Paula W. Shirley. *Understanding Chicano Literature.* Columbia: University of South Carolina Press, 1988. Surveys Chicano literature. Provides information in literary genres and helps readers understand Chicano literature by pointing out useful information on each topic.

• Tatum, Charles, ed. *Mexican American Literature.* Orlando, Fla.: Harcourt Brace Jovanovich, 1990. Covers Mexican American literature in well-defined literary categories including oral tradition, Spanish and Mexican periods, and contemporary short fiction.

• Trambley, Estela Portillo. *Rain of Scorpions and Other Writings.* Berkeley: Tonatiuh International, 1975. This literary work is a landmark in Chicano literature because the author was one of the first major Chicana prose writers to publish her work. There is a strong feminist strain in her stories.

Literature, pre-Columbian: Of all the arts practiced by the Mesoamerican civilization, literature is the most difficult to study, because most manuscripts were destroyed by the conquering Spaniards. Some manuscripts survived in the vaults of the cathedral in Mexico City, but most of those were burned by Pancho VILLA's soldiers during the MEXICAN REVOLUTION (1910-1921). The manuscripts, called codices, were written on paper made by pounding and burnishing strips of bark; some codices were made from deer or jaguar skins in parchment form. A codex was made of a single long sheet of paper that was folded accordion style, inscribed with hieroglyphs on both sides, and bound at both ends with thin slabs of wood or skin. Codices were generally read from top to bottom and right to left. The manuscripts were produced by scribes specially trained in the business of painting and making pictorial symbols.

Topics addressed in the codices included ceremonies, prophecies, kings, gods, feasts, myths, laws, customs, and movements of heavenly bodies. Codices that contain literary matter reveal that the Mesoamericans were versed in religious, lyric, epic, and dramatic poetry; historical prose; legends; and moral teachings. Much pre-Columbian "literature" was oral rather than written, as it was widely believed that it was wiser and easier to preserve knowledge in the ear than in the book. Nevertheless, Mesoamerican literature was divided into prose, which was used for instructive treatises and mythical and historic narratives, and verse (usually trochaic), which was used for religious or profane poems. Descriptive passages were typically written in rhythmic verses. The richness of the languages allowed the "stacking up" of near-synonyms to describe one deed. Thus, if a sorcerer made his appearance as an old man, the narrative might be: "He transformed himself into a little old man, he changed himself, he disguised himself, he became very much bowed, his head became quite white, his hair quite white." Parallelism was constantly sought in poems and treatises, so that two phrases with the same meaning were often used side by side, as in, "Sorrow overflows—tears fall." To the Aztec poet, the word *Cuicáni* (the singer) meant that poem and song were synonymous. Poems were always sung or accompanied by musical instruments.

Literature, Puerto Rican: Puerto Rican literature is important both in Latin America and as part of the U.S. Latino literary experience. Unfortunately, a significant amount of information on Puerto Rican literature is available only in Spanish.

Historical Background. On November 19, 1493, Christopher Columbus landed on a Caribbean island called Borinquen by its native population. The Spanish conquerors renamed the island, first as San Juan Bautista and later as Puerto Rico. The Puerto Rican ethnic makeup and heritage was formed from the mix between the Taino Indians (the island's original inhabitants), the Africans who were brought to the island to work as slaves, and the Spanish conquerors who came with Columbus and later.

From the sixteenth to the eighteenth century, almost all written Puerto Rican literature was composed by the Spanish conquerors who established themselves on the island. Most of this literature was in the form of letters, called *cartas de relación*, or descriptions written to the king of Spain, called CRÓNICAS or *memorias*. These cent'uries were also rich in oral forms of literature, particularly poetry. Spaniards brought the DÉCIMA (a ten-verse poem), the *copla* (short poetic composition), and the ROMANCE (narrative or lyric poem).

The printing press was brought to Puerto Rico early in the nineteenth century. The first newspaper with a strong literary section was *La gaceta de Puerto Rico*. Noteworthy is the contribution of the first recognized Puerto Rican woman poet, María Bibiana Benítez, who wrote the poem "La ninfa de Puerto Rico" (1832) and the historical drama *La cruz* (1836).

Aguinaldo Puertorriqueño de 1843 (1843) was the first anthology of Puerto Rican literature. It was a source of inspiration for a group of Puerto Rican students in Barcelona. In 1844, this group published *Album Puertorriqueño* with the intent of rescuing the indigenous Puerto Rican heritage from Spanish colonial domination. Among the authors included in this volume were two great Puerto Rican writers: Manuel A. Alonso (1822-1889) and Santiago Vidarte (1828-1848). Overcoming many obstacles imposed by Spanish censorship, Alonso published the first book by a Puerto Rican author, *El gíbaro* (1849). In *El gíbaro*, he tried to bring the rural creole ways into the mainstream of literature.

Literary Movements. The neoclassic movement (conservatives) and the Romantic movement (liberals) coexisted without much animosity between the schools in Puerto Rico. Some authors used a Romantic style for one poem and a neoclassic style for another. The passionate writings of revolutionary romanticism were published by Puerto Ricans who lived far away from the island. For example, *La Virgen de Borinquén* (1859) was published originally in French by Ramón Emeterio BETANCES (1827-1898), and *La peregrinación de Bayoán* (1863) by Eugenio María de HOSTOS Y BONILLA (1839-1903) was published in Spain and confiscated by the Spanish authorities. It became available to the Puerto Rican public only after its second edition in Chile (1873).

The Romantic movement in Puerto Rico was represented by Alejandro Tapia y Rivera (1826-1882) and José Gautier Benítez (1848-1880). The works of Tapia y Rivera include historical dramas (*Bernardo de Palissy*, 1857), social and racial plays (*La cuarterona*, 1867), and historical legends (*La palma del cacique*, 1852). Gautier Benítez is known as one of the greatest Puerto Rican poets. His poems were published in several anthologies and in a volume titled *Coleccion de poesías* (1880).

The neoclassic movement in Puerto Rico included such nineteenth century poets as Ramón Marín ("A mi patria"), Juan Francisco Comas ("Preludios del Arpa"), and the most important of all, José Gualberto Padilla, better known as "El Caribe" ("El Canto a Puerto Rico"). Equally valuable is the neoclassic prose of Julio L. de Vizcarrondo (*El hombre velorio*).

Toward the end of the nineteenth century, as the Romantic and neoclassic movements declined, most Puerto Rican writers began to give critical accounts of their time. Using literature as a sword, they described political persecutions from Spain in works such as the "Compontes" (1887), which described tortures authorized by the government, and the struggles for the "Carta Autonómica" (1897), a document from the

Spanish authorities giving Puerto Rico the right to its own government. This right was interrupted by U.S. occupation of the island in 1898. Many writers of this period fought against colonialism not only in their writing but also through political struggle. Outstanding contributions were made by Eugenio María de Hostos (*Obras completas*, 1939, twenty volumes), Salvador Brau (*La campesina*, 1886), Lola RODRÍGUEZ DE TIÓ (*Mis cantares*, 1876), Francisco Gonzalo "Pachín" Marín (*Romances*, 1892), and Luis MUÑOZ RIVERA (*Tropicales*, 1902).

At the end of the nineteenth century, Latin American writers were involved in a renovation of language called *Modernismo*. It attempted to use language in a more sophisticated manner, often describing aristocratic or fantastic settings. It also highlighted the importance of the human senses. This movement, initiated by Rubén Darío of Nicaragua, continued into the 1920's.

As a result of the intensity of social and political events, *Modernismo* was slow in being absorbed into Puerto Rican literature. Many Puerto Rican writers, however, followed the movement. Characteristics of *Modernismo* are reflected in the titles of poems such as "La princesa Ita" (1904) by Jesús María Lago (1873-1927) and "Aromas del terruño" (1916, smell of the earth) by Virgilio Dávila (1869-1943). The high point of the movement came with the publication of the literary journal *Revista las Antillas* (1913), edited by Luis LLORENS TORRES (1878-1944), author of *Alturas de América* (1940). Other outstanding figures were José P. H. Hernández (*El último combate*, 1921) and Evaristo RIBERA CHEVREMONT (*Antología poética*, 1954).

Modernismo also included numerous writers of prose. These writers, however, did not always adhere strictly to the idea of writing only for the sake of art, an idea that was valued highly by the movement in the rest of Latin America. Instead, some used their writings to make social and political statements. Examples are Miguel Meléndez Muñoz (*Cuentos de la carretera Central*, 1941) and Nemesio Canales (*Paliques*, 1913).

Many new, but often short-lived, movements appeared on the Puerto Rican literary scene during the 1920's. Most of these movements sought to aid in the search for self-identity through revolutionary ways of writing. New uses of poetic language (such as metaphors) and new explorations of poetic combinations of sounds (such as onomatopoeia) within a political or social context were the most relevant characteristics of these movements.

The works of Luis PALÉS MATOS (1898-1959) and José I. de Diego Padró (1896-1974) are noteworthy. In Palés Matos' collection of poems *Tuntun de pasa y grifería* (1937) he incorporates sound into his lyrics, initiating what was later called *poesía negroide* (black poetry) for its incorporation of Afro-Caribbean themes. In 1923, the *Euforismo* movement appeared, headed by Vicente Palés Matos and Tomás L. Batista. This movement was extremely short lived because another group, the *Noísta*, appeared and dominated the literary scene until 1929.

Atalayismo and *Meñiquismo* were the last two literary movements of the decade. The most prominent figures in the former were Graciany Miranda Archilla, Alfredo Margenat, and Clemente Soto, who promoted the use of metaphors with more audacity. *Meñiquismo* originated at the University of Puerto Rico. Under the guidance and inspiration of Margot Arce de Vázquez, a group of students including F. Manrique Cabrera, María Teresa Babín, and Francisco Arrillaga published their writings. Their work started an important new era in Puerto Rican literature.

The 1930's and Later. Literary activity became concentrated at the University of Puerto Rico. The Department of Hispanic Studies flourished and was visited by intellectuals such as Américo Castro and Gabriela MISTRAL. Puerto Rican writers were successful in all types of literature: essays, novels and short stories, drama, and poetry.

Essays. The first essayist of this period to reach a wide audience was Antonio S. PEDREIRA (1899-1939). His most important work, *Insularísmo* (1934), has been extensively studied and criticized. His immediate critic was Tomás Blanco (1900-1974), who wrote *Prontuario histórico de Puerto Rico* (1935), in which he criticized Pedreira for denying the value of popular culture in *Insularísmo*. A passion for history and culture is reflected in the life and works of María Cadilla de Martínez (*La poesía popular en Puerto Rico*, 1933). She belonged to a group of writers who were deeply concerned with the documentation of historical facts. Lidio Cruz Monclova (*Historia de Puerto Rico*, 1952) in 1953 became the first professor to offer a class on Puerto Rican literature at the University of Puerto Rico.

Known for their essays on literary criticism are Concha Meléndez (*Asomante*, 1943) and Margot Arce de Vázquez (*Garcilaso de la Vega*, 1930). Other important essayists of this period include Rubén del Rosario (1907-1989) and Nilita Vientós Gastón (b. 1908), who also founded various literary journals. Essays with a strong social component were written by Josc Emilio González (b. 1918), Ricardo Alegría (b. 1921), Emilio S. Belaval (1903-1972), César Andreu Iglesias (1915-1976), José Luis GONZÁLEZ (b. 1926), and Arcadio Díaz Quiñones (b. 1938).

Novels and Short Stories. Possibly the most important Puerto Rican novel of all time was *La charca* (1894) by Manuel ZENO GANDÍA (1855-1930). When Zeno Gandía died in 1930, novelists and other writers started to concentrate on a search for national identity. Enrique LAGUERRE (*La llamarada*, 1935) was the first of these novelists. His many novels affirm Puerto Rican values and identity.

An interest in history and culture was apparent in novels such as *Isla cerrera* (1938) by Manuel Méndez Ballester (b. 1909). History and culture are explored more deeply in a novelistic subgenre called the testimonial. The testimonial was cultivated in Puerto Rico by Edgardo Rodríguez Juliá (b. 1946), author of *Las tribulaciones de Jonás* (1981).

Metropolitan life in New York City and the Puerto Rican immigrant experience in the United States were important literary themes cultivated by writers such as Guillermo COTTO-THORNER (*Trópico en Manhattan*, 1951), José Luis GONZÁLEZ (*Paisa*, 1950), Pedro Juan SOTO (*Spiks*, 1956), and Luis Rafael SÁNCHEZ (*La guagua aérea*, 1989).

Sociopolitical problems on the island were the topic of writings by Abelardo Díaz Alfaro (*Terrazo*, 1947), Emilio S. Belaval (*Cuentos para fomentar el turismo*, 1946), Ana Lydia VEGA and Carmen Lugo Fillipi (*Vírgenes y mártires*, 1981), Rosario FERRÉ (*Fábulas de la garza desangrada*, 1982), and Luis Rafael Sánchez (*La guaracha del Macho Camacho*, 1976).

Drama. The literary period immediately prior to the 1930's gave Puerto Rican literature some important, although not well-known, plays such as *El grito de Lares* by Luis Llorens Torres. Many plays became known to the public through Areyto, a theater group founded by Emilio Belaval. Among them are *Esta noche juega el joker* (1939) by Fernando Sierra Berdecía (1903-1962) and *Mi señoría* (1940) by Luis Rechani Agrait (1902-1980).

Among the writers of this period, Francisco Arriví, René Marqués, and Luis Rafael Sánchez deserve special mention. Arriví's work *Una sombra menos o María Soledad* (1946) presented profound psychological problems to the public in a poetic way. Marqués' play *La carreta* (1951) dealt with the sorrows and problems of Puerto Rican immigrants in New York City. Sánchez wrote the well-known play *Quíntuples*

(1985), which deals with unresolved problems of Puerto Rican national identity.

Poetry. In Puerto Rican literature, poetry has always been the genre that attracted the most writers. Poets who combined poetry and political struggle were Juan Antonio Corretjer (*Alabanza en la torre de Ciales*, 1953), Francisco MATOS PAOLI (*Luz de los héroes*, 1954), and Dolores "Lolita" Lebrón (*Sándalo en la celda*, 1964). Julia de BURGOS (1914-1953) was the foremost female Puerto Rican poet of this period. Other female poets included Carmen Alicia Cadilla (b. 1907) and Violeta López Suria (b. 1926). After 1960, many more female poets entered the literary scene, exploring the changing role of women in Puerto Rican society. Best known are María Arrillaga (*Desnudez*, 1984), Vanessa Droz (*La cicatriz a medias*, 1982), and Mayra Santos (*Febres anamú y manigua*, 1991).

Reacting against the preoccupation with social and political issues in Puerto Rican literature, a group of poets founded *Trascendentalismo*. These poets included Francisco Lluch Mora (*Del barro a Dios*, 1954) and Hugo Margenat (*Intemperie*, 1955).

After 1960, several poets focused their writing on the problems of minority groups in society. Among these poets, Manuel RAMOS OTERO (*El libro de la muerte*, 1985) is the best known. Joserramón Meléndes (*En Borges*, 1980) and Rafael Acevedo (*Libro de islas*, 1990) presented a new perspective on Puerto Rican colonial problems.

Puerto Rican Literature on the Mainland. Although literature of the island tended to be written in Spanish and that of the mainland in English, the two strains appeared to have many similarities. Many writers from the mainland traveled to the island to use it as a reference point, or they idealized Puerto Rico as their homeland. Bernardo VEGA, Tato LAVIERA, and Nicolasa MOHR are only a few of the important Puerto Rican writers on the mainland. Such writers described the struggle of adapting to a new culture as well as spreading Puerto Rican culture to the mainland.

—*Juana Iris Goergen*

SUGGESTED READINGS:
• Cabrera, Francisco Manrique. *Historia de la literatura puertorriqueña*. Río Piedras, Puerto Rico: Editorial Cultural, 1982. Surveys the various literary movements on the island.

• Cadilla de Martínez, María. *La poesía popular en Puerto Rico*. Madrid: Universidad de Madrid, 1933. Surveys and gives a historical overview of popular poetry. A second edition was published in 1983.

- Gómez Tejera, Carmen. *La novela en Puerto Rico.* San Juan, Puerto Rico: Junta Editora, Universidad de Puerto Rico, 1947. A survey of novelists and their works.
- Marques, Rene. *The Docile Puerto Rican: Essays.* Translated by Barbara Bockus Aponte. Philadelphia, Pa.: Temple University Press, 1976. Discusses aspects of various literary movements and periods. Includes analysis of short stories, folklore characters, and farce.
- Rodriguez de Laguna, Asela, ed. *Images and Identities: The Puerto Rican in Two World Contexts.* New Brunswick, N.J.: Transaction, 1987. Analyzes portrayals of Puerto Rican identities and the search for personal identity.
- Turner, Faythe, ed. *Puerto Rican Writers at Home in the USA: An Anthology.* Seattle, Wash.: Open Hand, 1991. An anthology of works by mainland Puerto Ricans.

Literature, South American immigrant: Historically, the literary writer in exile or as an immigrant is not new to the Americas. In the nineteenth century, writers were drawn to Paris, and in the twentieth century they went to the United States. Like other immigrants, South American writers move from their home to another country to flee problems or seek opportunities. Some must leave because they have been expelled for political reasons or can no longer accept their country's oppression. Others are looking for a more sophisticated artistic and literary center, or the chance to work in a place where greater financial and economic opportunities will permit greater freedom of intellectual expression.

South American writers representing various literary movements have worked and published in the United States since the early 1900's, most prominently in the 1970's and 1980's. Some have received international recognition, such as Gabriela MISTRAL (1889-1957), who won the Nobel Prize, and Isabel ALLENDE (b. 1942), who achieved best-seller status simultaneously in a number of languages. Other less well-known writers have contributed to Latin American studies programs at American universities and founded journals such as *Revista de Crítica Literaria Latinoamericana.* Common themes of South American writers in exile include sorrow for the lost paradise, solitude, contrasts between their present world and their homeland, and depictions of the émigré community. Their work has also made North American readers more aware of political repression and resistance under Latin American regimes in Brazil, Paraguay, Uruguay, Argentina, and Chile.

Chilean Writers. Perhaps the most prominent South American literary exiles are from Chile. They left en masse after the 1973 coup that toppled the socialist government of Salvador Allende Gossens. Some already abroad were simply banned from entering Chile, and others thought they could not work under a university system controlled by the military. Although the United States became home to only a minority of the exiles, American political action groups in solidarity with Chile offered networking and support to the Chilean American intellectual community. The important journal *Literatura Chilena en el Exilio (Chilean Literature of Exile)*, later known as *Literatura Chilena*, began in California in 1977 under the leadership of successful Chilean author Fernando ALEGRÍA (b. 1918).

Although Alegría lived in the United States beginning in the 1940's, he was the first Chilean to write a novel about the military coup (*El paso de los gansos*) in 1975. He returned to that theme in *Allende. Mi vecino el presidente* (Allende. My neighbor the president) in 1990 but has also written a trilogy about Latin American exiles in the United States.

Isabel ALLENDE (b. 1942), niece of the deposed Chilean president, is the best known of the Chilean exile writers and an outspoken champion of human rights in Latin America. She began her career as a journalist in Chile but was forced to flee to Venezuela in 1975 when she realized that her family was being shadowed. In the late 1980's she moved to California. Allende has published *La casa de los espíritus* (1982; *The House of the Spirits*, 1985), *De amor y de sombra* (1984; *Of Love and Shadows*, 1987), and other novels. The best-seller *The House of the Spirits* gave her worldwide recognition. *The Infinite Plan* (1993), her first novel set in the United States, is the story of a young man who grew up in a Latino barrio in Los Angeles.

The theme of exile appears in the novel *Paradise* by Elena Castedo (b. 1937), which was published first in English and nominated in 1991 for the National Book Award. The Spanish version, *El paraíso*, received the 1990 Cervantes Award in Spain and was named the 1990 Book of the Year in Chile.

The tradition of Chilean women writers in the United States dates back to Amanda Labarca (1886-1975), who worked with Eleanor Roosevelt in the United Nations. She analyzed the problems of Chilean women in *Impresiones de juventud* (1909), *Actividades femeninas en Los Estados Unidos* (1914), *La lámpara maravillosa* (1921), *A dónde va la mujer?* (1934), and *Feminismo contemporáneo* (1947). A novel

Gabriela Mistral. (AP/Wide World Photos)

that produced shock waves in the conservative society of the time was *La brecha* (1961) by Mercedes Valdivieso (1926-1993), a professor at Rice University. Chilean-born María Luisa Bombal (1910-1980) lived first in Argentina among the literary elite, then in New York City until 1970. Her two novels *La última niebla* (1934) and *La amortajada* (1938) made her famous. A more recent Chilean writer is Elizabeth Subercaseaux, who wrote of her dream for a free and democratic Chile in *Silendra* (1986). Lucía Guerra-Cunningham (b. 1942), a critic and author of *Más allá de las máscaras* (1984), focuses on the problems of women.

Other noteworthy Chilean writers in the United States include José Donosa (b. 1924), who wrote about the Chilean exile experience in *Casa de campo* (1978) and *El jardin de al lado* (1981); Antonio Skármeta (b. 1940), who wrote *Soñé que la nieve ardía* (1975) in praise of the people who worked for his freedom; and José Leandro Urbina (b. 1949), the author of *Las malas juntas* (1973).

Some South American writers divide their time between their native country and the United States. An example is Chilean Ariel Dorfman (b. 1942), who moved to Washington, D.C., in 1980 and began teaching at the University of Iowa in 1989, splitting his time between Iowa and Chile. His best-known novels are *Viudas* (1981), translated as *Widows* in 1983; and *La última canción de Manuel Sendero* (1982). His play *Death and the Maiden* also won critical acclaim. Roberto Ampuero (c. 1958) has divided his time between Miami and Chile pursuing a construction business and writing. He wrote the thriller and political novel *Quién mató a Christian Kustermann?*, which won the 1993 Premio Revista de Libros of Chile's *El Mercurio*.

Other Exile Writers. Writers in exile from other dictatorships have also come to the United States in search of literary freedom. Jacobo Timerman (b. 1923) and Alicia Partnoy (b. 1955) gave testimony about their incarceration in Argentina under the dictatorship. In *Preso sin nombre, celda sin número* (1981), Timerman tells his experience of being tortured. Partnoy is the author of *Little School* (1986) and *You Can't Drown the Fire* (1988). Another famous female writer from Argentina is Luisa VALENZUELA (b. 1938). In 1983, she published *The Lizard's Tail*, a novel based on real and imaginary events during the presidency of Isabel Perón. María Vaccaro (c. 1932), born in Argentina, in her novel *El brillante inmovil* (1967; *The Immobile Brilliant*, 1993) focused on the problems of a woman

from India. Novelist Marta Traba (1930-1983), author of *Conversación al sur* (1981), which was translated as *Mothers and Shadows* in 1986, focused on women's problems. Isaac Goldemberg (b. 1945) humorously recounted tales about the Jews in Peru in *La vida a plazos de Don Jacobo Lerner* (1976; *The Fragmented Life of Don Jacobo Lerner*, 1976).

—Sylvia P. Apodaca

SUGGESTED READINGS: • Alegría, Fernando. *La novela hispano-americana siglo XX*. Buenos Aires: Centro Editor de America Latina, 1967. • Alegría, Fernando. *Nueva historia de la novela hispanoamericana*. Hanover, N.H.: Ediciones del Norte, 1986. • Flores, Angel. *Spanish American Authors: The Twentieth Century*. New York: H. W. Wilson, 1992. • Franco, Jean. *Historia de la literatura hispanoamericana a partir de la independencia*. Caracas, Venezuela: Editorial Ariel, 1973. • Goic, Cedomil. *Historia de la novela hispanoamericana*. Santiago, Chile: Ediciones Universitarias de Valparaiso, 1980. • Solé, Carlos A., et al., eds. *Latin American Writers*. 3 vols. New York: Charles Scribner's Sons, 1989.

Literature, Spanish American: Major trends developed from the COLONIAL PERIOD (sixteenth century) to the present in the literature of the Spanish-speaking Americas. This area includes most countries south of the United States on the American continents with the exceptions of Brazil, British and French Guyana, Surinam, and some English- and French-speaking islands in the Caribbean Sea.

Native and Colonial Writings. A large number of indigenous cultures existed on the American continents prior to colonization. Some achieved a high degree of civilization and produced great literary works such as the Mayan sacred book POPOL VUH (English translation, 1950). Franciscan priest Fray Bernardino de Sahagún (c. 1499-1590) wrote the *History of New Spain* (1988, in Spanish), in which he included many poems in Nahuatl, the language of the Aztecs. In the Andes, two chronicles describing Inca life and the devastating SPANISH CONQUEST were written by mestizos: *Royal Commentaries* (1609-1617; English translation, 1869-1871) by Garcilaso de la Vega, el Inca, and *First New Chronicle and Good Government* (1615) by Felipe Guamán Poma de Ayala. Both include poems in Quechua, the language of the Incas.

The conquest and the early stages of colonialism were the subjects of a number of chronicles written by Spaniards, such as the letters of Hernán CORTÉS, conquistador of Mexico, and the *True Story of the Con-*

Hernán Cortés and his conquests in the Americas were topics of early chronicles. (Institute of Texan Cultures)

quest of Mexico (1632; English translation, 1956) by Bernal Díaz de Castillo. Fray Bartolomé DE LAS CASAS was the most distinguished critic of the conquest and the colonial establishment. In his *Brevísima relación de la destrucción de las Indias* (1552; *The Tears of the Indians*, 1953), he holds the Spanish Crown responsible for the ill treatment and eventual decimation of the indigenous population.

At the height of the colonial period, the baroque style of writing was adopted by many. Among authors of this period, the best known is Sor Juana Inés de la CRUZ (1651-1695), a Mexican nun of extraordinary talent who wrote poems, plays, and essays.

The Period of Independence. After several centuries of colonization, a new sense of patriotism was aroused in CRIOLLO intellectuals, the descendants of Europeans born in the New World. Out of this patriotism grew a deep desire for separation from Spain. This new pride is reflected in the "silvas Americanas" of Venezuelan Andrés Bello (1781-1865). Wars of independence early in the nineteenth century resulted in the independence of most of the countries of South and Central America. Literature was inspired by that war. Ecuadoran poet José Joaquín Olmedo (1780-1847)

wrote "La victoria de Junín" and "Canto a Bolívar" (1825), among other war-inspired poems. After independence, the *caudillos* (tyrants) rose to power in many of the newborn countries. Political extremism inspired the adoption of European Romanticism in literature. In Argentina, Esteban Echeverría (1805-1851; *El Matadero*, 1871) and Domingo Faustino Sarmiento (1811-1888; *Facundo: Civilización y barbarie*, 1845) wrote passionately against the dictator Manuel Rosas. Romanticism achieved its peak in the novel during the second half of the nineteenth century. Well-known authors in this style include Argentinean José Mármol (1817-1871; *Amalia*, 1855), Chilean Albert Blest Gana (1830-1920; *Martín Rivas*, 1862), and Colombian Jorge Isaacs (1837-1895; *María*, 1867).

Modernismo. At the end of the nineteenth century there appeared the first specifically Spanish American literary movement, *Modernismo*. It involved remarkable innovations in the content and form of poetry, primarily, but also affected fiction. One of its major exponents was Nicaraguan poet Rubén Darío (1867-1916; *Azul*, 1888; *Cantos de vida y esperanza*, 1905). Another was Cuban poet and journalist José MARTÍ (1853-1895), who lived most of his life in exile, fighting for the liberation of his country, one of Spain's last three colonies. In addition to his monumental volume of journalistic work, Martí wrote *Versos sencillos* (1891).

Literary Emancipation. In the early twentieth century, novels became increasingly realistic, depicting the land, its people, their way of life, and their fight against nature. A few of these novels are *Don Segundo Sombra* (1926; *Shadows on the Pampas*, 1935) by Ricardo Güiraldes (1886-1927) of Argentina, *Doña Bárbara* (1929; English translation, 1931) by Rómulo Gallegos (1884-1969) of Venezuela, and *La vorágine* (1924; *The Vortex*, 1935) by José Eustasio Rivera (1889-1928) of Colombia. During this period, the Mexican Revolution (1910-1921) took place. Mariano AZUELA (1873-1952) wrote *Los de abajo* (1915; *The Underdogs*, 1929), one of the most famous novels about the Mexican Revolution and the struggle of the oppressed. The same theme, the condemnation of oppression, appears in the *indigenista* novels of the period in Mexico.

These include *El indio* (1935; English translation, 1937) by Gregorio López y Fuentes (1897-1966) and *Balún-Canán* (1957) by Rosario CASTELLANOS (1925-1974).

In South America, the *indigenista* novel bloomed in the Andean countries—Ecuador, Bolivia, and Peru—because of their large Indian populations. Its major representatives are *Huasipungo* (1934; English translation, 1962) by Jorge Icaza (1906-1978); *El mundo es ancho y ajeno* (1941; *Broad and Alien Is the World*, 1941) by Ciro Alegría (1909-1967); and *Yawar Fiesta* (1941) by José María Arguedas.

There was a definite change in poetry as well. After *Modernismo*, poets were inclined to express their sentiments in a simpler and more accessible way. Three women were of great importance in this period: Uruguayan Delmira Agustini (1886-1914), Argentinean Alfonsina STORNI (1892-1938), and Chilean Nobel laureate (1945) Gabriela MISTRAL (1889-1957). European avant-garde movements made their way to Span-

Octavio Paz addresses reporters after receiving the Nobel Prize in Literature. (AP/Wide World Photos)

Gabriel García Márquez is among the world's best-known writers. (AP/Wide World Photos)

ish America and found expression in *Trilce* (1922) by Peruvian César VALLEJO (1892-1938) and in *Altazor* (1916) by Chilean Vicente Huidobro (1893-1948).

Contemporary Period. In general, twentieth century Spanish American writers of prose have ranked ahead of poets. An exception is Pablo NERUDA (1904-1973), a Chilean poet who won the Nobel Prize in Literature in 1971 and is the author of *Canto general* (1950). Mexican poet and essayist Octavio PAZ (b. 1914) wrote *El laberinto de la soledad* (1950; *The Labyrinth of Solitude*, 1961), along with other famous works. He was awarded the Nobel Prize in Literature in 1990.

Many twentieth century Spanish American novels of what is called the "boom" period of the 1950's and 1960's have been recognized worldwide for their personal style and distinctive voice. Jorge Luis Borges (1899-1986) and Julio CORTÁZAR (1914-1984) wrote of universalist themes. Alejo Carpentier (1904-1980), Augusto ROA BASTOS (b. 1917), and Nobel laureates Miguel Ángel Asturias and Gabriel GARCÍA MÁRQUEZ (b. 1928) incorporated Indian and African mythology in their works in a style called Magical Realism. Asturias received the Nobel Prize in Literature in 1967 in recognition of *El Señor Presidente* (1946; English translation, 1963), and García Márquez won the Nobel Prize in 1982 for *Cien años de soledad* (1967; *One Hundred Years of Solitude*, 1970).

Narrative works written in this vein include Carlos FUENTES' (b. 1928) *La muerte de Artemio Cruz* (1962; *The Death of Artemio Cruz*, 1964) and Juan RULFO's (1918-1986) *Pedro Páramo* (1955; English translation, 1959). One of the most popular Spanish American writers is Peruvian Mario VARGAS LLOSA (b. 1936). His novels *La ciudad y los perros* (1962; *The Time of the Hero*, 1966), which was made into a motion picture, and *Conversación en la catedral* (1969; *Conversation in the Cathedral*, 1975) offer a fine analysis of military authority and the dictatorship. Later he changed themes. *El hablador* (1987; *The Storyteller*, 1989) tells of the encroachment of modern life into a traditional Indian culture.

Female writers and their works became increasingly important and well known in Spanish America. They include Mexican journalist Elena PONIATOWSKA and her novel *Hasta no verte, Jesús mío* (1969), Puerto Rican poet and essayist Rosario FERRÉ and her autobiographical novel *Maldito amor* (1986), and, perhaps the best known in the United States, Chilean Isabel ALLENDE, author of *La casa de los espíritus* (1982; *The House of the Spirits*, 1985) and several other acclaimed novels. —*Sylvia M. Nagy*

SUGGESTED READINGS: • Carrera Andrade, Jorge. *Reflections on Spanish American Poetry.* Translated by Don C. Bliss and Gabriela de C. Bliss. Albany: State University of New York Press, 1973. • Englekirk, John E., et al., eds. *An Outline History of Spanish American Literature.* 4th ed. New York: Irvington, 1980. • Franco, Jean. *Spanish American Literature Since Independence.* London: Ernest Benn, 1973. • Klein, Leonard, ed. *Latin American Literature in the Twentieth Century: A Guide.* New York: Ungar, 1986. • Manguel, Alberto, ed. *Other Fires: Short Fiction by Latin American Women.* New York: C. N. Potter, 1986. • Rodriguez Monegal, Emir, with Thomas Colchie. *The Borzoi Anthology of Latin American Literature.* 2 vols. New York: Knopf, 1977.

Little Havana (Miami, Fla.): Large numbers of Cuban refugees settled in MIAMI following the Cuban Revolution (1959) led by Fidel Castro. Although some Cuban Americans later departed, the area remains a center of Cuban culture.

Little Havana encompasses approximately four square miles and is located about two miles southwest of Miami's central business district. The area has been revitalized by thousands of Cuban Americans who live and work there while maintaining their unique culture. It is the largest, best-known, and most studied Cuban American community.

The term "Little Havana" was first used by Anglos in the 1930's to refer to a small Cuban American neighborhood. This district, between S.W. Eighth Street (CALLE OCHO) and Flagler, became the core of contemporary Little Havana. The community grew explosively following the Cuban Revolution. Cuban immigrants chose to live in Little Havana for many reasons, including the comforting presence of other Cubans, the many Catholic churches and parochial schools, and the low cost of housing and commercial space.

Little Havana was an ethnic enclave that aided in the adjustment of recent immigrants. The area sheltered from harsh culture shock those who had recently arrived. Immigrants could communicate in Spanish and find employment in Cuban-owned enterprises.

As new waves of Cuban immigrants moved into the area, it became crowded. The neighborhood expanded into contiguous areas, particularly toward the west and south. Many wealthier residents moved to the suburbs. In the 1990's, Little Havana continued to house many long-established Cuban American residents in well-maintained middle-class houses and apartments. It was also the home of many more recent immigrants, some

Maximo Gomez Park in Little Havana hosts a domino club. (Martin Hutner)

living in substandard housing. Although the majority of Cuban Americans in Dade County did not live in Little Havana, it remained the center of Cuban American community life and culture.

Traveling along Calle Ocho, the main commercial strip in Little Havana, a visitor could mistakenly believe he or she was in Cuba. There are small Cuban grocery stores, Cuban bakeries, and Cuban-owned restaurants and night clubs. BOTÁNICAS sell special herbs and figurines to believers in folk medicine and to followers of SANTERÍA, an Afro-Cuban religion. Signs in Spanish advertise Cuban-owned clothing and shoe stores, car dealerships, and funeral homes. Many enterprises have the word "Cuba" or "Havana" in their names, and some businesses carry the names of well-known stores in Havana. Cuban flags and maps are everywhere, and wall murals decorate buildings. Some commercial buildings and street lamps are Spanish in style. Residences also sometimes show a Cuban influence, with Spanish tile decoration, iron grillwork over the windows, and yard shrines honoring Catholic saints.

Cuban cultural traditions are particularly evident at the CALLE OCHO OPEN HOUSE—CARNAVAL MIAMI, an annual street festival in March that features Cuban food, music, and dancing. Little Havana's parks are focal points for Cuban American social life. Many older men meet daily to play dominoes and talk politics at Antonio Maceo Minipark. Cuban Memorial Plaza, a park honoring the men who died in the BAY OF PIGS INVASION, has been the site of many anti-Castro rallies. In the early 1990's, there were plans to develop Little Havana into a sixty-block Latin Quarter that would celebrate the heritage of all Latinos.

Little Joe and the Latinaires: Tejano music group. Little Joe and the Latinaires was led by singer Little Joe Hernandez. Born in Texas to migrant farmworker Mexican parents, Little Joe decided in his teens to follow a musical career and joined his cousin's band, David Coronado y los Latinaires. After two years, he became head of the band, which gained great popularity in tejano music during the 1960's. The Latinaires later split up, and Hernandez formed Little Joe y la Familia, which continued to perform into the 1990's. Little Joe has been described as the "King of Brown Sound" and has recorded various hit records.

Llorens Torres, Luis (1876, Juana Díaz, Puerto Rico— 1944, New York, N.Y.): Poet. After spending his childhood in Puerto Rico, Llorens Torres went to Spain as an adolescent. He studied law at the University of Barcelona and the University of Granada. The eloquent Llorens Torres is said to have won his first case as a young lawyer with his verbal dexterity rather than with his legal skills.

Llorens Torres began his career as a poet while in Spain. Upon his return to Puerto Rico, he became active in the movement for Puerto Rican independence. He founded *La Revista de las Antilles*, providing a vehicle to publish many of his own poems. His literary reputation was established with *Al pie de la Alhambra* (1899, at the foot of the Alhambra).

Llorens Torres' work is characterized by vigor of thought, skilled use of the Spanish language, and his originality. Because of his "nativist" flavor, he has come to be known as "the poet of Puerto Rico."

Llorona, La: Female character of a Mexican folktale. In Mexican folk tradition, La Llorona (the wailing woman) is dressed in white and appears in places where there is water. She wanders in search of her children who died in childbirth. According to the Aztec version, La Llorona was an Aztec goddess who, after sacrificing infants, would disappear shrieking into riv-

ers or lakes. The Hispanicized version, popular in Mexico City, tells of a shrieking woman who seeks her children after having murdered them. The children, born out of wedlock, were murdered in revenge against her lover, who abandoned her to marry a woman of his own class.

Lobos, Los: Music group. Los Lobos formed in 1973 under the original name of Los Lobos del Este de Los Angeles. Members David Hidalgo, Conrad Lozano, Louis Perez, and Cesar Rosas had all played in Top 40 bands but decided to try traditional Mexican music they had heard as youngsters. They collected old recordings and Mexican instruments, using these to teach themselves how to play. Their music reflects the diverse styles of Mexican *MÚSICA NORTEÑA*, TEX-MEX, other Latin styles, rock and roll, blues, country swing, and rhythm and blues. In 1983, Steve Berlin joined the group. Los Lobos recorded several albums, performed as guests on various artists' albums, recorded on several major motion picture soundtracks (including that of *La Bamba* in 1987), and toured worldwide. The group had won two Grammy Awards by the early 1990's.

Lomas Garza, Carmen (b. 1948, Kingsville, Tex.): Artist. Many of Lomas Garza's creations reflect the racism and discrimination she suffered as a child in South Texas. She began producing art while in junior high school. Her images also show the everyday life and activities of a rural Chicano community, and she tries in her art to narrate typical experiences. During the 1960's, she attempted to apply the goals of the CHICANO MOVEMENT to the visual arts.

Lomas Garza received a bachelor's degree in art education from Texas A&I University in Kingsville in 1972. She also holds master of arts degrees from Antioch Graduate School of Education, Juárez-Lincoln Extension (1973) and San Francisco State University (1980).

Lomelí, Francisco (b. Apr. 13, 1947, Sombrerete, Zacatecas, Mexico): Educator, critic, and writer. Born in Mexico, Lomelí received his education in the United States. After earning his bachelor's and master's degrees from San Diego State University, he completed his doctorate at the University of New Mexico in 1978. Following his graduation, he accepted a position at the University of California at Santa Barbara, becoming a full professor in 1989.

Lomelí has received fellowships from the Fulbright Foundation in 1969, the Ford Foundation in 1974,

Rotary Club International in 1983, and the Rockefeller Foundation in 1989. In addition to publications in literary criticism, he has edited *Chicano Literature: A Reference Guide* (1985) and *Aztlan: Essays on the Chicano Homeland* (1989). The journals *The Americas Review*, *The Bilingual Review*, *Discurso Literario*, and *The Latino Studies Journal* have placed Lomelí on their editorial boards. He was also a coeditor of *Handbook of Hispanic Cultures in the United States: Literature and Art* (1994).

Lopez, Alfonso Ramon (b. Aug. 20, 1908, Tampa, Fla.): Baseball player and manager. Lopez, of Spanish descent, spent nineteen years in the major leagues as a player before beginning a long and successful managing career. A light-hitting catcher renowned for his defensive prowess, Lopez played for the Brooklyn Dodgers, Boston Braves, Pittsburgh Pirates, and Cleveland Indians before retiring after the 1947 season. He was twice named to All-Star teams, and he retired as the majors' all-time leader in games caught,

Al Lopez played for four major league teams, then began a successful career as a team manager. (AP/Wide World Photos)

Aurelio Lopez made his return to the major leagues with the St. Louis Cardinals. (AP/Wide World Photos)

a record that would last for four decades. In 1941, he tied a major league record by not allowing a passed ball in 114 games.

Lopez began his managerial career in 1948 with an Indianapolis minor league team that won the American Association pennant. After the 1950 season, the Cleveland Indians called on their former player to lead the team. Lopez took the Indians to the American League pennant with a league-record 111 wins in 1954. He also led the Chicago White Sox to the 1959 American League pennant, making him the only American League manager to lead a team other than the New York Yankees into the World Series from 1949 to 1964. In 1959, he was named American League Manager of the Year. Lopez was elected to the Baseball Hall of Fame in 1977.

Lopez, Aurelio (Aurelio Alejandro Lopez y Rios; b. Oct. 5, 1948, Tecamachalco, Mexico): Baseball player. A longtime star in the Mexican leagues, Lopez made his U.S. major league debut with the Kansas City Royals during the 1974 season, but he pitched in only eight games and was ineffective. Returning to Mexico in 1975, Lopez was named the most valuable player in the Mexican League in 1977 after posting a 19-8 record and a 2.01 earned run average. The St. Louis Cardinals signed him for the 1978 season, and he was traded to the Detroit Tigers a year later.

With Detroit, Lopez emerged as one of the best relievers in the American League, saving twenty-one games for the Tigers in each of his first two years with the club. A stocky, hard-throwing right-hander, Lopez led American League relievers in wins in 1980 and 1984 and earned an All-Star selection in 1983. In 1984, he won the deciding game of the World Series for the Tigers against the San Diego Padres. Nicknamed "Señor Smoke" for his powerful fastballs, Lopez became a free agent in 1985 and played for the Houston Astros before retiring at the end of the 1987 season.

López, Ignacio (b. March, 1908, Guadalajara, Jalisco, Mexico): Editor and civic leader. López moved with his family to the United States as a young boy. He attended Pomona High School in California. After two years at Chaffey Junior College, he earned his B.A. from Pomona College in 1931. After earning degrees in Spanish and history in 1932 at the University of California, Berkeley, he returned to Southern California to edit and publish a crusading bilingual weekly newspaper, *El Espectador*, which he oversaw until 1962.

López worked for the Office of War Information in the Spanish department during World War II. He was active in the greater Los Angeles area in the postwar years, establishing civic Unity Leagues, which were based on his experiences during the war organizing Liberty Leagues among East Coast minorities. In his ongoing efforts to gain political power and civil rights for Hispanics at the end of the 1940's, López worked with Fred Ross, Sr., with the American Council on Race Relations.

In the 1950's, López worked toward his Ph.D. at the University of California, Los Angeles. He was a leader in the COMMUNITY SERVICE ORGANIZATION, and from 1964 to 1967 was a crucial voice for Hispanics in his position as southern regional director of the MEXICAN AMERICAN POLITICAL ASSOCIATION. López worked for the Los Angeles Public Housing Authority and joined the Housing and Urban Development Southwest Area office in 1968.

López, José Dolores (1868-1937): Artist. Most of López's SANTOS, or religious figures, are from the last decade of his life. Between 1917 and 1929, López's primary occupation was furniture making. The Mexican American artist also produced window and door frames, coffins, crosses for grave markers, and small wooden figures. He expanded into production of santos and carvings of birds and other animals when he could no longer earn a living from his carpentry work and farming.

López's move into santo art coincided with a resurgence of interest in traditional Hispanic art. He continued to produce furniture, but most of his later pieces were unpainted, as the Anglo patrons who were his main source of sales considered his painted pieces to be too gaudy. López was deeply religious and acted as sacristan (caretaker) for his church. Many of his figures reflect passages from the Bible, particularly the story of Adam and Eve.

López's children also participated in santo art during its resurgence in the 1930's. George López began carving in the mid-1920's and devoted himself full-time to this occupation in the early 1930's. By the 1960's, he was considered to be the best active *santero*.

Lopez, Nancy (b. Jan. 6, 1957, Torrance, Calif.): Golfer. Lopez, a Mexican American, learned golf from her father at the age of eight, and she was soon winning youth tournaments in New Mexico. Playing for the boys' team at her high school, she led the team to

Nancy Lopez was a star player on the women's golf tour in the 1980's. (AP/Wide World Photos)

two state championships before enrolling at Tulsa University, where she earned All-American honors in each of her two years of competition.

In 1977, Lopez joined the Ladies Professional Golf Association (LPGA) as a touring professional, and she soon emerged as the tour's brightest star, winning the Rookie of the Year Award. The next year, she was even better; at one point, she won five consecutive tourna-

ments, a feat without precedent in either men's or women's golf. Lopez won the LPGA Championship in 1978, 1985, and 1989 and the Colgate Dinah Shore in 1981. She was named the LPGA Player of the Year in 1978, 1979, 1985, and 1988, and she received the Vare Trophy as the LPGA's lowest scorer in 1978, 1979, and 1985. In 1987, she was named to the LPGA Hall of Fame.